A Variable Harvest

A Variable Harvest
Essays and Reviews
of Film and Literature

by Jon Tuska

Ach, von jenem lebenwarmen Bilde
Blieb der Schatten nur zurück.
—Schiller

McFarland & Company, Inc., Publishers
Jefferson, North Carolina, and London

*The Schiller quotation on the title page: O, of that
picture once living/ now only the shadow remains.*

British Library Cataloguing-in-Publication data are available

Library of Congress Cataloguing-in-Publication Data

Tuska, Jon.
    A variable harvest : essays and reviews of film and literature /
by Jon Tuska.
        p.   cm.
    Rewritten or revised pieces originally published in the last
fifteen years.
    [Includes index.]
    Includes bibliographical references.
    ISBN 0-89950-454-X (lib. bdg. : 50# alk. paper) ∞
    1. Motion pictures.   2. Western stories—History and criticism.
3. Detective and mystery stories—History and criticism.   I. Title.
PN1995.T794   1990
791.43—dc20   90-42760
                                                                CIP

Manufactured in the United States of America

*McFarland & Company, Inc., Publishers
    Box 611, Jefferson, North Carolina 28640*

For My Mother
Florence Tuska

Table of Contents

Acknowledgments   xi
Introduction   1

Film Studies
Trader Horn: A Cinematograph   15
Rain: A Cinematograph   29
Visions of Armageddon: *War of the Worlds*   49
The American Western Cinema: 1903–Present   59
Yakima Canutt: A Career Study   87
Spencer Gordon Bennet: A Career Study   117
A Conversation with Dick Richards   147

Literary Studies
Rex Stout and the Detective Story   163
It's Murder, My Sweet   177
The American West in Fiction   191
The Westerner Returns   211
Eugene Manlove Rhodes: An Appreciation   227
Dane Coolidge: Western Writer   259
Fran Striker and the Lone Ranger   277
Luke Short and the Western   287
Louis L'Amour's Western Fiction   307
Will Henry's West   339
A Word After Reading Elmer Kelton's
   The Time It Never Rained   343
The Historians and Billy the Kid   349

Notes   355
Index   369

Acknowledgments

"*Trader Horn:* A Cinematograph" first appeared in *Views & Reviews,* Summer, 1971, Volume 3, Issue 1.

"*Rain:* A Cinematograph" first appeared in *Views & Reviews,* Spring, 1972, Volume 3, Issue 4.

"Visions of Armageddon: *War of the Worlds*" first appeared in *Views & Reviews,* Fall, 1974, Volume 6, Issue 1.

"The American Western Cinema: 1903–Present" first appeared in *Focus on the Western* (Englewood Cliffs, N.J.: Prentice-Hall, 1974), edited by Jack Nachbar.

"Yakima Canutt: A Career Study" first appeared in *Close-up: The Contract Director* (Metuchen, N.J.: Scarecrow Press, 1976), edited by Jon Tuska and Vicki Piekarski.

"Spencer Gordon Bennet: A Career Study" first appeared in *Close-up: The Hollywood Director* (Metuchen, N.J.: Scarecrow Press, 1978), edited by Jon Tuska and Vicki Piekarski.

"A Conversation with Dick Richards" first appeared in *Close-up: The Contemporary Director* (Metuchen, N.J.: Scarecrow Press, 1981), edited by Jon Tuska and Vicki Piekarski.

"Rex Stout and the Detective Story" first appeared in *Views & Reviews,* Spring, 1974, Volume 5, Issue, 3, and also appeared in *The Detective in Hollywood* (New York: Doubleday, 1978), by Jon Tuska.

"It's Murder, My Sweet" first appeared in *The West Coast Review of Books,* July, 1979, Volume 5, Number 4.

"American West in Fiction" first appeared in three parts in *The Roundup:* May, 1981, Volume 29, Number 5; June, 1981, Volume 29, Number 6; July-August, 1981, Volume 29, Number 7.

"The Westerner Returns" first appeared in *The West Coast Review of Books,* November, 1978, Volume 4, Number 6.

"Fran Striker and the Lone Ranger" first appeared as the Introduction to *The Lone Ranger* (Boston: Gregg Press, 1980), by Fran Striker.

"The Historians and Billy the Kid" first appeared under the title "Fabrications on the Life of Billy the Kid" in *Northwest Magazine* published by *The Oregonian,* February 22, 1987, and "Trailing Billy the Kid" in *The Roundup,* January, 1984, Volume 32, Number 1.

All are reprinted in revised form with permission.

Introduction

This book contains essays and reviews I wrote for various publications on a variety of occasions over the last fifteen years. However, each one has been rewritten or revised for its inclusion in this volume. The reasons for this are numerous. If it is a career study or a survey, it required updating, to make it as current as possible. On other occasions, where the essay was to serve as an introduction to a particular novel by a writer, I have dropped any such specific reference and, instead, expanded my remarks to include an overview of that writer's work. In one instance, "The Historians and Billy the Kid," which I wrote for the literary supplement of *The Oregonian,* I was given galley proofs of what I had written and was asked to cut the review from thirty-nine inches to twenty-nine. Since, in this book, I have no reason to be quite so conscious of space limitations, I have included the review of an additional book which had to be excised.

Rather than include a brief introductory comment before each of the essays and reviews I have selected, I thought it best to deal with them as an aggregate in a general Introduction. By this means, I hope to provide the reader with some indication as to how each piece came to be written and how it may have been altered for its inclusion here. The contents of this book rather neatly divide themselves into two general categories, film studies and literary studies. The earliest pieces have to do with film and appeared in the periodical *Views & Reviews.* I have often been asked how one goes about becoming established as a writer. I do not know if there is a single answer to this question. In my case the most logical course seemed to be that I would, at least initially, become my own publisher. In June, 1969, after several years of planning and preparing, I launched *Views & Reviews.* In the main, its contents reflected my own interests, but these were also interests, as it turned out, shared by a number of others. The magazine concerned itself with the popular arts and took as its province motion pictures, literary and cinematic biography, personality profiles, popular fiction

1

of the generic kind such as detective stories and science fiction, and cinematographs, which are reconstructions and critiques of various films from the past, in addition to reviews of books, phonograph recordings, contemporary films, essays in art theory and perspective, a quarterly report from the motion picture section of the Library of Congress, and regular newsletters from the Arturo Toscanini Society, the Bruno Walter Society, and the Serge Koussevitzky Society. Michael Wayne, John Wayne's son and president of Batjac Pictures, once told me how stunt man Cliff Lyons used regularly to bring the magazine to the Batjac office for everyone to read, and London Records, which was an advertiser, placed Leopold Stokowski, then under contract to the company, on our subscriber list. The first issue had a paid subscription of less than 100 persons. The final issue, combining paid subscriptions and newsstand copies, had a total press run of 5,000 copies, with issues being sent everywhere, from Singapore to Calcutta to Paris to Warsaw to Buenos Aires. Beyond serving as a market for what I might write, and a recruiting ground for new writers, the magazine also gave a credibility to the work I was doing and led to unprecedented cooperation from the motion picture industry, permitting me to have printed films that had been out of circulation two, three, and even four decades, so that I might write about them from a position of authority. Since my job on the magazine also included that of selling space, I was constantly brought into contact with potential advertisers. Virtually every non-theatrical motion picture distributor was represented and every manufacturer of classical music recordings with the exception of Columbia Masterworks. On a trip to New York, I once asked Pierre Bourdain, then director of advertising and promotion at Columbia Masterworks, why he would not buy space. "Because," he replied, "I just cannot see how in any magazine Bruno Walter and Ken Maynard fit together." I learned what a small world publishing was in those days when, following a review of one of my books in *The New York Times Book Review,* I wrote a letter in protest to the paper. Andrew Sarris had written the review and had spent a good bit of it complaining about my having dedicated the book, in part, to Roman Polanski, and going on to suggest several other individuals more worthy in his opinion. I was called from the *Times* by Pierre Bourdain's wife, who apologized and then commissioned me to write a film review for the paper.

"Trader Horn: A Cinematograph" is the earliest essay chronologically to appear in this book. It was first published in *Views & Reviews* in the summer of 1971. It was intended to supplement another article,

"Concerning *Trader Horn*," by Ray Cabana, Jr., which was a narrative on the filming of the picture. My cinematograph concentrated more on the film itself; but in preparing it I was first brought into contact with Duncan Renaldo who became a friend. In revising it for inclusion here I have included a vignette of him as he was at that time. What I have specifically excluded are any time-bound or extraneous references which had to do with the appearance of this cinematograph in the magazine while the contents themselves remain unchanged. I have followed this same procedure elsewhere, when the occasion demanded.

"*Rain:* A Cinematograph" had a more complicated genesis. In early 1970 a woman got in touch with me. It seems that her father, recently deceased, had been a projectionist and among his effects was a 35mm print of *Rain* (United Artists, 1932). The woman did not know if the print was acetate or nitrate, but did I want to buy it? Since I could not find the film to be in release, I agreed to her very minimal price. She delivered the print to the door of the suite I then had in the Clark Building in Milwaukee. How might I find out if the print was nitrate or not? Nitrate film stock is extremely combustible and can just suddenly explode. It was generally replaced by acetate in the late 1940s. I asked Karl Thiede, who was research editor for *Views & Reviews* and who worked for United Artists. He came over to the office and made a practical suggestion. Why not cut off a small strip of the film's leader, take it into the lavatory, and see if it could be ignited with a match? That is what we did; it went up in a whoosh. There were no 35mm processing labs in Milwaukee. The airlines would not transport nitrate film. When I finally located a laboratory in Tulsa, Oklahoma, that would make a negative from the positive print I had, my problem of transportation was still not solved. In the end, Greyhound agreed to carry the print.

My next step was to have a copyright search made by the Library of Congress. I learned that the copyright in the film had not been renewed. In those days, a copyright could extend for a period of fifty-six years, but the copyright holder had to renew the copyright sometime during the twenty-eighth year in order for the twenty-eight year extension to go into effect. *Rain* had not been renewed for contractual reasons having to do with the ownership of the literary property, namely the original short story by W. Somerset Maugham and the play subsequently based on that story by John Colton. I negotiated an assignment of the subsisting literary rights in the property, which was as strong a protection, perhaps even stronger, than the picture copyright, and placed the film into distribution. The nitrate print I had purchased turned out to be a seventy-seven minute, abridged version which had been reissued by the Atlantic Releasing Corporation in 1947. It took me some time to locate the original negative of the full-length version, which has a running time of ninety-one minutes. It was being kept in a vault by Mary Pickford who was then blind and virtually inaccessible. Eventually, however, I was permitted access to the original preprint materials. This film became the first of a number of feature films to which, over the years, I have acquired the copyrights and have put into distribution. My distributor, TV Cinema Sales Corporation, wanted me to prepare some publicity about *Rain* and I thought it would be best to write a cinematograph about the film for *Views & Reviews* and then run copies of it from the same plates for use by the distributor.

It was on the occasion of the sixth anniversary of *Views & Reviews* that we had our science fiction issue, a subject about which many readers had expressed an interest. It was in this context that I came to write the third, and last, cinematograph included here, that devoted to *War of the Worlds* (Paramount, 1953).

"The American Western Cinema: 1903–Present" was written in response to a commission from Jack Nackbar, who was and still is a professor of popular culture at Bowling Green State University. It was for inclusion in his collection of essays for Prentice-Hall titled *Focus on the Western* (1974). When I wrote it, of course, it ended in 1974. For its inclusion in this volume, I decided to add one final scene, bringing it nearly up to date. The occasion was that of the First National Western Film Festival in Ogden, Utah, at which both Jack and I were among the invited guests expected to give talks. That was during the summer of 1985, which coincidentally also marked the release of *Silverado* (Columbia, 1985) and *Pale Rider* (Warner's, 1985), the first theatrical Westerns to be made in a long time and maybe the last ever to be made.

Vicki Piekarski and I were married in 1980, although we had been working together since 1974. It was she who persuaded me to divest myself of my business interests, including *Views & Reviews,* so I could concentrate my resources and energy doing my own work, exclusively. I have never regretted that decision. At the time, however, I did not want simply to abandon *Views & Reviews*. Fortunately, I made the acquaintance of Eric Moon, who was the president of Scarecrow Press in the seventies. I proposed that the Press publish a volume about chapter plays, a book which eventually did appear as *The Vanishing Legion* (1981), but not from Scarecrow. What Eric wanted instead was a three-volume series devoted to film directors because one of his best-selling performing arts titles was *Film Directors: A Guide to Their American Films* (1974) by James Robert Parish and Michael R. Pitts. I agreed for a variety of reasons, among them the fact that the first volume would be offered to *Views & Reviews'* subscribers at a substantial discount and also because many of the writers who were regular contributors could make of this series our mutual *Schwanengesang*. The three career studies of directors, all of whom worked in the Western genre, contained in this volume appeared respectively in each of the three volumes of what I jointly titled the "Close-Up on the Cinema" series. The studies of Spencer Gordon Bennet and Dick Richards are substantially as first they were written; only that of Yakima Canutt has been extensively revised.

In the case of these three directors, and all the career studies I have written, Vicki Piekarski was of inestimable assistance because she transcribed our conversations, which allowed me to avoid a tape recorder. I have found as a matter of practical experience that men and women will reveal more when they are not being tape-recorded. A verbal, written transcription is as useful to me as a tape-recording — after all, I am not preparing a court case — and far more effective. Often the person being interviewed forgets that his or her words are being taken down. Initially, when we visited Yakima Canutt, he was only one of several people who worked in the industry that we had contacted for interviews on one of our periodic trips to Southern California. Some years later, when we came to live in Sherman Oaks, only a few blocks away from Yak's home, we visited him quite often. My portrait of him would be incomplete were I to have excluded these subsequent conversations.

It was also Vicki Piekarski who was responsible for my involvement in writing about Western fiction. With the exception of the essay on Rex Stout and the omnibus review-essay about critical and biographical books dealing with detective fiction, all of the literary studies in this book have to do with some aspect of the literary Western — even in the case of books about Billy the Kid, historians have been more wont to write fiction than history! However, I have placed the two essays about detective fiction first and should mention them first. The original version of "Rex Stout and the Detective Story" was the result of a letter-exchange with John J. McAleer, who was at the time working on his splendid biography of Rex Stout. It first appeared in the spring, 1974, issue of *Views & Reviews*, together with an interview of Stout by McAleer himself. I used my essay to form the basis for the section devoted to Nero Wolfe in *The Detective in Hollywood* (1978). When, subsequently, I came to revise that book, I found that, according to my new design, there was no room at all for Nero Wolfe. Yet, of all the detective stories I have ever read, for pleasure or in connection with my work, I have enjoyed those by Rex Stout the most. Hence, for its appearance here, I have combined everything I intend ever to write on the Nero Wolfe stories and the Nero Wolfe films. On the other hand, "It's Murder, My Sweet" first appeared as an omnibus review-essay for the *West Coast Review of Books,* initially inspired by the appearance of Dorothy B. Hughes' biography of Erle Stanley Gardner and the paperback reissue of the best of her mystery novels—Dorothy B. Hughes, the only woman who seems to have successfully mastered how to write in the laconic, hard-boiled style of Dashiell Hammett and the other pioneers of what has come to be known as the "Black Mask School."

Since the remainder of this book is devoted to various aspects of Western fiction, it seemed most appropriate for me to include "The American West in Fiction: An Introduction." This was written as an introduction to my collection of Western fiction published as a Mentor Book in 1982, but it exists in two versions. That was also the year I joined the Western Writers of America and Dale L. Walker, the editor of *The Roundup,* the publication of the society, asked me for a contribution. I revised my introduction for its inclusion in *The Roundup* and that is substantially the form in which it appears here. I should comment, however, that that essay, as with all I have written about Western fiction, is a direct consequence of having been coeditor-in-chief with Vicki Piekarski on the *Encyclopedia of Frontier and Western Fiction* (1983). It was after I had reviewed *The Encyclopedia of Mystery and Detection* (1976) by Chris Steinbrunner and Otto Penzler that Vicki suggested we ought to do a similar encyclopedia on authors of Western fiction. No such book had ever been done before and there was definitely a market for one. I proposed the book to McGraw-Hill, which had published *The Encyclopedia of Mystery and Detection,* and the publisher agreed with Vicki. There was only one problem in all this, but it was of monumental proportions. I had perhaps read no more ᵗhan ten Westerns, and Vicki had read fewer than that. Unquestionably, we had our work cut out for us. When I informed our editor at McGraw-Hill that we intended to leave Los Angeles, where we were then still living, and move to Portland, Oregon, he became trepidatious. He was convinced that civilization ended at the Jersey border and that Oregon had even less culture than ancient Gaul. He turned out to be mistaken. Since to do this book properly each of us would have to read close to a thousand Western novels apiece, there was no better place we could be than Portland which had far more book stores, and better ones, than could be found in Los Angeles and more book stores *per capita* than can be found in New York City. What is more, many of these book stores had large inventories of Western fiction. Thus we embarked on a three-year sabbatical, reading Westerns literally morning, noon, and night, taking notes on all that we read, and comparing notes. Vicki took ninety authors whose lives and works she would research; I took a similar number; and the rest we assigned to other contributors. It was slow going. Often, no bibliographies existed, and even agents and the authors themselves had none and we had to help prepare them both for the encyclopedia and for the authors and agents.

Yet, it was as a consequence of this toil that I not only became familiar with a vast amount of Western fiction, but devised classes that I taught on both the graduate and undergraduate levels at Lewis & Clark College, the University of Portland, and Portland State University. Vicki's anthology, *Westward the Women* (1984), and my own were an outgrowth of our research and because of it I also came to write the omnibus review-essay, "The Westerner Returns," for the *West Coast Review of Books*. Our reading of Western fiction had necessitated our familiarizing ourselves with Western history and from this came another major project, *The Frontier Experience: A Reader's Guide to the Life and Literature of the American West* (1984) which Vicki and I coedited.

A publisher agreed to reissue the best fiction by Eugene Manlove Rhodes, including some stories and a short novel which had yet to appear between cloth covers. W.H. Hutchinson, a fine writer and scholar and author of the definitive biography on Rhodes, had been a friend for some years. As literary executor for the Rhodes estate, he arranged the necessary clearances. Publishing, however, these days is not what it used to be. Editors come and go with extraordinary rapidity, whereas years ago an editor might work all his life for a single publisher and develop a stable of writers. We lost our editor on the encyclopedia before the book went to press, and I lost my editor at New American Library before *The American West in Fiction* could appear. In the case of the Rhodes anthology, something even worse happened. I was paid for writing the introduction, but the book was scuttled after a change in editors. Later, the University of Nebraska Press decided to reissue *The Best Novels and Stories of Eugene Manlove Rhodes,* a reprint of the 1949 anthology originally published by Houghton Mifflin. At least some of Rhodes' most important fiction is included in this reissue, now that the University of Oklahoma Press has allowed all of its Rhodes books to go out of print.

Vicki and I, by necessity, had to live a rather reclusive life while we were doing so much reading for the encyclopedia. Therefore, it was fortunate that Will Henry, after reading what I had said about one of his books in "The Westerner Returns," thought to write me a letter. For more than three years, we exchanged multiple-paged letters on nearly a weekly basis. Many of the conclusions and value judgments I formed regarding Western fiction were first voiced in this correspondence, now archived along with many other letters and original manuscripts of mine at the Special Collections of the Library of the University of Oregon in Eugene. When Dale L. Walker published his Will Henry collection, I was pleased to write a review of it for *The Oregonian,* included here under the title "Will Henry's West." Part of the book is made up of essays by Will Henry and I saw, although I did not mention it in my review, that he, too, had used our correspondence to concretize his own thinking about Western fiction in general and his own work in particular.

The Gregg Press began a Western fiction reissue series in cloth-bound editions in 1978, as mentioned in my review-essay "The Westerner Returns." The field editor for this series was Priscilla Oaks, a contributor to our encyclopedia, and both Vicki and I were assigned the writing of introductions to various books which were scheduled for reprint. The Press seemed to prefer a movie tie-in where possible and that is how Fran Striker's *The Lone Ranger* (1936) came to be chosen and Dane Coolidge's *Gringo Gold* (1939). This last did not itself inspire a film, but it was based on the life of the fictitious California bandit, Joaquin Murieta, which had been brought to the screen in William Wellman's *Robin Hood of El Dorado* (M-G-M, 1936). I had read virtually all of Dane Coolidge's Western novels for his entry in the encyclopedia and I certainly would not have chosen this book as being at all representative of him. Accordingly, in writing my introduction to it, I made a survey of all his fiction. I did the same thing with Luke Short's fiction when it came to writing an introduction for the reissue of *Savage Range* (1939). During the final year of its existence, because Priscilla was to spend a year teaching in the People's Republic of China, I took over as field editor of the Gregg series.

Louis L'Amour was very anxious for his fiction to appear in hardbound editions. He had submitted one of his novels to Doubleday, but he refused to revise it as the publisher suggested. The Gregg Press was willing to reprint some of his older titles which had appeared as paperback originals and I was asked to write the introductions to three of them. Of course, I had corresponded with L'Amour when preparing his entry for the *Encyclopedia,* but now I thought a personal interview would perhaps be advisable. Always affable, he acceded to my request. However, the interview was not exactly what the publisher wanted since, in the course of it, L'Amour put forth his vision of social Darwinism and the desirability of one-settlement culture. I had just finished working as special film consultant on the five-part television series, *Images of Indians* (PBS, 1980), and naturally I wondered what L'Amour's view might be on the subject. He commented succinctly that the Indians, as the buffalo, had to go to make way for churches, hospitals, schools—in brief, for the white man's civilization.

Vicki and I were in Los Angeles at that time working on a television pilot, based on my adaptation of *The Detective in Hollywood,* for which Orson Welles was the host/narrator. I told the director of this pilot, Fred Hutchison, about my conversation with L'Amour the next morning at breakfast. As fortune would have it, Los Angeles was in the midst of a second-stage smog alert. People were being told to stay indoors, if possible, although a few joggers were out. Our eyes watered, we gasped and coughed as we made our way to the car we had rented. After we were once inside, Fred turned to me and said emphatically, "You know, L'Amour's right. Hell, look what civilization has done for this place! Imagine what it would be like if we had let the Indians keep it?"

The Gregg Press, while paying me for my introductions which appear here as a single essay, decided to reprint the books without any introductions. The reason given was that some liberal-minded readers and critics might take umbrage and hurt the sale of the reprints. Yet, for me, L'Amour's novels are *the* embodiment of his political and social philosophy and I felt then, as I do now, that it is worthy of critical analysis.

I have the highest personal regard for Elmer Kelton and I meant every word when I wrote about his novel, *The Time It Never Rained* (1973), that it "is one of the dozen or so best novels written by an American in this century." When Texas Christian University Press decided it wished to reissue this novel in a clothbound edition, an editor for the Press wrote to me, asking permission to quote my feelings about the novel and to inform me that Elmer Kelton had proposed I should write an afterword to the novel. I replied to the editor that, while I had no objection to being quoted, I was probably the wrong person to write an afterword. From what I had seen of such afterwords, what was wanted was a synopsis of the novel's plot and then a critique of its characters, after the fashion of what is done in college literature classes. I wanted no part of that. I felt that I had retained my love for reading precisely because I avoided being "taught" literature and what to think about literature, how to rank authors, and how to discuss characters and plots. Moreover, my own inclinations in reading, aside from what I have read in connection with books I was writing, has always been toward classical literature, Shakespeare, and the European tradition. I was weary of writers of exemplary Western fiction — and Elmer Kelton is certainly such a one — being grouped together in a minor genre with everyone who has ever written a novel with a Western setting, something to be abstracted and isolated from the main stream of Western literature as a whole. Indeed, the closest one comes to the American frontier experience, as it really happened and not as legendry has made it, is in Homer, whose books were generated during a time when Greek civilization was undergoing a period of tremendous expansion.

The editor dismissed all my objections and insisted I write the afterword any way I wanted to write it. I should have known better. As in the case of my L'Amour introductions, but for an entirely different reason, I was paid for the afterword but it was not used. What the publisher ultimately preferred was a long plot synopsis — always ridiculous, it seems to me, when you presumably have just finished reading the story — and a more mincing assessment. "Deservedly, *The Time It Never Rained* has been widely acclaimed for its high merit as a work of literary art," Tom Pilkington concluded in his afterword to the novel. "...In 1982 Jon Tuska ... adjudged it to be 'one of the dozen or so best novels written by an American in this century.' Lack of space permits neither a defense nor a denial of Tuska's claim, but it is a judgment for readers to ponder. At the very least, I believe those who have come this far will acknowledge that *The Time It Never Rained* is one of the major achievements of recent Texas literature."[1] I sent a copy of my afterword to Elmer Kelton who was both delighted and moved by what I had written. I have included it here so that it might reach the wider audience for which it was originally intended.

In 1981 I was telephoned by a producer of a special for the ABC network who wanted my recommendation as to an appropriate film clip showing Billy the Kid to be featured in the program.

"How are you treating the Kid?" I asked him.

"Why, as a hero, of course," he replied. "How is it you ask?"

"For one thing, because it will tell me what kind of film clip to suggest."

"Are you implying that the Kid wasn't a hero?"

"No. I would state outright that the Kid wasn't a hero."

The producer assured me that he would get a research expert on the matter at once, that, since the special was to deal with the contrast between the legends and the realities of the Old West, if the Kid was not a hero, he would be presented as he was; in short, this television special was going to embody that worthy principle of German historian Leopold von Ranke, to reconstruct the past "as it really had been." Once again, I should have known better. When the special was aired, the viewer was informed that Billy the Kid's real name was William S. Bonney, that he was a savage killer who had murdered twenty-one men by the time Sheriff Pat Garrett gunned him down, and that he had killed his first man at the age of fourteen. There is not a single element of historical truth in this image. I complained bitterly about the episode to one of my publishers who proposed that I should write a book about the Kid. I did, and especially since the paperback edition, I have received letters from numerous readers who have spent years studying the life and times of the Kid. It was in connection with its appearance that, at Dale L. Walker's request, I wrote a short article for *The Roundup* on the Kid; and, later still, I wrote the review-essay to which I refer in the first paragraph of this introduction. For my present purpose, I have combined the two Billy the Kid articles into a single essay.

Not too long after, my brief article on the Kid for *The Roundup,* which proved to be my last for it, Robert J. Randisi, an author of porno–Westerns, decided to take me to task for dismissing his novels. It is not that to which I objected. He began his editorial with the statement: "I recently read Jon Tuska's *Encyclopedia of Frontier and West-*

ern Fiction. . . and would like to make a few comments on its contents,"[2] that is, omitting coauthor Vicki Piekarski's name. The same sort of cavalier attitude also plagued reviews written about *The Frontier Experience* (1984), which Vicki again cowrote with me, along with other contributors. There remains too much male chauvinism within the whole province of the American West.

I have added footnotes and citations throughout to assist those who might wish to refer to the original sources whenever these are quoted anywhere in this book.

Film Studies

Trader Horn: A Cinematograph

M-G-M, 1930 (The film was released on January 22, 1931, in a roadshow version; May 23, 1931, for general theatrical release. It was re-released May 7, 1937, and reissued in June, 1953, on a double bill with *Sequoia* [M-G-M, 1934]).

Producer	Irving Thalberg
Producing Company	Metro-Goldwyn-Mayer
Director	W.S. Van Dyke, II
Assistant Director	Redd Golden
Novel by	Alfred Aloysius Horn and Ethelreda Lewis
Screenplay	Richard Schayer
Adaptation	Dale Every and John Thomas Neville
Dialogue	Cyril Hume
Photography	Clyde De Vinna
Associate Photographers	Robert Roberts and George Nogle
Film Editor	Ben Lewis
Recording Engineer	Douglas Shearer
Production Assistant	James McKay

Cast

Trader Horn	Harry Carey
Nina Trend	Edwina Booth
Peru	Duncan Renaldo
Renchero	Mutia Omoolu
Edith Trend	Olive Fuller Golden
Storekeeper	C. Aubrey Smith

M-G-M expressed gratitude to the governmental officials of the Territory of Tanganyika, the Protectorate of Uganda, the Colony of Kenya, the Anglo-Egyptian Sudan, the Belgian Congo, and to the white hunters, Maj. W.V.D. Dickinson, A.S. Waller, Esq., J.H. Barnes, Esq., H.R. Stanton, Esq., for their courageous service through 14,000 miles of African veldt and jungle.

Running Time: 11,109 ft./123 minutes/13 reels. (Note: The original release contained a short introduction by Cecil B. DeMille in conversation with Alfred Aloysius Horn, attesting to the authenticity of the picture. This was deleted from the negative for the 1937 re-release, giving the film only 10,794 ft./120 minutes/12 reels running time. This is the negative as it exists today. Production began May 7, 1929, in Africa and continued until November of that year.)

Current owner of world rights: Turner Entertainment.

When I mentioned to an executive at Metro-Goldwyn-Mayer that I was preparing a cinematograph on *Trader Horn,* he hastened to respond that M-G-M was remaking the picture. I asked him if it would be filmed in Africa. "No," he replied, "probably in Jamaica. You know how it is nowadays. An African picture you shoot in Jamaica, and a Jamaican picture you go to Africa to shoot."

Of course, Africa has changed and the world out of which the book was born, and the first motion picture inspired, has vanished. M-G-M spent nearly $3,000,000 on the film before its release in 1931, and by the end of that year it had grossed approximately $1,700,000. The negative cost figure should be contrasted with the $325,000 that was M-G-M's average expenditure on a feature film in the early thirties. Against this average, the anticipated gross for a film distributed on the Lowe's circuit in 1930 was around $400,000 domestically, and nearly a million worldwide. Two reissues, television, and nontheatrical rentals doubtless amortized the original cost over a period of time.

Trader Horn is a great motion picture. Its greatness is not solely in terms of the fine performances of its principals, the effectiveness of its technical achievement, but, equally, it is the product of the time at which it was made, during the final days of darkness when the veil over Africa was being lifted after centuries.

The book consisted of Alfred Aloysius Horn's reminiscences of the Ivory Coast in the 1870s. Colonialism was at its height. The savagery of the land, the primitivism of its aboriginal peoples, the timelessness that accompanies a ritual culture where memory is erased and consciousness obscured by collective forgetfulness, these were the things Horn described — and the quest for a white girl who had become a tribal fetish.

It is this last part, the fetish, which bothers me. The South African novelist, Ethelreda Lewis, first met Horn in the mid-twenties when he tried to sell her kitchenware. She got him to write down what he recalled of the early times in Africa. Horn was not a totally untutored person. He was familiar with the Tarzan stories and mentioned them to her in conversation. He spoke frequently of the cinema and probably had seen more than a few of the pictures supposedly set in Africa. Warner Bros. had begun a cycle in 1921 with the release of the chapter play, *Miracles of the Jungle.* Elmo Lincoln, who had first played Tarzan in *Tarzan of the Apes* in 1918, continued the cycle in *The Adventures of Tarzan* (Weiss Brothers–Numa Picture Corporation, 1921), a fifteen-chapter serial which was edited to ten episodes and reissued in 1928 by

Weiss Brothers–Artclass with synchronized sound effects, in the wake clearly of the popularity of Horn's book. Universal in 1922 had brought *With Stanley in Africa* to the screen; but it was reserved for Colonel William Selig to produce the crowning achievement in the cycle in *The Jungle Goddess* (Export-Import Film Company, 1922). Selig spent money on *The Jungle Goddess,* including the use of some 470 wild animals. The story involved the young daughter of an English lord who is kidnapped and thrown into the basket of a balloon. Cut loose by accident, the balloon is shot down over darkest Africa and the girl, played by Vonda Phelps, is captured by cannibals who make her a tribal fetish. Worshipped as a goddess by the tribe, the lost heroine spends many years before her childhood friend, played by Truman Van Dyke, mounts a search for her and finally, after fifteen chapters and events and adventures too numerous to recount, effects her rescue. My point is, had Horn seen Selig's film? If not, it was nonetheless reissued in 1929, as had been *The Adventures of Tarzan* before it, to take advantage of the intense interest in things African which *Trader Horn* engendered. It would be amusing to learn that the film gave birth to Horn's tale, just as the publication of his tale should have brought new life to the film.

The abduction of Nina T—and her ultimate rescue by Horn and Peru occupy precisely three of the book's twenty-six chapters. "'The English set a great deal of store by facts,'" Horn told Ethelreda Lewis, "'but if a book's to be sold in America you must keep your eye on the novelties.'"[1] Elsewhere he remarked: "'I think I told you that that girl Nina T—will be the pivot of the book. It sure was a bit of a shock to find the daughter of a good English family doing her duty as a goddess to Isorga.'"[2] Ethelreda Lewis was kind enough to follow each chapter written by Horn, retaining his misspellings and outrageous syntax, with quoted conversations between them. Horn appears to have been quite concerned over the prospects of producing a best seller. "'Aye,'" he said. "'Come to Nina's story, I would have crammed the whole narrative into three ... chapters. There was little enough of it.'"[3] In the end, that is all it took, but with a lot in between.

The motion picture screenplay concentrated on those three chapters. A story, after all, should have a plot, and the plot in *Trader Horn* was the drama of Nina's rescue. Regardless of how Horn came to it, whether at the cinema, by legend, by reading, or, least likely, because it had really happened, the plot sold the book. Simon & Schuster, which marketed the American edition, published a total of

7,000 copies in June, 1927, 9,000 in July, 10,000 in August, 20,000 in September, 25,000 in October, then 20,000 in November, 10,000 in December, and so on.

What, for certain, Horn did remember was life in Africa as he had known it: predatory, animals preying upon each other for survival, tribes preying upon the animals, white men preying upon both and the natural resources. It was a world characterized by murder, by death, and by a silence across the veldt beneath the blazing sun. European authors, the English in particular, were horrified by the spectacle of the slaughter. Joseph Conrad recorded his recoil in *The Heart of Darkness* (1901). Horn spoke more fundamentally, if with less poetry: "Best not to throw too high a light on some of my experiences on the Coast. It never does to give good folk a shock. Aye. Talk of dreadful scenes... A young lad brought up never to think of evil nor read it in a book — and he gets to the Coast at eighteen... Seventeen, it might have been... He feels Revolt... The shock of it's like to make him sick."[4] Horn considered himself safe among the "cannibals" and "Woody" Van Dyke, who was selected by Irving Thalberg to direct the picture because he was good at action and conscious of budget, thought a white woman safer in the wilds of Africa than in any of the large cities of civilized America.

For the most part the colonialists now are gone; the animals are diminishing through sport, carelessness, plunder, and the indifference accorded the European-sponsored game preserves upon the establishment of independence. Making a picture in Jamaica today would not matter as greatly as it did in 1929. M-G-M made a small fortune selling stock footage shot by Van Dyke on location to many of the studios making jungle pictures. The world long since has forgotten Alfred Aloysius Horn and the view of the human condition he put forward in his final years, before the cloudiness of senility and the blankness of death. "Aye," said Horn. "The first thing education teaches you is to walk alone. ... You can sure stand on your own spear when you've learnt the word goodbye, and say it clear."[5]

Thalberg was impressed by the book and perceived its cinematic possibilities, especially if filmed in Africa. L.B. Mayer agreed. Together they decided Wallace Beery would be perfect for the role, probably on the basis of *The Lost World* (First National, 1925). Beery would have nothing to do with it. So Harry Carey, who was playing vaudeville in East Hampton to recoup losses he suffered to his $750,000 ranch during the St. Francis Dam break in California, was contacted. Thalberg said his top price was $600 a week. Olive Fuller Golden, Carey's wife, thought it too little. They argued, took the argument to their friend Will Rogers, who took it to his wife, a practical soul. Carey was signed.

Horn, somewhat ironically, had commented to Ethelreda Lewis that Americans would likely be surprised to hear that his elocution instructor at St. Edward's was Edwin Booth, "'the brother to the feller that shot Lincoln.'"6 It was while Thalberg was testing several contenders for the female role of the goddess, Bessie Love, Thelma Todd, and Jeanette MacDonald among them, that a young starlet created quite a commotion at the administrative office about not being paid for having posed for a series of stills, a job that was generally done for nothing even by name actors. But Edwina Booth, from the beginning, thought she was a great star, or would soon become one, and she wanted instant compensation. Thalberg had her tested. He liked her. Mayer liked the price, $75.00 a week and found. The "found" in this case was all of the trappings of an M-G-M cinema queen. Van Dyke found her obnoxious. The finished picture did not have her mouthing a single word of comprehensible dialogue. It was Edwina Booth's first and last major motion picture and her career, primarily because she was incapable of giving a convincing portrayal, proved extremely short-lived.

Byron Riggan, who wrote an article on *Trader Horn* for *American Heritage,* quoted the late John McClain, M-G-M press agent for the expedition, as saying of Edwina: "'She was a pleasant enough woman, pretty, but frankly I thought she was a bit of a bore. She was such a proper do-gooder. I don't think she had much sense of humor.'"7 Olive Carey and Duncan Renaldo, interviewed for the same article, were more charitable in their remarks. Renaldo indicated that he had cared very much for Edwina Booth and claimed that he recalled with pleasure their association from those days. During the interview, Olive Carey produced Edwina's telephone number and Renaldo called her. When he rang off, Riggan quoted Renaldo as saying, "'I don't altogether understand Edwina. Although she was a very determined young woman, she was naive. She thought that good work and honest effort are always justly rewarded. She had worked so hard, under such difficult conditions, she felt she deserved better treatment than she got. But instead of accepting it gracefully, Edwina, I think, has just tried to blank out her whole life during those years.'"8 Duncan was not being entirely candid. There was much more to it.

When the troupe returned to the States from Africa, Edwina

**Edwina Booth as the Jungle Goddess in *Trader Horn* (M-G-M, 1931).
Photo courtesy of Metro-Goldwyn Mayer.**

Booth insisted that she had contracted a mysterious jungle disease and
she even brought a $10 million law suit against M-G-M. A visit to the
Medical Clinic for Jungle Diseases in London, however, elicited
negative results. Edwina was signed together with Harry Carey to appear in two chapter plays for Mascot Pictures, *The Vanishing Legion*
(Mascot, 1931) and *The Last of the Mohicans* (Mascot, 1932). The
M-G-M law suit was settled for $10,000 between the attorneys while she

was at work on these serials. She made a low-budget picture next with Duncan Renaldo, *Trapped in Tiajuana* (Mayfair, 1932). The private gossip around Hollywood claimed that Edwina had had an abortion while in Africa and was only suffering from some unfortunate side-effects. Duncan Renaldo's name was linked with hers and at least Renaldo's estranged wife placed sufficient credence in the rumors to institute an alienation of affection suit. She also informed the Federal authorities that Renaldo had lied on his passport when going to Africa by claiming to have been born in the United States when, in fact, he had been born in Romania. "'I am penniless,'" he had confessed to Lynn Fairfield for an article in *Movie Classic*. "'I have worked only once since *Trader Horn,* and they had to finish the picture in six days because I was arrested. For two years I have been harried as if I were a criminal....'"9 Edwina quit pictures after Renaldo's arrest during the filming of *Trapped in Tiajuana* and a new legend arose, that she had in fact died of a mysterious disease, when in fact all she had done was to change her name and to fashion a new life for herself in Los Angeles. Always a practicing Mormon, she worked in behalf of her religion. According to Renaldo, he and Carey helped collect money for her anonymously so she could pay off the many doctor and legal bills she had accumulated as a result of her unsuccessful suit against M-G-M. She did win, however, the alienation of affection suit filed by Renaldo's wife. The occasion for Lynn Fairfield's article was that Renaldo had just been fined two thousand dollars and was to be sentenced to two years in Federal prison unless he was deported instead. Renaldo intended to appeal the decision. "'My parents took me to Romania when I was a child and I grew up there,'" he was quoted as saying in the *Movie Classic* article, "'but I was born in Camden, New Jersey. I have proof of it—a copy of the birth certificate in the records. I was recognized as an American citizen when I served in the Army. I have an honorable discharge from the Army. Does the United States enlist citizens of other countries in its Army? My name is Duncan Renault. That is the name that appears on the birth certificate.'"10

White-haired, his countenance lined and ruddy with persistent youthful impishness, is the way I remember Duncan Renaldo. He had long ago remarried to a most gracious woman and had had two children. His well-proportioned ranch house in Santa Barbara contained in the living room two large oil paintings he had done while in Africa, of a Masai chief and his wife. There were also an African spirit drum and numerous other mementoes he had saved from the time of

Mutia Omoolu, Harry Carey, and Duncan Renaldo moving down an artificial river on M-G-M's back lot. This sequence is at the opening of the film,
Trader Horn (M-G-M, 1931). Photo courtesy of Metro-Goldwyn-Mayer.

Trader Horn. We became very good friends and he would always urge
me to move to Santa Barbara and once even went apartment-hunting
with me. He had grown rather stout and used to grin sheepishly as he
confessed to frequently getting up at night to have a snack. He liked
best to sit at the dining room table, smoking cigarettes and talking
about life on this planet in the twentieth century.

"Duncan," I said to him during one of these conversations, "you
will probably want to ask me to leave, but what nationality are you
really?"

He smiled quietly.

"I do not know, Jon, and that is the truth."

"At the time of your hearing," I said, "it was suggested that you
may have been Romanian."

"That's entirely possible," he conceded. "I had six different birth
certificates but I did not know if any of them was valid. I had worked

aboard a ship as a coal stoker and entered the United States on a temporary ninety-day seaman's permit. I told the judge that one certificate indicated that I was born in China. He said, were that the case, I would fall under the Exclusion Act. Had I been Russian, I might be politically dangerous. You see, I never knew my parents, but my name was Renaldo Duncan. Might I be Portuguese? I was sent to prison. All my money had gone to fight it. At last, by special amnesty from President Roosevelt, after nearly two years I was released."

He had been making $2,000 a week when working for M-G-M. When he returned to motion pictures, he never rose again above the status of a "B" player, cast as a Latin type mostly in Westerns.

Olive Carey came out the best of all of them. When the original expedition got back to the States, Mayer fired everyone. He had been looking for weeks at useless rushes and was fed-up with the expense. Seven months in British East Africa (*not* the Ivory Coast), and still they were no closer to having a finished picture than when they began. Once studio executives Bernie Hyman and Paul Bern viewed the footage at Culver City and convinced Thalberg the picture could be saved, and Thalberg convinced Mayer, the principals were all re-hired at their same salaries, all, that is, except Olive Carey. She had had only a small part as a woman missionary. Thalberg thought he could dispense with her entirely, only he couldn't and keep the valuable footage of her death and supposed burial at Murchison Falls (something the original Horn would never have done since, if they had wanted, the natives could have dug up her remains and made a fetish of her anyway). Thalberg offered Olive Carey $300 to complete the sequence, the same she had been paid for the whole expedition. She balked. Thalberg had first planned to replace her with Marjorie Rambeau, whom he had been willing to pay a thousand dollars a day. Ollie would not do the part for less. Thalberg finally gave in. She received $5,000 for as many days' work. To put the film in finished form required extensive retakes in Mexico, where Thalberg had assembled a zoo to equal Colonel Selig's for *The Jungle Goddess,* although the matter was kept secret for fear it would ruin the publicity value of an all–African film.

Van Dyke, who subsequently wrote a book about the picture, *Horning into Africa* (1931), revealed himself to have been a director interested primarily in action and not subtle emotional interplay. When the scene came that called for the principals to steal a lion's kill for food, Van Dyke recorded: "I wedged in between camera cases, film boxes, and my staff. I gallantly ordered Carey, Renaldo and Edwina Booth to charge the lion and drive him off the carcass, and the idiots did."[11] Notwithstanding the absurdity of this hyperbole, he managed to get a good picture.

Trader Horn opens with a long shot of natives paddling a large boat up a jungle river. The river is real, the jungle a matter of special effects. As the journey continues, with Horn and Peru in conversation, scenes of authentic animal life are adroitly intercut, hippos raising massive heads, swarms of crocodiles scurrying into the water. Horn, as portrayed by Harry Carey, is a man no longer young (as he claimed to be during this adventure in the book), an aged trader introducing Peru, the son of Horn's former partner played by Renaldo, to the mystery and wilds of Africa. They arrive at a village and the camera tracks the activities and crafts of the natives. Here, and elsewhere, as on the veldt, the style and technique are clearly documentary. Peru is delighted by the primitives and describes them to Horn as harmless children, until he espies a dried skeleton, fixed in the agony of crucifixion, foreshadowing things to come. "That's just a childish prank," Horn comments. Any hope for trading for ivory is dispelled by the arrival of fierce Masai warriors. Drumming indicates that the Ju-Ju has been put on the jungle. Every heathen in the bush, according to Horn, will become a homicidal maniac. The white men, returning to their boat, find two of their "boys" dead, but they manage to escape.

After setting up camp along the river, they encounter a midnight safari headed by a female missionary, Edith Trend, played by Olive Carey, who is in search of her daughter Nina, stolen some twenty years before by bushmen. She has had word that a white woman is being kept as a fetish by the Isorga in the unexplored region above the Falls. Despite Horn's warnings about the danger, she will not be put off. Pausing only long enough to have tea, she does make Horn swear to follow her should she die in the attempt. He gives his word. The safari, torches glowing in the inky darkness, resumes its trek. A few days later, Horn and Peru find her body beneath the Falls and bury her, Peru pledging to accompany Horn to rescue Nina. There was no more effort made to present the variety of native African cultures than Hollywood films ever tried to distinguish among the four hundred tribes of Native Americans.

Amid countless examples of jungle life which they meet on the journey, the two finally arrive at the camp of the Isorga where they are taken prisoner. The Ju-Ju is still on and the tribes have congregated to commit a sacrifice, or, in this case, three of them, Horn, Peru, and

Mutia Omoolu, as Renchero, Horn's native guide. "The Good Lord gives you only one death to die," Horn tells Peru, "and a fellow mustn't bungle it."

In the book, Miss Lewis recorded the following conversation:

"'Mr. Horn, tell me—what—how did they look?'

"He came a step nearer, an expression on his face which, in a young person would be called shy.

"'Ma'am, there's some things it's difficult to capture with a word. I should say her eyes were kind but piercing. Aye. Kind but piercing.'"[12]

In the film, Peru sees her first. She enters their hut, her eyes protruding from her head in hysterical, fanatical frenzy, naked beneath her flimsy garments, whipping savages from her path. She beats Peru when he dares to touch her; he does not flinch and she is impressed. Yet she orders three crosses prepared and she has the prisoners tied to them, upside down, ready for burning alive. The drums beat with great intensity. Suddenly, looking again and again at Peru, she orders the captives freed. Over the protests of the gaily painted, animal-like witch doctors, she departs with the trio in a boat headed across the lake.

From this point the remainder of the picture consists of an exciting chase, the natives in pursuit of their goddess. Snakes hanging from trees, leopards roaming the jungle, the incredible scene of stealing a lion's plunder, drinking muddy water from a spring frequented by a herd of elephants, the plot becomes complicated by Horn's objections to Peru's embracing Nina. A fight ensues between them, interrupted by the sounds of the approaching Isorga. Horn tells the others to flee while he diverts the Isorga on a fruitless quest. Peru and Nina dash into the underbrush, but Renchero chooses to stay behind with Horn. They light a fire and run for their lives, swinging across a river onto a small island by means of vines, crocodiles circling below them. The Isorga lose one of their party to the snapping reptiles before they camp and satisfy themselves with the rituals of war. Horn and Renchero float past, camouflaged on a log, while the natives practice throwing spears. One of the spears accidentally kills Renchero, who is lying atop Horn. When Horn reaches safety, in a sorrow quite moving he buries his friend.

Peru and Nina, in their rush to flee, find themselves entrapped by pygmies. Fortunately, these natives turn out to be friendly and assist the pair in reaching a trading post where they are reunited with Horn. Horn realizes by now that Nina belongs to Peru by right of love and he sees them off on a paddleboat, bound for civilization. It is a fond

A good part of the cast of *Trader Horn* (M-G-M, 1931) posed at Panyamur on the banks of the Victoria Nile. Harry Carey whittles a stick, Edwina Booth smiles demurely, Olive Golden studies the crown of her hat, and Duncan Renaldo glowers. Photo courtesy of Ray Cabana, Jr.

moment, with Horn remarking, "I'll still be beholdin' the wonders of the jungle that'll never grow old before your eyes, the way a woman does."

What, for me, makes the original *Trader Horn* such an entertaining experience is not the racial fantasy of its plot, which is, after all, only a variation on James Fenimore Cooper's *The Last of the Mohicans* (1826), but the actual African footage as Africa then was, and Harry Carey's performance. He was indeed a fine actor who was so persuasive in his role that you are never aware that he was acting. His wisdom, his tenderness, and his sense of fun invest the picture to this day with the vividness of an exceptional human being, easily the match for the violent surroundings in which he has chosen to live.

Van Dyke in his book claimed that Mutia Omoolu was a natural actor who stole the picture. If he does not do that, he comes very close to it. His quiet person, infused with a loyalty to the values of an inner civilization and culture that his world would deny him externally, leaves the viewer with an image of spiritual fortitude, the way Van Dyke felt about him when he asked of "the white and black men of our country . . . who laugh," how many "would step in front of their employer and take the thundering charge of a rhino, . . . would stand fast and firm with a huge lion hurtling at them in the air, . . . would ever be ready to stop drinking water themselves that the man for whom they carried a gun might not lack. . . ?"[13] A later generation of Americans, invested with the "me first" ethic of the late twentieth century, might term this simply "Uncle Tomism." It was otherwise for Van Dyke. The happy ending for Peru and Nina was written in Hollywood. Van Dyke, with Mutia Omoolu's help, created another ending, told by the camera and the man himself. Not love, but human nobility, white and black alike, surely this was Van Dyke's intention when, at the end, Horn heads once more up the river, Renchero's face superimposed on the horizon making the wild denizens less wild and the heart of man less dark.

Rain: A Cinematograph

United Artists, 1932 (Released October 22, 1932).

Producer	Joseph M. Schenck
Producing Company	Art Cinema Corporation
Releasing Company	United Artists
Director	Lewis Milestone
Assistant Director	Nate Watt
Original Story	W. Somerset Maugham
Stage Adaptation	John Colton and Clemence Randolph
Screenplay	Maxwell Anderson and Lewis Milestone
Music	Alfred Newman
Art Director	Victor Ray
Film Editor	W. Duncan Mansfield
Sound Engineer	Frank Grenzbach

Cast

Sadie Thompson	Joan Crawford
Reverend Davidson	Walter Huston
Sergeant O'Hara	William Gargan
Mrs. Davidson	Beulah Bondi
Doctor MacPhail	Matt Moore
Mrs. MacPhail	Kendall Lee
Joe Horn	Guy Kibbee
Quartermaster Bates	Walter Catlett
Griggs	Ben Hendricks, Jr.
Hodgson	Fred Howard
Passport Agent	Edward Peil, Sr.

Running Time: 91 minutes/12 reels.
Current owner of world rights: Jon Tuska

The Great War was still raging when W. Somerset Maugham set out for the South Sea islands. He was recovering from a lingering lung ailment contracted during the period of his war work which resulted in the Ashenden stories. An American publisher had spoken fondly of Honolulu and recommended that Maugham go there in his forthcoming travels. Maugham had originally planned to embark directly from San Francisco to Tahiti. He had a preference for French colonies. A character in the film version of *The Moon and Sixpence* (United Artists, 1942) remarks that the French are not "quite so technical" as the

29

English. The French were not out altogether to remake the world; that was only the initial excuse. As with the Jesuits in Indochina, which Maugham would visit in 1930, once religion had subdued the native leaders, the governing authorities could then take over and, despite incompetent administration, encourage unembarrassed exploitation. The English were more conscience-stricken. The Americans were even more so.

Maugham decided to visit Hawaii. He was accompanied by his secretary-companion of those years, Gerald Haxton. Aboard ship, they sedulously avoided their fellow-passengers. Upon arrival, Maugham acquainted himself with island life. He had been a playwright for years. The money was better and the royalties came in with a reassuring frequency. He was over forty when he began his South Sea travels. The time had come, he felt, to turn to writing short stories. He became uncommonly adept at it; at his best, few can equal him.

The religious zealots were in the process of cleaning up the red-light district in Honolulu. To Wilmon Menard, who later wrote *The Two Worlds of Somerset Maugham* (1965) about Maugham and his travels, Maugham remarked that Iwelei was laid out as a garden city "and in its respectable regularity, its order and trimness," it gave the impression of "sardonic horror." "Never can the search for love have been so planned and systematized...."[1] One-sheets outside the Liberty Theatre in downtown Honolulu advertised Chapter 17 of *The Iron Claw* (Pathé, 1916) with Pearl White, Creighton Hale, and Warner Oland. Coming attractions boasted of Theda Bara in *Gold and the Woman* (Fox, 1916). Theda Bara was a screen vamp whose films had put William Fox's studio on the map. In Iwelei each prostitute's den was exactly alike, consisting of a small parlor decked out with chairs and a gramophone mounted with a morning-glory flower horn, blaring out the latest hit tune from their respective homelands for there was no discrimination by race, Japanese, Chinese, Blacks, Germans, Spaniards, Portuguese, Hawaiians, Filipinos, and so on endlessly. The din was deafening. The bedroom was off from the parlor, furnished with a workmanlike double-canopied bed, a chest of drawers, a bar of coat hooks on the wall, opening into a tiny kitchenette. Beer, gin, whiskey in bottles stood on the sink, together with dirty glasses; no food was visible. When the blinds were drawn, that meant there was a man inside the house in the bedroom and probably another drinking and waiting with the exigencies of love in the parlor.

At one bungalow, there was a long line of "doughboys," biding their time in fitful mutterings, scuffing their feet, jingling the change in their pockets to let the "soiled doves" know that they were there, urgently containing their congested sexual energies as best they could. The silver dollars, as they clanked, created a sordid medley, until the prostitute within yelled at them to cut out their racket. In the windows of the unoccupied bungalows, brightly painted faces leered, or smiled, or called out the words of lust to passers-by stumbling about in the poorly lit sector searching for love. Out of curiosity, Maugham entered one of the bungalows. "She ceased her professional seductiveness when she learned I had come in only for a pleasant little chat," Maugham told Menard. "I refused a drink, in sharp awareness of the countless microbes no doubt incubated on the rims of the dirty glasses on her sink, and I didn't want my ear-drums rattled by the gramophone. She sat down, ill at east, and studied me with increasing disfavor.

"'You lookin' for a virgin, or young boy?' she suddenly asked.

"I assured her, neither.

"'Well, if you ain't in here to do nothin,' she informed me impatiently, 'then you'll have to pay double—which is two dollars. Bed-work is fast, talk is slow.'"[2]

Maugham handed her two dollars and walked out into the night. "Bushwah!" the insulted whore shouted after him.

It was the intention of the zealots to destroy Iwelei. Maugham talked to one of the circuit court judges and remarked that (recalling his early medical experience in London) should they succeed, there would be no controlling the spread of venereal disease and the incidence of rape would increase. The judge was blasé. He was not concerned with human suffering but rather with what he regarded as human morality. The attitude of the religious zealots became embodied in the Reverend Davidson in "Rain." Dr. MacPhail, Maugham's point-of-view character, describes a typical harangue in the short story.

"He came over to the table and stood in front of it as though it were a lectern.

"'You see, they were so naturally depraved that they couldn't be brought to see their wickedness. We had to make sins out of what they thought were natural actions. We had to make it a sin, not only to commit adultery and to lie and to thieve, but to expose their bodies, and to dance and not to come to church. I made it a sin for a girl to show her bosom and a sin for a man not to wear trousers.'

"'How?' asked Dr. MacPhail, not without surprise.

"'I instituted fined. Obviously the only way to make people realize that an action is sinful is to punish them if they commit it. I fined them

if they didn't come to church, and I fined them if they danced. I fined
them if they were improperly dressed. I had a tariff, and every sin had
to be paid for either in money or work. And at last I made them
understand.'

"'But did they never refuse to pay?'

"'How could they?' asked the missionary.

"'It would be a brave man who tried to stand up against Mr.
Davidson,' said his wife, tightening her lips.

"Dr. MacPhail looked at Davidson with troubled eyes. What he
heard shocked him, but he hesitated to express his disapproval.

"'You must remember that in the last resort I could expel them
from their church membership.'

"'Did they mind that?'

"Davidson smiled a little and gently rubbed his hands.

"'They couldn't sell their copra. When the men fished they got no
share of the catch. It meant something very like starvation. Yes, they
minded quite a lot.'"[3]

The judge invited Maugham to be present in his court while he
meted out sentence to the prostitutes. He adjudged *their* conduct im-
moral. He ignored their customers. He ignored the political machine
which, induced by bribes, had allowed Iwelei to flourish; and he ignored the fact that he was outlawing natural human behavior. One
hundred and two prostitutes were given suspended sentences, provided
however that they did not practice their trade for thirteen months (or
imprisonment), and that they lead model lives defined as not practicing
their trade. Six were deported. One of them booked passage aboard the
same ship as Maugham, bound for Pago Pago.

In his introduction to the first volume of his short stories, in view
of the fact that Maugham had netted over a half million dollars from
"Rain," he supplied the reader with a facsimile of his original notes
transcribed during that voyage. They bear a surprising closeness to the
characters as they came to be described in the story. Maugham was
hated for this reason. True, he shaped his stories and his characters'
destinies to suit his own pattern; what happened to them was by his
design; but the characters all too often were directly from life and people as he had known them. Occasionally, someone saw himself where
Maugham had had no intention of describing such a person; this
amused him. He believed that we know our fellowmen primarily
through their vices. Whether or not he was right, it goes without saying
that as readers we are primarily interested in their vices, and so in the

end it works out to the same thing. Maugham, in his notes in preparation for writing "Rain," gave a rather concise statement of the plot. It
is just as well that it be quoted since none of the three motion picture
versions, neither the play nor the musical comedy, follows it exactly nor
with quite the same emphasis as in the short story.

"I talked with the missionary and his wife but once," Maugham
wrote, "and with Miss Thompson not at all. Here is the note for the
story: 'A prostitute, flying from Honolulu after a raid, lands at Pago
Pago. There lands there also a missionary and his wife. Also the narrator. All are obliged to stay there owing to an outbreak of measles. The
missionary, finding out her profession, persecutes her. He reduces her
to misery, shame, and repentence; he has no mercy on her. He induces
the governor to order her return to Honolulu. One morning he is found
with his throat cut by his own hand and she is once more radiant and
self-possessed. She looks at men and scornfully exclaims: 'dirty
pigs.'"[4]

The story ends on just that note. Every other work based on an
adaptation of the story mitigates Sadie Thompson's observation in an
attempt presumably to make her more human, more conscious of a
suffering humanity of which she is a part, or just more acceptable (if
the truth be told) to the audience. Four years after his return to where
he lived in the south of France, Maugham wrote the story and titled it
"Miss Thompson." Maugham's American agent sent it to a number of
magazines which then were paying excellent money for short stories,
but they all turned it down. The editors reasoned that their readers
would object to a story in which a man of God succumbs to sexual relations with a blonde whore. Finally, the dauntless H.L. Mencken, editor
of *Smart Set,* accepted the story for publication in the April, 1921
number; it was the first of Maugham's South Sea stories to find its way
into print. The title was later changed to "Rain." It remains his most
successful short story.

Burton Rascoe, editor of *The Smart Set Anthology* (1924), told the
following story in his introductory remarks to the first edition of that
volume. "I remembered. . .going up to [George Jean] Nathan's apartment at the Royalton for a visit and cocktails," he wrote. "Nathan said
he had just bought a short story he would like me to read, it would only
take a few minutes. He passed the manuscript to me with the title page
already folded over, along with the slipcover of the manuscript, so I
could begin the text at once. When I had finished I let out an exclama-
tion of delight and told him it was a 'whizz' or a 'knockout' or

something of the sort. 'Another version of *Thais,*' I remarked, 'but what a beauty.'

"'I think it is the best story we have ever received at *The Smart Set,* don't you?'

"'I don't know what you have received at *The Smart Set* but it will be one of the best you have ever published.'

"''Guess who the author is?'

"''No idea.'

"''Somerset Maugham.'

"'Naw. How can you pay Somerset Maugham's prices? I thought your top was about a hundred dollars and you pay Ben Hecht and me thirty-five to fifty.' (Maugham was . . . a highly successful playwright; he was famous as the author of *Of Human Bondage;* his *Moon and Sixpence* had been a best seller; and he was selling to *Cosmopolitan;* and Ray Long was supposed to be paying him $1,500 to $2,500 for every story or article he sent in.)

"'We got this for $200. Long turned it down and after him so did everybody else. We are the last ones Paul Reynolds thinks of because of our word rate, so he came to us last. We offered him two hundred, and there it is.'"[5]

In 1921, having secured magazine publication for several of his stories, Maugham arranged for their American and English hardbound publication in book form. He was staying at a hotel in Hollywood, introducing himself to motion picture producers with a mind that some of his very successful stage plays might serve as suitable stories for cinematic treatment. He was about to start on another trip, this time to Australia, the Federated Malay States, and Borneo. The galleys for the first six stories in book form, titled *The Trembling of a Leaf,* had recently arrived. The conferences with the motion picture companies had not been all he had anticipated and his mind was on the imminent voyage when, one night, John Colton, whom he had previously met and who was staying in a room across the hall, knocked on his door. Colton was wondering if Maugham had anything he might read, preferably fiction, as he was having trouble sleeping. Since he had no magazines or detective stories with him, Maugham gave Colton the galleys to read instead.

The next morning Colton was again at Maugham's door. He was very excited. He wanted to make a stage adaptation of "Miss Thompson" if Maugham himself had no intentions along those lines. Maugham was somewhat irritable, being awakened early, but readily,

William Gargan and Joan Crawford with director Lewis Milestone in the center preparing a scene for *Rain* (United Artists, 1932). Photo courtesy of TV Cinema Sales Corp.

if somewhat coldly, gave his permission. The bargain was sealed with a handshake and Maugham went back to bed. It was a curious affair. Once the book was in print, Maugham was besieged with offers from many who saw dramatic possibilities in the story, several offering him large cash guarantees for the stage rights. Of these, quite a few had far more experience and evident theatrical success behind them than John

Colton. Yet Maugham stuck by his word and Colton retained the stage rights.

   Rain, as Colton titled it, became one of the most successful plays in American theatrical history. It opened in New York City on November 7, 1922 with the famous Jeanne Eagels as its star. Wilmon Menard described Maugham as initially distressed by the success of *Rain* as a stage play and, in view of the fact that he had not thought of the theatrical potential himself, as chary to praise the Colton version. He quoted a conversation with Maugham in which Maugham related, "I went to see it with John Colton for the first time, and when it was over I felt it had been a mistake to turn my short story into a play. John Colton and the coauthor, Clemence Randolph, had made a lot of changes. Stagewise I suppose they were commercially sound. But when John turned to me at the final curtain and asked: 'Well, what's your opinion now?', I had to tell him honestly: 'I still think "Miss Thompson" is a better short story.'"[6]

   I am doubtful if the success of the play and the impact of this on Maugham's vanity had anything to do with his attitude. Colton and Randolph rather abruptly, and significantly, altered the entire meaning of Maugham's original pattern; they wrote in a sentimental love affair for Sadie with the idea that she was now going to settle down and raise a nice little family in Australia; the validity and integrity of a human being's right to be himself — in this case Sadie's misandry and Maugham's possible misogyny — were altered to accommodate the emergence of a new Sadie, sadder but wiser, for whom domesticity was a desirable personal goal — which meant changing Sadie's personality. Above all, the ideology of the story — the power fantasies of the righteous and the suffering which they impose on the rest of us; the loneliness of the human soul, sealed off from any sense of community by fears, ambitions, lusts, and perversions — is excluded so as to turn the entire undertaking into a slightly off-color romance. To a man of Maugham's sympathies, for whom this story represented a statement of his own perception of the world and of life, the play had to be a disappointment, if not also a brilliant illustration of the farce of commercial success. It was the Colton adaptation which became the basis for the later musical version and all three motion picture screenplays. In the process, the meaning of the story was lost.

   In addition to its long Broadway run, *Rain* played in a London engagement and in several roadshows. Tallulah Bankhead tried to make a Broadway revival of the play in 1935, but she was personally rejected for the London production by Maugham himself, an action for which she never forgave him. June Havoc sang and danced in the 1944 musical version. Bette Davis played Sadie in a sketch for her revue *Two's Company* in 1952. Juliet Prowse performed the "Sadie Thompson dance" on television and, shortly before her death, Marilyn Monroe had been signed to play the role in a television spectacular. Marilyn had blonde hair, as does Sadie; she was fat, as Sadie is; but Sadie is not stupid in life the way Marilyn had been and, again unlike Marilyn Monroe, Sadie has guts, character, and fortitude. Perhaps it is just as well Marilyn did not play the part.

With the exception of the *Rain* sequence from *The Jeanne Eagels Story* (Columbia, 1957) starring Kim Novak, Sadie Thompson has been played on the screen by Gloria Swanson, Joan Crawford, and Rita Hayworth. *Sadie Thompson* (United Artists, 1928) was made by Gloria Swanson Productions and was not available since its initial release until after Gloria Swanson's death. When, at last, it was reissued, the final reel had decomposed and still photos were substituted to bring the film to its close. The plot deviated from the stage play. The character of the Reverend Davidson was changed to Alfred Atkinson, played by Lionel Barrymore, more a reformer than a missionary. Raoul Walsh, who had got his start with D.W. Griffith and would later become an important film director in his own right, was cast as Sergeant Tim O'Hara. Joe Horn, the trader, was played by James Marcus and Charles Lane portrayed Dr. MacPhail. Blanche Frederici was Mrs. Atkinson, Florence Midgley was Mrs. MacPhail, Sophia Artega was Ameena Horn, and Will Stanton was Quartermaster Bates. In addition to acting in the film, Raoul Walsh was also credited as its director and for the screen adaptation. C. Gardner Sullivan did the titles. The picture was released on January 7, 1928 in black and white, silent, running nine reels, 8,600 feet. Gloria Swanson played the Sadie Thompson role to the hilt, turning her seductive charm on Atkinson, the reformer, rather than snubbing him as the role more conventionally has been played. The picture stirred up a great deal of unfavorable comment.

Joseph M. Schenck, four years later, decided to make a talking version of *Rain*. He contracted Lewis Milestone, who had scored a box-office success with *All Quiet on the Western Front* (Universal, 1930), to direct it. Schenck wanted Joan Crawford for the Sadie Thompson role. She was under contract to M-G-M, then a subsidiary of Loew's, Inc., of which Schenck's brother, Nicholas, was president. Further, Schenck was a good friend of studio manager Louis B. Mayer. A rare thing, indeed, was an M-G-M loan-out with virtually nothing in return, but that is how it happened. Joan Crawford was signed.

William Gargan was appearing in a stage play, *The Animal Kingdom*. He had made two pictures for Paramount at its Astoria studios, the second one, *Misleading Lady* (Paramount, 1932), he claimed in his autobiography, *Why Me?* (1969), was directed by Lewis Milestone and it was on this basis he was engaged by Milestone to appear as Sergeant O'Hara in *Rain*. As released, *Misleading Lady* credited Stuart Walker as the director. Walker was a stage producer who became a contract director at Paramount in the early thirties. However, as David L. Parker and Burton J. Shapiro pointed out in their career study of Lewis Milestone for *Close-up: The Contract Director* (1976), "the *New York Times* issue of April 19, 1932, reviewing *Misleading Lady,* carries on the same page a news item in its 'Picture and Players' column about Milestone's arriving in Hollywood to direct several pictures for United Artists, including *Rain,* . . . so there may be something in these recollections" of Gargan's.[7]

Walter Huston, who had played a grim Calvinist in *A House Divided* (Universal, 1932), was cast in the role of the Reverend Davidson. All around, it was excellent casting.

When it came to the scenario, Milestone did again what he had done in filming *All Quiet on the Western Front:* he went back to the original source, the short story. While still ostensibly using the play as his reference and the basis for the screenplay, Milestone added a number of highlights from the story which helped to alter the meaning so as to restore some of the original emphasis that Maugham had intended. Maxwell Anderson, the Broadway playwright, collaborated with Milestone on the adaptation and was given screen credit.

Milestone knew his actors well. This point cannot be stressed too strongly. I believe that he went outside the confines of the motion picture and cast his principals in terms of the kind of people *they really were.* Sadie may seem to be in love with O'Hara, according to their romantic scenes together, but the viewer is wiser by the time of the fade-out; Sadie Thompson's disillusionment is complete. It is an impression which does not need to be stated because it has become inevitable through the entire development of the characters throughout the course of the film. Gargan's O'Hara is a simple, sincere lush who knows so little of life and the world that he is able to delude himself into believing he can actually settle down with Sadie. Gargan tells his reader in *Why Me?:* "They say it is false energy you get from the bottle, and undoubtedly false courage. But some reality is too real, too terrible to be borne, so we seek our escape. I can't change the reality, so I change myself. I take a snifter, and the strange faces that loom up become friendly faces. I lie to myself this way, but such delusion may be necessary. It is the old. . . theme; take away man's illusions, and you kill his hopes, and eventually kill him."[8] After decades of self-abuse, smoking and drinking excessively, Gargan lost his larynx to carcinoma. No sooner was the operation over than the nurse had to slip him a shot of whiskey to ease his nerves. At every opportunity, he sabotaged his career. When he finally landed a successful television role, taking over from Lee Tracy in *Martin Kane, Private Eye* which began on NBC in 1949, he gave it up, presumably for moral considerations, namely the shows seemed to contain sexually suggestive women. He had come some distance since he played opposite Joan Crawford's Sadie Thompson! "I am a beat-up Catholic, but I am a Catholic," Gargan wrote. "Never once in my bleakest moments had I contemplated suicide. My faith prevented it. . . ."[9] Faith and the bottle! This was William Gargan, and this was the way Lewis Milestone used him on the screen, without a change, true to his own personality and temperament.

Prior to filming, Gargan was a guest at a dinner at which were present among others, Louis B. Mayer, Joan Crawford, Lewis Milestone, and Walter Catlett. Gargan started off by telling Joan Crawford that he had never seen her on the screen. Then Catlett, who according to Gargan "had previewed the dinner with a couple of belts of Chicken Cock in our room," leaned over and remarked to Joan: "'Listen, fishcake, when Jeanne Eagels died, *Rain* died with her.'"[10] The incident embarrassed Gargan, whenever he thought of it, for the rest of his life.

For exteriors, *Rain* was shot on Catalina Island. "Before we ever shot a scene," Gargan recollected, "Milestone would call in a bevy of cartoonists and they would sketch the scene. Then the actors would be blocked in with the cameras, and we would begin rehearsing."[11] In his opinion, the scene he liked best was that with Joan as Sadie in which the two of them walked around the porch of Horn's trading post, O'Hara attempting to convince Sadie to flee to Australia and wait there for him. "It took place at night," he wrote, "in the rain (pipes overhead pumped salt water from the ocean down on us), and the electricians and cable carriers were in constant danger from electric shock."[12] They walked around the porch, which circled the entire building, and Milestone wanted the camera to follow them in one continuous take. Shooting of the scene began at nine one night and lasted until four the next morning when, on the fifteenth take, Milestone was satisfied. However, when the rushes were screened the next day, it was discovered that there was a scratch on the entire negative. Two days later the scene was shot again, this time being completed the way Milestone wanted it on the fifth take. Milestone's way of working nettled Gargan and, in the end, he little understood the picture and what it was about. He accused Walter Huston of over-acting. *Rain* was in production for ten weeks and he earned $15,000.

Joan Crawford's official account of the film in her autobiography, *A Portrait of Joan* (1962), is somewhat different, although she, too, was disappointed in the film. In her case, even when interviewed personally about *Rain,* her objection was mostly to the way in which the film was received by the public, the largely negative response to her and her portrayal of a whore on screen. She was a star at M-G-M, known then chiefly for flapper roles such as that in *Dance, Fools, Dance* (M-G-M, 1931), and her public had come to respect her as being a kind of ideal person, rather than an actress capable of playing totally diverse roles. This is unfortunate because Crawford was one of the very few stars from Hollywood's Golden Age who was truly an accomplished professional with a talent far in excess of that required for most of her screen appearances in M-G-M films before and after *Rain.* Perhaps something of Catlett's comment is reflected in her observation that "I was haunted by my inferiority to famous Sadie Thompsons of the past, Jeanne Eagels, who created the part on the stage, and Gloria Swanson, who appeared in the early silent-film version. I hadn't seen them, but they were constantly held up to me by my coworkers. Mr. Joe Schenck thought I was worried unnecessarily, he told me to listen to my director, but Lewis Milestone frightened me. I wasn't wise enough about acting to understand how brilliant a man this was or how talented a director. He had worked out blueprints for every scene, precisely what I was to do and how to do it; but to me, no actress worthy of the name could be a puppet in anyone's hands. I was no Method actress, I was an emotional one — in *Rain,* far too emotional."13

One need only recall the number of takes Milestone demanded in the porch scene with Crawford and Gargan to realize that *nothing* got into the release print that he did not want to be in it. "My fans wouldn't accept Sadie," Crawford went on. "They would accept me as Letty Lynton who was just as vulgar, but she had style. Cheapness and vulgarity they would not accept."14 This is the way she felt at the time and in retrospect, although it is probably irrelevant in evaluating her performance in the film. *Rain* was a motion picture forty years ahead of its time. By the time *Klute* (Warner's, 1971) was made, Jane Fonda could win an Academy Award for playing a prostitute without public opprobrium.

When *Rain* was made, movie-goers were different people living in a different era. They were naive and went to movie palaces to dream and see their wishes fulfilled. They were not ready for very much reality. Psychological drama in the deepest sense was nearly unknown in the cinema, especially the American cinema. *Rain,* as Lewis Milestone conceived of it, is the drama of pain, the agony of knowledge, the suffering that comes from understanding one's fellow human beings too well. It is a drama of human truth amid its attendant torments, its rank delusions, the destructiveness of the will to power, the twisted sexual energies so often at the bottom of moral bigotry, the misery of the lonely divided from the herd by an acquaintance too intimate with human motivations and psychological maladjustment.

Lewis Milestone saw Sadie Thompson exactly the way Joan Crawford played her. It all came to one affect, at the fade-out. Maugham described that terrible sensation again in his novel, *Christmas Holiday* (1939), when he wrote of the principal character's coming of age: "It was a fact that he had done nothing; his father thought he had had a devil of a time and was afraid he had contracted a venereal disease, and he hadn't even had a woman; only one thing had happened to him, it was rather curious when you come to think of it, and he didn't know what to do about it: the bottom had fallen out of his world."[15] Sadie Thompson, at the end of *Rain,* has attained that state of knowledge of the ways of the world which is above speech and can only be captured by the camera.

In his scenario, Milestone kept two significant alterations made in the play. The first is the love affair between Sadie and a Marine, with, however, the shift in emphasis I have already mentioned. The viewer readily perceives that O'Hara can never dispel Sadie's isolation. The second change is more subtle.

It is not known if Sadie was the rightful praenomen of the blonde whore who booked passage aboard the steamer *Sonoma* bound for Sydney on December 4, 1916. Wilmon Menard did at least establish that her surname was Thompson. The passenger list was carried in *The Pacific Commercial Advertiser* of Honolulu for Tuesday, December 5, 1916, and Menard reproduced it in his book. The missionaries were probably Mr. and Mrs. J.J. Mulqueen, the only passengers other than

Maugham, Gerald Haxton, and Miss Thompson. The ship had a forced layover at Pago Pago due to an outbreak of smallpox.

At the time, Pago Pago was under the administration of the United States Navy, but since has been transferred to the Department of the Interior. The combination trading post–hotel in which the travelers were compelled to stay was later renamed the Sadie Thompson Hotel, perhaps misspelling her praenomen but commemorating her memory. Maugham and Haxton roomed next to Miss Thompson who immediately took up with a native, playing her gramophone and making love to all hours. "'I no savvy his name,'" Iosefo Suafo'a, the lover, told Menard, "'but I know he make blentay touble for Sadie. We keep him 'wake all night, an' he swear like hell an' pound on wall wit' fist. Oh, he vairee damn sore man! But me an' Sadie jes' laugh an' keep on make lub. Sadie an' me, we sure have lots of fun!'"[16] Maugham asked the innkeeper to do something about the woman. Even with the gramophone silent, the bed springs cried with strain beneath the weight of the lovers' bodies. It was not until Maugham and Haxton departed that the whore tried to marry the Samoan only to find herself deported back to Honolulu by Navy officials. The islander was an enlisted man.

Maugham's feelings toward the prostitute in his short story were no more sympathetic than those he felt toward Davidson. The play made a heroine of Sadie. The audience's sympathies were drawn toward her in her persecution. It is only intimated in *Rain* that Sadie is a loose woman. In *Miss Sadie Thompson* (Columbia, 1953), it is stated emphatically that Sadie is *only* a singer who happened to work in a dive, which puts the onus even more on Davidson for thinking otherwise. Further, it gave Rita Hayworth in the role an opportunity to sing a couple of numbers. Joan Crawford may not have studied the work of her predecessors; Rita Hayworth quite obviously had studied Crawford's portrayal and probably had learned from Joan's experience not to overdo the stronger implications. Not only did Milestone carry over this affection for Sadie in his screen treatment but also, as in the stage play, the script took a positive attitude toward Sadie's conversion, reserving judgment on the existence of divine grace by only condemning Davidson as an improper agent. Sadie becomes radiant, aglow thanks to unearthly special lighting effects which took Milestone many hours of experimentation to achieve. The surface impression is that Sadie has become truly repentant.

Maugham was harshly realistic in his description of Sadie after her

Joan Crawford with Walter Huston as the Reverend Davidson after Sadie's conversion in *Rain* (United Artists, 1932). Photo courtesy of TV Cinema Sales Corp.

so-called conversion. "She had not troubled to dress herself, but wore a dirty dressing-gown, and her hair was tied in a sluttish knot. She had given her face a dab with a wet towel, but it was all swollen and creased with crying. She looked drab."[17] This is not the image on the screen; nor, had it been, could one think of Walter Huston's Davidson commenting, as he does, "Sadie. . . you're radiant. . . beautiful."

The religious question was a sticky one for Colton and Randolph and I can understand why Maugham was displeased by their compromises. It was not Maugham's intention that Davidson be perceived as a misguided missionary. He knew the island missionaries for what they were. In "Honolulu," another short story in *The Trembling of a*

Leaf, the narrator is shown about the island city and learns that all of Hawaii's richest families are descended from one-time missionaries who were first given land by the natives and then took still more in exchange for promises of heavenly forgiveness or reward. "'Heaven helps those who help themselves,'" he remarks scathingly.[18] It was unthinkable to Maugham that Davidson's hocus-pocus represented anything more than a desire to exert power over Sadie, to bend her to his will and then to satisfy himself in her. He drew Davidson as a weak man whose wife frequently must bolster him against the depths of despair. As written, it is a finely wrought psychological portrait. Milestone's direction, on the other hand, is nowhere more evident than in his handling of the conversion. Nietzsche once quipped that if men wanted him to sing better songs to their Redeemer, His disciples would have to look more redeemed. Sadie, in the story, appears squalid in her redemption. On the screen, Milestone followed the format of the play but notwithstanding had Joan Crawford's acting undermine clandestinely the apparent visual impression. When Maugham wrote the story, he added a complication to his original sketch of the plot. Davidson persuades the Governor to have Sadie deported on the next boat which, by accident, happens to be bound for San Francisco. If she returns there, she faces a three-year prison sentence. The play retained this complication, as did Milestone's film. With Joan Crawford in the role, the inference is made, by means of fleeting facial expressions and a momentary hollowness, that perhaps the conversion is a sham, a final desperate ploy on Sadie's part to get Davidson to change his mind.

I have said that Gloria Swanson in her performance as Sadie went out of her way to tempt the reformer into fornication. That was one way of dealing with the problem. Jeanne Eagels in the stage version underwent an actual conversion. Joan Crawford's Sadie leaves the viewer somewhat in doubt as to the total sincerity of her change in character. All the time she manages to become increasingly dependent on Davidson, needing him, calling to him, alone with him nearly always. This was Milestone's master stroke. Davidson, as he conceived of the role, would not have succumbed to Sadie in the circumstances in which Maugham had described her; but he might very well succumb once she was transformed into a shining angel. Sadie did it for her survival; and, even as she did it, she regretted having to do it, and was only made sadder by it. Milestone needed precisely Crawford's emotionalism to make Sadie's mood swings at once credible and sufficiently ambiguous.

Milestone's underlying philosophy in *Rain* was the same as it had been in *All Quiet on the Western Front:* the inalienable right of the individual to be himself amid all the destructive pressures and counter-forces of a conformist social order. If this is not a new point of view, it is nonetheless a refreshing one and one definitely out of step with the United States in 1932. *Rain* broke even; it did not make money.

Physically, Walter Huston is the embodiment of the Reverend Davidson as Maugham described him, "very tall and thin...hollow cheeks and curiously high cheekbones; he had so cadaverous an air that it surprised you to notice how full and sensual were his lips. ... His dark eyes, set deep in their sockets, were large and tragic.... But the most striking thing about him was the feeling he gave you of a sup-pressed fire."[19] Huston dramatized the Davidson character, made him a self-dramatist, as religious leaders so often are, so that he could make an example of himself. After he fornicated with Sadie, he killed himself. Why? Maugham was too clever a playwright to show us Davidson in sexual congress with Sadie. Instead, he let the reader wonder. Did guilt drive Davidson to do it? Or did Sadie laugh at him, ridicule him, spit on him? When Columbia Pictures remade the film in 1953, the screenplay insisted on showing Jose Ferrer, totally miscast as Davidson, lunging at Rita Hayworth's Sadie, consumed with passion. Even Colton and Randolph were not such novices as to commit so evident a blunder. The imagination of the reader or the viewer is an artist's greatest asset and he must know how to use it effectively.

"Each one of us is alone in the world," Maugham wrote in *The Moon and Sixpence* (1919). "He is shut in a tower of brass, and can com-municate with his fellows only by signs and the signs have no common value, so that their sense is vague and uncertain. We seek pitifully to convey to others the treasures of our heart, but they have not the power to accept them, and so we go lonely, side by side but not together, unable to know our fellows and unknown by them. We are like people living in a country whose language they know so little that, with all manner of beautiful and profound things to say, they are condemned to the banalities of the conversation manual."[20] In "Rain" there is really no person with whom one can become wholly sympathetic, not even Dr. MacPhail who is fundamentally indifferent. The revisions in the stage play sought to overcome the dreadful isolation true of the characters in the story and, due in large measure to the effectiveness of these revisions, the property went on to earn a million dollars. The ma-jor revision was to give Sadie a love affair. The compromise is not realistic. The sense of hope dies hardest and the anguish of its passing is nearly unendurable. So inevitably, compromises always are more popular than the reality. Henrik Ibsen regarded love as a life-sustaining illusion and found it preferable therefore to the actuality. Yet, just sometimes, as fleeting and fraudulent as it so frequently can be exposed as being, it does have its hour. Jeanne Eagels lived in a tower of brass. For this reason, I believe, her stage performance was especially moving. Joan Crawford, whose childhood was as lonely and as fraught with bitter pain as that of any of Maugham's characters, refused to let her Sadie abandon completely the hope that her tormented and suffering soul might still press far enough beyond her so as to affect another human being. The audience, wrapped up in the implied criticisms of organized religion, missed the central point in Milestone's film and Crawford's portrayal: that there is in Sadie's struggles the suggestion of a humanity to which most, regrettably, remain oblivious.

For Rita Hayworth *Miss Sadie Thompson* was intended to be a comeback picture. Her marriage to Aly Khan had ended in disappointment with Rita broke. She returned to work for Harry Cohn and Columbia for $3,500 a week. Her first film under the new contract was *Affair in Trinidad* (Columbia, 1952) which did good business. Then came the two expensive blockbusters, *Salome* (Columbia, 1953) and *Miss Sadie Thompson*. They were financed by Columbia but produced by Rita's Beckworth Productions to provide her with a greater share in the profits. While filming *Miss Sadie Thompson* in Hawaii, Rita fell in love for the fourth time with singer Dick Haynes.

One asset this version of the story has is the genuine location shooting in the South Seas, the tropical backdrop, the sparkling Pacific, the verdant paradise of that seemingly enchanted clime with its volcanic mountains rising from the ocean's floor. Another asset was Rita Hayworth. Whatever the perpetual instability of her personal life, she had lost little of her ravishing beauty and photographed well even when disheveled. During her song and dance sequences at Chung's saloon, Rita was costumed in a bright orange dress, performing to a jive beat amid a haze of tobacco smoke. Rita so much relished the role she insisted on not wearing a girdle and Harry Cohn, who termed her antics malingering, demanded that the cameras be kept waisthigh.

What failed miserably was the screenplay by Harry Kleiner, filled with hackneyed compromises and blushing niceties. Dr. MacPhail, played by Russell Collins, was altered completely to a pompous bigot. Maugham's story described the emphasis Christianity so often puts on outward appearances and he enjoyed juxtaposing this with the unhappy facts of mortal existence. Kleiner did not know how to adjust this view to the world of 1953, following a second orgy of global war and the terror of a third. Davidson accuses MacPhail of reading Freud, Adler, and Jung and of adopting a position of moral relativism. He storms off to bed while MacPhail engages in a Freudian diagnosis of Davidson's inner motives.

Davidson's attempts to seduce Sadie are so clumsy as only to incite amusement and scarcely justify his suicide. When O'Hara, played by Aldo Ray, learns from Davidson that Sadie sang at the Emerald Club in Honolulu, he dresses her down for her moral lassitude and calls her unclean. Later, he repents this lapse into conventionality, reasserts his undying love for her, and begs her forgiveness. From the outset, he has been panting after Sadie. It is rather comic when he proposes marriage to her, then is repelled, only to renew the offer after second thoughts. Sadie's acceptance reduces the story to farce. The conversion is redefined as self-discovery. The implication is that Sadie, as a result of fornicating with Davidson, has learned to live with herself and is now prepared to settle down in Australia with a Marine she has known for only three days and who himself, besides having changed his mind once, has not seen a white woman for years. In the 1932 version, responding to Davidson's fanatic intolerance, Dr. MacPhail comments that the founder of Davidson's religion wasn't so squeamish. The line was changed in *Miss Sadie Thompson* to "our" religion and MacPhail is himself a devout Christian. At the end of the film, in an effort to provide Sadie with a better perspective on her sexual congress with Davidson, MacPhail recommends to Sadie that she separate in her own mind what Davidson said, which supposedly was valid, from what he did which was presumably unrelated to his convictions and a betrayal of them. *Miss Sadie Thompson* failed at the box office and it has not stood the test of time because it sought to combine the musical and stage Sadies with that saccharine Hollywood sense of total unreality that makes the celluloid dramas of the fifties particularly unappealing.

Even if I were to agree with Maugham that "Miss Thompson" is best as a short story, I should not want to overlook Milestone's film as a penetrating example of motion picture art and an anomoly in American cinema history for its championing an individual's right to be himself and for its psychological realism. Human nature, in its contrariness, is best described by means of contradictions. Maugham showed it thus in the short story and Milestone, in his own way, managed to bring something of that vision to the screen.

Visions of Armageddon:
War of the Worlds

Paramount, 1953 (Released October, 1953).

Producer .... George Pal
Associate Producer .... Frank Freeman, Jr.
Producing Company .... Paramount Pictures
Director .... Byron Haskin
Assistant Director........................... Michael D. Moore
Original Story .... H.G. Wells
Screenplay..................................... Barre Lyndon
Music.. Leith Stevens
Photography .... George Barnes, A.S.C.
Special Effects .... Gordon Jennings, A.S.C.
Wallace Kelley, A.S.C.
Paul Lerpae, A.S.C.
Ivyl Barks
Jan Domela
Irmin Roberts, A.S.C.
Art Director .... Hal Pereira
Albert Nozaki
Film Editor........................... Everett Douglas, A.S.C.
Sound Engineer............................ Harry Lindgreen
Gene Garvin
Technicolor Color Consultant .... Monroe W. Barbure

Cast

Clayton Forrester .... Gene Barry
Sylvia Van Buren .... Ann Robinson
General Mann .... Les Tremayne
Dr. Pryor .... Bob Cornthwaite
Dr. Bilderbeck.................................. Sandro Giglio
Pastor Matthew Collins.......................... Lewis Martin
Aide to General Mann .... Houseley Stevens
Radio Announcer .... Paul Frees
Wash Perry...................................... Bill Phipps
Col. Ralph Heffner .... Vernon Rich
Cop .... Henry Brandon
Salvatore .... Jack Kruschen
Commentary by .... Sir Cedric Hardwicke
Introductory Narrator .... Paul Frees

```
Professor McPherson............................ Edgar Barrier
Buck Monahan ............................... Ralph Dumke
Bird-Brained Blonde ........................... Carolyn Jones
Man ......................................... Pierre Cressoy
Martian.................................... Charles Gemora
Sheriff...................................... Walter Sande
Dr. James..................................... Alex Frazer
Dr. DuPrey ...................................  Ann Codee
Dr. Gratzman ................................ Ivan Lebedeff
Ranger ..................................... Robert Rockwell
Zippy ........................................ Alvy Moore
Alonzo Hogue.................................. Paul Birch
Fiddler Hawkins ................................ Frank Kreig
Well-Dressed Man During Looting ................... Ned Glass
M.P. Driver ................................. Anthony Warde
Woman News Vendor ...................... Gertrude Hoffman
Secretary of Defense .......................... Freeman Lusk
Fire Chief ................................... Sydney Mason
Lookout ..................................... Peter Adams
Reporter..................................... Ted Hecht
Japanese Diplomat ............................ Teru Shimada
Chief of Staff USA ............................ Herbert Lytton
Staff Sarge ............................. Douglas Henderson
Looters ...................................... Dave Sharpe
                                           Dale Van Sickel
                                            Fred Graham
```

Running Time: 85 minutes
Current owner of world rights: Paramount Pictures

It was during the silent era that Paramount Pictures purchased screen rights from H.G. Wells to his novels *The Island of Dr. Moreau* (1896) and *The War of the Worlds* (1898). *The Island of Dr. Moreau* was brought to the screen as *The Island of Lost Souls* (Paramount, 1933) in an effort to duplicate the extraordinary success Universal was having with its horror films. In addition to *Frankenstein* (Universal, 1931), *Dracula* (Universal, 1931), and *The Mummy* (Universal, 1932), the studio cast Boris Karloff and Charles Laughton together in an eerie film based on a novel by J.B. Priestly titled *The Old Dark House* (Universal, 1932). Having cleared rights for H.G. Wells' *The Invisible Man* (1897), Universal produced it as a film in 1933 with Claude Rains in the lead directed by James Whale.

Charles Laughton was cast as Dr. Moreau and was splendidly ghoulish in the role of the sinister vivisectionist who, at one point in the screenplay, when reflecting upon his deformed creatures compares himself to God. Bela Lugosi was cast as the Ape Man who, in the novel, gave forth the Big Thinks but who in the film was confined merely to leading a chorus repeating the Law. The Law was devised by Moreau

Top to Bottom: The Striding Terrors as described by H.G. Wells and depicted by artist Frank R. Paul, on the cover of *Amazing Stories* for August, 1927. A jacket illustration for one LP recording of the original Orson Welles broadcast of *War of the Worlds.* An original art board for George Pal's *War of the Worlds* (Paramount, 1953) showing the Martian war machines with the electrical legs Pal wanted to have but which proved too dangerous in practice. Photos courtesy of *Views & Reviews* Magazine.

to prevent his animal-beast-human creatures from spilling blood and going on the rampage. The screenplay made Moreau a madman whose work in artificial evolution has little merit, thus diminishing much of the substance of Wells' story. The novel had been a premonition of the Great War, nearly two decades before it occurred. Moreau's creatures revert to their bestial instincts half way through the novel and overrun his island, killing him and bringing havoc. In the film, the creatures, chanting that they are part man, part beast, drag Laughton as Moreau to the House of Pain where he has conducted all of his operations without benefit of anaesthetics and, breaking open the glass cases, draw out scapels and other instruments so they can operate on him. The novel is no such melodrama; it has a far more sobering message. "Then I look about me at my fellow men," the narrator concludes. "And I go in fear. I see faces keen and bright, others dull and dangerous, others unsteady, insincere; none that has the calm authority of a reasonable soul. I feel as though the animal was surging up through them; that presently the degradation of the Islanders will be played over again on a larger scale."[1]

No one at Paramount, however, dared attempt *The War of the Worlds,* and so the property remained dormant until 1951 when George Pal resurrected it.

Wells had had a social axe to grind when writing this novel. He was born on September 21, 1866 of a shop keeper and a lady's maid, the offspring of a lower class family in a highly class conscious society, growing up in Kent, a British subject during an era when Great Britain was the greatest imperial power the world had seen. One third of the world's people and one fourth of the Earth's land surface was under British rule or suzerainty. Wells grew up to become a liberal thinker who strongly disapproved of the fashion in which the peoples of Africa and Asia were denied any determination of their own destinies. He concentrated the entire conflict between the Martians and the Earthmen in a pitched battle on the small surface of the British Isles. When, finally, the British capitulate, the first part of the novel ends and the second part begins, titled "The Earth under the Martians." Wells was an opponent of imperialism and he conceived of this war between creatures with fabulous machines and men with little more than sticks as a parallel to the colonial skirmishes between the technologically advanced Europeans and the primitive aborigines of the Earth's darker sectors.

If you were to read Wells' later novels which are not science fiction and his *The Outline of History* (1920) which he published after the Great War, you will find, especially in the latter, an optimism that is absent from his early adventures in pure fantasy. The ambiguity of *The War of the Worlds* is surpassed by the outright despair with which *The Time Machine: An Invention* (1895) is seen to conclude, his first and probably his finest science fantasy novel. In it, human life comes to nothing but futility and predatory co-existence, and then, at long last, to nothing at all. While Wells tended to show some sympathy for the Martians—excusing their penchant for tasting human blood, there is yet another dimension: not only the destruction of human civilization but, as well, a lament for the sudden and credible crumbling of the fabulous Martian offensive. The Martians are described as "minds that are to our minds as ours are to those of the beasts that perish, intellects vast, cool, and unsympathetic. . . ."[2] Basing his views on scientific theory at the turn of the century, Wells regarded Mars as a planet much older than the Earth because of its greater distance from the Sun. Therefore, life processes had begun earlier and life would have reached its climax and subsequent exhaustion sooner. For Wells the termination of life was exhaustion. This vision is consistent with that expressed earlier in *The Time Machine.* "That last stage of exhaustion," he wrote of the Martians, "which to us is still incredibly remote has become a present-day problem for the inhabitants of Mars. The immediate pressure of necessity has brightened their intellects, enlarged their powers, and hardened their hearts. . . . The Tasmanians, in spite of their human likeness, were entirely swept out of existence in a war of extermination waged by European immigrants, in the space of fifty years. Are we such apostles of mercy as to complain if the Martians warred in the same spirit?"[3]

Howard Koch, who in the mid–1960s would be in charge of production at Paramount Pictures, wrote the radio adaptation of Wells' novel for the Mercury Theatre of the Air broadcast on October 30, 1938. It had been Orson Welles' notion to bring *The War of the Worlds* up to date and it was presented in a modern format via news broadcasts and on-the-scene interviews over network radio. The program instigated riots in New Jersey, where Koch's version was set, with people seeking shelter from the invaders having tuned in on the show too late to hear that it was all a fictionalization. Welles was greatly criticized for some years but the program is still available on recordings and cassettes. Welles set the scene by describing world conditions as they were in 1938. "It was near the end of October," he narrated. "Business was better. The war scare was over. More men were back at work. Sales were picking up. On this particular evening, October 30, the Crossley service estimated that thirty-two million people were listening in on radios." The Martians on this Mercury Theatre broadcast were not as severe as those in Wells' novel. Two characters talk about the future on Earth under Martian rule. The Martians are presumed to be intent on perhaps breeding humans, making pets of some, training them to hunt those who have not been subjected by the Martian war effort. Men, however, might conceivably seek Martian protection and even experience an improvement in the quality of life. "Nice roomy cages," says one character, "good food, careful breeding, no worries. After a week or so chasing about the fields on empty stomachs they'll come and be glad to be caught."

George Pal may have produced a fine film in his *War of the Worlds,* but the screenplay lacks any of the social, political, psychological, or cultural overtones of Wells' novel or Orson Welles' broadcast. There is no subtlety in this presentation of the Martians, certainly no sympathy. The overpowering ecological issue, which preoccupied Wells fifty years before it became more commonplace, is significantly absent. Human beings are terrified of mass destruction. It was to this fear, and to it alone, that the argument of the screenplay was addressed. There is a point in the film when the invincible technological power of the Martians infuses the viewer with a tremendous sense of inflation. Despite the fact that it is the future of humanity that is threatened and the Martians are portrayed as repellent monsters, their fantastic military might is as shocking and awesome to watch as newsreel footage of the German Blitzkrieg during the invasion of the Ukraine, tanks rolling across meadows, fighter planes swooping down from the clouds, bombers darkening the sky overhead. Not even the atomic bomb can stop the Martians' terrible advance.

George Pal, born in 1908, was a puppeteer who went to Hollywood in 1940 and began by producing a series of Puppetoons and specialized in trick photography. His first science fiction enterprise was *Destination Moon* (Eagle-Lion, 1950) followed by *When Worlds Collide* (Paramount, 1951). Both films earned Academy Awards, as did *War of the Worlds* after its release. "I was stimulated by the problems it posed," George Pal said in an interview. "Although written fifty-six years before, in many respects it had withstood the advances of time remarkably well and remained an exciting and visionary story of the future. It offered me my greatest challenge up to that time to figure out

The way the Martians looked in *War of the Worlds* (Paramount, 1953). Photo courtesy of Paramount Pictures.

how to film the Martian machines, their heat and disintegration rays, and the destruction and chaos they cause when they invade the Earth." *War of the Worlds* cost $2,000,000 to produce, contrasted with only $586,000 for *Destination Moon* and $936,000 for *When Worlds Collide*. The special effects required six months' shooting time, the opticals another two months, after forty days' working with the actors at the Paramount studios in Hollywood and on location in Arizona. Nearly half the film needed some kind of special effect. Paramount mounted a brilliant promotion for the film which spurred a tremendous box-office response.

War of the Worlds opens with a narration by Sir Cedric Hardwicke describing the dilemma of the Martians and how all the planets in this solar system, other than Earth, are unsuited for habitation. Martian civilization is declared to be far older than that on Earth while, curiously, Venus is ignored completely as a possibility for colonization. In modernizing Wells, Pal was aware that contemporary audiences were familiar with the basic concepts of nuclear physics, atomic fission, and

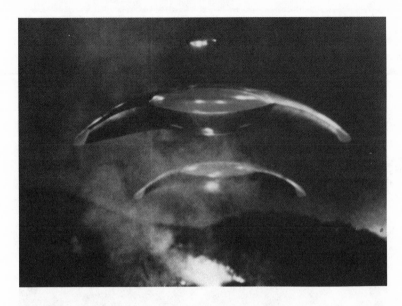

The Martian war machines as finally photographed in *War of the Worlds* (Paramount, 1953). Photo courtesy of Paramount Pictures.

gravitational fields. Ingeniously, the basis of Martian power was magnetism which called upon the electrical foundation of the universe. I do not know where else in science fiction films this has been presented so matter-of-factly and yet it is a concept far-reaching in its implications. The Martian war machines are suspended by reversing magnetic polarities; everything in their midst and for miles around is magnetized. Wrist watches no longer function; power plants are knocked out. But the screenplay overlooked the most obvious consequence of the Martian use of magnetism: none of the motorized vehicles shown in the film, not cars, trucks, or tanks, could use their ignition systems because they are based on magnetism and in most cases so are military launching and firing systems. Interference with the Earth's magnetic field would literally incapacitate our technology.

Wells based his concept of space travel on the rather primitive notions of Jules Verne. The Martians commence their attack by firing a series of missiles toward the Earth. In the film, these missiles are meteor-like and land according to a definite formation all over the planet — which makes the conflict global. However, these missiles in the film are in no way powered or fueled and, apparently, the Martians themselves have made no effort at interplanetary exploration. The mechanical tripods which Wells imagined have been replaced by machines which use magnetic force fields for locomotion, albeit flight *per se,* even within the Earth's atmosphere, is something evidently unknown to the Martians.

Originally, Pal wanted to give the Martian machines electrical legs. It had been his intention to have the miniature machines rest on three pulsating beams of static electricity. Some one million volts were fed down wires to the suspended miniatures from an overhead rig on a sound stage. A high velocity blower was employed to force the sparks down the thin wire legs, but the apparatus proved too dangerous. Not only might the stage itself catch fire, but there was the very real possibility of electrocution. However sound the idea may have been in principle, in actuality it might have proved as disastrous as it would be pictured as being on screen. Yet, it was intriguing to speculate on Martian science based on electro-magnetism rather than nuclear power.

The special effects people built three war machines, forty-two inches in diameter and constructed from copper to be consistent with the iron oxide hue of the Red Planet. They were flat, semi-disc shaped objects with a long cobra neck which emitted the devastating heat ray, an electrical television scanner at the end of a snake-like metal coil which emerged from the body of the machine and wing-tip flame throwers. The machines were controlled by fifteen hair-thin wires connected to a device on an overhead track. This variation of standard puppetry permitted the machines to function realistically. The heat rays were produced by means of welding wire backed by a blow-torch. The sounds of the ray were manufactured through striking chords on three guitars, amplifying them, and then playing them backwards with reverberation.

The Martians were the creation of Paramount art director Albert Nozaki. Wells had pictured them as clumsy, with truncated tentacles by which they radioed their machines. The clumsiness was due to the variance in gravity. Pal's Martians were crab-like, huge, with one Cyclops eye with three separate lenses, a gigantic head encasing an over-sized brain and long, spindly tentacles with suckers on the end for arms and fingers. The final forms were built out of papier-mâché and sheet rubber with arms that actually pulsated via rubber tubing; the entire organism was painted lobster red. Charles Gemora, a man of short stature, got inside this rig, moving around on his knees with his hands coming just to the elbows of the Martian tentacles. The creature is only

seen for a few seconds. Pal estimated that the effect would be more terrifying if used in extreme moderation.

The Paramount story department insisted on a love theme between the principals played by Gene Barry and Ann Robinson. Even
when the air force drops the atomic bomb on the Martians, their
machines prove inviolable due to protective magnetic fields which,
dome-like, encompass them, permitting the heat ray to penetrate out-
wards but allowing nothing in from the outside. Human society and
human love are doomed confronted by such a menace.

To get the Earth out of this crisis, Pal resorted to the same device
Wells had used in the novel. The Martians, totally unequipped for the
bacteria and disease-ridden atmosphere of the Earth, succumb to
natural causes, their fabulous machines crashing to the ground as they
expire. One might well wonder how the Martians, after their centuries
of observation and their staggeringly advanced science, should have
failed to take into account bacterial and ecological matters; nor would
this necessarily stop them ultimately, unless their entire population
had been involved in the initial invasion—which is nowhere implied.
Notwithstanding, this solution is more satisfying than that the Earthmen should triumph out of sheer courage or by some divine right.

In George Pal's *War of the Worlds,* it is not war that inspires awe,
although it depends for its effectiveness on the vivid scenes of destruction. The awe most truly derives from our own secret worship of
machines, incredible, miraculous, supreme machines which, by extension, place human beings in much the same position as that occupied
by Dr. Moreau: able at last to dominate matter through intelligence.
The Martians' machines are but extensions of their genius and their
dominion. I suspect Wells quite consciously intended to have these
splendid, extraordinary products of scientific vision fall and clank into
the dust because, in final contrast to even the most minute forms of living plasma, all man-made machines are as nothing. At the close of the
1980s, with all the hoopla about what is called the Strategic Defense
Initiative, I am reminded of the vision of the protective domes surrounding the Martian war machines. Could it be that this science fantasy, instead of counseling against hybris, rather only lent support to
the conviction that the sole salvation from human destructiveness
might be in technologically more sophisticated machines? Saddest of
all to relate, Pal's film gave rise in 1988 to a syndicated series produced
by Paramount Pictures Television in which the Martians are restored to
life and continue their attempt at conquest on a weekly basis.

The American Western Cinema: 1903–Present

...denn Geschichten müssen vergangen sein, und je vergangener, könnte man sagen, desto besser für sie in ihrer Eigenschaft als Geschichten and für Erzähler, den raunenden Beschwörer des Imperfekts. — Thomas Mann[1]

I

The Red Pony was remade as a motion picture for television and broadcast over NBC on March 18, 1973. You may not care for the short novel by John Steinbeck, but he gave his character of the Grandfather a brilliant soliloquy. Grandfather once led a wagon train west. He tells twelve-year-old Jody, his grandson, about his adventures. According to the screenplay based on Steinbeck's dialogue when Jody suggests that maybe someday he, too, could be a leader of the people, Grandfather shakes his head, no. "There's no place to go, son. There's the ocean to stop you. Every place is taken. It's all done now. Westering is finished."

It is difficult, if not impossible, to draw theoretical conclusions about the significance of the Western cinema when so little that is accurate has been written about its history, nor have most critics seen what remains of the films spanning eight decades. I believe in being thorough. I have screened more than 8,000 Westerns. I would not recommend that anyone else do it. There has been no appreciable change in my personality or temperament as a consequence. My moral convictions — or utter lack of them — remain unassailed. Yet you cannot undergo an experience of this kind and not come away without some impressions.

I cannot pretend in this essay to clear up the countless fantasies and delusions which have come to be accepted as facts about Western film production and personnel. However, there are a few observations

I should like to pass on to the reader as to how one best approaches a motion picture and in particular a Western as an object of critical study rather than as an entertainment. The truth of film is emotional truth. When you get right down to it successful pictures, as all successful stories, are about individual people. Whatever the location, or the historical setting, or the great events used as a backdrop—and these may be very important to the film as a composite unity—it is the people in it who matter most and the action that centers around them. The traditional Western has celebrated American individualism.

John Ford won four Academy Awards for direction and subsequently, when he could no longer find work, became the subject of academic interest. Many critics have complained that he refused to answer their questions directly or, at times even, intelligently. They expected him to be analytical about his films. He could not be. He had not made them that way. His films are about the characters in them. All of the bits of business he invented on the cuff, or the spontaneous dialogue he achieved by emending the printed script, were things intended to amplify peculiarities of personality. A good director intuitively *feels* these things. They are planned; they have an instinctive rightness; but they are the result of a creative synthesis, not analysis.

A film is a collective and necessarily corporate enterprise. Every person working on a picture contributes his share to its effectiveness. When one person fails, you can spot his blunder more readily than you ever can see the working parts when everyone does his best and the illusion of the film is uniformly sustained. Motion pictures are produced in order to make money. It is successful cinema—does business at the box office—when the story told fills the public's emotional needs in such a way as to induce it to pay hard cash for the experience of it. Grosses cannot, and do not, determine artistic quality or technical achievement, but grosses are a reflection of popular sentiment. And popular sentiment is a filmmaker's stock-in-trade. A film may occasionally be a personal expression. So long as the personal expression parallels popular sentiment, the financial results will be favorable. Often filmmakers seek to impose their vision on an audience. This can be dangerous. Frequently, when popular sentiment changes, so must a filmmaker's orientation, or he may be done.

The Western film from 1903 until the end of the Vietnam War was a safer bet withal than any other kind of picture. Americans preferred it among genre films. What the French or the Egyptians may have

Candid of movie cowboy Hoot Gibson. Photo courtesy of Hoot Gibson.

thought of Westerns was not very important to American filmmakers — not because of any narrow chauvinistic bias, but simply because, then as now, for foreign and domestic films, the United States remained *the* primary market. Economic conditions prior to World War II were such that the foreign market alone could maintain Greta Garbo as a star. It is not so any more. Films may be produced abroad but, usually, they cannot be financially successful without the American movie-viewing public.

Were you to have spoken with men such as Col. Tim McCoy or directors such as John Ford who straddled the silent and sound eras, or interviewed John Wayne, or could you have known Ken Maynard or Hoot Gibson, it would not surprise you to learn that the concern had never been to depict the West as it once was, but rather to interpret its spirit and give it a new meaning. For them, the Western represented an enduring myth and they were part of a living tradition bound up in the articulation of that myth. Duke Wayne's objections to *High Noon* (United Artists, 1952) came to this: rugged men of the frontier,

men who had battled hostile Indians and a harsh nature, who had scrat-
ched a living from barren land, clawed at rock to survive would not
cower as a group before three thugs. They would unite, as they had
united in the past to make the land habitable, to build a town on dust,
to drive their cattle a thousand miles to the railhead. The spirit of the
West that *High Noon* depicted was outside the mythical promise of the
land. It may have been emotionally true for some in 1952, but not
before that.

Following World War II, there arose a new generation of
filmmakers who set out to redirect the impulse inspiring the theatrical
Western. For them it was a vehicle for social protest, a platform for
radical political ideas, a forum for special pleading, while the traditional hero increasingly became an object of ridicule. By way of contrast, Duke Wayne was the last of the great traditionalists. Once he
passed from the scene, there was no other Western hero to replace him.
As he mounted his horse straight of body as Tom Mix mounted Tony
when Duke was a prop boy at Fox; when in *The Searchers* (Warner's,
1956) John Ford had Duke imitate a gesture characteristic of Harry
Carey; when Duke's weathered face was photographed with lines of
granite resolve reminiscent of Buck Jones with whom Duke worked
when they were both at Columbia Pictures: there you had the embodiment and epitome of almost a half century of Western filmmaking.

For better or worse these predominant trends — the heroic and the
socially disillusioned — serve as a rather convenient line of demarcation
between the Western before World War II and what followed. On the
one hand you have the mythical, the man enlivened by faith or, barring
that, still capable of envisioning the hope for a better world. On the
other you have a bleak cognizance of innate human savagery, a brutal,
"realistic" portrayal of human and social failure. These are not pure
cultures; but you find almost nothing of the latter before 1945 and far
less of the former since.

II

Edwin S. Porter was a technician and a mechanic rather than a
resourceful and creative filmmaker. Notwithstanding, his one-reel *The
Great Train Robbery* (Edison, 1903) was the first narrative Western and
it established the basic cinematic pattern for subsequent Western film
production: crime, pursuit, retribution. *The Train Robbers* (Warner's,
1972) differed only in that it ends before the retribution is
consummated.

Tom Mix and Tony as they appeared at the time of *Destry Rides Again* (Universal, 1932). Photo courtesy of MCA-Universal.

Although he may never have been on a horse before, G.M. Anderson, who had been hired by Porter, managed to play four roles in the film. He was impressed by the financial prospects of the Western, especially in view of the continuing box-office success of *The Great Train Robbery*. By 1908 Anderson was in partnership with George K. Spoor of Chicago and their Essanay Film Company was in the process of producing a series of one-reel Westerns being shot on western locations. Anderson was the first to attempt location shooting. Eventually others followed suit. California, it seemed to Anderson, offered the best climate. As the teens began, most of the eastern film companies were sending troupes to the West Coast or were opening studios there expressly to film outdoor dramas.

Anderson's impact on the screen treatment of the West is surely the equal of any of the technical innovations employed by D.W. Griffith. It was Anderson's conviction that a Western must have a

Buck Jones showing "Uncle Carl" Laemmle how a bolt-action rifle works when they were both at Universal. Photo courtesy of Dell Jones.

central character. In 1909 he purchased for $50 screen rights to the character "Broncho Billy" whom Peter B. Kyne had featured in a story he wrote for *The Saturday Evening Post*. Anderson's first starring Western, *The Bandit Makes Good* (Essanay, 1908), was not a Billy film. The character made its debut in 1910 in *Broncho Billy's Redemption*. The name became a moniker and Anderson played the same character in all of his subsequent films until he left Essanay in 1915. Anderson later claimed that during the years 1908–1915 he had produced and appeared in some 375 short Westerns. Few of these survive, although more are at the British Film Institute than at the Library of Congress and other American archives. Fortunately, two of his better films, made at the twilight of his career, *Shootin' Mad*, a two-reeler from 1918, and *The Son-of-a-Gun* (Sperry, 1919), his last Western and second feature-length picture, can still be viewed.

Billy's favorite role was that of a good bad man. Anderson constantly strove to improve the production values of his pictures and so his last are his best. Yet, in terms of contents, he stayed entrenched in the traditional melodrama typical of the pulp fiction of his time. I think we are inclined to forget today the degree of snobbery with which films were met in the beginning. The pay was good, but low social esteem made seeking work in them a last ditch compromise. Anderson had been an unsuccessful stage actor. D.W. Griffith had been a failure as a playwright. William S. Hart did not have a wholly illustrious time before the footlights, nor did Francis Ford who became a serial hero. When these men came to make movies, they brought with them all the heavy sentimentality of the American legitimate theatre of the previous century. The cynicism following the Great War altered public sentiment and brought much of this excessive sentimentalism to an end. John Ford, Francis' younger brother, was one of the few survivors.

Probably the single most important figure in the history of the silent Western was a man of whom no one seems any longer to be aware. It was his character and temperament which shaped and influenced nearly all Western production in Hollywood from 1915–1935. The Fords worked for him. Jack Holt starred in the first Western serial for him. Thomas Ince got his start with him. At one time or another Harry Carey, Hoot Gibson, Art Acord, Roy Stewart, Tim McCoy, Ken Maynard, Buck Jones, and Tom Mix all worked on his lot and in nearly every case made their most memorable films on his generous budgets. This was because no man in the motion picture industry loved Westerns as much as emigrant, five-foot, beaming Carl Laemmle, the "Little

Champ," president of the Universal Film Manufacturing Co. Laemmle had arrived in the New World virtually penniless, unfamiliar with the American language or with American customs. He did have daring, perseverence, guts, and charisma. He battled against the Film Patents Trust and won. He hired Edwin S. Porter on the basis of *The Great Train Robbery*. When he opened Universal City in 1915, he introduced the assembly-line concept to film production. He gathered together stock companies of players.

Laemmle signed Harry Carey to make a series of Westerns to compete with the Billy films just as Anderson was leaving Essanay. John Ford cut his teeth as a film director on the Carey pictures. Hoot Gibson got his main chance with Carey, first as a double and then worked himself into leading roles. The format of the Carey Westerns was soon changed from two-reelers to features. John Ford's first feature film survives, *Straight Shooting* (Universal, 1917). It is by no means a great Western. Ford savants have seen in it techniques Ford supposedly learned while playing a Klansman in D.W. Griffith's *The Birth of a Nation* (Epoch, 1915). I find this sort of speculation preposterous. We have an insufficient number of silent films intact from the teens—much less easily accessible to be viewed by these critics—to say anything very intelligent about who borrowed what from whom. It makes good copy, but it has no historical foundation.

Whatever his pardonable failings, Uncle Carl (initially called this because of the number of old country relatives he employed) loved cowboys and Western films. He gave his directors extraordinary freedom. By the mid-twenties, actors such as Hoot Gibson, and later Ken Maynard, Tom Mix, and Buck Jones, had incorporated their own production units and were directly responsible for the production of their Westerns. Universal financed and had general story approval. Hoot Gibson's films from 1925 to 1930, Ken Maynard's from 1929 to 1930 and 1933 to 1934, Tom Mix' from 1932 to 1933, and Buck Jones' from 1934 to 1937 were extremely personal vehicles and were made the way these stars intended them to be made. No series Westerns subsequently produced by any studio show the individual stamp and distinct personality of the lead players as these Universal entries. Rightly or wrongly, Uncle Carl felt that movie cowboys knew most about how Westerns should be made.

Nearly the whole of Universal's silent library is unavailable. In the mid-fifties, when MCA had assumed control of the company, the decision was put to the executives to finance transfer from nitrate to acetate film stock or destroy all prints and negatives. After much deliberation, the latter course was chosen. I believe it was probably financially sound as a business decision, but in terms of historical assessment and study it remains a tragedy. The sound Westerns of Gibson, Maynard, Mix, and Jones, most of which have been saved by MCA, deserve attention and I shall come back to them.

The assembly-line concept of Western film production had wide influence. Universal and the independent companies in the twenties specialized in producing "B" or budget Westerns as well as, in Universal's case, specials or "A" feature Westerns. In the forties and fifties, John Ford persisted in the stock company concept; as, later, did Duke Wayne in his films. Universal maintained its "B" line of Westerns and serials until 1946 when it shut down all units; other firms continued the practice theatrically until 1954 and then applied it to television production. Universal City Studios, which depends heavily on televison markets currently, has but refined concepts Uncle Carl first borrowed from Detroit automobile manufacturers in 1915.

III

D.W. Griffith, whom Porter hired at the Edison company, left and began directing one- and two-reelers for Biograph in 1908. By subsequent standards, he had a chaotic way of working. He avoided scripts. No one, including Griffith, could foretell what a film would look like until it was edited. In a time of unlimited enthusiasm, guaranteed box office, and a general air of improvisation, Griffith made a staggering number of "bombs" — this has long been a *technical* term for failure in the industry — but, when everything coalesced, whipped into a frenzy by D.W.'s passionate zeal, he raised the art of the silent film above the need for spoken language.

Griffith took his company to California in 1910. He was dissatisfied with New Jersey locations for his Westerns. He borrowed his horses from a group of wranglers, among them Hoot Gibson who did occasional stunt work and appeared on camera as Henry B. Walthall's double in *Two Brothers* (Biograph, 1910). Harry Carey began his career in films working for Griffith in the same year. Walthall, Gibson, and Carey would appear together in the final important Western for all of them, *The Last Outlaw* (RKO, 1936), based on a screen story by John Ford from Carey's Cheyenne Harry days at Universal.

There has been some debate over whether or not Lionel Barrymore appeared in D.W.'s *Fighting Blood* (Biograph, 1911). I have seen it forty times and I cannot tell you. What *is* significant about this film is Griffith's staging of an Indian attack on a block house and a rescue by the cavalry. What he learned from this one-reeler, Griffith applied ingeniously in *The Battle at Elderbush Gulch* (Biograph, 1913), among surviving materials unquestionably Griffith's most effectively staged Western. Technically both *The Battle at Elderbush Gulch* and *The Birth of a Nation,* if they did not innovate, at least incorporated a number of devices which became staples in Western film production. Both build up to climaxes in which seemingly doomed characters are saved at the last minute from certain death. The editing of the ride of the Klan to create breath-taking suspense was utilized in many Westerns henceforth and especially in the Hoot Gibson Specials made during the twenties by Universal. One of the Midwestern franchisees of *The Birth of a Nation* was Harry "Pop" Sherman who became a Western filmmaker himself in the 1930s, first with the Bar 20 series based on Clarence E. Mulford's novels about Hopalong Cassidy and numerous other characters and then producer of the last entries in the Paramount Zane Grey series plus several "A" Westerns later for release by United Artists. "Pop" admitted his indebtedness to Griffith. He once summed up his successful formula for Westerns as, "Open big, forget the middle, and come to a terrific finish." It worked. "Pop" personally made some $15,000,000 using that one idea.

William S. Hart for all the prestige he continues to enjoy was an anomaly. When he came to pictures, he was forty-four years old. Thomas Ince, for whom he worked, did *not* discover him nor did he even want Hart to star in a Western. However, after much deliberation, Ince did contract with Hart and backed his films for theatrical release. Hart was a better actor than G.M. Anderson and his portrayals had greater substance. Hart caught on rapidly with the public and as the teens closed ranked prominently at the box office among Western players.

I call Hart an anomaly because, while he did have a distinctive and individual screen style, his influence on Western filmmaking was negligible. I mentioned that very few Westerns from the teens survive. No one can depend on anything but memory or the trades to tell you what Tom Mix' early Fox Westerns from 1917–1919 looked like. When Hart made his first feature, *The Bargain* (New York Motion Picture Company, 1914), his only real competition came from the Anderson two-reelers and they were nearly at the end. You'll find the same crudity of dress, dilapidated town sets, dusty streets, rough interiors—

signs of the "realism" praised by recent critics in the Hart Westerns — in Anderson's pictures of that period and in a Universal film such as *Straight Shooting* or the Selig short Westerns with Tom Mix. Since most of Hart's Westerns survive, in lieu of any ready contradiction, he is given credit for introducing these elements. To me this appears more the consequence of hindsight come of the absurd gaudiness of the musical Western that began in the mid-thirties and, earlier, the glamour introduced by the Ken Maynard virtuoso vehicles commencing in 1926 with First National's *Señor Daredevil*. If contrasted with these later Westerns, the Hart films are a novel, even startling experience. Had we more documentation by means of which to trace stylistic evolution, I suggest it might well turn out that Westerns were so "realistic" in the teens because any other way of filming them had not yet occurred to filmmakers. They were still too near the nineteenth century to dare conceive films as brazenly idiotic as the Autry fantasies of the sound era.

Ince had not made a starring Western series before Hart's. He thought little of Hart as a person at the beginning of their association and he took minimal interest in the production of the Hart films for the duration of Hart's contract. The fortune Triangle amassed from the Hart Westerns was wasted on films with New York stage players that died at the box office. Unlike Carl Laemmle, Ince cared nothing about Westerns, regarding them as a necessary, if slightly embarrassing, commodity the revenues from which could be used to finance more ambitious artistic projects. For the time, Ince permitted Hart relatively generous budgets. The Hart features cost between $13–15,000 and went at least a month in production. This figure ought to be compared with the $125,000 budgets at Paramount in the 1920s for its first Zane Grey Westerns, $500,000 at Universal for Hoot Gibson's *The Calgary Stampede* in 1926, and then with Sam Katzman's $8,000 budgets for Tim McCoy's *sound* Westerns in 1938–1939 with McCoy getting $4,000 of it as salary on pictures filmed in two days and a night!

Curiously, those critics who prefer Hart's Westerns tend to favor his early work at Triangle for Ince as opposed to his later films for Paramount on $150,000 budgets. Ince initially gave Hart a good crew with Reginald Barker directing and C. Gardner Sullivan doing the scenarios. In 1915, Hart directed a series of short Westerns and began to develop his concepts of Western filmmaking, moving on in October, 1915, to the feature *The Disciple* and following with *Hell's Hinges* in 1916. Hart's career in Hollywood proved that, whatever else he may have been, he was no director. If you divorce from his Westerns their physical austerity and the raw reproduction of panchromatic film stock on which they were photographed, Hart's films are unique but in a somewhat unexpected way. Hart's plots as plots are *not* realistic. They are keenly romantic, sentimental, melodramatic, and occasionally ridiculous—albeit ridiculous in the spirit of Don Quixote. You do not doubt for a moment the knightly sincerity with which Hart undergoes his religious conversions or emotes in the throes of a throbbing self-recrimination. Not until his last film, *Tumbleweeds* (United Artists, 1925), did Hart alleviate somewhat this heavy emotional atmosphere with less oppressive moments of bright comedy. Hart was obsessed with his personal conception of the West and his vision of its heroes—gripped by the same frantic thraldom in which Clarence E. Mulford in his home at Freyburg, Maine dreamed of a solitary meal on the prairie, a noisy cattle town, or tinkered with the small pieces of wood from his facsimile of the Alamo. History and romance were inseparable, even beautiful, to them as they sometimes are for essentially lonely men.

For my taste, I would choose Hart's Paramount titles, *Wagon Tracks* in 1919 and *The Toll Gate* in 1920—and, of course, above all *Tumbleweeds*. *Wagon Tracks* had nowhere the astonishing response engendered by *The Covered Wagon* (Paramount, 1923), but it was, frankly, a better film. Hart steeped himself in the lore of the West. More important than his "realism" or his romanticism was his factuality. His comment on seeing *The Covered Wagon* was that no responsible wagon master would camp his train in a box canyon. His observation of the stage race across the salt flats in *Stagecoach* (United Artists, 1939) was that an intelligent Indian would have shot one of the horses and ended the chase. He knew what he was doing factually and *Wagon Tracks*, splendidly photographed by Joseph August and codirected by Hart and Lambert Hillyer, wove a spell of poetic grandeur about a long trek westward through Indian lands. Yet it has a documentary feel in its attention to detail.

The probable reason James Cruze's *The Covered Wagon* did so well, or John Ford's *Stagecoach*, even with their discrepancies, is that you can readily identify with the actions and feelings of the characters in their respective stories. The characters are cinematic and yet human. What ruined Hart in actually a very short time was his dogged insistence on overstated, fragrant, idealistic, and sentimental plots. Hart overplayed all of his scenes. On screen he *feels* too much. He does not let the audience feel. If the screenplay calls for an emotional close-up of Hart's face, there is no ambiguity; the tears stand in his eyes. When, for exmaple, in *Rio Grande* (Republic, 1950) John Ford wanted a close-up of Duke Wayne, he instructed Duke to show nothing and to *think* nothing. Let the audience project the misery and determination accented by the harsh lighting with the silver, moonlit water of the great river casting a pale hue on haggard features. The emotion arose in the audience — where it was supposed to be — not on the screen. For all of his many virtues, William S. Hart was not a consummate filmmaker. He never learned how to thrill audiences at the same time as he might impress them.

IV

I do not wish to spend much more time on the silent Western. By the 1920s the star system was solidly entrenched. The plots of films mattered less than *who* appeared in them. Tom Mix had the largest public following. Sol Wurtzel was in charge of the Fox West Coast studio. He let the Mix unit make Westerns as it pleased. Mix himself was a flamboyant, fun-loving personality who stressed excitement, stunting, and cavalier bravado in his films. His cinematographer Daniel Clark was one of the best in the business. Clark, as much as Mix, helped to create the superhuman qualities in Mix' heroes through subtle camera setups and flattering oppositions. Mix sought out unusual locations and national park sites for many of his Westerns. When John Ford joined Fox, he directed several Mix Westerns.

William S. Hart had made his horse, Fritz, into nearly a costar although he temporarily "retired" him until his contract with Ince expired. Mix latched on to the idea and used Old Blue and then Tony in a similar manner. Mix had a theatrical flair that other movie cowboys did not — and in flagrant abundance. Tony was not only a pal, he dazzled audiences with amazing equestrian feats. Yet a movie cowboy's relationship to his horse wasn't all for the camera. Ken Maynard loved Tarzan as he never did a human being, although, when drunk, he would beat the animal. When Buck Jones died, Silver stopped eating and his demise followed soon after. It is almost ludicrous to think that Hart's principal influence on later movie cowboys should have come to no more than this.

Not many of Mix' feature Westerns from the twenties survive and some that do, such as *Just Tony* (Fox, 1922), are not readily available. *Sky High* (Fox, 1922) has some precarious footage with Mix pictured doing stunts on the rim and along the narrow trails of the Grand Canyon. *The Great K & A Train Robbery* (Fox, 1927) employed a railroad setting, always a Mix favorite, with a story that moved, filled with humor and action.

Mix made repeated importunities for more money so that by 1919 he was earning $10,000 a week and more than that if combined with his personal appearances. He went on strike for $17,000 a week. His pictures were supporting the studio and he felt well within his rights. Buck Jones, who was working for Fox as a double and had had minimum exposure in a few Franklyn Farnum independent two-reelers, was then offered a contract. Winifred Sheehan wrote to him on October 9, 1919, advising him on his vice-presidential stationery among other things (he had seen Buck's screen test), "your teeth require proper attention with polishing and cleaning by a dentist once every two months and very careful attention several times daily. It should be a practice of yours to open your mouth a little wider when you smile so that your teeth are seen more."

These considerations had not been important previously. Mix had changed that. Buck Jones proved popular with audiences and kept Mix in line (although he did get his $17,000 a week) as long as they were both at Fox. Only a few of the Jones Westerns from this period are known to survive. As might be expected, Mix was at first rather hostile. Later, during the sound era, the two became friends.

The finest surviving Mix Western we have is *Rider of Death Valley* (Universal, 1932), one of nine all-talking films he did before he quit pictures altogether. His return in 1935 for Mascot's *The Miracle Rider,* a fifteen chapter serial, was an indifferent affair done strictly to publicize the Tom Mix Circus. I rank *Rider of Death Valley* with *The Vanishing American* (Paramount, 1925) in which Lois Wilson was also the heroine, *Stagecoach, My Darling Clementine* (20th-Fox, 1946), *Shane* (Paramount, 1953), and *True Grit* (Paramount, 1969) as one of the finest Westerns ever to be made, singularly without pretension, and what is more — as with the others — a film capable of being enthusiastically enjoyed by an audience that does not especially like Westerns. The principals, including Mix, Lois Wilson, Fred Kohler, Sr., and Tony, find themselves stranded in the desert without water fighting a desperate battle against the elements. The simple drama of its story inspired John Huston's later *The Treasure of Sierra Madre* (Warner's, 1948); it was not coincidental, surely, that Huston was employed in the Universal story department when the Mix film was produced. Daniel Clark was the cameraman. Every shot is conceived with a sustaining visual poetry. I find it exceedingly fortunate that one of Tom Mix' brightest moments should be preserved so that future generations can realize his reputation and fame were not merely adventitious.

Also among survivors, beyond a handful of Mix films, are two rather exceptional John Ford vehicles of the silent era, *The Iron Horse* (Fox, 1924) and *3 Bad Men* (Fox, 1926). The land rush sequence in *3 Bad Men,* as that in the two versions of Edna Ferber's *Cimarron* (1931) (1960), is well-staged but perhaps not the equal of that in Hart's only epic, *Tumbleweeds.*

Universal competed with their Hoot Gibson series with Gibson, as Buck Jones, stressing a comic, off-handed, seldom serious approach to the Western format. When sound came, Jones became very serious (a total bankruptcy not of his own doing being a contributing factor) and revealed himself to be not only a capable action player but a better actor than most movie cowboys. Gibson never changed, and this proved to his detriment. Jones made his best sound films in the mid-thirties for Universal, beginning with the serial, *The Red Rider* (Universal, 1934). *The Ivory-Handled Gun* (Universal, 1935), *Ride 'em Cowboy* (Universal, 1936) the story to which Jones wrote, *Sunset of Power* (Universal, 1936), *Left-handed Law* (Universal, 1937), and *Smoke Tree Range* (Universal, 1937) are compact, intelligent "B" Westerns with a more mature appeal than was usually the case among other entries in this prolific sub-genre. I could wish the same had been true of Hoot Gibson. Perhaps only *Cowboy Counsellor* (Allied, 1932) and *The Fighting Parson* (Allied, 1932) contain a glimmer of the quality of his silent Universal Jewels and Specials.

I am puzzled by those critics who claim that Ken Maynard's most outstanding Westerns were his silent series for First National. Only 1927's *The Red Raiders* survives — in the abridged Kodascope version — and five of six reels of *Somewhere in Sonora* (First National, 1927). I would rather opt for *Wheels of Destiny* (Universal, 1934), which I once had Universal reissue nontheatrically, and *Strawberry Roan* (Universal, 1933). The latter was built around Curley Fletcher's popular ballad and gave rise to the musical Westerns of the thirties and forties. The only real drawback was Maynard's inability to sing.

From what remains of them, Paramount's Zane Grey series from 1925–1939 may be the most consistently impressive group of Westerns ever made not centered around a single personality (save a loose connection with Grey's stories). This series went from a film of the stature of *The Vanishing American* to the brilliant *Man of the Forest* (Paramount, 1933) directed by Henry Hathaway. Many of the entries are remarkable.

I cannot hope to describe the hundreds of modestly budgeted Westerns made in the sound era until 1954, or the chapter plays, or the many specials that might be worth viewing again. Republic developed an extremely resilient formula for what I call the standard formulary Western, as did Columbia, stories with heroes, heroines, and villains with completely predictable endings. In terms of action sequences, many of the Republic Westerns are as thrilling today as then, as in the case of *The Bold Caballero,* a 1936 resumption of Zorro, or *Riders of Whistling Skull* (Republic, 1936) based on William Colt MacDonald's Three Mesquiteer novel of the same title, a series begun by RKO in 1935 with *Powdersmoke Range* starring Harry Carey, Hoot Gibson, Tom Tyler, Bob Steele, and a plethora of other Western players. In 1940 on a $750,000 budget Republic with *Dark Command* inaugerated a policy of issuing one "big" Western a year that united its incredibly slick production techniques with interesting stories and competent casts. *Hell-Fire* (Republic, 1949) proved that Bill Elliott was capable of playing more of a character than "Wild Bill" or "Red Ryder," although he himself would have preferred to remain in the Red Ryder series.

As convenient as it is to comment that the "B" Western ended in 1954 with Allied Artists' *Two Guns and a Badge,* in truth it happened much earlier, perhaps already by 1940. The "B" Westerns after World War II just are not as carefully made as those from before. Gene Autry's features for Columbia in 1947-1953 are something of an exception, as are the Tim Holt RKO series and several Repulic entries; but, on the whole, the passion and dedication expended in the "B" units in the twenties and thirties were henceforth generally confined to major productions. I must also confess my conviction that neither Producer's Releasing Corporation nor Monogram ever made a notable Western.

On behalf of the "B" product of the thirties—the Universal Westerns with Mix, Maynard, and Jones, the Columbia series with Jones and Tim McCoy, the RKO George O'Brien series, the Republic Westerns with John Wayne and the Three Mesquiteers—let me say this: in many ways they achieved a uniquely American perfection of the well-made story. Dramatists and storytellers over the centuries have not been fools. The tradition of a story of classical proportion with a beginning, middle and exciting and suspenseful ending has always pleased a certain segment of the public. It did so again here, albeit briefly and unexpectedly, only to be replaced by a later generation with a wholly different iconology and imagery while the essential plot varieties have remained pretty much the same.

V

In order better to assess Western films since 1945, critics tend to discount players and concentrate on directors. I do not object to this practice but I ought to remind the reader that this is only an arbitrary procedure. It comes about not as a result of observation but rather as a framework *for* observation. In this shift of emphasis, it is nonetheless true that a director was often not as good or bad as his last picture whereas an actor very well might be. A successful Western was still dependent on a great deal more than its director, including star attraction, a fact widely accepted in the industry but at times only begrudgingly outside of it.

However, I am not about to say that a director's influence cannot be decisive. You need only look at *Frontier Marshal* (20th-Fox, 1939) with Randolph Scott and contrast it with John Ford's remake *My Darling Clementine*. Ford's film is clearly superior. No scene is extraneous; it does not sag; it is not self-indulgent, as many of his later films would be. Everything pushes forward to the shoot-out; nothing distracts. The characters exude confrontation with savagery and sudden death. Yet, there is humor and humanity, friendship and hope. Together with *Stagecoach,* I believe it Ford's finest work in the genre. In part, Ford worked from the lies Wyatt Earp had told him; but more importantly he wanted to make a dramatic and coherent film — history be damned! — and he brought it off. He brilliantly created the polarities, the emotions around an historical event, even if the emotions really had nothing to do with that particular historical event, and he meticulously etched the sensibilities of his screen characters. It has the incomparable virtue of brevity and the white heat of unflagging inspiration — the players, the technical crew, the screenplay have all been welded together by the very personal vision of the director. Yet it is not always so. To erect a cult around only a director is to obfuscate a thousand contributing nuances. It is far more noteworthy in evaluating *Western Union* (20th-Fox, 1941) that Harry Joe Brown was the associate producer — he had supervised or directed Maynard's First National Westerns and his Universal series in 1929–1930 — than that Fritz Lang directed it. For Lang, a recent emigré from the brutal

realities of European political chaos and the director of such Expres-
sionist masterpieces as *Metropolis* (German, 1927) and *M* (German,
1931), *Western Union* was but a typical example of American naiveté,
with its stock characters and obligatory happy ending.

Because of the disparateness of the post–1945 Westerns, I cannot
possibly condense them into so limited a space as I have at my disposal.
Eschewing the *auteur* principle, I think that two distinct trends are
discernible. The one was summed up by Sam Peckinpah when he said,
"'the Western is a universal frame within which it is possible to comment on today.'"[2] The other was formulated by Howard Hawks: "'To
me a Western is gunplay and horses. . . . They're about adventurous
life and sudden death. It's the most dramatic thing you can do.'"[3] You
may feel the Peckinpah principle didactic in the extreme, rather as in
practice going to see a Bernard Shaw play and getting the preface read
to you first and sometimes not getting to see the play at all. Yet,
whatever, it has had its proponents. The fundamental idea is "today."
Authenticity and history can be warped to serve contemporary causes
as much as they have been warped to provide entertainment or to
articulate a legend.

I do not deny the power of Stanley Kramer's *High Noon*. It is an
excellent film and deserved the awards it won. Gary Cooper's resigned
but desperate persistence, Dimitri Tiomkin's music and especially the
ballad sung by Tex Ritter, the ingenious editing — these are factors that
must receive their due. But setting this story in the Old West is irrelevant. It is a Western only incidentally. *The Chase* (Columbia, 1966)
with Marlon Brando is an even more telling presentation of social decay
in a modern Texas township with a screenplay by Lillian Hellman, who
was every bit as infuriated by *Huac* as *High Noon's* screenwriter Carl
Forman was. *High Noon's* pastness is an example of intemperate
escapism. Our ancestors had many imposing social problems, but
cowardice and indecision were scarcely foremost among them.

High Noon fits Peckinpah's principle. Ultimately, it is a matter of
taste if you can accept such incongruities with equanimity. There have
been numerous Westerns socially relevant to the period depicted and
not without significance now. *The Ox-Bow Incident* (20th Fox, 1943)
directed by William Wellman and starring Henry Fonda is a splendid
instance. *Silver Lode* (RKO, 1953) directed by Allan Dwan and featuring John Payne and Lizabeth Scott is another. No performance in either
of them can surpass Gary Cooper's in *High Noon,* but their shared basic
premise derives from their natural setting rather than being imposed

upon it. One advantage to the methodology I devised in *The American West in Film: Critical Approaches to the Western Film* (1985) is that by contrasting any Western against the historical reality we can decipher just what the distortions are and what may have been the ideological and dramatic reasons for making them. One very important point to remember is that while a Western film was made to attract an audience and make money the ideology in it tells us virtually nothing about who went to see it and what they might have been thinking but a great deal about what the filmmakers themselves were thinking and were trying to persuade audiences to think.

Howard Hawks' *Rio Bravo* (Warner's, 1959), although a total antithesis to *High Noon,* is ironically as much a ready candidate for the directors' cults as Peckinpah's *Ride the High Country* (M-G-M, 1962). Duke Wayne was cast as a sheriff whose superiority to his environment and basic heroism can inspire men to rally around him. I believe it is an important distinction to make that both in *High Noon* and *The Chase,* the sheriff-protagonist walks away from his job at the conclusion. In *Rio Bravo,* that is not a feasible alternative. I am reminded of a comment made by the character played by Gary Merrill in *Mysterious Island* (Columbia, 1961) upon arrival at Captain Nemo's retreat: "When are we going to stop escaping *to* places that need escaping *from?*"

John Ford was of the opinion that *Stagecoach* made John Wayne a star, but Hawks' *Red River* (United Artists, 1948) showed him to be an actor. Hawks had no response to this, but he did relate to me once how he had told Wayne when he wanted him to play the part of Tom Dunson, "You're *gonna* be an old man pretty soon, and you ought to get used to it. And you also better start playing characters instead of that junk you've been playing." Short of *True Grit* (Paramount, 1969), I regard it as Wayne's best Western.

Henry Hathaway has unfortunately been underrated. This may have been due in part to the unavailability of many of his fine Westerns of the thirties. There is a generating line of sorts that unifies *The Thundering Herd* (Paramount, 1933) with Harry Carey and Randolph Scott, *Man of the Forest* with these same principals, *Go West, Young Man* (Paramount, 1936) with Mae West and Randolph Scott, *Shepherd of the Hills* (Paramount, 1941) with Wayne and Carey, and *True Grit.* His Westerns were always marked by a cognizance of human isolation and his heroes by a stubborn *Innigkeit.* More than a little of John Ford's irascibility crept into Wayne's portrayal of Rooster Cogburn.

What most of us are inclined to overlook in connection with Westerns since 1945 is the separation of generations. The players and directors who were working in the industry prior to that year belonged to a rough and tumble world where a man with talent could cut a deep niche for himself in his profession. For them the United States was really a land of nearly unlimited opportunity and they were openly grateful. For those who have come on the scene since, they have made as much money; they have had as many — or more — opportunities. But their films reflect their unhappiness and dissatisfaction. In several cases they have propounded ideologies which, should a viewer be interested, can be used as a guide to the multiple causes of their unhappiness; but in the process you very well might not be as well entertained.

VI

The Europeans, especially the French, almost from the advent of military forays into the New World were possessed of an *idée fixe* glamorizing the American Indian as a god-like pagan, a fierce but un-tutored ally in whom barbarism, while deplorable, may be forgiven due to a childish simplicity. Maurice Tourneur propounded precisely such a romantic view in his *The Last of the Mohicans* (Associated Producers, 1920). Thomas Ince, as early as *The Invaders* (Bison, 1912), was touched by the spectacle of a crushed Indian civilization. Col. Tim McCoy, who worked as an Indian agent in Wyoming, became technical consultant first on *The Covered Wagon* and then on *The Vanishing American*. If the trades from the twenties are to be believed, the latter is more com-pelling today than at the time of its initial release.

It is now the custom to point to these films and perhaps McCoy's own vehicles *War Paint* (M-G-M, 1926) and *Winners of the Wilderness* (M-G-M, 1927) as rare instances of compassion amid hundreds of Westerns picturing Indians as mindless savages. Other critics call atten-tion to *Broken Arrow* (20th-Fox, 1950) as a renewal of this trend right down to the anti–Anglo-American films of the seventies. This assertion ignores entirely features such as McCoy's *End of the Trail* (Columbia, 1932) or Gene Autry's *The Cowboy and the Indians* (Columbia, 1949) which fall during the decades of ostensible neglect and are exceedingly strident if sentimental in their sympathies — directly from the "B" units where you would least anticipate finding them.

Critical barnstorming in this manner strikes me as ill-advised. Before I knew better, I thought John Ford's *Fort Apache* (RKO, 1948) did justice to both sides in the conflict. Unfortunately, I had only sat down with men such as Tim McCoy who seemed an authority because he had lived among the Indians and had learned the Plains Indians' sign language. When he was signed at M-G-M, W.S. Van Dyke, the director on his early pictures, said, "Now, Tim, tell me about the Indians. Just talk about them. Everything you know about them." Van Dyke wanted an interesting story and McCoy gave him one. It was not until I worked on *Images of Indians* (PBS, 1980) with Native Americans that my own education began.

Carl Laemmle kept Chief Thunderbird, Chief John Big Tree, and All-American Jim Thorpe under contract at Universal for years. From them he got "zany savages" movies by the bushel, such as the serials *The Indians Are Coming* (Universal, 1930) with McCoy and *Battling with Buffalo Bill* (Universal, 1931). Uncle Carl's Indians, as their forebears in the Wild West shows, were apparently happy to be working and in their way did their best to put together an exhilerating cinematic story. The preponderantly Jewish management of the film industry would have, perhaps, predisposed executives to promote tolerance, had that been an issue. It wasn't.

About the time of Sam Fuller's *Run of the Arrow* (RKO, 1957) — comparable ideologically in the sound era to the silent *Vanishing American* — you find the impulse for social criticism in filmmaking addressing itself increasingly to the so-called "Indian problem," at least the version of it which appealed to some filmmakers at the time. It did bring about some interesting Westerns, but you can never forget your audience. Pre–1945 audiences were inclined to view Indians as appropriate villains without any consciousness of prejudice. The celluloid battles were just a further elaboration of the routines of the Wild West shows and what might be termed the "Buffalo Bill" approach to history: namely, the taller the tale, the more exciting, the more spectacular, the better. I do not think the situation would have changed so suddenly or so dramatically had it not been for the Vietnam War. This brought a new national awareness of genocide in American history and with it a revisionist view of the winning of the West as depicted in Western films. But even so, as I suspect may by now be obvious, whether the picture playing is Griffith's *The Birth of a Nation* or Stanley Kramer's *High Noon* or anything since, one ought not go to the movies — and Westerns most of all — to obtain either a balanced view or accurate history.

Is there no Western that depicts Native Americans adequately? I

cannot think of one. I know that many Native Americans favor *One
Flew over the Cuckoo's Nest* (United Artists, 1975). Some may argue
that this film is *not* a Western. However, it was based on Ken Kesey's
novel, a book cited by Leslie A. Fiedler in *The Return of the Native
American* (1962) as supporting his thesis that any story featuring a
Native American is *a priori* a Western. For me, *One Flew over the
Cuckoo's Nest* is that most elusive of all types of fictional narrative, an
allegory. In it the whites have imprisoned themselves in an insane
asylum from which there is no escape and from which a Native
American, named Chief Bromden, breaks out and seemingly alone can
gain freedom. When working on *Images of Indians*, I asked Will
Sampson, who had played Chief Bromden in the film, if he felt this
ending to be tragic. Not at all, he assured me. He interpreted the picture to mean that the white man is destined to live in a world of his
own creation which must ultimately deny him his liberty, whereas the
Native American lives in the world of Nature and can only be destroyed
if he remains in the white man's world.

I must confess that I do not find this kind of mutually exclusive
ideology any more palatable than the old Anglo-American idea that
color lines are inviolable. I have learned much in my life from my
association with Native Americans and I would hope that in the future,
with a more accurate understanding of their various cultures, a truly
meaningful dialogue would develop. No statement I have ever made
has led to so many attacks on me by the "Western as myth" school of
thought than what I must say now again here. I would hope that we
may once and for all recognize that images of killing "mythical" Indians
are only so much "newspeak" for enjoying genocide and that the
Western films which have indulged in this deserve the strongest censure
for the lies that have been told.

VII

For me the chronicle of the Western motion picture is very much
the lives, passions, struggles, and beliefs of the men who made the
films. I regret that I have not been able to say more about them as people. Many of them had an enduring, unshakable love affair with the
land and the spirit of the men who, as they were idealized, were
reputed to have pioneered it. As the United States became increasingly
an urban culture, the Western film helped the American people to remain enraptured by an agrarian dream of the past, precious because of
the hope it had once held.

John Wayne on the set in Mexico during the filming of *Cahill, U.S. Marshal* (Warner's, 1973). Photo courtesy of Warner Bros.

Let us go to Durango, Mexico. It is just before Christmas, 1972. Two production companies were there filming Westerns. Sam Peckinpah was at work on *Pat Garrett and Billy the Kid* (M-G-M, 1973). This was to be no fantasy. "This is the real *fucking* story!" Peckinpah asserted.

John Wayne was filming *Cahill, U.S. Marshal* (Warner's, 1973). Andrew McLaglen, Victor's son, was the nominal director; but Duke was everywhere on the set, giving orders. The Peckinpah camp was relatively quiet. There were few reporters around. Most of Peckinpah's company planned to hitch a ride home for the holidays on Wayne's chartered plane. "If you haven't that much money to spend," Duke commented, "I don't think you should make the picture." At one point Sam was fuming because Rona Barrett had called him a drunk; then, drinking heavily as was his custom, he lashed out at Pauline Kael for saying he was a Fascist. One night he said to me: "Are you going over to Duke's camp later?"

"Yes."

"Do me a favor. It's funny, you know, but I've never met him. I'd like to."

"I'll see what I can do," I assured him.

The next day when I returned to the Peckinpah camp Sam wanted to know if I had been able to set up a meeting for him with Wayne. I shook my head, no.

"He said that he wouldn't let that Commie son-of-a-bitch within six feet of him. When I asked him if that meant no absolutely, he gave me such a hard stare I shut up. You might as well pack it in, Sam. To Pauline Kael you're a Fascist and to Duke a Commie. You can't win."

The Wayne camp was usually swarming with reporters with Duke answering questions between scenes. The reporters were not friendly. Often they would bait him, hoping he would let slip some political comment that would make good news copy.

"What do you think of Kissinger?"

"There is a very fine dust in here," Wayne remarked, coughing. It was a dry cough; there was no phlegm. Wayne was living on part of only one lung. "Can you see the dust up there, a fine, white dust?"

"Do you smoke very much?"

"Only three cigars a day. I try to keep it down."

He has smoked more than that while answering questions.

"What do you think of Kissinger?"

"Do you inhale?"

"I try not to but . . . that's hard for an inveterate smoker—but I try not to."

Wayne spoke very slowly; he was relaxed. He did not give the impression of being a complicated man.

"Did your doctor tell you about the cancer right away?"

"No, he didn't have the guts. He wouldn't tell me. I was going through the pictures [X-rays] with an intern. He showed me the latest one of my lungs.

"'This is the cancer,' he said. Then he looked at me. 'Didn't your doctor tell you?'"

"How did you feel when you found out?"

"Like somebody had hit me in the stomach with a baseball bat."

"What did you think about?"

"Well, I have enough faith in that Man up there. I thought about my family, about what they would do without me, about getting my things in order."

"Have you met Kissinger?"

This reporter had been at it for an hour. Wayne had answered others' questions. He did not become irritated.

"Yes."

"What did you think of him?"

Wayne was cautious.

"I felt he was a nice man."

"Why did you start smoking again?" another asked.

"I used to chew, but it began to affect my voice."

"What do you think of Kissinger?"

It is enough. We must leave Durango, for my time is nearly gone. The only notable Western to be released in the eighties was *The Grey Fox* (United Artists, 1982) directed by the Canadian, Phillip Borsos. The film purports to tell the story of Bill Miner who, in history, robbed a stagecoach in 1869, was captured, and was sent to San Quentin for ten years—not thirty-three years as the screenplay by John Hunter has it. After his release in 1879, the real Bill Miner joined Billy LeRoy's gang in Colorado. After a series of robberies, Miner fled the country, ending up in the Middle East and then in Turkey where he became involved in slave trade of desert women for Turkish harems. Back in the United States in 1880, Miner resumed robbing stagecoaches. Late in 1881 he was caught and sentenced to twenty years at San Quentin. He was released in 1901, as shown in the film, and, as shown in the film, in 1903 he held up a train near Corbett, Oregon, although I doubt his inspiration was, as in the film, seeing *The Great Train Robbery*. Two train robberies in British Columbia followed which got him sentenced to life in New Westminster Penitentiary in Victoria. The film shows Miner escaping, as he did in 1907, and asserts that he then went on a European tour with Kate Flynn, a feminist frontier photographer played by Jackie Burroughs. This he did not do. Instead, in 1909 he robbed a bank in Portland, Oregon, and in 1911 he held up a train near White Sulpher, Georgia, after which he was captured and sentenced to life in the Georgia State Penitentiary at Milledgeville. He broke out three times and was recaptured three times. The last time he broke out he was sixty-six and, upon being caught, remarked, "'I guess I'm getting too old for this sort of thing.'"[4] He died quietly in his sleep in 1913, but he died in prison.

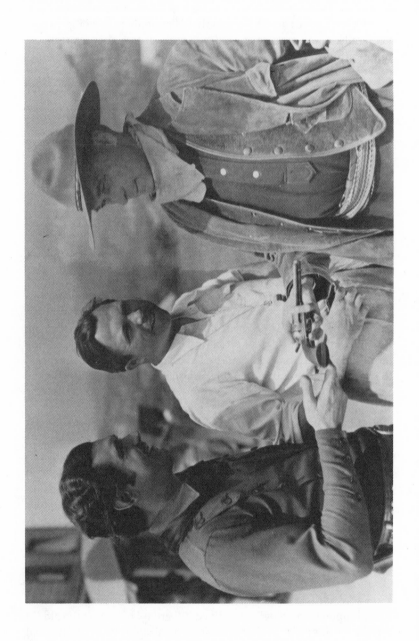

Originally Harry Dean Stanton had been slated to play Bill Miner, but he bowed out at the last minute and was replaced by Richard Farnsworth, a truly ideal choice. He had been working in the motion picture industry since 1937 but this was his first starring vehicle. His unique voice, his gentle manner, his expressive eyes and countenance bring his screen character imperishably to life. I first interviewed Farnsworth when he was touring with the film in the Pacific Northwest. After the interview, I told him I thought he would be perfect in the role of Charlie Flagg in Elmer Kelton's *The Time It Never Rained*. Farnsworth asked me to send him a copy of the novel. I wrote at once to Kelton and had him send a copy as well to Phillip Borsos.

I did not meet Farnsworth again until I was invited to speak at what was called the first National Western Film Festival in Ogden, Utah. For all I know, it was also the last. The entire project, including Western players and writers and critics of Western films along with screening Westerns, was undertaken to interest young people in the Western film as an art form and the young people were staying away in vast numbers. Farnsworth was almost the first person to whom I spoke. We were at lunch and Wilfred Brimley joined us. Brimley claimed that *The Grey Fox* was the greatest Western he had ever seen and told of how he enjoyed playing repeatedly a cassette of it, especially of the scene where Bill Miner handles a gun for the first time after being released from prison. I participated in a press conference that afternoon where I made the statement that the majority of Western films had habituated American audiences, and audiences everywhere, to a degree of falsehood I did not regard as healthy. The conference was filmed by the local media. Brimley rebutted me by saying that he was a red-neck and proud of it and that Westerns were the last bastion for red-necks. Once the conference was over, Ben Johnson approached me, smiling. He said if Mr. Ford were still alive and present, he would want to string me up. I could remember when Mr. Ford was alive and had wanted to string me up for far more innocuous comments.

The entire affair ended with an awards ceremony. All the recipients of the awards—the players who had been invited—were old men. Pat Buttram was the master of ceremonies. He recalled how once a man had said to him: "You and Gene Autry sure made an awful lot

Passing the mantle: William S. Hart presents Johnny Mack Brown with a pistol reputed to have belonged to Billy the Kid on the set of *Billy the Kid* (M-G-M, 1930) with director King Vidor in the middle. Photo courtesy of King Vidor.

of pictures together." "Wrong," he said. "Gene and I made a lot of *awful* pictures together!"

Two theatrical Westerns had been issued the summer of that film festival — *Silverado* (Columbia, 1985) and *Pale Rider* (Warner's, 1985). It did not initiate a new trend. Young people, for whom the majority of films are made, seemed to prefer fantasies about the present and the future to fantasies about the past, at least the past of the Old West.

The character actor, Royal Dano, told me a story. Recently he had gone with Gene Autry when Autry was to be made a thirty-third degree Mason.

"Gene can no longer stand up without assistance," Dano said. "So I stood alongside him, with my arm around his shoulders, propping him up. After the ceremony was concluded, all those old Masons began approaching the stage on which we were standing. They kept asking if Gene was going to sing. 'No,' I told them, 'I'm sure Gene is *not* going to sing.' They didn't really see the old man up there. They saw the man they remembered from his films."

Yakima Canutt: A Career Study

I

The closest Yakima Canutt ever came to being an American Indian was his first name. He was born Enos Edward Canutt at Colfax, Washington on November 29, 1896 and he died in Los Angeles on May 25, 1986. His lineage was Scottish, Irish, Dutch, and German. While still a youth, he learned to ride and then to use a rope. By thirteen, he was employed as a ranch hand; at seventeen, he joined a Wild West show as a trick rider. The show toured the country. At every available opportunity, he entered as a contestant in rodeos. In 1917 he won the title of World's All-Around Cowboy at the Pendleton Round-Up in Oregon. Already at that time he was known as "Yakima" Canutt. In the Pendleton competition for 1914 an error was made by a reporter. Canutt had been raised in the Yakima Valley of Washington. A photo in a newspaper identified him as the "cowboy from Yakima." It became his moniker. He went on to retain the Pendleton championship for seven years.

Once on the rodeo circuit, Canutt met others who would come to prominence in the film industry. Ken Maynard was first. Maynard also specialized in trick riding. The two were at the top of the field in terms of amazing dexterity and supple control of their performances in the arena. Canutt also met Tom Mix. Mix had begun working in motion pictures as early as 1909. He was already the most popular Western player on the screen when Ken Maynard first went to work for the Fox Film Corporation, where Mix was under contract, making his screen debut in *The Man Who Won* (Fox, 1923) directed by William Wellman.

Canutt was awarded the *Police Gazette* Cowboy Championship Belt in 1917, 1918, 1919, 1921, and 1923. He was presented the Roosevelt Trophy in 1923. Following other illustrious examples, he sought motion picture work during the off-months, beginning first as an extra and then as a stunt man. Ben Wilson was a production super-

87

visor on Westerns at Universal where Canutt frequently worked. Wilson admired Canutt's athletic prowess and his expert horsemanship. He proposed to feature Yak as a player in a series of inexpensive independent Westerns he planned to produce for release on the state's rights market as Arrow Productions. State's rights pictures were leased for a specified number of years for an exclusive territory to one or another independent film exchange servicing the area. Prior to this offer, Canutt's only acting credits had been in supporting roles in some Neal Hart Westerns made for independent release by William Steiner.

Under the new agreement with Wilson, Canutt's first role was in support of Ed Lytell in *Sell 'em Cowboy* (Arrow, 1924), a story about a saddle manufacturer. Yak starred in the next feature, *Ridin' Mad* (Arrow, 1924), and performed all his own stunts for the camera. Wilson then starred himself in *The Desert Hawk* (Arrow, 1924) with Yak as the second lead. *Branded a Bandit* (Arrow, 1924) with Canutt again in the lead closed out the year.

Very few independent films of any kind survive from the silent era. This is probably nowhere more true than of Ben Wilson's Arrow Productions. I would not wish to imply, judging from what I have seen of them, that they were personality vehicles. Dick Hatton, a heavy in low-grade Westerns and serials in the early thirties, starred in an entry like *The Cactus Cure* (Arrow, 1925) with Yak as a bullying foreman. The character name Canutt was given in this film was Bud Osborne; it was also the name of a rodeo wrangler who would make a career as a featured player in Westerns. Yak was cast as the rugged hero in *The Human Tornado* (Arrow, 1925). Neither who was cast as what nor the story-line mattered very much. Wilson had contracted to supply a series of Westerns. And that is what they were, a series of Westerns without distinction. Nor was Wilson very particular about distribution. If Film Booking Office was impressed with one of his Westerns, such as *The Ridin' Comet* (FBO, 1925) with Canutt, he would sell it to the company and let FBO distribute it through its exchanges. But Ben might also write, direct, and star himself in a Western, as in *West of the Law* (Rayart, 1926), or take just a bit part in a major studio production like *Rainbow Riley* (First National, 1926). Irritated by this situation, Canutt began to free-lance himself.

Hal Roach featured Canutt in *The Devil Horse* (Pathé, 1926). Rex, King of the Wild Horses as he was billed, was an unruly black stallion that became quite popular in a series of pictures Roach was producing with him. Rex played the devil horse. It remains one of the memorable equestrian films of the twenties, primarily for the battle Yak helped stage for the camera between Rex and a rival pinto stallion. This footage was so exciting it was used over and over as stock for years, showing up in Ken Maynard's *The Strawberry Roan* (Universal, 1933), or Yak's own use of it in serials such as *The Vanishing Legion* (Mascot, 1931) and *The Devil Horse* (Mascot, 1932); and Yak employed it again in the Three Mesquiteer Western, *Hit the Saddle* (Republic, 1937).

Canutt received credit during the twenties for performing stunts for himself or for another player in some forty-eight films. It was becoming a specialty. Even when he was appearing as the lead in independent Westerns for a small producing company like Big Four Productions, he still engaged in stunt-work assignments on his own.

Nat Levine came to Hollywood in 1925. He had begun in the film business with theatre-owner Marcus Loew. His first efforts at independent production were fraught with problems, but he turned a handsome profit when he co-ventured in a ten-chapter serial with Sam Bischoff. It was budgeted at $70,000 and was titled *The Silent Flyer*. Universal bought it. Levine then had sufficient working capital to commence making state's rights serials on a regular basis. He founded Mascot Pictures Corporation in 1927.

Levine hired Canutt to handle the stunt work on his initial chapter play, *The Golden Stallion* (Mascot, 1927). It proved a success. Whatever Levine's difficulties with finding adequate directors or his tendency to cut corners by employing actors whose popularity had tarnished or who were raw beginners, it was to Canutt that he was indebted for the hectic, frantic pacing of his serials which led to such immediate and enthusiastic endorsement by matinee audiences. Levine made three serials in 1927, two in 1928. Boris Karloff starred in the initial entry for 1928, *Vultures of the Sea,* Yak in the second, *The Vanishing West.* Harry Webb was Levine's director in 1927. He was replaced by Richard Thorpe in 1928. Webb had a drinking problem. Levine did not like that. Canutt never interfered. He did his second unit stunt and action work adeptly and minded his own business. Harry Webb liked that. He wouldn't be the last one. Webb had produced a series of low-budget Jack Perrin Westerns for Aywon release in the mid-twenties.

After parting company with Levine, he went on to another series with Perrin, this time for John R. Freuler's Biltmore Productions distributed by Big Four. Webb brought Canutt along. Although he might assign Canutt a part in a film like *Ridin' Law* (Big Four, 1930), Webb relied on Yak principally for stunting and action sequences.

Canutt had contracted bronchial pneumonia during the great influenza epidemic. His bronchial tubes bled for days. His voice changed. It got weak. He had to shout to be heard. In the silent era, Yak's hard, intense eyes, his chiseled features did not make him ideal to play heroes, and he did so only sporadically. After sound came in, his voice quite definitely limited him to character roles. He made stunt work his major occupation. In this way he could preserve the integrity of his income. He would star in a sound Western such as *Canyon Hawks* (Big Four, 1930) for the same $125 a week he demanded and received from Nat Levine for working the full three weeks it required to make a chapter play. The consistency of his Mascot efforts enhanced his reputation as a creative stunt director.

Levine's serials rapidly earned for Nat a name among exhibitors, exchange managers, and patrons as producing the best chapter plays among serial manufacturers. Their superiority was due to the constant action and truly daredevil stunting. A cutting continuity from any Universal serial from 1927–1931, put alongside one from a Mascot serial, would reveal the difference: the Mascot chapter plays got twice as many thrills into a chapter; things were always happening; and there was always too much plot, not too little. Herbert J. Yates, who had his start in the tobacco industry, now owned a conglomerate of film laboratories huddled beneath the corporate holding company of Consolidated Film Industries. He believed Levine to be a comer.

During the silent era, Levine was accustomed to spending between $30,000 and $35,000 for a chapter play. The addition of some spoken dialogue, synchronized music, and effects in *King of the Kongo* (Mascot, 1929) ran him approximately another $5,000. Yet he had the courage to attempt a sound serial in advance of Universal. Henry MacRae, head of Universal's chapter plays, had to fight studio boss Carl Laemmle and Laemmle's sound engineers before finally winning out in *The Indians Are Coming* (Universal, 1930), proving once and for all that sound could be used in making outdoor dramas. Levine worked hard, and he worked all the time, especially while in production. In this he proved an example to his cast members who were characteristically asked to work overtime and Saturdays in order to complete the picture on schedule. Levine sought to be a pathfinder and he was invariably willing to innovate. Olive Carey, Harry Carey's wife, once told me that as long as Levine ran his office out of his vest pocket he was without equal. Nat himself admitted to me that probably no one was as integral to the success of the Mascot serials as Yakima Canutt.

In 1930 Levine signed Rin Tin Tin to star in a serial titled *The Lone Defender*. He paid Lee Duncan, Rinty's owner, a flat $5,000. Since Rinty had been earning so much more while a Warner Bros. star in the twenties, Duncan suppressed the actual amount Mascot paid him when, some time later, he wrote his autobiography. What with this "star" cost and full sound recording equipment which he leased from Walt Disney (consisting of one mobile truck unit for location work and a dubbing service which Disney rented out when not preparing one of his cartoons for Columbia release), expenses were edging dangerously above the $40,000 mark — two to four thousand dangerously. D. Ross Lederman, who had directed Rinty at Warner Bros., was engaged for Mascot's second serial that year, *Phantom of the West*, starring former FBO player Tom Tyler. Notwithstanding, to close out the season, Levine wanted a real blockbuster. He engaged both Harry Carey and Edwina Booth who had just returned from several months in Africa shooting *Trader Horn* for M-G-M. He had a jungle story fashioned for the two in hopes of cashing in on M-G-M's massive publicity campaign. Carey and Booth were signed for one serial each, with an option for two more. However, production problems at M-G-M prevented them from coming to Mascot to make *King of the Jungle* (Mascot, 1930). Instead, the two were starred in the initial entry the next year, *The Vanishing Legion*.

The Mascot formula had by this time become established. Each chapter play had its leading player or players; they could be either familiar names or someone such as "Red" Grange, the football hero, who would guarantee public interest. Flanking the lead players were one or two supporting actors who could be hired cheaply and yet would add much to the finished product. The remainder was customarily made up of free-lance character actors who specialized in working for the independents. The better known among them would be placed on a weekly salary, according to the length of the part; others were paid either weekly or daily, as needed.

Levine borrowed. He borrowed has-beens from Universal and other studios. He borrowed the two-director concept from Pathé with one director working on interiors, another on exteriors, and Canutt handled all the action. He slashed budgets. Whereas Pathé in the years 1926–1929 spent an average of $10,000 an episode, Levine making *sound* serials spent $5,000 on the first chapter of three reels with a running time between thirty and forty minutes and $3,000 for every additional chapter lasting between fifteen and twenty minutes in duration. Wyndham Gittens was made story supervisor. His job involved the development of scripts that could be shot in twenty-one days, that amplified the story characteristics which appealed to Levine: the super-real and the fantastic, and that had plots so loosely conceived that the script need only indicate for action sequences: "See Yak."

In subsequent years, process screens, special effects, and optical printing would minimize the danger in most stunt work. Yet, when Canutt was working for Levine such techniques were very primitive and he avoided them. What the camera recorded and the frequently enthralled viewer saw was really being done by a man dependent only on his own amazing dexterity and ingenuity. Canutt's presence began increasingly to make itself felt with *The Vanishing Legion*. His exceptional skill working with horses was emphasized in the screenplay. Frankie Darro, a talented action player at twelve and an excellent rider who did not require a double, joined the cast for a flat $1,000. He teamed up with Yak for some astonishing sequences. Levine also signed Rex so Yak could make use of previous footage he had shot with the horse. Rex and Darro played off Harry Carey's reserved and charming screen style to provide the serial with what charisma it has. Edwina Booth was the problem. She saw herself as a great star. She was driven to the location every morning in a hired limousine. She remained aloof from other cast members and talked mostly with Ollie Carey whom she had come to know while making *Trader Horn* and who had to drive Harry Carey to work every day because he adamantly refused to have anything to do with cars. Unfortunately for Levine, *The Vanishing Legion* had a complex, dramatic part for Booth. Her acting wasn't even passable. Yak paid no attention to any of this. He concentrated on the stunts and the horses. He was also given a credited role. Reaves "Breezy" Eason joined Mascot with this serial. He and Canutt shared the direction of *The Vanishing Legion*.

Eason had a serious drinking problem. It had already showed up in the late twenties when he had directed Hoot Gibson at Universal. Levine assigned him to direct the next serial, *The Galloping Ghost* (Mascot, 1931). After it, he fired him for drinking and absenteeism. Only it didn't stick. Levine tried him again the next year for Carey's second serial with Booth, *Last of the Mohicans* (Mascot, 1932). This time it did stick. Nat not only fired Eason, but he kept him fired until *Law of the Wild* (Mascot, 1934). Why did Levine put up with him? He did it because Eason had talent as an action director which few in Hollywood could equal. David O. Selznick thought so too. He assigned all the action sequences in *Duel in the Sun* (Selznick, 1947), his colossal high budget Western, to Breezy Eason and another Mascot alumnus, Otto Brower.

Rin Tin Tin's second serial and his last motion picture was for Mascot. It was called *The Lightning Warrior* (Mascot, 1931). Armand Schaefer directed. Outdoor cameraman Benjamin Kline was Schaefer's co-director. Kline worked closely with Yak. It did not matter to Canutt that he was not always credited with the co-direction; he was paid well and regularly, while the others came and went. Henry MacRae borrowed Yak for the chapter play, *Battling with Buffalo Bill* (Universal, 1931), with Tom Tyler in the lead. It was one of the fastest-paced Western serials that studio ever made, with much the same hectic action to be found in the competitive Mascot entries.

When Warner Bros. released *The Clash of the Wolves* in 1925 with Rin Tin Tin and June Marlowe (the same principals Levine cast in *The Lone Defender*), the *Photoplay* reviewer commented on how human and sympathetic Rinty seemed, so much so that at times it appeared as if the dog actually shed tears. At Mascot, however, Rinty was an action player and, because of his age, this meant mostly a dependence on doubles. Lee Duncan had a whole retinue, including a stuffed wolf dog for harrowing stunts. *The Lightning Warrior* may well rank highest among Levine's early serials because of the action sequences Canutt designed for Rinty and Frankie Darro. To bring much of this off, Yak had assembled a group of competent stunt performers. Helen Gibson was among them. She had once shared a room with Hoot Gibson at the Pendleton Round-Up. Her name then was Helen Wenger. She never married Gibson, but she assumed his last name. Subsequently she claimed to have once been his wife, but she never was. In *The Lightning Warrior,* she doubled the female lead, Georgia Hale, who had played opposite Charlie Chaplin in *The Gold Rush* (United Artists, 1925). Richard Talmadge and Cliff Lyons became Canutt's understudies. Later, they would build substantial careers for themselves as doubles, stunt men, and second unit directors.

The sites were carefully selected. Bronson Canyon, located a short distance from Hollywood, was known for its "Indian Caves." These were caverns in the canyon walls, running clear through the mountain in some cases, originally made while the quarry was active supplying stone for the bricks used in the construction of the Los Angeles streetcar system. Motion picture companies had begun in the late twenties to use the caves as scenic backgrounds. It was here that Canutt created the Wolf Cave, the hide-out for the mystery figure in the serial known as the Wolf Man. The Prudential studio was a large lot outside Kernville used in the twenties and thirties in the production of Westerns. It had a town, a series of shacks, the Kern River, the arroyo featured in such Rex pictures as *King of the Wild Horses* (Pathé, 1926) and *The Vanishing Legion,* a rough and undulating terrain for chases, a high cliff overlooking a lagoon for dangerous jumps. The town set was named Sainte Suzanne for *The Lightning Warrior* and nearly all the exteriors were shot there or elsewhere on the Prudential lot. Minimal interior sets were located at Tec-Art studios in North Hollywood and at Universal City studios.

George Brent, who had come to Hollywood from the Broadway stage, had been signed by Levine to play the lead. Kermit Maynard, who worked frequently as a double for his more famous brother, Ken Maynard, was assigned by Yak to the second unit to double Brent. A friendship began between Maynard and Canutt that lasted until Kermit's death in 1971.

Rinty's screen farewell was totally in character with his fabulous career, retrieved from the trenches in France and brought to the United States by Lee Duncan. The public accorded him a unique place among Hollywood luminaries. Much of what Rinty earned was lost by Duncan through unwise investments. One afternoon, shortly after *The Lightning Warrior* was completed, Rinty, then fourteen, jumped into his master's arms and collapsed. Duncan in the meantime had trained several offspring and subsequently Levine would feature Rin Tin Tin, Jr., in a number of serials. Personally, Yak thought little of the dog. He felt that Rinty was at his best in close-ups. Once the dog bit him, missing entirely the protective pad Yak wore on his arm. Rinty's double struck Yak as a better action player. However, he did not approve of Duncan's treatment of Rinty, often hitting him to get him to obey and once beating him with a chain. Levine, for his part, was buying the dog's name, not his ability.

Typical of the stunts Canutt prepared for this serial is the ending to the first episode. The camera is mounted on the front of a runaway wagon with Canutt and Helen Gibson aboard, doubling Brent and Georgia Hale. They are being pursued by hostile Indians. The camera tracks to where the wagon hits a stump, mounted on the driver's seat right to the moment of impact. The horses pull forward, taking the lip and harnesses with them, while the wagon rolls back slowly and gains momentum as it hurtles down the hillside.

Another parlous moment is when Frankie Darro is fighting with the Wolf Man in an ore car supposedly suspended high up in the air. Rinty jumps from a wooden beam as the car passes, landing on the cloaked mystery figure. Frankie is thrown from the car and hangs on from below. Yak, as the Wolf Man, then sees Yak as George Brent starting toward him, hanging onto a hook attached to the cable. The Wolf Man jumps across into another ore car, going in the opposite direction. The loss of his weight causes the car he has left to dump over. In the nick of time, Frankie grabs hold of Rinty. Now the two are dangling. Yak jumps aboard the overturned car, pulling both the boy and dog to safety. All of this was accomplished only a few feet above the ground, but the illusion of its being hundreds of feet in the air is successfully sustained. When the ore car dumped over, audiences must have gasped and screamed. I heard college students react in this fashion when as a guest speaker at the University of Indiana I had occasion to have this chapter screened for them.

II

We were standing in Yak's study in his home on Riverside Drive in North Hollywood in the summer of 1975. Everywhere on the walls were action stills of Yak's doing various feats. I was flipping through the pages of his autobiography, then a work in progress.

"When the late Gabby Hayes was an old man," I said, "I talked to him. As you know, he had worked at one time or another with most of the Western players of the thirties and forties. He told me he had worked with only one cowboy player worth anything as an action performer: You."

I showed him the page I was at in his manuscript. The chapter heading read, "I Meet John Wayne."

"He didn't think Duke much of a cowboy," I said.

"That's probably because Duke doesn't like horses," Yak said.

John Wayne was six feet four inches tall. Were you to have met him, you might well say that he loomed; he dominated the space around him. Wayne's screen career did not begin at Mascot, but it got its second wind there. He started as a prop boy for Tom Mix in 1927 at the Fox Film Corporation. John Ford took a liking to him and used him in several capacities in the films he directed for Fox. Wayne got his first big break when Fox starred him in its 70mm super Western, *The*

**Roy D'Arcy (left) and Yakima Canutt in a scene from *Shadow of the Eagle*
(Mascot, 1932). Photo courtesy of Columbia Pictures-Screen Gems.**

Big Trail (Fox, 1930). It turned out a box office bomb. Fox then gave
him the fast shuffle. In 1931 he was out looking for work. His agent
managed to get him signed on at Columbia Pictures as a contract
player. Wayne dislike playing "second" lead to Tim McCoy and Buck
Jones in their series Westerns. He was saucy, sullen, hard to get along
with, and unhappy. He wanted to be a star. Levine heard about this

and found a way to take advantage of it. His three serials for 1931 had done so well on a state's rights basis that he felt secure in his decision to increase his production budget by another $15,000 while cutting the individual budgets on all entries, thus having not three but four serials for 1932. Distributors were subjected to block booking whereby they had to agree to take all four if they were to get any one. If John Wayne wanted to be a star, all right, he would have his chance at Mascot. With Harry Carey and Edwina Booth on an option for two more chapter plays after *The Vanishing Legion,* Levine offered Wayne a contract while he was still at Columbia to make three serials for Mascot at a total compensation of $2,000. The contract stipulated that Wayne was to be on call anytime during the three respective months the chapter plays were in production. The payments were divided into shares of $666.66 per serial. Wayne agreed to the terms. Yak, at $250 a week, was earning more than the star.

Shadow of the Eagle (Mascot, 1932) went into production first. Wayne had to work six days a week, twelve hours a day. Once the cast and crew worked seven days consecutively and some days for as long as eighteen hours. In a single day there might be as many as one hundred and fourteen camera setups. Ford Beebe was the director, but Nat still had Breezy Eason handle some of the action.

While out on location, Eason announced that next day everyone was to report to Bronson Canyon at six in the morning. Returning home some distance away for so few hours did not appeal to Wayne. He decided to stay the night on location. The crew had built a fire as a shield against the late night cold. There was no place to stay, no cabins, no tents. A few had brought bed rolls. There was no commissary truck. There was only bread and cheese and whiskey.

Wayne sat by the fire and pulled out a pint bottle of whiskey. He was cold and disgusted. His weary body ached. Yak sauntered over to the fire and crouched down. He did not speak. Duke handed Yak the bottle. Yak uncorked it and took a long pull. He wiped his mouth with the back of one hand.

"Well, Duke," he said, "it don't take very long to spend the whole night here."

Wayne chuckled. He took a pull at the whiskey.

"Sure don't," he said.

They laughed. They were friends.

The Last of the Mohicans came between *Shadow of the Eagle* and Wayne's second serial, *Hurricane Express* (Mascot, 1932). As might be deduced from its title, this opus had a railroad setting. Canutt had had to work out complex motorcycle antics for *Shadow of the Eagle*. *The Last of the Mohicans* had put him into a Colonial setting with wagon stunts and plenty of water action in the Kern River. For *Hurricane Express* he put his mind to railroad thrills.

The Devil Horse was the final entry for the year. Levine dropped Edwina Booth after *The Last of the Mohicans*. Having lost her suit against M-G-M, she was without money to pay her legal fees. Harry Carey sought to assist her. Duncan Renaldo by this time was about to be imprisoned by the immigration authorities for illegal entry into the United States. Carey would star alone in *The Devil Horse*. However, funds were short so Levine scrapped the idea of using Rex. Instead he bought a wild three-year-old black stallion from Tracy Layne. Otto Brower was assigned the direction. He had been an assistant director at Paramount on its silent Zane Grey series and he had directed Harry Carey and Hoot Gibson in sound Westerns. He had also worked with the Tim McCoy unit at Columbia. Much of *The Devil Horse* was to be shot on location in Arizona. Levine dispatched Brower with the cast and crew. Carey refused to go, so Yak did all his scenes for him except for close-ups. Richard Talmadge whose principal experience had been as Douglas Fairbanks' double in the twenties went along as Canutt's second unit assistant.

This serial is important because its opening chapter contains one of Canutt's most fabulous stunts. Originally planned with Rex in mind, the stunt with the horse Levine bought, named Apache, almost cost Yak his life. The script called for Canutt, dressed as Carey, to grab hold of Apache's mane with his hands. He was then to clamp his legs around the horse's neck, as the animal reared and bucked and continually tried to shake him and dash him beneath his hooves. A pit shot was arranged, placing a camera in an indentation in the ground with boards on top. It was to capture the hooves rearing and stamping on the earth. Another camera with a long-range lens focused on the action from in front. The horse went berserk and shook violently, Yak hanging on for all he was worth.

It made for fantastic footage, but Apache proved almost impossible to work with and the serial went way over budget. Canutt remained so impressed with the scene, however, that he later put the encounter with Apache and the fight between Rex and the pinto into a subsequent Gene Autry Western with Autry dressed as Carey, *Comin' Round the Mountain* (Republic, 1936). Levine tried to get rid of

Apache by donating him to the University of Arizona in exchange for the University's kindness in letting him use a herd of horses it owned. The University ultimately did not thank him for the favor and ended up selling the horse to a private interest. Yak had two uncredited parts on screen in *The Devil Horse*. He was done in by Apache in an early chapter only to re-appear later on in the serial as another character altogether. Evidently the incongruity of this was accepted by audiences with equanimity, if in fact it was noticed by them at all.

Levine produced five chapter plays in 1933. He also leased the Mack Sennett studio lot in North Hollywood. He had tried his hand the previous year at a feature, *Pride of the Legion* (Mascot, 1932) with Barbara Kent and Rin Tin Tin, Jr. It did business. Nat thought the time right to embark on feature production as well as to increase the number of serials annually. Now that he had lot space, he endeavored to rent it out when it was not in use for one of his own productions. Trem Carr, who had been producing a series of low grade Bob Steele Westerns for Tiffany release, founded Monogram Pictures together with W. Ray Johnston. They set up their offices at Mascot. Levine signed Bob Steele to star in the serial *Mystery Squadron* (Mascot, 1932), while Trem Carr contracted John Wayne to appear as the lead in a series of Lone Star Westerns for Monogram release.

Wayne had just finished starring in a series of cheap remakes of silent Ken Maynard Westerns at Warner Bros., films originally made by First National, now a wholly owned Warner subsidiary. Wayne appeared in these sound Westerns in close-ups, with Maynard interpolated in medium and long-range action footage. Their apparel matched if their physical proportions did not. Carr's idea was to budget the Wayne Westerns at $5,000 to $8,000 a picture. Canutt was to be in charge of all stunt work, was to double Wayne, and was to have a featured role, usually as a villain. Paul Malvern was hired to be production supervisor. Robert N. Bradbury, Bob Steele's father, directed most of the entries and even wrote many of the original stories. Armand Schaefer, when he was available, was occasionally borrowed from Mascot to substitute for Bradbury.

The Three Musketeers (Mascot, 1933) was Wayne's final chapter play. Ruth Hall was the heroine. The story had a French Foreign Legion background. The company went on location to Yuma, Arizona, for the desert footage. No sooner had it arrived than the banks closed. President Roosevelt had begun his one hundred days. The company was suddenly without funds. Because it was Mascot, Ruth Hall had to do all her own make-up. Exposure and severe sunburn made it all the more difficult and, as the serial progresses, her face darkens noticeably. There is a mystery man. Yak doubled Wayne and stood in at times for the mystery man, El Shaitan, as did several other cast members in order to make his identity difficult to guess. Canutt also worked out a number of transfers from one horse to another and, additionally, some harrowing sequences back at the Bronson Canyon location. It is an entertaining serial and probably the best of the three that Wayne made.

Riders of Destiny (Monogram, 1933) was Wayne's initial Lone Star Western. Cecilia Parker was the girl. Gabby Hayes, still billed as George Hayes, had a featured role. He became a regular fixture as the series continued, playing either an outlaw or the girl's father, although increasingly he would work himself into the role of a sidekick. In *West of the Divide* (Monogram, 1934) he was sympathetic support to the hero. In *The Lucky Texan* (Monogram, 1934) he added much to the comic effect of a chase involving a Model T, a railroad handcar, and some horses. Canutt, of course, was the heavy in *The Lucky Texan*. During this chase sequence, Yak was to be pumping away on the handcar. Duke was to ride up alongside, do a transfer from his horse to the handcar, fight it out with Yak, and finally throw Yak off into a ditch. Duke felt he could do the transfer, but he was worried lest he miss the handcar and break both his legs. He stood around tensely on the set, getting up his courage. He wanted to show Canutt that he was his equal.

"Well," Yak said finally, "are you gonna do it? Or would you rather *double me?*"

As the series progressed, Yak frequently wound up chasing himself during the final reel, playing both himself and doubling Wayne.

While they were shooting *Sagebrush Trail* (Monogram, 1933), Canutt began to observe that Wayne was following him around all the time. At last he stopped in his tracks. He asked Duke why.

"I'm trying to get down that walk," Duke replied. "You roll on the balls of your feet. I want to walk like that."

If Wayne imitated the way Tom Mix mounted a horse and Buck Jones' look of granite resolve, his ambling lope and his horsemanship once in the saddle, huddled close to the saddlehorn, he owed to Yakima Canutt.

Jack Mulhall, Francis X. Bushman, Jr., and Raymond Hatton were cast as the Three Musketeers in the Levine serial. With them, Nat began his first promotion of the concept of a trio of heroes in action films. It prompted William Colt MacDonald to write his Three Mesquiteer novels which Levine eventually brought to the screen at Republic. Even more far-reaching in its impact was Levine's exploitation of the musical Western. Nat was visibly impressed by what Ken Maynard had been doing at Universal. When Junior Laemmle, Carl Laemmle's son and heir apparent, ousted Maynard from his Universal contract, Maynard and his wife went on a European vacation. Levine contacted Maynard in London via long distance. It was his intention to produce a series of musical Westerns in both serial and feature form. Maynard agreed to Levine's offer of $10,000 a week for each week that he worked. Levine wanted him for an undetermined number of pictures. Yet, signing Maynard was not the significant thing. The truly momentous decision Levine made was to bring Gene Autry to Hollywood. Perhaps no personality in the history of the American cinema presents a greater paradox to critic, historian, or modern viewer alike than Gene Autry. One quality about Autry must be kept in mind above all: he divorced himself utterly from reality. No one before him developed quite the thorough-going and consistent fantasy world he did, as no one for better than a decade and a half would be quite the same in Western programmers because of his influence. I am not speaking here so much of the musical content of the Autry films as I am of the prospect of Gene Autry as a Western hero.

Nat Levine had a reputation for giving young, inexperienced talent a chance with his company. "I received a dozen letters from Autry during 1933," Levine once remarked to me, "asking for an opportunity to work for me in anything I would suggest in pictures. Autry's name value at the time was limited to a radio station in Chicago, practically an unknown with questionable ability. On one of my trips east, I stopped off in Chicago, not to meet Autry but for business I had with my distributor. But I did get to meet Autry and he virtually begged me for an opportunity to come to Hollywood and work in pictures. While he was nice-looking, it seemed to me he lacked the commodity necessary to become a Western star: virility! I wasn't impressed and tried to give him a nice brush-off, telling him I would think about it. For a period of six months he wrote to me continually, conveying that he would do anything for the opportunity."

Autry had a recording contract with American Records. Herbert J. Yates was president of the company. Yates' laboratories were still processing all of Levine's films and Yates knew Levine well enough to lend him money. Autry enlisted Yates to put in a good word for him. Yates informed Levine that Autry was selling a lot of records. When Ken Maynard signed with Mascot, Levine went ahead and put Autry on salary with a three-year option. It was Levine's notion to use Autry, who *could* sing, to support Maynard who really could not.

"Gene was completely raw material," Levine continued, "knew nothing about acting, lacked poise, and was awkward. A couple of days after his arrival I had him at my home and invited my production staff to meet him. The next day all of my associates questioned my judgment in putting him under contract. They thought I was slipping. But I persisted, and for the first four months he went through a learning period. We had at that time, in our employ, a professional dramatic and voice teacher, and Autry became one of her pupils. He wasn't much of a horseman either, so I had Tracy Layne and Yakima Canutt teach him how to ride."

The riding lessons did not leave Yak with a positive impression. He did not particularly like Autry, although subsequently he was more than willing to acknowledge Autry's acumen in industries unrelated to motion pictures.

Autry had a singing role in the Ken Maynard feature, *In Old Santa Fe* (Mascot, 1934), and a small acting part in Maynard's serial, *Mystery Mountain* (Mascot, 1934). By that time Maynard's unruly ways had got the better of Levine. Maynard was dropped. Levine then took a desperate chance. He chose to star Autry in his next serial, *The Phantom Empire* (Mascot, 1935). It proved almost as successful at the box office as had *Mystery Mountain*.

It would be useless to conjecture what might have happened to Mascot had it not merged in 1935. The company was both reputable and profitable, which is why Yates wanted it. Yates' Consolidated laboratories also did the lab work for Monogram Pictures. By 1935, Monogram had nineteen company-owned exchanges and twenty franchisees for the distribution of its pictures. What Yates proposed came to this. Mascot, Monogram, and Consolidated would combine their assets. Monogram would bring the John Wayne Westerns and its distribution network to the merger. Mascot would contribute its serial production, the projected singing Western features with Gene Autry, and its lease on the Sennett lot. Yates would provide additional capital and a total laboratory service. The parties involved thought the merger a good idea and by March, 1935 Republic Pictures was born. Mascot completed its serial production for that year under its own logo, but its last chapter play, *The Fighting Marines* (Mascot, 1935), was distributed via the Republic exchanges. Gene Autry's first feature, *Tumbling Tumbleweeds* (Republic, 1935), referred to the releasing company in the publicity as a "Mascot brand name." John Wayne's first Western for the new company was *Westward Ho* (Republic, 1935).

Canutt was still free-lancing, but now he was placed in charge of the stunt work and second unit direction on the Wayne and Autry Westerns and the four Republic serials produced annually by Levine. He continued for some years to sign a series of short-term contracts with Republic. There was little he could do with Autry, but it was the intention of the production personnel — namely Levine, director Armand Schaefer, and the writers — to keep plenty of action in the films. About this Canutt could do something.

John Wayne wanted his movie fights to be realistic. To achieve this end, he did not pull his punches. The result was that Canutt or any other heavy he was fighting would emerge from the scene black and blue. It was the director Robert N. Bradbury who happened upon a solution. "He said," Duke once remarked, "that he thought if he placed a camera at a certain angle it would look as if my fist was making contact with Yak's face, though my fist was passing his face, not even grazing it. We tried it out one day. When we saw the rushes, we saw how good it looked. Bradbury invented this trick which he called the pass system. Other stunt men and directors picked up on it and it became the established way of doing a fight." When sound effects were added, the fights in the Wayne Westerns seemed the most real on the screen.

Canutt found Wayne a more able pupil than he did Autry. He taught him how to float over a horse's head when the horse buckled beneath him as if shot; how to make a transfer from horse to horse, horse to stage, train to horse, or horse to train; how to ride up alongside another man on horseback and jump him; and how to drop in a slump from a horse when supposedly bushwacked. Wayne came greatly to admire Canutt. He would remark to friends that if only he were the stunt man Yak was, he could quit acting and complained teasingly that Yak was still getting paid more than he was.

The scriptwriters for the Republic serials, as their predecessors at Mascot, allowed Canutt to work out all the action sequences, no matter what the setting. Yak perfected the running W for tripping horses, since outlawed in the United States. He only injured one animal in his entire career. He invented tricks such as rigging a wagon with fine wire so it could disintegrate on cue. With wires he could also make dangerous stunts safe, such as climbing up a suspension bridge as it collapsed. For the serial *The Vigilantes Are Coming* (Republic, 1936) which starred Robert Livingston, Canutt devised an elaborate stagecoach stunt to be used in the eighth or ninth episode. The hero was to ride up alongside a moving coach and transfer onto it. He would then be knocked off onto the tongue of the stage, between the racing horses. He would, gripping the shaft, lower himself down between the horses' pounding hooves and let himself go. As the coach rolled over him, he would grab onto the luggage carrier, pull himself up, and climb up over the top of the coach again to engage the villain in a fight. Levine, once he saw how brilliantly this was executed in the dailies, thought Canutt crazy to put a stunt like that in a late episode. He wanted it in the first chapter. Yak would repeat it frequently in other Republic productions and in Westerns for other companies. When John Ford was preparing *Stagecoach* (United Artists, 1939), he viewed a print of *Riders of the Dawn* (Monogram, 1938). Robert Livingston's brother, Jack Randall, was the star. At the conclusion of the picture there is a terrific race across the salt flats up at Victorville. Canutt did his famous stagecoach trick, doubling for Randall. Ford decided he wanted such a race in his own film and he contracted Canutt to perform the stunt in *Stagecoach*.

Yates ultimately was not a man to have partners. Once the merger was completed and the company consolidated with a fixed market for its product, he began eliminating the men he had invited to join him. Trem Carr was first. Yates bought out both Carr and Ray Johnston. Before newly organizing Monogram Pictures, Carr went to work briefly for Universal, now itself under new management. When Wayne's contract with Republic expired in early 1936, Carr invited him to come to Universal to star in a series of non–Westerns that he was producing. Wayne was pleased with the chance. Once Carr resumed operation of Monogram, Wayne returned to Republic and Westerns.

Next Yates moved against Nat Levine. He bought out his interest in 1937. Gene Autry went on strike against Yates and Republic, demanding more money. All Yates had was the Three Mesquiteer series Levine had started with Robert Livingston, Ray Corrigan, and Max Terhune. He attempted to fill the gap in his release schedule by releasing, and then finally producing, A.W. Haeckle's independent Westerns, one series with Johnny Mack Brown, another with Bob Steele.

While all this was occurring, Canutt branched out, working for other companies in order to keep busy. He did second unit work on some of the Tex Ritter singing Westerns for Grand National and even had a substantial part as a ranger in *Riders of the Rockies* (Grand National, 1937). When Trem Carr began again to produce Westerns for Monogram release, Canutt also occasionally worked for him. When Columbia Pictures entered the chapter play field, Yak found work there, both doing the second unit work as well as appearing in a featured role in a serial such as *The Secret of Treasure Island* (Columbia, 1938).

Canutt regarded Yates a hard man with a contract. He was primarily a businessman interested in little else except saving on costs. "Working at Republic," Yak remarked to me, "you were always fighting for something you should have had to begin with." When word got out that there were to be general pay cuts, Canutt took the script for the latest Republic serial to the executives. He told them he had analyzed the stunts. They were too difficult. He would only do them if he received a hundred dollar raise. By this time, John Wayne was playing the part Robert Livingston had had in the Three Mesquiteer series, a suitable punishment for his brief defection to Universal. He could not get a better deal out of Republic. But Canutt knew how important *he* was; he got the raise.

Yak was hired to double Clark Gable in *Gone with the Wind* (M-G-M, 1939) and even had a small part in the finished film. His most harrowing stunt was leading a blindfolded horse through the scenes of the burning of Atlanta. When he was hired to work on *Stagecoach*, it would be Ford's first sound Western. Ford had decided to include John Wayne in the cast and on the set he tended to belittle him incessantly. This rankled Yak. Wayne used to tell the story of how, one day, Ford invited him to screen rushes and evaluate Andy Devine's performance as the stage driver. "I thought," Wayne said, "that Andy held the reins too loosely and I told Ford I thought so. Ford said to me that it was an important point and he wanted everyone to hear it. Well, he called everybody to him, the cast, the technical crew, the wardrobe workers, the grips, even the electricians. 'I want you to know,' he told them, 'that Duke thinks this is a great picture and that we're all doing one helluva job—but he can't stand Devine's performance.'" Obviously Ford felt, even then, that Wayne too often took the point of view of a director rather than that of an actor. Ford intended to develop Wayne as an actor. At night when on location in a motel room Wayne would

Yakima Canutt in the plaid shirt heading up the second unit for *Man of Conquest* (Republic, 1939). Photo courtesy of Yakima Canutt.

rehearse his lines repeatedly with Canutt as his critic. He resented the way Ford kept after him.

The race across the salt flats was shot at the same California location used in *Riders of the Dawn*. Ford told Canutt that he was an expert on how fast horses could run and, therefore, on how fast the camera car should be moving during the chase. Yak insisted horses could not run as fast as Ford said they could. Ford would hear nothing of it. He tried racing the camera car across the flats at a high speed only to watch the horses begin slowly to trail behind. Ford became highly agitated and told Yak to shoot the sequence any way he wanted. When Ford saw the rushes of the horse falls, he was elated; and when he saw Yak's stunt of falling beneath the stagecoach horses he feigned outright disbelief, although he had hired Canutt with that very stunt in mind. Ford also called on Canutt's engineering skill to assist him in the sequence where the stage must be floated across the Kern River.

Once the film was completed, the cast and crew were assembled for a wrap party. Bert Glennon had been the cinematographer. Ford overheard someone remark that it was an excellent Western.

"Thanks to Yakima Canutt," Glennon responded.

"It was the first time I worked for John Ford," Yak commented to me, smiling, "and it was the last." Subsequently he would do the second unit work on *Mogambo* (M-G-M, 1953) which Ford directed, but he did not so much as see the director on that occasion.

III

Stagecoach was previewed at the Village Theatre in Westwood. Wayne saw to it that the Republic brass attended, especially Sol and Moe Siegel. He spotted them sneaking out of the theatre afterwards, so he knew they had come. And why not? Wayne was readily the best Western player Republic had. Now he was to be seen in a major Western. Yet, no one said anything the next day, nor again on the next. At last Wayne broke down and asked Sol Siegel what he had thought of the picture.

"If it's a Western they want to make," Siegel snapped, "let them come to Republic to learn how to make it."

Wayne had four more Three Mesquiteer pictures to make for the current season. His Republic contract had four more years to run. Wayne's agent got Yates to agree to let him appear in pictures for other companies. It was due to his popularity in these major productions that Wayne himself could get Yates to agree in 1941 to pay him ten percent of the gross profits on his pictures above his contract salary.

Allegheny Uprising (RKO, 1939) again co-starred Wayne with Claire Trevor who had appeared opposite him in *Stagecoach*. Yates felt that the time was now ripe for Republic to attempt a major motion picture. The property he selected was *The Dark Command* (Republic, 1940), based on a novel by W.R. Burnett. The budget was set at $750,000 and Raoul Walsh was contracted to direct. After a decade, this picture reunited Wayne with the director who had worked on his first bid for stardom in *The Big Trail*. Claire Trevor was signed and by contract received top billing; Wayne was second; Walter Pidgeon was third. Republic insured the production with Lloyd's of London for $670,000. When Claire Trevor fell ill, production was suspended on December 23, 1939, after a month of shooting. Republic had paid $30,000 for the insurance policy and was paid $250,000 by Lloyd's as a settlement for the delay. Production was resumed on February 1, 1940, and completed in sixteen days on February 17, 1940, at a total cost in excess of a million dollars, or twice as much as *Stagecoach* had cost. Canutt headed up the second unit. He surpassed himself in a stunt where he and three other stunt men went over a cliff and into a ravine in a buckboard. Yak used a ninety-foot chute, well-soaped, and breakaway harnesses on the horse team. He also supervised the tense scene of the burning of Lawrence, Kansas with which the film concludes, utilizing techniques he had learned while at work on *Gone with the Wind*.

In the late thirties Warner Bros. began a series of high budget Westerns. Errol Flynn starred in *Dodge City* (Warner's, 1939). After several more pictures in this same romantic and optative mood, the studio decided to cast Flynn as General George Armstrong Custer in *They Died with Their Boots On* (Warner's, 1942). Raoul Walsh was the director. Walsh kept having trouble with the stunts during battle sequences. People were getting hurt. Walsh called in Breezy Eason to assist him and Eason called in Yak. Yak was to double Flynn. Together Canutt and Eason master-minded the elaborate stunting. There were over three hundred running Ws used in the course of the film and only once was a horse so much as stunned. Canutt and Eason would rehearse the action so thoroughly that all Walsh had to do was film it. Flynn in his autobiography, *My Wicked, Wicked Ways* (1959), tells of how he violently objected to the use of running Ws while filming *The Charge of the Light Brigade* (Warner's, 1936). He felt using a series of wires to trip a horse while running was brutal and he complained about it to the Society for the Prevention of Cruelty to Animals. It was not running Ws that he recalled about *They Died with Their Boots On*, though. It was the death of Bill Meade, who was thrown from his horse and fell on top of his sabre.

Breezy Eason, in addition to the chariot race in *Ben-Hur* (M-G-M, 1926), directed the land rush in *Cimarron* (RKO, 1931), the jousting in *Robin Hood* (Warner's, 1938), the burning of Atlanta in *Gone with the Wind,* and the battle scenes in *Sergeant York* (Warner's, 1941), to name just a few of his most illustrious credits. "You can have a small army of people charging across the screen," he told Ezra Goodman in *The Fifty Year Decline and Fall of Hollywood* (1961), "and it won't matter much to an audience. But if you show the details of the action, like guns going off, individual men fighting, or a fist hitting someone in the eye, then you will have more feeling of action than if all the extras in Hollywood are running about. That is why real catastrophes often look tame in newsreels. You need detail work and close shots in a movie. Only then does it come to life."[1]

Yates had rapidly settled with Autry concerning his money demands. In the early forties, however, he saw that he would have to increase and vary Western film production, particularly now that John Wayne was becoming a name star and Autry was inducted into the Air Force. Yates personally negotiated with Bill Elliott for him to leave Columbia and join Republic. He promised Elliott full star treatment. After completing *Vengeance of the West* (Columbia, 1942), Elliott's last series Western which teamed him with Tex Ritter, and his third and final chapter play, *The Valley of Vanishing Men* (Columbia, 1942) directed by Spencer Gordon Bennet, Elliott was welcomed onto the Republic lot. Gabby Hayes, who had been playing a sidekick to Roy Rogers, was now assigned to the Elliott Westerns. His place in the Rogers series was then taken by Smiley Burnette who had always been Gene Autry's comic stooge. The Sons of the Pioneers, a group Roy helped found, appeared with Roy the first time in one of his starring vehicles in *Red River Valley* (Republic, 1941). Rogers wanted the Republic management to promote alcoholic, peculiar Pat Brady of the Pioneers into the role of his comic sidekick. The proposal was turned down and it was not until Rogers began his television series that Brady would play his sidekick. Instead, in such films as *Heart of the Golden West* (Republic, 1942), besides a mixture of station wagons and steam-powered river boats, both Gabby Hayes and Smiley Burnette were in comic support, with the Sons of the Pioneers for musical backup. After Elliott's first season, Hayes was reassigned to the Rogers unit.

Donald Barry had starred in the serial *The Adventures of Red Ryder* (Republic, 1940). Beginning that same year, billed as Don "Red" Barry because of the serial, he was given his own Western series. It lasted for two seasons. Barry wanted to emulate James Cagney and kept pestering Yates to star him in gangster roles which were more or less the kinds of parts he had been playing when he first came to Republic. Barry's contract paid him the same whether he was cast as a hero or a villain. Yates also tried to start another singing cowboy series in 1943 by signing Eddie Dew and co-starring him with Smiley Burnette, but the series proved unpopular and was hastily dropped.

When Robert Livingston's contract expired with Republic, he joined Producers' Releasing Corporation for a series that was intended to capitalize on his appearance in the serial *The Lone Ranger Rides*

Again (Republic, 1939). This new character was called the "Lone Rider." Livingston was soon replaced by a virtual unknown, George Huston, who added singing to the role, something Livingston could not do. So Livingston returned to Republic and began to star in a new series with Smiley Burnette, after which he turned to playing villains and character roles, first at Republic and then for other studios.

Tom Tyler finished up the Three Mesquiteer series in the old Livingston/Wayne role of Stony Brooke for one more season before Yates admitted the idea was played out and scrapped it. *Riders of the Rio Grande* (Republic, 1943) and *Outlaw Trail* (Monogram, 1944), the final entries respectively in the Mesquiteer series and in the ill-fated Trail Blazer series at Monogram, in both of which Bob Steele played one of the leads, marked the demise of the trio concept of Western film production.

Most of these new Western series at Republic were shot on accelerated seven-day schedules. Canutt was placed in charge of all the second units on every picture and chapter play. As many as seventy scenes a day would be shot for various pictures in production. Yak had to chart all his crews' assignments and oversee all the action footage shot.

Livingston was replaced in his solo series with Smiley Burnette by tall, athletic Sunset Carson. About Carson's only qualifications to play a movie cowboy were his Texas drawl and his winning a championship cowboy title in Buenos Aires in 1941. He was a wretched actor whose delivery of the simplest dialogue proved an embarrassment. Yates was so unsure of him on the basis of his screen test that he released his first pictures giving Smiley Burnette top billing. Notwithstanding, Carson caught on with audiences, particularly in the South. To compensate for his total incompetence as a believable player, his pictures had to be packed with more than the usual apportionment of action sequences and had very strong plot-lines.

In 1944 Yak signed a four-year contract as a full director at Republic and his first assignment under the new agreement was one of the Carson pictures, *Sheriff of Cimarron* (Republic, 1945). He found Carson nervous and indifferent to acting. For the first four days Carson was sober. The fifth day he showed up hopelessly drunk. Near the end of shooting, there was a fight sequence. Once it had been shot, Carson disappeared from the set. Yak found him outside, sitting on a step, sobbing. He turned his tear-stained face to Yak and whimpered that he thought his arm had been broken.

One of the better Carson Westerns, *Rough Riders of Cheyenne* (Republic, 1945), featured Monte Hale in a supporting role. Hale would soon replace Carson. The leading lady was Peggy Stewart, her callipygian figure resplendent in tight riding breeches. The action sequences are fantastic. Ted Mapes, doubling for Carson, actually jumps from an overhanging tree limb onto the top of a moving stagecoach, something usually handled by means of rear-view projection. Alcoholism and sexual indiscretions, however, soon created such adverse publicity for Carson that Yates was compelled, finally if reluctantly, to fire him.

Thanks to Canutt's streamlined second units, Republic was able to transform the reckless, continuous action format of Mascot and polish it to an incredible degree. It was this tremendous technical capacity which permitted the studio to make a starring series with a character actor like Donald Barry into a modest box-office success, that entertained so consistently that by keeping Sunset Carson riding no one guessed what was missing. It is a measure of Eddie Dew's inadequacy that with all this going for him he still did not make it!

Bill Elliott's first film on his new contract was *Calling Wild Bill Elliott* (Republic, 1943) directed by Spencer Gordon Bennet. Bennet had been right behind Elliott coming from Columbia. The two were frequently teamed over the next two years at Elliott's request. The studio did right by Elliott. Not only was his name used in the title of the picture but, as Autry and Rogers, he played himself in the story. Bennet stressed action. Yak doubled Elliott. In one sequence, Elliott had to jump from the roof of a hacienda onto his pinto below. Yak constructed a wooden platform and attached it to the rear of an adobe arch out of camera range. The camera tracked Elliott running across the stucco roof to the arch. He stopped, poised above his horse. Then he jumped off the arch onto the platform. A split second before Elliott landed on the platform, Yak continued the jump onto the back of the horse. On screen, it appeared to be a single action.

Once Elliott began to star in "A" productions, there was no thought of his resuming series Westerns. Gene Autry had returned. Yates had been preparing himself for this moment and felt well-armed. It was true that his efforts on behalf of Donald Barry and Sunset Carson had come to little, but with John Wayne and now Bill Elliott he was marching forward into the ranks of the majors. Yates had seen a production of *Oklahoma* in New York and had put out a general memo that the studio's Roy Rogers Westerns were to be extravagant musicals.

When Yak broke both of his legs performing a stunt in one of Rogers' pictures, he was glad of the chance to leave stunting increasingly to others and concentrate on direction. Yates was able to control Rogers. Autry's first picture after he was released from the service was *Sioux City Sue* (Republic, 1946), produced on a modest budget. Throughout the war, Yates had been re-releasing eight Autry Westerns a year. Autry's contract was coming up for renewal. Yates warned him that he had best not be unreasonable in his demands. Military life, however, had changed Autry.

"I don't think I ever appreciated money until I had been in the service," Autry once confided to me. "I learned what it was like to work for almost nothing, and I didn't like it."

As a consequence, Autry was intent on being as unreasonable as he could be. He had signed his seven-year contract with Yates in 1938. He considered the contract up. Yates countered that Autry's time in the service could not be deducted from the time he owed on the contract. Autry took him to court. While the suit progressed, Autry made three more Westerns for Republic, the last being *Robin Hood of Texas* (Republic, 1947). All are firmly in the tradition of what I call the Autry Fantasy where everything adverse in life can be readily overcome with either a joke or a song. Yates put Roy Rogers in his first "A" budget feature, *My Pal Trigger* (Republic, 1946), and promoted Monte Hale into starring vehicles of his own as a singing cowboy, including *Out California Way* (Republic, 1946) in cinecolor which also featured Roy Rogers, Dale Evans, Allan Lane, Bobby Blake, and Donald Barry as guest stars. Bobby Blake was playing Little Beaver in the studio's Red Ryder series, first opposite Bill Elliott and then Allan Lane in the lead role. Autry felt that as a Western player he was worth more than any one else on the screen. When the lower court found in his favor, he negotiated himself an excellent package with Columbia Pictures and checked off the Republic lot. He also signed a lucrative radio contract and was able quickly to regain his preeminence in the field. Yates, of all people, apparently understood least about the secret magic of the Autry Fantasy.

Allan Lane had appeared as Tim Holt's partner in crime in *The Law West of Tombstone* (RKO, 1937). He played mostly nice young men in all kinds of films until he came to prominence as a Western star when he replaced Bill Elliott in the Red Ryder series. He continued in this series through 1947 when Republic sold the property to Eagle-Lion and developed Lane into a performer in his own right under the name

Rocky Lane. There may have been a bit of irony dubbing him "Rocky." He was most difficult to direct. Yak was assigned to one of his pictures.

"I'm the director," he told him. "You're the actor, Remember that."

All went well until the third day. Lane kicked up a storm. Yak only got him back in line by threatening to go to Yates and have him replaced on the picture. Henceforth, Yak tried to avoid working on Lane's pictures.

Ben Johnson was Bill Elliott's double on his high budget Westerns. Yak was called in to supervise a stunt where Johnson was to leap from atop a stagecoach to the ground, a variation of Canutt's original stunt from a decade earlier. "Sorry," Johnson said, "but old Ben would like to stay around a while yet." Yak decided to do the stunt himself. He got as far as pulling himself up on the luggage carrier. He had gained twenty pounds. Johnson had to take the stunt from the pull-up to completion. After this episode, Yak retired totally from stunt work. When his Republic contract expired in 1948, he returned to free-lancing.

Rocky Lane became an expert rider and did most of his own fights. He had a specially vicious round with Roy Barcroft in *Code of the Silver Sage* (Republic, 1950) in which Barcroft complained about how mean Lane could be and how, sometimes, when he did not pull his punches, he only laughed at the physical damage he caused. Republic had an ample supply of stock footage from its previous Westerns. When the script required Lane to leap onto the back of a wagon, or jump from a tree onto a moving wagon, a cut of a double doing it from a Sunset Carson or Red Ryder picture was used. The problem was that Rocky Lane wore dark blue shirts. The stock shot frequently featured a light-colored shirt. Lane would not alter his garb for the sake of any intercut. Yet, perhaps by that time no one cared any more. Films such as Lane's *Covered Wagon Raid* (Republic, 1950) drew its central sequence — the raid — from former wagon train raids in several Republic Westerns. Yak had done his work well. It was all recorded on celluloid for perpetual reuse.

Canutt was charged with running a herd of sheep off a cliff for *The Devil's Doorway* (M-G-M, 1950). He felt the censors would insist on its deletion; nor was he wrong. He was asked to reshoot the sequence. He went on to handle the second unit on a vast number of top-flight productions. He worked on *Ivanhoe* (M-G-M, 1950) with Robert Taylor;

Knights of the Round Table (M-G-M, 1953), again with Taylor: *El Cid* (Allied Artists, 1961) with Charlton Heston and Sophia Loren; *Spartacus* (Universal, 1962) directed by Stanley Kubrick; *Fall of the Roman Empire* (Paramount, 1964); and *How the West Was Won* (M-G-M, 1964), but not on the Civil War sequence directed by John Ford and starring John Wayne as General Sherman.

Undoubtedly one of Yak's finest achievements was directing the chariot race in the remake of *Ben-Hur* (M-G-M, 1959). It will be re-called that Breezy Eason had directed it in the first version. Canutt asked M-G-M to be allowed to use six key men. He wanted a one-year contract. M-G-M wanted Yak to use Italians when on location in Italy. A series of hassles ensued, but Yak finally got what he demanded. His son, Joe Canutt, stunted in the race. Yak constructed a handle on the back of Joe's chariot for him to hang onto when his chariot was supposed to leap over another chariot. The horses had been specifically trained for this stunt. Joe grabbed onto the front instead. The chariot thundered and lurched. He was nearly killed; but he had the Canutt luck. His lot was a few stitches in his chin.

We were sitting in Yak's trophy room. Yak was petting his German shepherd. He was older, of course; but his voice had the same distinctive nasal intonation.

"I ran into old man Yates when I was in Italy," he said. "He had sold Republic. Now he was living comfortably with Vera Ralston, whom he'd married. He threw his arms around me and treated me like a long lost friend. He told me that when I got back to California I should come and visit him. When I did get back, I said, 'What the hell! I might as well go see him.' And I did. I went out to his house and told the servant who I was and that I had come to visit Mr. Yates." Yak paused and a smile played around the corners of his mouth. "The servant came back and I was told: 'Mr. Yates can't be disturbed.' It was probably Vera's doing. During his last years, she wouldn't permit anyone from the old days to see him." Yak reclined in his chair. "I never did see him again."

In the years that followed, I kept in touch with Yak. In 1976 I even made the attempt to video-tape an interview with him. I brought Peggy Stewart with me for the taping session, hoping she would help jog his memory. This was almost standard operating procedure in those days when I was recording oral history of the motion picture industry. If you could get more than one person in a room and screen a film they had worked together on or just to talk, one person's memory would kindle memories in another. Yak was charmed and pleased by Peggy's presence and did his best for the camera.

When I moved to Sherman Oaks in that same year, I was only a mile or so away from Yak's house and we could visit more conveniently. He was still at work on his autobiography and on more than one occasion he asked me to help him write it and find a publisher for it. I recall once visiting with him only to find him studying a book about the making of *Gone with the Wind.* "I know I worked on that picture," he confessed to me, "but I've forgotten just what I did on it and I was hoping this book would help bring it back to me." By that time, he had found a publisher for his book and veteran screenwriter Oliver Drake had agreed to polish the manuscript for him. The publisher wanted the book to open with *Gone with the Wind,* and Yak's memory, being what it was, could recall the twenties and early thirties more vividly than what came later.

I left Sherman Oaks in 1978. The last time I saw Yak was in 1979 in St. Louis where he was an invited guest, as was I, at a conclave of Western buffs. His autobiography, titled *Stunt Man: The Autobiography of Yakima Canutt* (1979), had appeared. I was asked to interview him again for video tape, this time for a half hour. His memory was sharper than once it had been, because he had had to read his manuscript so many times prior to submission and in galleys. We were old hands at it by this time. I knew what questions to ask him and he knew the answers to give. He added one thing for the camera. He had received an Academy Award in 1966 and the citation mentioned the tremendous importance he had been in developing safety devices to protect stunt men everywhere. We closed the interview as he closed the story of his life. "I think my safety record is what I am most proud of."[2]

Spencer Gordon Bennet:
A Career Study

I

He was an adventurous, athletic man of nineteen when he was told by a friend that the Edison Film Company had run an advertisement in the newspaper seeking someone to perform a sixty-two foot jump from a cliff into the water. He was born of Anglo-French parents in Brooklyn on January 5, 1893; he would die in Los Angeles on October 8, 1987. What would come between was inevitably shaped by his decision to make the trip to Fordham, New York and apply for the job. It was scarcely out of character since he had been interested in theatricals from his earliest youth, playing hooky from school in order to appear in Wednesday matinees at a Brooklyn theatre where he worked nights as an usher when he was without a small part in whatever play was being performed. Nor did the danger particularly bother him; he had quit school in 1909 to strike out on his own into the wilds of Canada. Two years elapsed before he returned home. The Edison offer intrigued him.

When he arrived at the location where the picture was being filmed, Bennet was asked to get into a full dress suit, with a top hat, tails, and patent leather shoes. A wooden frame building had been erected on a steep cliff overlooking the ocean. Bennet, who had asked his brother to accompany him, had him position himself in a canoe at the foot of the cliff in the event anything went wrong. It was January, 1912 and a thin layer of ice covered the water.

Bennet perched himself on a window, ready to make the jump. He turned to the director.

"How much do I get for doing this?"

The Edison Company was accustomed to pay for stunts involving jumps at the rate of a dollar a foot.

"Sixty-two dollars," the director said.

Bennet nodded and followed with a beautiful jump, cutting the water with precision. Returning to the top of the cliff, Bennet was surprised to learn that the director wanted him to repeat it. He asked him what had been wrong with the jump he had just made. The director assured him that the jump had been fine but that the film had buckled in the camera and so another take was required.

Bennet did the jump again, only this time his hands hit the water, knocking him out. His brother on shore climbed immediately into the canoe and paddled out toward him. In his excitement, the canoe capsized and Bennet's brother, who could not swim, began splashing about and screaming. Fortunately, Bennet regained consciousness in time to witness what had happened; he swam toward his brother and brought him safely to shore.

When Bennet once more arrived back on top of the cliff, the director, who carried his production money with him, handed the youth one hundred and twenty-four dollars. Since bread was five cents a loaf and eggs nine cents a dozen, this seemed an excellent profession to be in. Bennet went to the Edison management and said he wanted to work for the company regularly as a stunt man. Impressed by his uncommon courage (or foolhardiness), the studio accepted Bennet's proposal.

While at Edison, Bennet tried to find out as much as he could about filmmaking, doing stunts, devising action sequences, working as a prop man and as an assistant director (the two jobs were nearly one in those days), and, occasionally, appearing before the camera as a player. In 1914 Bennet left Edison and joined Pathé, working as both stunt man and actor. Charles and Emile Pathé had established themselves in France shortly after the turn of the century in the business of film processing; they soon expanded into international distribution. The brothers felt that all the risks in the motion picture industry were in financing new production, so their firm always kept this aspect secondary to processing and distribution. A large, modern processing plant was started in Bound Brook, New Jersey, and in Jersey City a small studio was built managed by Louis J. Gasnier who came to the States from France. Eventually additional studio space was acquired in Edendale, California for the production of Westerns and comedies. Edison and several other pioneer film manufacturing companies, to stem competition, formed a trust called the Motion Picture Patents Company and insisted that all film producers submit to having their pictures distributed by its wholly owned subsidiary, the General Film

A scene from *The Fatal Ring* (Pathé, 1914). From the left: the director George B. Seitz; the property man, Frank Redman; and Spencer Gordon Bennet. All had roles in the film. Photo courtesy of Spencer Gordon Bennet.

Company. By early 1914, the trust was near collapse and Pathé, which had early become a member, seceded in May of that year, opening up sixteen independent exchanges in key American cities. These exchanges were exclusively to distribute product either produced by Pathé or produced independently but purchased outright by Pathé. The Pathé specialties remained short subjects, principally the Pathé newsreels and, beginning with the fabulously successful twenty-chapter serial *The Perils of Pauline* (Pathé, 1914) starring Pearl White, chapter plays released in installments on a weekly basis. Pathé consolidated its position in 1916 by merging with the Hearst syndicate, jointly producing, with Pathé distributing, the Pathé-Hearst News. The emblem of the company was a crowing rooster, as famous in the twenties as a symbol for quality as the bison had been for the New York Motion Picture Company in the teens or Leo the lion was becoming for Metro-Goldwyn-Mayer.

Although Louis Gasnier was credited with the direction of *The Perils of Pauline,* George B. Seitz had provided much of the shooting script. Seitz' first love was playwrighting and, based upon his prolific if uneven efforts in this realm, he had applied at Pathé as a scenarist. By 1916, cognizant of both the huge profits to be made from chapter plays and Pathé's persistent reluctance to become overly involved in company-financed production, Seitz formed the Astra Film Corporation and simultaneously signed a contract with Pathé to produce serials for it independently and to lease its Jersey City studio facilities. Seitz' reputation in serial production began with his popular *The Exploits of Elaine* (Pathé, 1914) with Gasnier credited as the co-director and again starring Pearl White. It ran to thirty-six episodes. From the Pathé staff, Seitz hired the talented Frank Leon Smith as his principal scenarist, Bertram Milhauser as an adapter and director, Edward Snyder as cameraman, and Spencer Gordon Bennet as stunt man, second unit director, and prop man.

Bennet's first assignment at Pathé had been stunting and doubling in *The Perils of Pauline.* The theatrical serial was then only two years old, having begun with the release of *What Happened to Mary?* (Edison, 1912). It was Seitz who altered the focus from sentimental and romantic themes and devised the startling and hectic action format which, when combined with Pearl White's attractive charm and daring acrobatics, set the tone for all future serial production from that time until Spencer Gordon Bennet directed the last commercially produced chapter play, *Blazing the Overland Trail* (Columbia, 1956). Seitz fancied himself an actor, as well as a screenwriter and director, and soon decided to star in his own productions. Becoming frustrated with any supervision whatever from Pathé, he moved out of the Pathé facilities and formed his own production unit in a Harlem dance hall. He starred opposite Marguerite Courtot as well as directed *Bound and Gagged* (Pathé, 1919). Bennet understudied him and, increasingly, functioned in the capacity of an assistant director. Seitz pursued his winning streak with *Private Gold* (Pathé, 1920) and *Velvet Fingers* (Pathé, 1920), two more vehicles in which he co-starred with Marguerite Courtot before departing for Spain for his first feature appearance with Courtot in *Rogues and Romance* (Pathé, 1921). The picture ran into a number of difficulties and was met with indifference upon its release. Having invested all of his money in this feature, Seitz had no choice but to ask Pathé to hire him back as a serial director.

The notion never occurred to Seitz that one of the reasons *Rogues and Romance* may have failed was his leading role. Under the new agreement, he starred opposite June Caprice in *The Sky Rangers* (Pathé, 1921). When this chapter play did less than was expected, the notion quite definitely did occur to Pathé. Seitz' next three chapter plays found him working solely as a director and starred Pathé's most popular male serial player, Charles Hutchinson. Bennet continued as Seitz' assistant, handling almost all the second unit work.

There was no more prestige attached to chapter plays in the early days than there is now. Within the industry itself, and by critics, they were considered the lowest and most vulgar sort of entertainment. To be type-cast as a serial player frequently meant that one's career would start in serials and end there. Accordingly, most actors who were at all successful in them tried as soon as possible to get into feature work. Pearl White was no exception. In 1919, battered and physically broken from having done her own stunts for so long, she left Pathé and signed with Fox Film Corporation to star in a series of features. She was fundamentally an action player and seemed inept and unconvincing in straight dramatic roles. When Fox refused to renew her contract, as Seitz before her, she returned to Pathé. Seitz directed her in *Plunder* (Pathé, 1923).

There is a scene in this serial where Pearl White is being chased and, in her flight, jumps atop a bus. Running along the top of the bus, she was supposed to grab onto an elevator structure when the bus passed beneath it. She would not have to jump far, but she would have to jump sideways; otherwise she would hit her head. The bus came so near the elevator structure that it was impossible for her to stand straight. Although he received no credit as co-director, this was now very much the capacity that Bennet filled. When he was not directing part of the action himself, he was assisting Seitz. He was present when this scene was being rehearsed. The light was failing and Pearl White's eyesight had become impaired. Her timing was off since she had been away from Pathé and a back injury incurred in making her first serial was by now seriously troubling her. Seitz wanted her to grab onto the elevator structure and then swing onto a passing train. Her chauffeur, John Stevenson, volunteered to double for her. Seitz agreed to let him do it. Seitz was in a hurry and he was certain Fortune would smile on him. Stevenson's wife and teenage daughter were extras in the picture and they joined the rest of the cast and crew to watch him, dressed in woman's clothing, leap from the bus top and grab hold of the elevator structure. It was oily and greasy and his hands slipped; he fell on his head eighteen feet below, dying instantly. Seitz was so shaken that he refused to go on with the picture, nor would he shoot the scene again. Bennet was assigned to the sequence. The next day he rehearsed the scene with an experienced stunt man — something Stevenson had not been — and completed it. Seitz finally agreed to return to the picture, but neither he nor Pearl White were any longer much interested in it. It was finished hurriedly and proved a box-office disaster. Pearl White retired permanently from the screen and went to live in France, where she died in 1938.

Whatever else might be said about serials as a genre, one of the most unusual aspects about them in the late teens was the pre-eminence of women playing leads without co-stars and without any exaggerated emphasis on their sexuality; in fact, women in chapter plays were more times than not superior to the male foes against whom they struggled. Kathlyn Williams, Pearl White, Ruth Roland, and to a lesser extent Helen Holmes, Grace Cunard, and Marie Walcamp dominated the field. It was not until the mid-twenties that men took over almost completely. There was then just one reigning serial queen where in years past there had been several: her name was Allene Ray. When she entered films in 1919 for Harry Myers in a series of two-reel Westerns, she was eighteen, five foot three, one hundred and fourteen pounds, with golden blonde hair and hazel eyes. After appearing in a very low budget series of Westerns produced by Louis Weiss — he called his company Artclass, nearly an anagram for William S. Hart's Artcraft (but there the similarity ended) — Pathé signed Ray in 1923 and Seitz introduced her to chapter play audiences in *The Way of a Man* (Pathé, 1924). The studio declared she was another Pearl White and embarked on what was the most significant publicity campaign in its history. Seitz filmed this chapter play and the next two with Ray on the West Coast at the Talisman studio for interiors and at Newhall for exteriors. He then took Ray east to finish *Galloping Hoofs* (Pathé, 1924), her third serial. Next he joined Ray with Walter Miller and went with them to Florida for location shooting for *Sunken Silver* (Pathé, 1925). This chapter play catapulted Miller and Ray to overnight fame as a "serial team," a wholly new and completely novel idea. In the years that directly followed, Miller and Ray won the kind of following for their serial exploits that Vilma Banky and Ronald Colman enjoyed as screen lovers in Samuel Goldwyn productions.

Seitz did not go along for the ride. For some time he had been negotiating with Paramount to direct outdoor features and, after completing *Sunken Silver,* he left Pathé for good. With Seitz and Bennet directing and Frank Leon Smith scripting, Pathé had outdistanced every independent manufacturer of serials and maintained a considerable edge over its strongest competitor, Universal Pictures. Without Seitz, Pathé was fearful of losing this advantage. If he was replaced at all, it would have to be by a name director. Frank Leon Smith objected vociferously. Spencer Gordon Bennet was the best replacement Pathé was likely ever to find. The company thought the notion worth a try. Bennet was assigned to direct Ray and Miller in *Play Ball* (Pathé, 1925), returning to Florida (where it rained) to film the baseball sequences and concluding in New York.

At Paramount, Seitz went on to direct some of the most memorable Westerns of the silent era, among them the first and best versions of *The Vanishing American* (Paramount, 1925) and *Wild Horse Canyon* (Paramount, 1925). He fared less well during the sound era, relegated (as Bennet would be) to Poverty Row features and series Westerns such as directing Buck Jones in *The Thrill Hunter* (Columbia, 1933) before a long and basically stagnating contract at M-G-M found him specializing in directing Andy Hardy pictures. Yet in departing Pathé it can be said that he had taught Bennet well. The Pathé serials Bennet directed throughout the mid and late twenties still rank with the best of that time and, in terms of human interest and dramatic projection, superior to many of the more fantastical and outlandish productions of the sound era.

The Green Archer (Pathé, 1925) was Bennet's second serial. Based on a novel by Edgar Wallace adapted by Frank Leon Smith, it teamed Ray and Miller in a setting at Bellamy Castle on the Hudson River near Kingston, New York. A mysterious figure moves in the castle and part of the suspense is created by the moving finger of suspicion as it points first at one character and then at another. While the sixth episode was being filmed, Pathé threw an elaborate party at the castle for Allene Ray during which she was crowned "Queen of Serials." Bennet placed a small coronet, symbolic of the honor, atop her head.

Pathé maintained its hold on the serial market despite new competition coming from Mascot Pictures. Pathé budgeted each chapter play at $125,000. The average length was ten chapters and each played in well over eight thousand theatres. Universal, although it sought to achieve comparable serial production, began as many studios to market economy features with its chapter plays to be included as part of a double bill. It was this trend toward what became the double feature that would eventually relegate the chapter play to weekend matinees and also contributed significantly to a modification of story content.

Bennet went to the West Coast to film *Snowed In* (Pathé, 1926), arriving in Los Angeles on January 3, 1926. He had had scouts everywhere searching the state for enough snow to serve as a background for the serial, but it was a drought year and even the high mountains were bare. Desperate, Bennet finally asked a railroad conductor where snow could be found. He was advised to go to Idaho. Packing up snow machines along with the cast and crew, Bennet departed, working on location in Idaho for three weeks. By double-exposing the film, Bennet was able, once he returned to California for the studio interiors, to match shots photographing the actors against a black screen. The effect worked so well that Walter Miller could disappear entirely into what was a swirling blizzard merely by retreating toward the black screen.

In the wake of the immense publicity provided by the press for the impending bout between Jack Dempsey and Gene Tunney for the World's Heavyweight Championship, Pathé signed the contender, Tunney, to star in a serial. It was a real gamble because Tunney was no actor and little popular interest would exist were he to lose the fight. Frank Leon Smith hurriedly assembled a story from material already being worked on in the Pathé story department in New York and Bennet filmed the serial at the Talisman studio in Los Angeles. The first chapter opens to Tunney standing at night beneath a street lamp reading a paper. He notices an advertisement in the paper asking for someone with a Marine background to apply at eleven o'clock that night. Being down on his luck, Tunney goes to the address, an office building, and walks into the vacant lobby. The elevator does not work and, since he is to apply on the third floor, he decides to take the stairs.

On the first landing, he is jumped by three toughs and a terrific fight ensues, with Tunney emerging victorious. When he arrives at the second landing, three more toughs jump him with similar results. By the time he reaches the third floor, he cautiously looks around. At the end of the hall, he meets a dapper little man in a business suit and is about to rough him up when the man congratulates him.

"You're the first man I've seen tonight," he tells Tunney on the title card. "You've got the job."

Bennet's next serial was *The House Without a Key* (Pathé, 1926), the first of Earl Derr Biggers' six Charlie Chan novels and the film which marked the Oriental detective's screen debut.

"No prints of *The House Without a Key* are known to survive," I once remarked to Bennet in conversation. "I guess I'm going to have to rely on your memory."

"Well, I can tell you this," he responded, "it was no Charlie Chan picture. Chan was just a detective. He wasn't that involved in the action. In fact, we were a couple of chapters into the story before he even made an appearance."

"Didn't Warner Oland suggest himself to you for the role?"

"Not to me, no." Bennet shook his head negatively. "Of course, he specialized in playing Orientals, usually villains. I was at Pathé in New York when he worked on *The Yellow Arm* [Pathé, 1917]. I remember I was given the job of finding him when he disappeared. Warner was a heavy drinker and might vanish for days on end. I spent nearly a week going through every bar on Third Avenue before I finally found him. We were then able to sober him up and shoot his scenes. He was a splendid actor. The part in *House Without a Key* would have been too small for him, even if somebody had suggested he be cast in it. Instead, we used George K. Kuwa as Chan."

Frank Lackteen was a familiar villain in the twenties, especially in Pathé serials. He menaced Miller and Ray in *House Without a Key* and returned in a similar role in *Melting Millions* (Pathé, 1927), but for me his best role in any silent serial was as the notorious Montana bandit, "The Hawk," in *Hawk of the Hills* (Pathé, 1927). It was Bennet's first Western and it became a pacesetter in future decades, primarily because of its substantial plot and inherent drama. Not only were story elements borrowed from it for later serials such as *The Indians Are Coming* (Universal, 1930) — the first chapter play to top a million dollars in film rental — and *Battling with Buffalo Bill* (Universal, 1931), but even more frequently footage was lifted and interpolated in subsequent chapter plays. It was because of her performance in *Hawk of the Hills,* appearing quite attractive in period costume, that Universal chose Allene Ray to star opposite Tim McCoy in *The Indians Are Coming,* which was her first talking picture. Unfortunately Henry MacRae, the head of Universal's chapter play department, knew nothing of the difficulties Bennet had had getting any emotional displays from Ray whatsoever. She was incapable of registering any emotion at all except terror or variations of fright. To get this out of her Bennet would have a prop man sneak behind the set and fire a gun loaded with blanks. The sudden sounds worked every time and Allene Ray's eyes would widen with horror. It would not really have done MacRae much good to have learned this about Ray *after* she had been signed since *The Indians Are Coming* was a sound serial and such devices would have been prohibitive. Moreover, her voice was high and uncontrolled and recorded poorly on the primitive sound equipment. Despite her international fame as a serial heroine in the twenties, talking pictures proved an insurmountable obstacle for her.

In addition to his work on serials, Bennet also directed his first feature for Pathé release in 1928, a programmer called *Marked Money* starring Virginia Bradford. George Duryea, who in the thirties would star in Westerns for RKO and Monogram as Tom Keene, had the male lead. Cecil B. DeMille had left Paramount to produce and direct films independently for Pathé release. After a few minor appearances in the mid twenties, Virginia Bradford was cast as the heroine in the DeMille Pictures' production of *The Wreck of the Hesperus* (Pathé, 1927) and was absolutely convinced by the time she came to make *Marked Money* that she was a major star. She told Bennet that Edward Snyder, the cinematographer, would have to be very careful how he lighted her, since she did not want her protuberant jawbone visible in the least. She also informed Bennet that it was her habit to make suggestions to the director as they went along and she trusted he would not object. She became so insistent about her suggestions that Bennet, in retaliation, had the musicians—frequently in silent films romantic scenes were acted to musical accompaniment—perform "Me and My Shadow" during each sentimental interlude.

Bennet also proposed to Bradford that he was willing to arrange with the front office for her to be paid a dollar for each suggestion that she gave him which he adopted, but that she must be willing to reciprocate by paying him five dollars for every suggestion of hers which he rejected. The suggestions soon stopped.

The Pathé management was alarmed by the prospect of sound films, particularly what it would add to production costs. Nat Levine's Mascot Pictures were being produced on much smaller budgets, a saving passed on to exhibitors. Cecil B. DeMille, who owned a large block of Pathé stock, was all for selling out the Pathé production facilities and exchange network to Film Booking Office. Joseph P. Kennedy, who managed FBO, had worked out a scheme whereby the Keith-Orpheum theatre circuit and Pathé could merge with Radio Corporation of America. Existing Pathé contract obligations, including the newsreels, would be released by RKO-Pathé, whereas the new corporation would be known as Radio-Keith-Orpheum. When this merger became a reality, production on the Pathé serials ceased. Bennet's contract was not renewed and he had no alternative but to free-lance.

II

It was somewhat generally accepted in Hollywood that the advent of talking pictures meant the finish for outdoor dramas and Westerns. There was a total reshuffling of Western players and production schedules. Tom Mix, who had been starring in a series of silent Westerns for Film Booking Office, left the screen and joined the Sells-Floto Circus. Bob Steele and Tom Tyler, who were also starring in Western series for FBO, were dropped. Tyler began appearing in chapter plays and Bob Steele was signed for a low budget series by Trem Carr for independent release. Tim McCoy was not renewed at M-G-M and signed to make serials at Universal. Hoot Gibson and Ken Maynard were released by Universal and had to seek work on Poverty Row. Buck Jones had been off the screen since 1928.

What surprised everyone was the eminent success of *In Old Arizona* (Fox, 1929), a talking Western, the first, starring Warner Baxter as the Cisco Kid. Baxter won an Academy Award for his portrayal of the dashing caballero. Cliff Broughton, who since 1923 had been manager of Mrs. Wallace Reid Productions (the famous silent actor's widow went into film production on her own after his death), furthered this trend by producing *The Dude Wrangler* (Sono-Art, 1930) with George Duryea and Lina Basquette. It was on the basis of the success of this picture that Duryea was signed by RKO to make a series of Westerns. This only convinced Broughton all the more of the viability of sound Westerns.

For his second picture, Broughton approached Sono-Art Productions directly. His idea was to star José Bohr, an Argentine actor, in a role similar to the Cisco Kid, namely a glamorous road agent dressed in black and bedecked in tooled leather and silver who steals from the rich and provides for the poor and who is finally reformed from his wayward life through the love of a beautiful señorita. Sono-Art was loosely affiliated with World-Wide Pictures, Tiffany Productions, and Trem Carr Productions, releasing through E.W. Hammons' Educational Pictures exchange network. Sono-Art bought Broughton's concept and Spencer Gordon Bennet was engaged to direct. Myrna Loy was cast as the beautiful señorita, Raymond Hatton as Bohr's sidekick Pedro, Walter Miller as the sheriff, with Carmelita Geraghty, a well-known character actress of the silent era, and Wallace Ford in supporting roles. Technically the picture was no match for talking Westerns such as Hoot Gibson's *Spurs* (Universal, 1930) and artistically it was many times inferior to either *In Old Arizona* or the sequel of the next year, *The Cisco Kid* (Fox, 1931). Bohr spoke in a labored, exaggerated accent and this only made the long, static indoor sequences move even more slowly. Myrna Loy sang a couple of songs specially composed for her by the screenwriter, Oliver Drake, but they were ineptly staged and proved tedious. All of this notwithstanding, *The Rogue of the Rio Grande* (Sono-Art, 1930) was sufficiently successful upon release that Cliff Broughton was placed in charge of all Sono-Art production, Oliver Drake was hired by RKO to script the George Duryea Westerns (perhaps becoming the most prolific contributor of Western screenplays in the thirties and forties), and Bennet was hired by a producer at RKO to direct a series of theatrical two-reelers titled *Nick Harris* and consisting of dramatized stories based on the files of the Nick Harris detective agency in Los Angeles. Harris acted as a consultant on this series, portrayed on screen by Walter Miller. *The Rogue of the Rio Grande* did not help José Bohr who was henceforth finished in pictures or Myrna Loy who had to wait for *Manhattan Melodrama* (M-G-M, 1934) and the subsequent Thin Man series co-starring William Powell before achieving popular recognition.

When the producer of the *Nick Harris* short subjects got into financial difficulties, RKO contracted Bennet to direct *The Last Frontier* (RKO, 1932) which was produced experimentally to see if the studio should resume serial production in the Pathé tradition. The chapter play starred Creighton Chaney, son of the late Lon Chaney, in one of the few roles where he played a straight part as opposed to the grotesque monsters and werewolves with which he was later identified. His role in *The Last Frontier* had him appear both in buckskins and in a

Zorro-like costume. The action called for him to don this latter get-up to play the "Black Ghost" in order to confuse villain Francis X. Bushman and his gang. The serial did so dismally at the box office that RKO never made a second attempt to produce one.

In terms of his future career it was opportune for Bennet that he met Larry Darmour while directing at RKO. Darmour had long been associated with the production of theatrical short subjects and, as he told Bennet, he was now intent on branching off into feature films. Based on the success of his Mickey McGuire short subjects starring Mickey Rooney, Darmour set up Continental Pictures which would release independently on a state's rights basis variously using the logos of Empire, Mayfair, or Majestic Pictures. He required a director who could shoot films quickly and economically with a minimum of waste and few retakes. Bennet, since his days at Pathé, was accustomed to fast, slick production work; he had learned early to cut in the camera; and already in 1933 he possessed that remarkable ability to add sophistication and polish to a very low budget enterprise so that the final release print often belied the rather limited financing. The two men got along instantly and Darmour placed Bennet under a personal contract.

The Midnight Warning (Mayfair, 1933) was Bennet's first assignment. The film starred William "Stage" Boyd. He had been a character actor of considerable stature at Paramount until scandal brought about his ruin (due to confusion in the press the same stigma frequently was attached to William Boyd, the former DeMille player who would later portray Hopalong Cassidy). Claudia Dell, a young blonde actress who had played opposite Tom Mix in his talking picture debut in *Destry Rides Again* (Universal, 1932), was cast as the heroine. Darmour rented space on the sound stages of the newly formed Monogram Pictures. Overcoming adverse public sentiment about Boyd would be Darmour's problem. Bennet had his hands full with Claudia Dell who could not fake a fall. There was a morgue scene in which Dell was supposed to faint. She simply collapsed, knocking her head against the cement floor, losing consciousness and cutting open her scalp.

Bennet had better luck with Jack LaRue who starred in *The Fighting Rookie* (Mayfair, 1934). Paramount had purchased film rights to William Faulkner's novel *Sanctuary* (1931), retitling it for the screen *The Story of Temple Drake* (Paramount, 1933). Originally the studio wanted George Raft to play the psychotic Popeye who rapes a girl with a corncob and then murders her feeble-minded son, but Raft categorically refused. Jack LaRue got the part instead and caused such a stir with his performance that for a time he was much in demand to play character roles for the majors and lead roles for the minors. Darmour hired LaRue again the next year to play the lead, with Bennet directing, in *Calling All Cars* (Empire, 1935).

There was a strong market in the mid thirties for non–Western action melodramas in the style and after the fashion of Jack Holt's starring series for Columbia release. In fact, the demand reached such proportions that in 1933 Buck Jones, who had been appearing in a series of Westerns produced by Sol Lesser at first distributed by Columbia and then finally financed by that studio directly, retired from the sagebrush to battle lawless elements in modern dress. Columbia also retired Tim McCoy from his series Westerns for the entire 1933–1934 season to cast him in films of this kind, playing pilots, policemen, firemen, or brilliant trial lawyers.

Buster Crabbe, who had appeared in the serial *Tarzan the Fearless* (Principal, 1933) and who was featured in a number of major Paramount productions, was signed by Darmour to star in *The Oil Raider* (Mayfair, 1934) and *Badge of Honor* (Mayfair, 1934), both of which Bennet directed. Leon Ames, who had debuted in pictures in *Murders in the Rue Morgue* (Universal, 1932) as Pierre Dupin who fights desperately to prevent Bela Lugosi from breeding his pet ape with Sylvia Fox, found work so scarce that he opened a Chevrolet dealership (which he retained even when times got better); he was cast by Bennet together with Ralph Forbes and Verna Hillie in *Rescue Squad* (Empire, 1935). Wallace Ford, who had accidentally fallen backwards into a cactus when shot by José Bohr in *Rogue of the Rio Grande*, was cast in the lead for *Get That Man* (Empire, 1935).

Bennet became an increasingly competent action director of economy features over these years and this was one of the essential ingredients accounting for Darmour's unusual success as an independent producer. Bennet did experience one anomaly, *The Ferocious Pal* (Principal, 1934), yet the failure of the picture had nothing directly to do with him. Kazan was a German shepherd in the Rin Tin Tin vein that had a brief vogue in the early thirties. He belonged to Bert King, a friend of Bennet's. King talked Bennet into directing a picture with Kazan and the two of them struck a deal with Sol Lesser's Principal Pictures: in exchange for financing the production costs Lesser could distribute the film with both King and Bennet receiving a percentage of the profits. No sooner had production begun than Kazan developed an infection in his tail which caused it to be amputated. Bennet did not know quite how to get around the problem so he tried tying a phony tail on the dog, but the phony tail kept falling off, requiring more retakes than the $9,000 budget would allow. Frustrated, Bennet finally let the dog do his tricks bob-tailed. Lesser, when he saw the work print, nearly burst a vessel. For a long time he refused even to release the picture and once he did no one saw any money.

When Ken Maynard was fired by Nat Levine after making a serial and a feature Western for Mascot Pictures, Larry Darmour opened negotiations with him. He wanted to star Maynard in an unspecified number of Western features for Majestic Pictures release. Maynard signed the contract which guaranteed him only $8,000 a picture in contrast to the $40,000 a picture he had been getting at Mascot and the almost $10,000 a week he had been earning previously at Universal. When Majestic Pictures joined the merger of Mascot, Monogram, and Consolidated Film Industries to form Republic Pictures, Darmour was left without a releasing company. Fortunately for him, Universal hired Buck Jones away from Columbia to replace Maynard and Darmour took advantage of the situation. He approached Sam Briskin at Columbia Pictures. Maynard was under a personal contract to Darmour. If Columbia would finance and release the series, Darmour promised the studio a series of program Westerns the equal of the Westerns Buck Jones would be making at Universal. Briskin liked the idea and thus began a short, albeit profitable, cooperative venture between Columbia and Larry Darmour Productions.

Darmour opened his own studio on Santa Monica Boulevard and had the interiors for most of his productions filmed there. Columbia agreed that if the Maynard series was a success in 1936 Darmour could also take over a number of the studio's "B" melodramas. He would receive an annual budget from which, after subtracting his producer's share, all production costs were to be paid. What was left over, if anything, would be Darmour's profit. It was this situation which would generate a violent friction between Darmour and Maynard. Bennet was still working on *Get That Man* when the first Maynard Western went into production, *Western Frontier* (Columbia, 1935), but he was assigned to the unit beginning with the second film, *Heir to Trouble* (Columbia, 1935), and directed all the subsequent Maynard entries.

Maynard's penchant for improbable or downright incredible plot construction had got him in trouble at Universal in *Smoking Guns* (Universal, 1934) in which the viewer was expected to accept Maynard and Walter Miller as identical twins! Initially, Darmour allotted

$75,000 budgets to the Westerns, but he objected to the kinds of stories Maynard wanted to film. In *Heir to Trouble,* Maynard had his horse Tarzan act as a nursemaid to a baby, boiling eggs, rocking the cradle, and sounding an alarm should visitors come to Ken's prospector's shack. Darmour thought the whole thing preposterous.

Possibly the best staged, most carefully photographed, and most consistently entertaining Western Bennet directed with Maynard was their second feature together, *Western Courage* (Columbia, 1935). It is set on a dude ranch where frosty, pompous, attractive Geneva Mitchell arrives with her parents. In filming the requisite fight sequences, Bennet began using the device of having a punch thrown directly into the camera and then cutting to the punched actor falling away from the camera. He also used a variation of the double exposure technique he had employed in *Snowed In.* When Ward Bond and his gang leave Maynard tied up in a shack, the shack catches fire and at the last minute Tarzan rushes in and unties the ropes binding Ken, then pulls him to safety. Bennet shot Ken's rescue against a black backdrop and then superimposed the image of the burning shack so that it appears that both Ken and Tarzan are in the midst of the conflagration.

Maynard had introduced songs and music into his Westerns as early as 1930 and in his series for Universal in 1933–1934 he would frequently build an entire picture around a popular ballad. Once Gene Autry became immensely popular it was generally believed that singing was an essential ingredient in a sound Western. Darmour's productions followed suit and Maynard was called upon to play the guitar, piano, banjo, harmonica, or fiddle (on all of which he could perform with some proficiency although, as Autry, he could not read a note of music). At times Maynard would even sing. Bennet took little interest in these obligatory musical numbers and, as a result, they slow down the action even more obviously than otherwise might have been the case. One who did enjoy the music making was Gene Autry. When he was not working on one of his own pictures, he would usually visit the set and sit near Bennet behind the camera. Ken Maynard had long been his idol among movie cowboys.

Ken Maynard (black hat) and Spencer Gordon Bennet sitting next to each other, surrounded by the crew, during the filming of the Larry Darmour series of Ken Maynard Westerns in the mid thirties. Photo courtesy of Spencer Gordon Bennet.

Maynard complained that he was not being paid enough to work so hard. This, combined with his excessive drinking, showing up for work at noon when on location (forcing Bennet to shoot around him, using Ken's double, Cliff Lyons, to stand in for him), and his indifference to putting on weight, tended to make the films in retrospect much less than they might have been and considerably less than Maynard's earlier series for Universal. Ken would become despondent at what he perceived as his slumping career and he would often explode in rage or take to beating his horses. He had a secret door put in his dressing room at Darmour's lot and would have prostitutes visit him in the mornings and afternoons. Darmour was appalled by this behavior. Bennet, who liked Ken, tried to ignore it.

Avenging Waters (Columbia, 1936) is memorable for two reasons. First, in the titillating emphasis Bennet placed on callipygian heroine Beth Marion, the viewer became more aware than ever of sexual overtones. Even the fade is a shot of her riding double behind Ken, her posterior clad in tight light-colored riding britches. Second, the picture demonstrates what Bennet could do using miniatures and stock footage to introduce elaborate special effects into a picture that would otherwise have required a larger budget to achieve the same results. Cliff Lyons was engaged to marry Beth Marion. However much he may have shared Bennet's erotic appreciation of the heroine, he did not like in the least the amorous attentions Maynard paid his fiancée off camera and the two men nearly came to blows. The plot of *Avenging Waters* finds Ward Bond damming up a river high in the mountains, only to have the dam break during an electrical storm, sending giant waves of water crashing down to the valley floor. Bennet included another double exposure, shooting first in miniature the water destroying Ward Bond's ranch house and then superimposing a shot of Cliff Lyons, doubling Ken, sweeping Beth Marion into his arms atop Tarzan and racing for safety, closely followed by a tidal wave of foaming water.

The Fugitive Sheriff (Columbia, 1936) was Maynard's last picture for Darmour, after which they agreed to part company. Bennet cast Walter Miller in the role of the principal heavy. Since the very early thirties, Miller increasingly had had to take villain roles. He would die relatively young on March 28, 1940, after a fight sequence in a Gene Autry Western proved too great a strain on his heart. Bennet, who had directed Miller during all the fluctuations in his career, was deeply shocked at his sudden death.

To replace Maynard, Sam Briskin proposed that Darmour try Bob

Allen. In Tim McCoy's series Westerns, Allen had frequently been given second lead. He was good-looking and had an infectious charm before the camera. Darmour had a talk with Allen and agreed to complete the remaining complement of six Westerns he had contracted for with Columbia with Allen as the star. The films were known as the Texas Ranger series and the title of each had the word Ranger in it somewhere. What Darmour did not know was that one of the reasons McCoy quit when his Columbia contract was up at the end of 1935 was because he could not stand working with Bob Allen. Bennet found Allen sensitive and willing to take suggestions, but he could also behave much differently off camera than when before it. In *Rio Grande Ranger* (Columbia, 1936) and *The Unknown Ranger* (Columbia, 1936), Bob Allen, exuding charm, falls in love with the rancher's daughter and is embracing her by the fade. Darmour had tightened up the budgets on the Allen series and this often called for the unit to shoot certain interior sequences at night. While on location at a private ranch near Newhall, California Bennet was busy rigging a shot for a fight sequence between Allen and the heavies. Allen was sitting in Bennet's director's chair. The real ranch owner's daughter came over to Allen while he was reviewing his lines and attempted to engage him in conversation. Allen gave her a resounding slap on the behind and told her to get lost. Bennet, who was looking down at his script, looked up when he heard the commotion and was surprised to see the ranch owner himself on the set, yelling at Allen about the way he had mishandled his daughter and actually start to swing at him.

It would be difficult to say which of the Allen series was the better, since they are all so uniformly bad. The fault was not only the direction. The scripts were a hackneyed rehash of the worst clichés to be found in "B" Westerns. What was Bennet to do when, in *The Rangers Step In* (Columbia, 1937), a lynch mob is chasing Allen and the script calls for him to hesitate in front of his horse until a rope is thrown around him? What is interesting is what Bennet could accomplish with a single camera and a variety of setups. However, part of the blame no doubt was due to Bennet who had become as disenchanted working for Darmour as Maynard had become. The arrangement whereby Darmour could increase his personal profits by cutting on the budgets could only lead to an inferior product.

Bennet's contract with Darmour came to an end with the Allen Westerns. Columbia decided to engage another producer to produce a series of Buck Jones Westerns now that Jones had quit Universal.

Columbia had also just entered the chapter play market and had hired
Louis Weiss as associate producer on the serial unit. Weiss asked Bennet
if he would be willing to direct the forthcoming chapter play, *The
Mysterious Pilot* (Columbia, 1937). It was to star Captain Frank Hawks,
a noted aviator who in 1933 had flown the distance of the continental
United States in thirteen and a half hours, beating his previous world
record by four hours. Bennet accepted the assignment and went on
location to Bass Lake. Although Bennet had Hawks doubled in all the
dangerous flying sequences, Hawks could not be prevented from doing
his own stunts in real life. He almost killed himself one night while taking off in a make-shift seaplane and several months after the serial was
completed he did kill himself while flying a non-commercial aircraft.
Dorothy Sebastian, a star of some magnitude a few years earlier during
her successive marriages to director Clarence Brown and then William
Boyd (when he was out of work due to the William "Stage" Boyd scandal), was cast as the heroine. For the villain, Bennet engaged none
other than Frank Lackteen, his favorite menace from the old Pathé
days. *The Mysterious Pilot* was Columbia's second chapter play and
reviewers and audiences alike found it a vast improvement over the
initial entry with its stunning scenic locations, the exceptional aerial
photography, and the well-paced action. Columbia, on the other
hand, was disgusted by the cost and the way in which Weiss inflated
the payroll, among other outrages hiring his son Adrian at one thousand dollars a week as an assistant director.

Weiss was fired and the serial contract for three chapter plays a year
was offered to Larry Darmour. Darmour agreed to produce the serials
provided he could also continue producing feature melodramas. Probably Darmour's most notable feature series for Columbia would begin
with *Ellery Queen, Master Detective* (Columbia, 1940) in which Ralph
Bellamy played Ellery Queen and Margaret Lindsay was cast as Ellery's
secretary, Nikki Porter. When Darmour died suddenly in 1942, his
widow, Alice Darmour, announced to the trades that she would carry
on production of both the chapter play then in production and the two
Ellery Queen films scheduled for release that year.

At the very beginning of this serial contract, Darmour approached
Bennet with a new contract for a much longer term than had been true
of their previous one, a raise in salary, and a clause specifying that he
would direct all of the Columbia serials. Bennet, however, would have
none of it. He did not want to become involved again with Darmour
under any circumstances and he was being troubled by a nervous dis-

order induced by depression at where his career was going. He did not want to go on indefinitely directing chapter plays and low budget features. For almost a year and a half, he did not work, nor did he accept any of the jobs offered to him. One day in mid 1939, Bennet woke up and felt fine. He had reconciled himself to the kind of picture he could direct well and would never be plagued again by self-doubt.

Edward Finney, while he was still working in publicity for Grand National Pictures in 1936, had placed Western singer Tex Ritter under a personal contract and had begun producing a series of singing Westerns for Grand National release. Finney was offered a more attractive financing and releasing arrangement by the recently reorganized Monogram Pictures Corporation in 1938 and so signed a production agreement with that studio. Monogram increased the budgets on the Tex Ritter Westerns from $12,000 to $15,000 over what they had been at Grand National. Finney had been impressed with the Westerns Bennet had directed for Darmour and engaged him to direct *Riders of the Frontier* (Monogram, 1939) with Tex Ritter. In view of the indifference with which Gene Autry was reputed to walk through his Republic Westerns and the trouble there had been with Ken Maynard, Bennet was pleasantly surprised to find Ritter deeply concerned about his work as an actor and enthusiastic about doing his own stunting.

Scott R. Dunlap, in charge of production at Monogram, hired Bennet to direct an entry in that studio's Jack Randall series Westerns. Bennet began to alternate between Randall and Ritter Westerns until Dunlap invited him, for an increased salary, to direct the first entry in a major new series that Monogram would be releasing, featuring a trio known as the "Rough Riders" and starring Buck Jones, Tim McCoy, and Raymond Hatton. The company producing these Westerns was owned jointly by Buck Jones, Scott Dunlap, and Trem Carr. The budgets were set at $65,000 and *Arizona Bound* (Monogram, 1941) introduced the three leads as United States marshals called in to protect Luana Walters' stageline. Dunlap was a red-necked Irishman with a fiery temper. He and Buck Jones were continually at odds as to how a particular scene was to be handled. Dunlap would tell Bennet what he wanted. When Bennet would try to direct the scene accordingly, Jones would object, reminding Bennet that he was the president of Great Western Productions, not Dunlap, and what he said went. Bennet got on especially well with Tim McCoy who was invariably a gentleman and stayed aloof from all the squabbling. In the second picture, *The Gunman from Bodie* (Monogram, 1941), Bennet directed two rather notable sequences with McCoy. The first occurs when McCoy is at the bar with heavy John Merton and where, just by taking off his gloves and putting them on again while describing a hanging, he is able to fragment Merton's composure. The other is the shoot-out with heavy Charles King, filmed in relative shadow, the blazing spurts of gunfire alone visible until someone lights a lamp and, first as a silhouette and then as a full figure, McCoy is ominously revealed as the harbinger of doom.

In 1942 Alice Darmour renewed her late husband's importunities to Bennet to direct a chapter play. She sent him the completed script for *The Secret Code* (Columbia, 1942) which would star Paul Kelly and Anne Nagel. Bennet conceded, but first he had to complete work on *They Raid by Night* (PRC, 1942) with Lyle Talbot, an obvious imitation of Raoul Walsh's tremendously successful *They Drive by Night* (Warner's, 1940) with George Raft, Ann Sheridan, and Humphrey Bogart. *The Secret Code* was to be another imitative film, Columbia's response to *Spy Smasher* released earlier that year by Republic. The scenario called for Paul Kelly to dress entirely in black, even to a hood and gloves. The publicity advised audiences to thrill again to spy smasher's biggest chase, even though Kane Richmond and not Paul Kelly had appeared in the Republic opus. In its streamlined action and harrowing stunts, *The Secret Code* turned out not to need a reference to any other production. It was celebrated by critics as the equal of Republic's best serials and played in more theatres than had any Columbia serial before it.

III

After nearly a decade of playing minor roles and assorted heavies, chiefly at Warner Bros., Gordon Elliott was cast in the lead for the serial *The Great Adventures of Wild Bill Hickok* (Columbia, 1938). Henceforth, he altered his screen name to Bill Elliott. Columbia wished to have two series of feature Westerns in release each season. Between Elliott's first serial and his second, the elaborate *Overland with Kit Carson* (Columbia, 1939), the studio cast Elliott in a series of "Wild Bill" Saunders Westerns, replacing the short-lived Bob Allen series Darmour had produced. Elliott's third and last serial was *Valley of Vanishing Men* (Columbia, 1942), in terms of story continuity probably the weakest of the three but it did bring him together with Spencer Gordon Bennet who stayed on at Columbia to direct it.

Herbert J. Yates at Republic was in the midst of corralling a stable of Western stars both to fill the gap created by Gene Autry who had enlisted in the Air Force and so to diversify Republic's line-up that when Autry did return he would no longer be in such a dominant position. Elliott was one of the players Yates succeeded in signing up. Yates offered Elliott a major exploitation campaign and to give him bigger budgets for his pictures. At Columbia since 1941, Elliott had been forced to co-star in feature Westerns with Tex Ritter once Ritter succeeded in breaking with Edward Finney. When Bennet was signed by Republic as a contract director, Elliott asked for him to direct his first entry, *Calling Wild Bill Elliott* (Republic, 1943).

Despite the number of Westerns he had already been in, Elliott would still spend hours in a saddle tied to a carpenter's horse, perfecting for the camera the way in which he sat astride a mount. "Bill was a great admirer of Buck Jones," Bennet recalled, "and when we were working together, knowing that I had recently directed Jones, he would talk to me about him, finding out all I knew."

Since the days of the merger with Mascot Pictures, production of four chapter plays a year was a staple at Republic. In the late thirties most Republic serials had been directed by the team of William Witney and John English. Yates figured that in view of Witney's imminent departure for active duty and English's desire to direct features, Bennet, who was over military age, would make an excellent replacement. Joseph Kane who by 1942 was the top contract director at Republic had years before worked with Bennet as Bennet's principal film cutter at Pathé. Yates put Bennet in charge of the two serials remaining on the 1943 production schedule (Witney and English had been split up, each alone assigned to one of the two prior serials for that year) and apprenticed Wallace A. Grissell's to Bennet. Grissell, much as Kane in former years, was an experienced film editor and assistant director and Yates hoped that the apprenticeship would lead to Grissell's becoming an action director in his own right. When Yates subsequently hired Lesley Selander to direct at Republic, Grissell formed an even closer working relationship with him than he had with Bennet, eventually following Selander when Selander left Republic to direct Tim Holt at RKO. Grissell's problem as a director was hereditary epilepsy which led to his early retirement; while directing a picture he might be seized by an attack at any time.

Concurrently, Columbia Pictures hired Sam Katzman to take over its serial unit. Katzman since the early thirties had gained a reputation for bringing to low budget films even lower budgets and embarrassingly identical scripts. He had produced more thoroughly uncreative and technically shoddy vehicles than anyone else would have dared. In 1936 he founded Victory Pictures with himself as president, producing eight Tom Tyler Westerns for a per picture cost of $6,000. His Tim McCoy Westerns for the 1938–1939 season had increased budgets of $8,000 a picture because McCoy required a guarantee of $4,000 a picture and Sam Newfield, the director, wanted $1,200. With these expenses at the outset, the only way Katzman could bring in the pictures according to his budget allocation was by shooting them without retakes over a maximum of three days and two nights—and that is exactly what he did. Katzman also produced two serials prior to his somewhat more ambitious series at Monogram with the East Side Kids: *Shadows of Chinatown* (Victory, 1936) and *Blake of Scotland Yard* (Victory, 1937). Not only did Katzman assure Columbia that it need not fear from him any of the abuses committed by Louis Weiss, which did not show on the screen, but that he would cut Darmour's budgets by half (Darmour had spent $200,000 on *Overland with Kit Carson*) and yet not have *that* show on the screen.

Yates was confident that with this change in management at Columbia, Republic would easily retain its foremost position in the chapter play market. It was characteristic at Republic, in both its features and its serials, that frantic action and plot development were stressed over all other dramatic considerations. This suited Bennet because what excited him most in filmmaking was discovering new ways to portray visually convincing and novel action sequences; and at Republic, for the first time since Pathé halted production, Bennet could direct and originate *all* the action rather than have to shoot around stock footage interpolations.

Of the many chapter plays he directed during the sound era, Bennet always preferred the first he made for Republic, *Secret Service in Darkest Africa* (Republic, 1943). "We spent around $160,000 on it," Bennet recalled. "It had fifteen episodes and good actors: Rod Cameron, Duncan Renaldo, Joan Marsh forming a trio battling against Nazi agents. It was a fine production. It stands out to me because I thought I worked out the fights better than usual. When I went over to Republic, the other directors and the stunt men told me I must shoot a full panorama of a fight routine. They would knock up and break everything, then stop and set up everything again so that we could get close-ups. I knew how to match shots better than that. I would say to a stunt man, 'Now, I want you to start from here . . . it's going to take a minute . . . a minute and eight seconds to do that. But I want it done well.' So I would set them up and they fought in a corner. Then I would cut to my principals, right while I could remember their positions, and we wouldn't have to set up all the props again. Now I would match shots and bring my principals out of it and take them right into the next routine — cut — put in the doubles and go on. All the editor had to do was assemble the footage. The other way fights took twice as long."

The Masked Marvel (Republic, 1943), Bennet's next serial, had seven writers working on the screenplay. The idea of a masked hero was only a variation of the Lone Ranger serials made earlier. This masked man, righting wrongs perpetrated by a former Japanese envoy, is one of four special agents of the World-Wide Insurance Company. His identity is revealed to heroine Louise Curry only in the final episode. Bennet may have lacked the players he had had in *Secret Service in Darkest Africa* to develop an engaging interplay between the characters, but he more than compensated for this in terms of pacing, excitement, and staging.

In 1944 Bennet had a heavy schedule, directing five Western features and three chapter plays. He directed Bill Elliott in *Mojave Firebrand* and *Tucson Raiders,* the latter a Red Ryder entry which retained Gabby Hayes, Elliott's regular sidekick in the 1943 starring series, and cast Bobby Blake as Little Beaver. Bennet genuinely liked Blake and thought him a gifted actor. In *Tucson Raiders,* during a fight in a blacksmith shop, Blake was to keep score by chalking up blows with a horseshoe for Elliott or for the villains. The same skit was repeated later the same year in another Red Ryder picture with Elliott and Blake, *Sheriff of Las Vegas* (Republic, 1944). It is interesting because this skit was the keenest remembrance that Lesley Selander, who directed *Sheriff of Las Vegas,* had of his time at Republic and it proved only slightly less memorable for Bennet although audiences may have been less than pleased to see it twice in the same year in the same series.

Code of the Prairie (Republic, 1944) with Smiley Burnette billed above nominal star Sunset Carson had a memorable sequence of another kind. Roy Barcroft, the principal heavy, is a barber. He murders a man in cold blood in his barber chair but he is interrupted before he can dispose of the body. Barcroft has no alternative but to pretend he is shaving the corpse, volubly carrying on a one-sided conversation while his shop is searched. The suspense is effective and, surprisingly, a viewer's sympathy is with Barcroft.

Among the three studios producing serials, Sam Katzman at

Columbia came to rely largely on B. Reaves Eason, an experienced veteran; Universal customarily used Ray Taylor (fired by Yates in 1937 for drinking while on location filming *The Painted Stallion* and replacing him with William Witney); and Republic, with the exception of John English who returned briefly to serials to co-direct *Captain America* (Republic, 1944) with Elmer Clifton, employed Bennet while listing Grissell on the credits as co-director. Republic hoped to promote serial heroine and former model Linda Stirling into another Pearl White and the publicity department got a lot of mileage from the fact that Stirling had once studied at an acting school run by serial queen Ruth Roland's widowed husband. Because of his background at Pathé, Bennet was charged with properly grooming her. In *The Tiger Woman* (Republic, 1944), Stirling was cast as a mysterious white jungle queen frequently rescuing Allan Lane and his associate, Duncan Renaldo, from the evil schemes of villain George J. Lewis. For *Zorro's Black Whip* (Republic, 1944) Lewis returned, this time as the hero, but the serial was really an attempt to cast Stirling as a female Zorro. More often than not Lewis found himself in jeopardy and in need of help from Stirling.

The mode of operation in Hollywood has always been blatant and shameless imitation and this was no less true for serials. Bennet's direction of Stirling in *Tiger Woman* won such enthusiastic endorsement from matinee audiences that the next year Universal felt compelled to make *Jungle Queen* with Ruth Roman in the title role and Sam Katzman borrowed Lesley Selander on loan-out from Republic to direct *Jungle Raiders* (Columbia, 1945) which put Janet Shaw through all the horrors inflicted on hero Kane Richmond. Bennet was not to be outdone and in *Manhunt of Mystery Island* (Republic, 1945) he readily surpassed the competition. Yakima Canutt joined Bennet and Grissell as a co-director to assure that the thrills and dangers experienced by Stirling exceeded anything in previous chapter plays. But this was nothing compared to the narrow escapes Stirling would have in *The Purple Monster Strikes* (Republic, 1945) in which Roy Barcroft was cast as an advance scout for a Martian invasion.

What had changed since the twenties was the sexual emphasis. Linda Stirling had as many scrapes and near catastrophes as Pearl White or Allene Ray once had had, but she had them clad in body-tight clothing, stressing the fullness of her bosom, the seductive curve of her hips, and the enticing slope of her derrière. Alas for Republic, Stirling did not want to be a serial queen; she wanted to work in "A" budget features. Yates tried to pacify her by alternately casting Peggy Stewart in *The Phantom Rider* (Republic, 1946) only to have Stewart complain loudly that she, too, wanted to be in "A" features and that Linda rightfully belonged in serials. Yates finally decided in favor of Stirling and consigned Stewart (and Bennet, who was in the middle placating as much as directing) to another serial, *Son of Zorro* (Republic, 1947). Stewart quit Republic and, somewhat defiantly, had a baby.

Bennet first directed Kirk Alyn, whom he would later cast as Superman, in *Daughter of Don Q* (Republic, 1946). The plot concerns LeRoy Mason's attempts to murder all the descendants of Don Quantero (for whose portrait Bennet posed, clad in the costume of a Spanish nobleman) only to be frustrated by Alyn, playing a reporter, and Adrian Booth, one of the heirs. The last serial Bennet directed for Republic on his four-year contract was *The Black Widow* (Republic, 1947) which was filmed at the old Pathé-DeMille studio where Bennet had not shot a picture in nearly twenty years. Universal had ceased serial production altogether and Sam Katzman was more determined than ever to have Bennet join him at Columbia. The negotiations proceeded smoothly until Bennet told Katzman what he expected to get paid. When Katzman visibly blanched, Bennet made him a proposition: if he did not save Katzman what he was asking on the lab bill alone, by economically cutting in the camera, Katzman did not have to pay him anything. Katzman did not have to think twice about a proposition like that.

Katzman preferred to base his serials on newspaper cartoon-strip characters to give them a tie-in with an existing audience. *Brick Bradford* (Columbia, 1947) starring Kane Richmond was the first chapter play Bennet directed for Katzman. Sam usually screened the previous day's rushes when a serial was in production and would then communicate his thoughts to the director. When he saw Bennet's rushes, he became alarmed and telephoned him on location to say that there wouldn't be enough footage. Bennet countered that Katzman was too accustomed to waste, that there would be more than enough. Once the serial was assembled, Bennet became the hero of the day. Katzman congratulated him, agreed to his salary stipulation, and cut the budget for the next chapter play. It was Katzman's corner-cutting which, in time, distressed Bennet almost to the point where he lost interest in what he was doing. Katzman would have Bennet screen stock footage and action sequences from previous Columbia serials even before the scripts were written so that Bennet could incorporate it in his visualization of various scenes and shoot with it in mind. Katzman started out by budgeting each chapter at $8,000 and then, over the years, constantly cut back on this figure.

"It was partly my fault," Bennet confessed. "Katzman would give me a budget and I would meet it. If I was given so many days to film a serial and did it, Katzman would only figure, if I could do it in that time, then cut off a day or two on the next one and see if I could still do it. It got so bad that I knew going in I couldn't make it, but Katzman wanted to know I was trying. Unfortunately, I usually did it, and that was my mistake.

"When we were shooting *Superman* in 1948, I wanted to use animation to show him flying. The artist came to Katzman and told him he could have really effective animation for $64 a foot. Katzman asked the artist how much it would cost to have not so effective animation. When the artist said $32 a foot. When the artist said $32 a foot but that no one would believe it, Katzman ordered animation at $32 a foot.

"Katzman also liked to use a retrospect episode which was nothing more than a recapitulation of what had happened so far. Then he started using two of them in a fifteen-chapter serial. At Pathé and even at Republic, serials were shot more in continuity. Katzman changed that. He would put up all the episodes on a board and select the key sets, shooting all those scenes at once. I had to block the serials for a single camera. There was usually only one rehearsal and one take. As I got the crew geared up, I found that you couldn't even sit down and figure out a shot, or they would let you down, go and have a smoke until you were ready. The minute I would finish a scene, I knew exactly what the next set was going to be. I would have it all mapped out ahead of time. I would say 'Cut!' and then 'over here,' keeping the crew busy. That was the only way I could meet Katzman's schedules, sometimes twenty-one days, sometimes as few as eighteen. If I wanted to get any quality into a scene, I had to rush through several days ahead of it so that when I got to that particular scene I could take my time, work on camera placement, angles, things like that."

By the time Bennet came to direct *Blazing the Overland Trail* in 1956, Columbia was the only studio still making serials. Katzman had Bennet build almost the entire serial out of footage from *Overland with Kit Carson,* dressing Lee Roberts and Dennis Moore in costumes identical to Bill Elliott and Richard Fiske in the earlier chapter play. It was a wholly predictable, if sad, last act for an entertainment form which had spanned four decades and to which Spencer Gordon Bennet, with fifty-two serials to his credit, had contributed more than any other single director.

In addition to the Columbia serials, Bennet also directed various features for Katzman, primarily the Jungle Jim series with overweight Johnny Weismuller. Bennet retired in 1959 at the age of sixty-six. He was brought out of retirement in 1965 by Alex Gordon, a low budget entrepreneur who outdid Katzman in providing cheap, vulgar, disappointing production standards. Bennet agreed to direct two pictures for Gordon because they would feature many of the old-time Western players from previous decades, Broncho Billy Anderson and Tim McCoy among them.

When I met Spencer Gordon Bennet for the first time at the General Service Studio on Las Palmas Avenue in February, 1969, we were congregated for a closed screening of a low budget feature, *Big Foot* (American-Gemini, 1970).

"Do you recognize this old cowpoke?" *Big Foot's* director, Robert F. Slatzer, asked Bennet.

"Sure," Bennet said.

It was Ken Maynard; he had a small part in the picture. Ken was then seventy-four, Spencer seventy-six.

Every time I came to Hollywood after that, I made it a point to visit with Bennet. I marveled at how he remained in fine condition, his skin a healthy tan, seldom ill even with a head cold. We met once at the old Columbia Pictures lot to screen *Avenging Waters* and it was astonishing to see how Bennet remembered when and where every sequence had been filmed. Max Lamb, then associated with Robert Wise's Filmmaker's Group as a story editor, stopped in to watch the picture with us. It was that way in those days at Columbia where Stanley Kramer, Jack L. Warner, and so many others rented office space— people were constantly wandering about from office suite to office suite to office suite, snooping around or just wanting to chat.

Bennet was with me when I went out to the Motion Picture Home in Woodland Hills to see Ken Maynard for the last time. Ken was dying of intestinal carcinoma, but he joked with us and I think he was decidedly pleased to see Bennet again. It was in part one-sided. It dismayed Bennet to see the ravages of age, the withering of the body and the emaciation of the mind.

Max Lamb was with us and we wanted to go to a store to buy Ken a pair of carpet slippers. Spencer begged off. He hurried on his way. As they kept dying, one after another — Ken Maynard, Tex Ritter, Bill

Elliott, Allan Lane, Dennis Moore, Lon Chaney, Jr., Jack LaRue, following after Buck Jones, Walter Miller, Pearl White, Sam Katzman, Larry Darmour, George B. Seitz—with each fatality I noticed Spencer hurried off more quickly.

When in 1976 I video-taped an interview with him, I remarked, once it was over, "You know, Spencer, it wasn't so long ago that you remembered everything with much greater clarity."

When he became excited, Bennet had a tendency to stammer. "Well Jon," he replied, "I ... I th-think an octogenarian has a right *not* to remember, d-don't you?"

I could not help but agree with him. After all, even though everything I have written of film history has been made possible only because of the numerous people I have talked to who were able to remember, I suspect from my association with so many men and women over seventy-five that longevity in some obscure yet inextricable way is the inevitable result of being able to forget.

A Conversation with Dick Richards

Dick Richards was born in New York City on July 9, 1930. Growing up in New York, he went to the movies frequently and enjoyed genre pictures, Westerns, adventure and detective films. He attended several Ivy League schools but discovered that his real interest was in still photography. During the Korean conflict, Richards served in the U.S. Army as a photo-journalist. After his return to civilian life, he embarked on a career as a commercial photographer. His photographs appeared in *Life, Look, Vogue, Time,* and *Esquire,* as well as in other places. He started photographing for commercial advertisers such as Levi's and Volkswagen. From this it was an easy transition to filmed commercials for television.

Richards wanted to try his hand at a theatrical film. While researching a spot for the Heinz Company which would feature a cattle drive as a background, on location in the Southwest, Richards came across an old man in a rest home whose stories about his boyhood in the Old West when combined with E.C. Abbott's *We Pointed Them North* (1955) became upon release *The Culpepper Cattle Company* (20th-Fox, 1972). Richards sketched out his ideas and took them to Gregory Prentiss, a student teacher at New York University, and asked him for help on it. Eric Bercovici, a veteran screenwriter, helped Richards polish the rough draft. When the script was finished, Richards gave it to agent Paul Helmick who showed it to Elmo Williams, then head of production at Twentieth Century–Fox Film Corporation. Williams liked it and wanted to schedule it for production. As far as Richards was concerned, his Western would depict what it was like in the not so good old days, without romance and without female characters.

For its exteriors *The Culpepper Cattle Company* was shot in Mexico. Richards set up a working formula he would follow in all of his subsequent films. "What I do," he told me, "is I visit all of the existing sets, and I photograph them from different angles. Then I go away with

147

the script for several weeks, go over it and break it down into shots. Using the photographs, I set up a kind of war-room, so that I can figure out all my camera angles and coverage. In this way, I have time on the set to work with my actors and to make changes if I feel I have to."

Richards had long been an admirer of John Ford and he wanted to assimilate the Ford "look" in *The Culpepper Cattle Company*. He even went so far as to hire one of Ford's old cutters and with every scene he would ask the cutter how Ford would have done it. "There was a whole feeling," Richards recalled, "in the Charles Russell paintings and the Remington paintings—soft, always late day and long shadows, an early morning feeling. I tried to match those feelings. I tried to marry all the feelings of the early John Ford, Remington, Russell, Hawks—all the classics, all the people who had created the Western mystique."

Of course, any Western centering its primary action around a trail drive and seeking to imitate a classic structure invites comparison with Howard Hawks' *Red River* (United Artists, 1948). Hawks in making his film had in mind the basic plot of *Mutiny on the Bounty* (1932) and John Wayne, as Tom Dunson, achieved the proportions of the tyrannical Captain Bligh. This plot orientation was due at least in part to Borden Chase who wrote the novel on which the screenplay was based, *Blazing Guns on the Chisholm Trail* (1946), and who worked on the screenplay with Charles Schnee. "It had everything going for it," Donald C. Willis wrote of *Red River* in *The Films of Howard Hawks* (1975). "It's what you wish every movie could be and what very few are: exciting, funny, moving, beautiful, majestic. I think it's successful on all levels and in almost every area: the mythic level, the interpersonal level, *mise-en-scène*, acting, dialogue, detail, music, characterization, plot, theme, photography, setting, humor. And it's more than the sum of those parts."[1]

"Quand j'ai fait Red River," Howard Hawks told Jacques Rivette and François Truffaut in an interview for *Cahiers du Cinéma*, *"j'ai pensé que l'on pouvait faire un Western adulte, pour grandes personnes, et non pas un de ces quelconques 'cowboys'...."*[2] Hawks pursued his customary technique of weaving together a number of individual stories and interpersonal conflicts against the background of a cattle drive and finally resolved them when John Wayne and Montgomery Clift confront each other for a climactic showdown at the end. The milieu, as much as anything, compelled these two central characters to assume an enlarged stature.

Richards went to the opposite extreme in making his cattle-drive

Western. Not only were there no women and no romance, as there had been in all of Ford's and Hawks' Westerns, but there were no heroes and, in fact, no heroic deeds. "Our history and our being, I feel, really started with the opening of the West," Richards remarked, "and I felt that this culture should be told as it really was."

That there were no heroes and no heroic deeds — or that there should not be in a "modern" depiction of frontier times — was scarcely original with Richards, but rather epigonal. Budd Boetticher in his exceptional series of Randolph Scott Westerns in the late fifties introduced an innovation whereby the villains were far more spectacular and interesting than the isolated and introverted hero invariably cut off from the social order around him in a state of existential exclusiveness which the villains envied and, at times, sought to emulate. From this evolved the attempts to demythologize the treatment of the Old West in the sixties and seventies. William Fraker, a cinematographer turned director for *Monte Walsh* (National General, 1970), cast Lee Marvin and Jack Palance (both formerly heavies in Westerns) as two obsolescent cowboys during the range depression of the 1890s and credited Charles M. Russell for the art work on the titles. The notion of combining a story with anti-heroes in the Old West with photographic nostalgia reminiscent of Remington and Russell was also evident in *Will Penny* (Paramount, 1968) which stars Charlton Heston as a quiet, self-sufficient, aging wrangler desperately trying to eke out a livelihood in a profession that is dying. The film has no glamour. John Ford told Peter Bogdanovich that he liked *She Wore a Yellow Ribbon* (RKO, 1949) because he had "tried to copy the Remington style there — you can't copy him one hundred percent — but at least I tried to get his color and movement, and I think I succeeded partly."[3] Apparently others thought so as well since *She Wore a Yellow Ribbon* won an Academy Award for Best Photography. In his effort to capture the same pictorial quality in *The Culpepper Cattle Company,* Richards did not fall very far short of the mark and his Western is in many ways quite striking visually. The effects with sunlight bathe the entire production in a burnished glow and many of the tracking shots are memorable. Richards' cattle drive may be dustier and grimier than the one in *Red River* (with Richards using fewer steers), but that is consistent with his basic intention in making the picture. The shortcoming of the film is to be found in its fragmentary plot.

The story concerns sixteen-year-old Gary Grimes who signs on with Billy "Green" Bush, playing Culpepper, to learn how to be a

Gary Grimes, standing, in a scene from *The Culpepper Cattle Company* (20th-Fox, 1972). Photo courtesy of Twentieth Century–Fox.

cowboy. Grimes is involved in a stampede perpetrated by rustlers which results in the rustlers getting shot down; a raid on the trail herders' cavvies by horse thieves which results in the horse thieves getting shot down; and an attack on a group of settlers which results in the attackers getting shot down. After this last episode, the Grimes character drops his gun belt and rides off toward home, having decided *not* to become a cowboy.

Even here a few contrasts come to mind. In *Cahill, U.S. Marshal*

(Warner's, 1973) Gary Grimes was cast as one of John Wayne's two screen sons. However, this is a traditional Western with the dominating Wayne persona and in it the Wayne character suggests that the only possible response of a true Westerner to the Grimes' character's foolish and cowardly antics is that he ought to drop his pants instead of his gun belt and receive a good licking. Although nominally directed by Andrew V. McLaglen, *Cahill, U.S. Marshal* came the year after *The Culpepper Cattle Company* and it represents, certainly, Wayne's personal reaction to the Grimes character as depicted in Richards' pseudo-documentary. Nor was such a reaction totally isolated. The most obvious contrast with *The Culpepper Cattle Company* is *The Cowboys* (Warner's, 1972) directed by Mark Rydell in which John Wayne recruits a group of youngsters to help him on a trail drive. When Bruce Dern and his gang of rustlers shoot and kill the Wayne character and run off with the herd, the youngsters rise to the occasion and through strategy and ruthlessness wipe out the cattle thieves and reclaim the herd, getting it to market safely.

Richards' intention was for there to be no heroes in *The Culpepper Cattle Company* but even critics who were sympathetic to this approach and who were willing to admit the visual beauty of the film had to complain about the ending which consists of a five-minute bloodbath followed on the sound track by a heavenly choir singing "Amazing Grace." Philip French, who in his book *Westerns* (1974) tried to reduce all recent Westerns to manifestations of various political ideologies, managed—the ending notwithstanding—to read a profound message into Richards' film when contrasting it with *The Cowboys*. "Here we see a sixteen-year-old Texan," French wrote, "joining an arduous cattle drive out of a romantic desire to live the cowboy's life. He too becomes a man, but the film's authors—and to a lesser extent the boy himself—show real awareness of the kind of man he is becoming as he is initiated into the squalid pleasures, the self-seeking, the random violence around him. Without ever making it too explicit, Richards seems to be implying that the Culpepper Cattle Company is America—a business ploughing relentlessly on, totally amoral, fighting when it must, compromising when it can, a few deranged or misguided members galloping off from time to time to pursue 'idealistic' Vietnam-like missions on the side which neither adversary nor apparent beneficiary justifies."[4]

This kind of political interpretation leaves me cold. For one thing, such film analysts are too quick on the draw with analogies about what "represents" America. Jim Kitses in *Horizons West* (1970) said of Sam Peckinpah's *The Wild Bunch* (Warner's, 1969) that "the Wild Bunch is America."[5] I imagine that both the Culpepper Cattle Company and the Wild Bunch can be viewed this way, but, if so, they are this primarily in the minds of critics who wish to editorialize on these conjectures and were not intended to be such according to their respective directors.

Richards did what he really wanted to accomplish in *The Culpepper Cattle Company*. He made a Western with documentary realism. The film won a gold medal from the Spanish Film Institute for its photography. By remaining cognizant of the limited box office such films have — *Monte Walsh* grossed $2,300,000; *Will Penny* grossed $1,314,130 — Fox budgeted *The Culpepper Cattle Company* at a little over a million and was able to come out with a profit. Richards, who had spent so many years in advertising in an effort to persuade the American television culture of the desirability of all manner of products, in this film had an opportunity to shatter what he regarded as a glamourous myth and reveal the life of the average cowboy to have been filthy, violent, and without reward. As opposed to the stress his models, Ford and Hawks, always placed upon story, Richards neglected story and, therefore, failed ultimately to engage his viewer emotionally and intellectually. Richards belongs to that group which introduced dubiety and ambiguity into the treatment of the American westward expansion, but he is scarcely among those who have excelled at it. *The Culpepper Cattle Company* comes off best when seen as a strictly visual experience and, as Arthur Penn's later *The Missouri Breaks* (United Artists, 1976), can be enjoyed only perhaps on a pictorial level.

Rafferty and the Gold Dust Twins (Warner's, 1974), Richards' next film, is again both generic and epigonal. Produced by Michael Gruskoff, who had produced the ecological protest film *Silent Running* (Universal, 1972), and Arthur Linson, a rock manager and music publisher, it is a formula road picture. It came hard on *Scarecrow* (Warner's, 1973) directed by Jerry Schaltzberg and starring Gene Hackman and Al Pacino as a pair of itinerants. "Rafferty," Richards himself summed up the plot of his film, "is about a fifteen-year-old girl, played by Mackenzie Phillips, a thirty-five-year-old would-be singer, played by Sally Kellerman, and a twenty-year career veteran and former Korean War Marine played by Alan Arkin. This guy doesn't know what to do with his life. He's working as an instructor at the Motor Vehicle Bureau, and the two women kidnap him because they want to

Sally Kellerman and Dick Richards posing on the set of *Rafferty and the Gold Dust Twins* (Warner's, 1974). Photo courtesy of Warner Bros.

go to New Orleans and they've got no way of getting there. The girl pulls out a gun, puts it to his head, and says, 'We want to go to New Orleans.' And it's about their experiences together. It becomes very funny."

Only, according to most reviewers, *Rafferty and the Gold Dust Twins* wasn't very funny and the blame was placed on Richards' direction which was unable to make comic the misadventures in the script. Certainly one of the gravest oversights in the film and one which Richards sought to correct in *Farewell, My Lovely* (Avco-Embassy, 1975) where Philip Marlowe is given a friend is that there is no friendship in the film as there is in *Scarecrow* between Hackman and Pacino. Sally Kellerman deserts Arkin before the picture is over, completely destroying the "family romance" which the first part of the film is at pains to build. However amusing Arkin's madcap drive across the grass outside the orphanage at the end may be, with Phillips in the car, it is anticlimactic and somehow the viewer is left with the feeling that the adventures of this duo will not be as interesting as when they were a trio.

Shot in and around Hollywood, then on location in Las Vegas, Phoenix, and Tucson for five weeks, *Rafferty and the Gold Dust Twins* depicts the outlandish threesome of Arkin, Kellerman, and Phillips cheating others out of money, liquor, gasoline, and food — the staples of the American way of life if kept in that order — until they wind up, not in New Orleans, but in Kellerman's home town of Tucson. Mackenzie Phillips plays a fugitive from an orphanage. In her attempt to get money, she thinks of trying prostitution but satisfies herself with petty larceny. She is arrested and Kellerman runs off with a country and western singer. Arkin decides to follow Phillips to the orphanage and bail her out, although his motive in doing so is far from clear.

"Casting," Richards said, "has always been a hobby of mine and even when I was doing commercials I was well-known for it. I think it's true, as a lot of people have said, that it's as much as ninety percent of the movie." Yet, casting alone is insufficient. Alan Arkin possesses a splendid capacity for both comedy and drama, but it was not utilized in *Rafferty and the Gold Dust Twins.* Mackenzie Phillips was somewhat typecast; in her personal life (which has included her having been found unconscious on Hollywood Boulevard from an overdose of narcotics) she has surpassed in disorientation the alienated roles she has had. Yet, in *Rafferty and the Gold Dust Twins,* her brittle characterization needs Kellerman's softening presence to balance it properly. The direction and the script have to be in accord with the casting or the entire enterprise will falter.

"I used to like this town," Philip Marlowe remarks in Raymond Chandler's *The Little Sister* (1949). "A long time ago. There were trees along Wilshire Boulevard. Beverly Hills was a country town. Westwood was bare hills and lots offering at eleven hundred dollars and no takers. Hollywood was a bunch of frame houses on the interurban line. Los Angeles was just a big dry sunny place with ugly homes and no style, but good-hearted and peaceful. It had the climate they just yap about now. People used to sleep out on porches. Little groups who thought they were intellectual used to call it the Athens of America. It wasn't that, but it wasn't a neon-lighted slum either."[6]

When Richards came to film *Farewell, My Lovely,* he was convinced that it worked best as a period piece. Yet, to do so presented numerous problems. "There were no red-painted curbs to restrict parking," he commented. "Even the traffic lights and corner stop signs were of a different design. The fire hydrants in 1941 were unlike those we use today. We had to rip out all the modern stuff so nothing would seem incongruous—and then we had to replace it when we were through. In fact, what appears in the movie to be a single continuing walk down a couple of blocks is, in actuality, a compendium of maybe ten to fifteen briefer shots, photographed at separate locations in order to avoid the intrusion of visuals that wouldn't fit the period."

Elliott Kastner and Jerry Bick who had packaged *The Long Goodbye* (United Artists, 1973) based on another Chandler novel with Robert Altman directing had had to take Elliott Gould as part of the package in order to get financing. The improbability of Gould playing Marlowe had not concerned Altman in the least. In fact, Altman had talked himself into directing the picture while trying to convince Jerry Bick of Gould's "rightness" for the part. When *The Long Goodbye* grossed $959,000 at the box office, United Artists turned an unsympathetic ear toward Kastner and Bick's proposal for a third make of *Farewell, My Lovely* (1942). Kastner was finally able to get the British financier, Sir Lew Grade, and the British-based International Television Corporation to co-finance. Dick Richards was asked to direct. He would sign to do the picture provided Robert Mitchum was cast as Marlowe. Kastner got Mitchum for Richards.

When we had our conversation together about his career, Richards was in preproduction on *March or Die* (Columbia, 1977). *Farewell, My Lovely* had been released and had proven both a critical and a commercial success. We were in the office suite Richards was then occupying at what was then the Samuel Goldwyn studio on Santa Monica Boulevard. Richards sat poised at his desk, his blue-green eyes attentive.

"Robert Altman updated his treatment of Marlowe. Why didn't you?"

"I was given an updated script when I was offered the picture," he replied. "I turned it down. I thought it was sacrilegious to screw around with that book."

"What happened then?"

"It was the same producers as on *The Long Goodbye,* Elliott Kastner and Jerry Bick. They told me to make any changes in the script I wanted to make. David Goodman and I rewrote the whole thing, making it a period piece." David Zelag Goodman had received Academy Award nominations for his scripts for *Monte Walsh* and *Lovers and Other Strangers* (ABC Films, 1970) and had written the screenplay for Sam Peckinpah's *Straw Dogs* (Cinerama, 1971).

"I have to admit that the way you did it, it worked," I said. "When *The Long Goodbye* was in preproduction, I didn't think it was possible for it to be brought off as a period piece."

"*The Long Goodbye* is very late Chandler," Richards said. "*Farewell, My Lovely* is from Chandler's early period. I think he wrote well in that period. His dialogue is sharper. Everything was better. I tried to stay true to Chandler. The dialogue is what makes Chandler stick. That I wanted to keep. There was a lot about the book that was unbelievable, but not the dialogue."

"You changed the plot. You substituted a cat house for the asylum Chandler used in the novel and a madam for the psychic, Jules Amthor."

"I didn't like Amthor as a villain. That's one of the things I found unbelievable in the novel. It played better, I thought, the way we changed it. And we created a sub-plot. We gave Marlowe a friend. In the novels, he has no one."

"In the novels," I interjected, "he can't trust anyone enough to make him a friend."

"Well, that's where Bob Mitchum came in. He played Marlowe like a man of his age. He's tired. Marlowe is tough, smart, but fallible. He can say, almost at the end, 'Now, I get it.' It's nearly too late. But he knows how to get information."

"How did Mitchum take to the role?"

"Oh, he liked the role. But he worried about how he would be accepted, playing Marlowe. Bob Mitchum is a great sardonic character. That's the way I wanted him to play Marlowe. We talked over the role quite a bit. But we agreed what kind of guy Marlowe was. We even improvised on the set when something didn't sound right."

RKO Radio Pictures had originally purchased screen rights to *Farewell, My Lovely* and had used it as the basis for *The Falcon Takes Over* (RKO, 1942) with George Sanders in the starring role. The Falcon series had its own successful formula for crime detection with a high comic tone, and the only real flaw of *The Falcon Takes Over* is Chandler's rather convoluted plot. The characters belonged to Chandler's stark, albeit melodramatic, view of Southern California and were out of place in New York City being investigated by the debonair Sanders. The police, played by James Gleason and Edward Gargan, were buffoons compared to the brutal and secure men Chandler had drawn.

Edward Dmytryk brought the novel to the screen as the first film to feature Philip Marlowe by name as the detective, with Dick Powell in the role. Principally because of Powell's reputation as a singer and dancer, the title of the film was changed to *Murder, My Sweet* (RKO, 1944). It is perhaps the best Marlowe film other than *Lady in the Lake* (M-G-M, 1947) which was directed by and starred Robert Montgomery. Powell's flippant yet hard tone was appropriate, although he lacked the biting sarcasm Montgomery could occasionally get into his characterization.

"Did you look at *Murder, My Sweet?*" I asked.

"I looked at *Murder, My Sweet* and at the Falcon picture. I wanted Los Angeles to be seedy in my film, the way it had been when Chandler described it. We shot the whole picture right here. I used the *Queen Mary* for the gambling ship."

"Chandler based Bay City in the novel on Santa Monica. Eddie Dmytryk told me they used to lock up Santa Monica at night. Chandler drew his cops as corrupted men. You didn't."

"No. For me, the picture was about Marlowe. In *The Culpepper Cattle Company,* there were no heroes. Marlowe is a hero. We debated for months on how to handle the last scene where Marlowe gives money to the widow. I wasn't so concerned with corruption. There's plenty of that in the picture. I wanted to stress Marlowe's honesty."

To play the cop who is sympathetic to Marlowe, Richards cast John Ireland. One might almost regard him as much of a friend as Jimmie Archer is, playing Georgie, the newsstand proprietor who helps Marlowe and even gives him a place to stay. It is the Ireland character who at the denouement decides for once to put duty before the pay-offs the force receives and to see the case through. Maybe that could have happened in 1941. As for Marlowe's turning over the two grand paid him by the gangster Brunette, *Newsweek* commented that that was the film's final unspeakable horror: Chandler's hard-boiled hero had been turned into a soft-boiled liberal.

In more than one way, *Farewell, My Lovely* is a comic novel, a satire, the closest Chandler ever came to imitating the hectic humor of Nathanael West at his finest. When Marlowe meets Mrs. Grayle for the first time, there is hyperbole, the comic tone approaching the grotesque. The absurdity of the characters and the situation in which they find themselves is nowhere more evident and, if a reader is inclined to laugh out loud, sitting alone in a room with nothing but a book before him, this scene might provoke it. None of the film versions brings it off. Richards' handling of the sequence is marred because of his shift from the ridiculously sensuous to the tantalizingly erotic. If there is little more annoying to a woman than the sexual pretensions of a man toward whom she is not even remotely attracted, there is for Chandler's hero nothing quite as idiotic as the sexual advances of a female who is a murder suspect and, therefore, morally dubious.

"I saw what Bob Altman had done with *The Long Goodbye*," Richards concluded. "I was impressed to see him try to do what he thought was something fresh with Chandler. I said to myself that I'd like to see if I could come up with a style for Chandler."

The style Richards came up with went farther than expert casting, including Mitchum. He retained the back-telling technique which is the only way a screenplay can preserve Chandler's caustically disrespectful and incisive descriptions of people and places. There was something peculiar about indoor light in the forties and Richards managed to capture it, a moody, soft glow rather than the harsh illumination to which we have since become accustomed. Mitchum's presence, so reminiscent of his work from the forties in such films as *Out of the Past* (RKO, 1947), stands almost as a critique of the era. If it wasn't as bleak, desolate, misbegotten, and corrupt as our own, it was nonetheless all of these things to a lesser degree, and Mitchum's Marlowe makes certain that we realize it.

Another thing Richards overlooked in the dramatization of the Chandler novel, primarily because he was limited to the John Ireland character, is the reason the police always brutalize Marlowe. Robert Altman caught it. The police are so often paid not to exercise power, not to make arrests, to look the other way, that it is natural to hunt for opportunities to flex one's muscles. Ultimately the powerless—petty criminals, the homeless, traffic violators, private detectives—afford these opportunities. Chandler said it over and over in his books: as long as the public is going to stand by and tolerate crooked politicians and big league mobsters, it cannot expect more from the police than to have law and order rammed forcibly down its throat and occasionally for some bystander to stop a bullet.

Farewell, My Lovely was filmed in thirty-seven days at a cost of $2,300,000, in contrast to *Murder, My Sweet* which required forty-four days and cost $450,000. Even as we talked, Richards had just returned from scouting locations for *March or Die* and had been this time entrusted with a $9,000,000 budget. David Zelag Goodman had again been engaged to write the screenplay.

Yet, upon release, *March or Die* proved another epigonal, generic film, devoid of any real story value. It deals with the French Foreign Legion in North Africa and has an international cast headed by Gene Hackman, icy and expressionless Catherine Deneuve, Max von Sydow, Ian Holm, and Terence Hill. The production was once more a joint venture between Sir Lew Grade and International Television Corporation with Columbia Pictures releasing. Perhaps the most promising aspect of the film might have been the characters, but they turned out to be clichés. Gene Hackman plays an American major in the Legion who spends his time being bitter with dialogue like, "There are no heroes in war, only survivors," and, to the Arabs, "Let the French bring you into the twentieth century." Catherine Deneuve is always perfectly coiffured and attired despite being thousands of miles distant from boutiques and beauty parlors and is otherwise undistinguished. Ian Holm is a murderous but ostensibly noble Arab chieftain. Max von Sydow portrays an inhuman, monomaniacal archeologist and Terence Hill is Marco the Gypsy, momentarily attracted to Deneuve's wooden personality and, following the Hackman character's death, the man destined to take his place leading the Legion. Having set out to make *March or Die* a formulary combination of *Gunga Din* (RKO, 1939) and *Four Feathers* (United Artists, 1939), Richards may have been thrown off by the fact that the colonial French embodied objectives different from those of the colonial British. What he came up with was a movie with characters and situations as predictable as its dialogue.

The most notable shortcoming in Richards' screen work to this point was his reliance on generic ideas. He had only one qualified success. Nor have matters improved much since. *Death Valley* (Universal, 1981) is a slasher film with Peter Billingsley cast as a city boy who returns to Arizona only to become entangled with a psychotic killer played by Stephen McHattie. *Man, Woman and Child* (Paramount, 1983) is a sentimental drama with Martin Sheen cast as a happily married man with two children haunted by an affair out of his past with a French woman which has left him with an orphaned son. One thing is certain. Richards is a competent and technically proficient filmmaker. Should he come to acknowledge that there is no escape from the necessity for a strong, compelling, integrated story-line, his best films may well still lie before him.

Literary Studies

Rex Stout and the Detective Story

The first detective story I ever read was *The Bishop Murder Case* (1929) by S.S. Van Dine. I was impressed at the legitimate way in which it was plotted, the manner in which the clues concealing the identity of the murderer were all set forth before the reader and, by using one's wits, it was possible to arrive at the solution to the case ahead even of the detective, Philo Vance. When Willard Huntington Wright chose to write detective stories he adopted the *nom de plume* S.S. Van Dine — so he claimed — because the steam ship initials summed up his desire to travel and he hoped that at last "dine" would become a verb for him since, prior to that time, it had not been in his vocabulary at all. In a collection of detective fiction which Wright assembled and published under his own name, titled *The World's Great Detective Stories: A Chronological Anthology* (1927), he included an historical survey of the entire field of such fiction by way of an introduction, current as of the time he prepared the book. "There is no more stimulating activity than that of the mind," Wright wrote in that Introduction; "and there is no more exciting adventure than that of the intellect."[1] I still regard this as the principal justification for reading a detective story, although I have found, over the years, in my study of the genre that playing fair with the reader, providing precisely that stimulation of the intellect, is something most authors have tended to ignore. As a consequence, I came to the conclusion that, however much I might personally endorse Wright's precepts, the majority of readers of detective stories obviously did not; and that the reason, apparently, so few were bothered by an author's sleight-of-hand concerning who had done it was because they preferred being surprised to actually solving an intellectual puzzle.

Van Dine also believed that characterization in a detective story should be minimal. "Think back over all the good detective stories you may have read," he suggested, "and try to recall a single memorable personality (aside from the detective himself). And yet these characters were of sufficient color and rotundity to enlist your sympathetic emotions at the time, and to drive you on to a solution of their problems."[2] In this I believe he was absolutely right. I have frequently forgotten the solution of a particular detective story, but what has always remained firmly in my memory, especially when he has been a cleverly drawn and intriguing character, has been the personality of the detective.

Some years ago I received a letter and a series of questions from John J. McAleer. A covering letter from Rex Stout announced that Professor McAleer of Boston College had a contract with Little, Brown to write a biography about him and the recipient, while exercising discretion, should provide McAleer with whatever assistance he could. I confess that I was disinclined to answer all of his questions. I could not list then, or now, anything like the ten Nero Wolfe stories I most enjoyed in order of preference. I have read all of them, some more than once, but only two or three really stand out, perhaps the short novel "Cordially Invited to Meet Death" (1942) and perhaps, as well, more for their comic scenes than for any other reason, the novels *Some Buried Caesar* (1939) and *Over My Dead Body* (1940).

Sir Arthur Conan Doyle stumbled into most of the pitfalls that later writers of detective fiction have wisely tended to avoid. He murdered his detective and had his narrator marry. Later, when Dashiell Hammett and Dorothy L. Sayers had their detectives marry, they had reached the nadir of their productive contributions to the genre. Raymond Chandler, too, attempted marrying off his detective, Philip Marlowe, with unsatisfactory results. Rex Stout made no such mistakes. He created a fantasy world, one with sufficient coordinates with the real world in which you and I live that we are not always aware of it. Agatha Christie narrated Hercule Poirot's death and she showed Miss Marple ravaged by old age. Neither Nero Wolfe nor Archie Goodwin ever ages. They cannot. This was part of Stout's literary compact. He was not going to allow Wolfe to develop a cardiac disorder any more than he was about to expose Archie Goodwin to venereal disease. Personally, Stout suffered from ulcers which prohibited him from enjoying in the flesh the exquisite cuisine he invented for Wolfe's consumption. In the Wolfe stories, Archie's life is his job and he is so little troubled by contrary urges and emotions that one can almost accept his reluctance to ask no more of life than occasionally to show up Wolfe.

Stout, in the beginning as a prodigy of the Depression, put all of his passion and vituperative wit into his detective stories. This became less pronounced after the Second World War. Later it was only intermittantly apparent amid the boredom he found in his formula. A reader may reasonably ask an author not to age his characters or alter their lifestyle, but he cannot expect an author to prevent these things from happening in himself. In *Rex Stout: A Biography* (1977), John J. McAleer made the point that Stout had the ability to continue his saga over decades without having his characters grow stale. I believe this is true when it comes to his principal characters, Wolfe and Archie, but even the other regular characters in the saga, such as Inspector Cramer, are more attitudes of mind than rounded human beings and a reader will never learn, not even in *Red Threads* (1939), presumably Inspector Cramer's own case without so much as a mention of Wolfe and Archie, what Cramer's first name might be and he is never seen at home with his family or separate from his function as a homicide inspector.

Wolfe's house and his life are like a persistent dream, one man's romantic vision of a life of order, freedom from interruption, and, within its confines, peace. It is a wholly masculine environment. This of itself is very unusual, when you think about it. Women have always read Rex Stout's books, but I suspect they have not read him as avidly as they have read Erle Stanley Gardner or Agatha Christie. Women are the great readers in modern civilization: any publisher will tell you as much. Since women buy and read more books of fiction and story collections than men, they have every right to request that an author address himself specifically to women, at least some of the time. This Rex Stout could never do because he was unable to draw female characters convincingly in the fiction he wrote prior to the Wolfe saga and after he had begun his saga Archie's first person, subjective narratives to an extent relieved him of the obligation of having to do so. His sole effort to create a woman detective, Dol Bonner in *The Hand in the Glove* (1937), is one of the slowest moving, even turgid detective stories he ever published.

In a satirical essay, Stout once suggested that Dr. John H. Watson may have been a women. He acknowledged Archie's sexual needs when he introduced Lily Rowan into the stories with *Some Buried Caesar* and during the Second World War and henceforth the two continued to keep company. Conversely, Wolfe's intense dislike of women and female hysterics keeps his home an andromorphous paradise with a Belgian chef, a German gardener who tends to Wolfe's ten thousand orchids, and, of course, Archie. I have always been astonished at the number of virgins in their early and mid twenties in Stout's fiction of the forties and fifties. Archie makes the remark in *Death of a Dude*

(1969) that he suspects a lot of little old schoolteachers and librarians read his accounts of Wolfe's cases, and he may have been correct. Perhaps what he had in mind was the furor raised in certain circles when in *The Mother Hunt* (1963) Archie goes to bed with Mrs. Lucy Valdon while on the case; it was the first and last time he ever admitted doing anything so bold as that. Yet I am disinclined to fault Stout for this reticence. Since his time such sexual episodes between the detective and various females have become almost obligatory while adding nothing to the story and very often providing little more than an intrusive distraction. In *The Godwulf Manuscript* (1973) Robert B. Parker has his detective, Spenser, go to bed with both the wife and daughter of his client. Richard Hoyt told me that in his first John Denson mystery, *Decoys* (1980), his detective sleeps with a former female acquaintance because his literary agent insisted upon it, not because of some exigency of the plot he had devised.

It was not until publication of Stout's next to last Nero Wolfe novel, *Please Pass the Guilt* (1973), that Wolfe's attitude toward women and their sexual behavior became overtly cynical. Orrie Cather, an operative who has long assisted Wolfe, was falsely imprisoned in *Death of a Doxy* (1966) for supposedly having murdered a Park Avenue whore. We meet Orrie's grief-strickened fiancée in *Death of a Doxy*. By the time of *Please Pass the Guilt*, Jill, an airline flight attendant, and Orrie are married. Orrie investigates at least two Continental Air Network female researchers by taking them to bed on Wolfe's expense account. For whatever the reason, Stout until he wrote this novel had ignored for the most part probing too deeply into questions such as who is sleeping with whom. In *Please Pass the Guilt*, Wolfe instructs Archie to seduce the two leading female suspects, and Archie comments breezily that there is "no evidence that either of them has any chastity to surrender."[3] As it turns out, neither of them has, although Archie has sexual congress with neither. I do not know how many crimes of passion can be traced to the confusions engendered by sexual intercourse in and out of marriage, but it is certainly responsible for a great many of them and, ultimately, Orrie Cather's promiscuity is his undoing in Stout's final mystery, *A Family Affair* (1975).

McAleer structured his biography of Stout around Stout's interrelationships with his family. He perceived this to be at the center of Stout's emotional and spiritual world and he felt that Wolfe's domicile is in effect an idealized extended family in which the dialogue between the father and the son, Wolfe and Archie, finally progresses to where "understanding grows between the two men. What is more remarkable, while the flow of Rex's traits into Archie gradually subsides, Nero Wolfe and Rex Stout come increasingly to share characterisics in common."[4] This is a valid observation, but it does not go far enough. David R. Anderson in *Rex Stout* (1984) made a considerable study of family relationships and the family as a symbolic unit in the saga and came to a conclusion in which I concur. ". . . The family, for all its violent undercurrents, has always been idealized in the vision of the Wolfe family. In the last novel of the series, however, that ideal collapses. The cynicism of politics merges with the already present dark view of the family to tip and finally to topple the scale which balanced the Wolfe family against the flawed families encountered in the novels. The bastion of order and justice and humanity had its comic cracks and flaws; here at the end of the series those flaws become serious, perhaps even tragic, and the order of Rex Stout's universe is gone."[5]

So skillful was Stout as a humorist that it is difficult to realize until the very late books that Nero Wolfe is actually a prisoner of his own fantasy, that the basis of his existence is a confession of the utter bankruptcy of love, of life in the world. It represents a cynical despair in one's fellows and all social structures; it is a retreat from the pressures, inadequacies, frenzies of reality. We can best laugh at life when we are least susceptible to being hurt by it, but we remember our former pain in our enjoyment, or when we have insulated ourselves from our own being to such an extent that we cannot easily be hurt by it again. Laughter is our release in the face of the inescapable futility of all that we do. It comes above suffering, before and after it, and it tells us that human relationships at their base can be funny because they may become meaningless. A man who makes you laugh does so by telling you half a story, but half a story is only one side of reality and not the whole of it.

The more conscious you become, the more aware you are of each person's separateness. Think of Theodore Horstmann in the plant rooms, encased in a chrysalis of glass, as he was in the early novels before Stout moved him out, with a tiny sleeping chamber enclosed by brownstone right next to the potting room, his cot, the flowers which he does not own, and Wolfe four hours a day. Archie doesn't tell it like this, because if he did the compact would break and the compact is supposed to keep us amused. But that is Horstmann's life. He's akin to a lunatic I once saw while visiting an insane asylum whose one joy consisted in scrubbing out ashtrays that had been soiled. I see her now, old, gray-headed, hobbling about, flashing me a quick, fleeting, impatient smile, and pointing mutely at the ashtray beside me, supplicating, would I please finish with it?

When I travel, I read Ross Macdonald's detective novels. When you know how much the author of these books suffered over the indirections, the torments, the disappearance of his own daughter, the wandering daughters which obsess the characters and the detective, Lew Archer, in his fiction take on a whole new dimension. And, recently, when I was away long enough to read three of them consecutively, and thinking so often of my own infant daughter and how much I missed her and how difficult life will surely be for her, the anguish Macdonald embodied in his detective fiction became palpable. This is a variety of the experience of finitude and helplessness and somberness which does not become manifest in Stout's books until nearly the end, and then never so poignantly, so desperately.

Rex Stout was born at Noblesville, Indiana, on December 1, 1886, and he died in his upper state New York home on October 27, 1975. In many ways, as McAleer has amply demonstrated in his biography, Stout's life was as extraordinary as any of the fiction he wrote. Following his birth, his parents, John Wallace Stout and Lucetta Todhunter Stout, moved to Topeka, Kansas. One of nine children, Stout was very precocious, having read the Bible twice by the time he was four; by the time he was thirteen, he was spelling champion for the state. He was a voracious reader. At eighteen, he joined the U.S. Navy and became a warrant officer on the *Mayflower,* President Theodore Roosevelt's yacht, a post he held until he left the Navy in 1908.

He checked the want ads in New York City and found employment as bookkeeper for *Pharmaceutical Era and Soda Fountain* for eighteen dollars a week. The job proved short-lived because he was found to be hustling advertisements on the side. He roamed the country as an itinerant bookkeeper, worked briefly in a smoke shop in Cleveland until his penchant for expensive Havana cigars caused him to be laid off, sold Indian baskets in Albuquerque, was a guide to the Indian pueblos near Santa Fe, a barker for a sight-seeing bus in Colorado Springs, a bookstore clerk in Chicago, Indianapolis, and Milwaukee, and a stable hand in New York. In four years he had held thirty jobs in six states.

He had his first literary success during these years. When he was twenty, he wrote a poem which was accepted by the *Smart Set* and for which he was paid fourteen dollars. It did not take him long, however, to realize that he could not make much of an income from writing poetry. More lucrative was an article he sold to the New York *World* analyzing the palm prints of William Howard Taft, then running for the Presidency, and Tom L. Johnson, a prominent Democrat. That earned him $200.

It was probably on the basis of these efforts that Stout decided in 1912 to become a magazine writer. Until 1916, he concocted and sold reams of fiction and articles to *Munsey's* and other popular magazines. Finally, he determined that this was getting him nowhere. According to McAleer, it had been a chance meeting with Eugene Manlove Rhodes in New York that had fired Stout's literary ambitions. He had been convinced that if Rhodes could do it, so could he. But simply making a living at writing was not all that Stout wanted. He wanted to write what he felt to be serious fiction. In order to do this, he opined, he would have to cease writing altogether and manage somehow to accumulate at least $200,000 so as not to be interrupted by economic pressures while writing. In tandem with his brother, John Robert Stout, he devised and proceeded to implement the Educational Thrift Service, a school banking system that was eventually installed in four hundred cities and townships across the country. The notion was so successful that he raised his goal to $400,000. He took time off to explore the high Rockies in Montana with two cowboys and thirty packhorses; these annual excursions would usually take three months during which time Stout fished, read, and walked. He went to Europe, and there, too, he walked, once 180 miles to see Thermopylae. Back in the States, he would visit schools on Bank Day and address the students on behalf of thrift.

When he felt he was near enough his goal to try it, he went to Paris to live for two years. He first novel, *How Like a God* (1929), was praised critically. He followed it with four more novels, all of which have come to be forgotten. Yet, he had made a fundamental discovery about himself: "I was a good storyteller, and I would never be a great writer."[6]

He had long had a tremendous fondness for Sir Arthur Conan Doyle's Sherlock Holmes stories and would reread them almost as often as he reread Shakespeare's sonnets. He became a Baker Street Irregular. The financial panic of those years dissipated his fortune. At forty-eight, he wrote his first detective story, the first Nero Wolfe novel, *Fer-De-Lance* (1934), which was featured in an abridged form in *The American Magazine,* a ready market for the Nero Wolfe stories as long as the publication lasted. The book proved to be popular and screen rights were purchased nearly at once, but for relatively little money, by Columbia Pictures. Before I say anything about the motion picture Columbia made, if it should happen that you have not read that first novel but only one of Stout's later stories, you may wonder how different Wolfe and Archie were in 1934. The answer is simple: not much. Horstmann, as I have indicated, slept near the orchids in the glassed-in greenhouses on the roof of Wolfe's brownstone. Fritz Brenner, the Belgian chef, slept across the hall from the plant rooms; he later moved to the basement. Archie and Wolfe were then both sleeping on the second floor; Archie later moved to the third floor. Archie kept a bottle of rye whiskey in his closet from which he would nip when particularly frustrated by Wolfe, and Archie liked smoking cigarettes. Later on in the saga he quit smoking. Wolfe detests the smell of tobacco and, no doubt, would not have enjoyed a visit from Rex Stout. "'I see him at meetings: He would sit there in a tan sports jacket from the pocket of which would protrude a row of cigars,'" Herbert Mitgang once recalled. "'It always reminded me of a bandolier of machine gun cartridges.'"[7] Harry Foster was the man at the *Gazette* who helped Archie with information; Lon Cohen only did so later. Ten thousand pages of the saga had been written before Wolfe and Archie made their final appearance in *A Family Affair*. Not very much was altered about them in all those years; we just got to know them better, or know them under varying sets of circumstances. Stout was eighty-eight at the time of his last book. He liked his characters and he liked the world in which they lived. "If I'm not having fun writing a book," he had said, "no one's going to have any fun reading it."[8] It was as much for this reason as any other that he was disgusted by what Hollywood did to his characters.

Meet Nero Wolfe (Columbia, 1936) cast Edward Arnold in the role of Wolfe. Arnold was born in New York City on February 18, 1890. He was five feet eleven inches and weighed in at two hundred pounds when he assumed the role, which scarcely made him the requisite one seventh of a ton. Lionel Stander played Archie Goodwin. The picture went into production under the title *Fer-De-Lance*. According to the screenplay, Archie is about to marry Mazie Gray, played by Dennie Moore. Joan Perry played Ellen Barstow, daughter of the college professor who is murdered on the golf links by a pin that is shot from the handle of a golfing iron. Rita Cansino, before she became Rita Hayworth, had a bit part as a bootlegger. Victor Jory was

Edward Arnold as Nero Wolfe in the plant rooms with Rita Hayworth and John Qualen from *Meet Nero Wolfe* (Columbia, 1936). Photo courtesy of Columbia Pictures–Screen Gems.

cast as one of the suspects. John Qualen was cast as Olaf, Wolfe's Scandinavian chef. Herbert Biberman directed. The screenplay was by Howard J. Green, who was rather well known at the time, Bruce Manning, and Joseph Anthony. B.P. Schulberg, who had been terminated at Paramount when that company went into receivership, was the producer. The film was actually one of Columbia Pictures' better efforts in the thirties, although it was hardly recognizable as having been based on a Nero Wolfe story. Arnold does not keep Wolfe's hours in the plant rooms, but he is shown there much of the time and, atypically, that is where he solves the case, with all the suspects gathered together.

Walter Connolly was cast as Wolfe in *The League of Frightened Men* (Columbia, 1937), the second and final theatrical film based on the saga. Connolly had been very successful on Broadway but in 1932 Harry Cohn, head of production at Columbia, persuaded him to come to Hollywood for the summer months. He was featured in pictures like Frank Capra's *Lady for a Day* (Columbia, 1933) and *A Man's Castle* (Columbia, 1933). He liked working in films so much he signed a long-term contract with Cohn. Subsequently he was featured in top-flight films such as Capra's *It Happened One Night* (Columbia, 1934) and Howard Hawks' *Twentieth Century* (Columbia, 1934). Playing Nero Wolfe permitted Connolly to *star* in a film. Lionel Stander was back as Archie Goodwin, even more of a comic bungler than in the first film. The plot follows the novel. A group of ten men is threatened by one of its members, and murders begin. The character played by Eduardo Ciannelli is the logical suspect since he was permanently crippled in a hazing while at college with the other men in the group. The love interest is delegated to Irene Hervey and Allen Brook. Alfred E. Green was the director. Perhaps it was felt to be in bad taste to have a detective who drinks a great deal of beer. Connolly's Wolfe confines himself to hot chocolate. The film was so bad that Stout refused to license any more of his properties to Hollywood and seemed for the rest of his life happy about his decision.

In 1930, after returning from France, Rex Stout put much of what was left of his fortune into building High Meadow, his home on a thousand-foot elevation at Danbury, Connecticut, fashioned after a palace he had seen on the Mediterranean which belonged to the Bey of Tunis. It was a concrete structure in a U-shape with fourteen rooms. Together with nine men and "three and a half boys," all amateurs, he worked on it for fourteen hours a day for months. On the surrounding fifty-eight acres, he grew all manner of things, but principally flowers (none of them orchids).

The Nero Wolfe mysteries proved a solid success. John Farrar of Farrar and Rinehart was his publisher. It was Farrar's idea that Stout should develop another series detective so that the reading public would not become overly sated with Wolfe. *Red Threads* and *The Hand in the Glove* were an outgrowth of this impetus, but Stout's most serious effort at creating a second detective was Tecumseh Fox who appeared in three novels. Fox is very much the country gentleman Stout had become, in contrast to the urban Wolfe, with a spacious house on a farm in Westchester county near Pleasantville. *Double for Death* (1939) was the first of the Fox mysteries. A wealthy businessman is thought to have been murdered only for the victim to turn out to have been a double he had hired. This means that the murderer is going to have to strike again. "'I don't think *Double for Death* is the best story

I ever wrote,'" Stout later said; "'I think it is the best detective story, technically, that I ever wrote.'"9 I do not know if I would go so far as that, but it is one of the best detective stories Stout wrote in terms of a legitimate plot. The clues are fairly presented to the reader so that it is possible to arrive at the correct solution to the mystery before Fox explains what happened and who is responsible. If there is a serious flaw in Stout's detective fiction generally, it is his tendency to conceal vital information from the reader so that many times the exposure of the culprit is done more through clairvoyance than through ratiocination. According to McAleer, Stout "termed 'nonsensical' the ironclad rule that the detective story writer 'must play fair with the reader.'"10 This is indeed unfortunate. As fine as many of his Nero Wolfe mysteries remain in terms of the interchanges between his principal characters, they are, notwithstanding, detective stories and the reader is denied all too often the satisfaction of being able to match his wits with Wolfe in arriving at the identity of the murderer.

Double for Death was an establishing novel. The reader is told something about Fox, about his lifestyle, and his country home is described in detail. *Bad for Business* (1940) is more of a straight detective story, dependent on its plot to carry the book, since Fox is rather thinly characterized and even the brief appearance of Dol Bonner does not excite much interest. *The Broken Vase* (1941) is ever more disappointing, set largely in New York, as is *Bad for Business,* only this time among the rich and cultured. The method of the first murder is preposterous: a concert violinist's instrument is tampered with just prior to a concert and his poor performance so drives him to distraction that he commits suicide. Tecumseh Fox is more than ever a cardboard figure. These novels, however, do point up the fact that it was the combination of Wolfe and Archie, and not Stout's expertise as an inventor of ingenious and engrossing plots, which would account for the success he had in the genre. Obviously the editors at *The American Magazine* thought the same since they agreed to serialize *Bad for Business* only if Stout would turn it into a Nero Wolfe story which Stout did. The Wolfe version of the story did not appear between covers until McAleer resurrected it for inclusion in *Death Times Three* (1985), but reading it in tandem with the original Tecumseh Fox novel provides ample proof of the color, vitality, and inherent fascination which Wolfe and Archie could bring to what, without them, remains a rather humdrum story.

During the Second World War, Rex Stout retired temporarily as a detective story writer and occupied himself with political advocacy. He wrote propaganda for the necessity of American involvement in the war, in favor of preparedness, and, once war came, for Lend-Lease and the draft. He was the master of ceremonies for the Council of Democracy's radio program "Speaking of Liberty" and chairman of the Writers' War Board. His civic-mindedness continued until the end of his life. He became chairman of the Writer's Board for World Government in 1949. In 1943–1945 he was president of the Authors' Guild and, after the war, he became president of Authors' League of America from 1951 to 1955, vice-president from 1956 to 1961, and then president again in 1962. Most significantly he lobbied in Washington on behalf of copyright revision. If his efforts in this direction were not so successful that a writer is better off having produced a book than having built an apartment house, subsequent legislation at least now promises him a slightly longer claim to his property before he must throw open the doors to public tenancy.

"The Adventures of Nero Wolfe" began as a radio series in 1943 with Santos Ortega in the role of Wolfe. A later radio series featured Sidney Greenstreet as Wolfe and Everett Sloane as Archie. Stout's distrust of movies after the two Columbia entries carried over to television and there was no Nero Wolfe series while he was alive to prevent it. Ultimately, I suspect his reservations were well-founded: the Nero Wolfe stories are basically unfilmable. They rely for their effectiveness on literary style and resist translation.

Stout resumed the Wolfe saga with *The Silent Speaker* (1946). It is a weaker novel than any of the pre-war books. Of course, most writers of detective stories have been baffled at how to retain a reader's interest for two hundred-odd pages with only one murder. S.S. Van Dine introduced the idea of a series of murders in some of his most popular books and the idea took firm root. It is unusual to find any detective novel in which the story is confined to only a single death, although Erle Stanley Gardner was able to do it more than most since the structure of his Perry Mason mysteries usually include a lengthy trial sequence. I do not know if I would agree with Julian Symons' charge that after the war the Nero Wolfe stories underwent a severe deterioration. They certainly were not as fleshed out as had been the earlier novels. One need only compare *Too Many Cooks* (1938) in which Paul Whipple is a young black man who works as a waiter at a posh resort with *A Right to Die* (1964) in which Whipple returns, now as a middle-aged professor of anthropology. The earlier novel is filled with colorful background material and Stout even went to the extreme of paying Sheila Hibben of *The New Yorker* $2,000 for the recipes which are included as an appendix. *A Right to Die* is spare, characterization and setting kept to a minimum, and, I am pleased to say, it is legitimately plotted so that a reader can discern the murderer before the denouement. In the post-war period, Stout wrote quickly, a single draft sufficing, taking on the average only thirty-eight days to produce a novel, twelve days for a short novel. "'My father won't retire,'" Barbara, Stout's oldest daughter, once told Clifton Fadiman. "'He has nothing to retire from.'"[11] For many of these years, Stout's personal quota was a novel *per annum* and one or two short novels. The rest of his time was spent in activities other than writing. No wonder Robert Van Gelder was prompted to remark in *The New York Times* that "one has the impression that he has lived more and worked less than the majority of his peers."[12]

Stout never reread his Nero Wolfe stories which permitted all manner of discrepancies to creep into the cycle. For example, in *Too Many Cooks* Wolfe calls Inspector Cramer from West Virginia to ask him to trace the murderer's actions in New York. In *A Right to Die*, Wolfe says to Cramer in conversation: "'I believe I have never told you of an experience I had years ago at a place in West Virginia.'"[13] Stout also could change his mind about the identity of a murderer. His stories were never so tightly plotted that they would allow only a single determination. "Murder Is No Joke," a short novel contained in the collection *And Four to Go* (1958), was expanded originally at the request of *The Saturday Evening Post* and it became "Frame-up for Murder" in its new incarnation. The basic plot is totally improbable in both versions, but the identity of the murderer is different! In the rewriting of the short novel "Counterfeit for Murder," contained in *Homicide Trinity* (1962), Stout so liked the character that was killed off in the first version that he decided on another victim altogether, although here the identity of the murderer remained the same.

The finest remark that can be said about any writer is that he is rereadable. That certainly is true of Rex Stout, whatever else may be said about his Nero Wolfe stories. After all, the stories are in the last analysis a splendidly humorous commentary on life and that is the true source of their subtle magic. When asked in old age what he thought about someone else continuing the Wolfe saga, Stout was succinct: "I don't know whether vampirism or cannibalism is the better term for it. Not nice. They should roll their own."[14] Now that another author, with the concurrence of the estate, has undertaken to do just that, Stout still has the last laugh. It cannot be done. Nero Wolfe and Archie Goodwin were too much a part of their creator ever to be duplicated.

In the Nero Wolfe stories, Stout constantly exposes hypocrisy and artifice. The detective story form was the perfect vehicle for him to do this. By its conventions, he could assemble a widely divergent assortment of people who, under an external and inexorable stimulus, are forced to show themselves for what they are. Sex, greed, power, and vanity motivate most human behavior. Stout specialized in ridiculing vanity. This was the impulse of his muse and it explains, I think, the delight we take in reading his fiction. Most of us cannot admire a man we cannot laugh at occasionally. Such laughter reminds us of our common humanity. Sadly, we are sufficiently absent-minded about it to stand in need of frequent reminders. To have managed to do that as well as Rex Stout did is no little achievement.

It's Murder, My Sweet

When I lived in Los Angeles, the book review section of *The Los Angeles Times* occasionally would include book reviews by Dorothy B. Hughes. She was born at Kansas City, Missouri. She attended the University of Missouri, Columbia University, and the University of New Mexico. Her earliest literary efforts were in the field of poetry. Then she wrote a mystery story, *The So Blue Marble* (1940). It received excellent reviews. During the next seven years, Hughes published eleven books, many of them memorable. Then came a tapering off, until an eleven-year gap followed the appearance of *The Davidian Report* (1952) and the publication of her last novel in 1963. According to Hughes, the reason she stopped writing novels was domestic. Her mother lived with her and was ill. Her children were getting started in marriages and there were grandchildren for her to help care for. She lacked the tranquility required to write, but she managed to keep her hand in by reviewing mysteries. Reviewing had always been very important to her. Then, in 1978 Bantam Books began reissuing her novels in paperback editions, starting with *Ride the Pink Horse* (1946) and *In a Lonely Place* (1947) and following up with *The Fallen Sparrow* (1942), *The So Blue Marble,* and *The Davidian Report.*

I do not know who first said it — I heard it at a cocktail party — but it has been remarked that women cannot write good suspense thrillers because their wombs get in the way! Not only is this male chauvinism, in Hughes' case nothing could be further from the truth. She is one of the very few authors, male or female, who proved herself a master of the hard-boiled style. Her prose often scintillates with dark metaphors, even as her male protagonists came to embody the torment and desperation of modern man's condition in post-war America. The agonies are not always the same, although they are related. The taut frustration of *In a Lonely Place* derives from the tension and anxiety of being found out, even by yourself; while that of *Ride the Pink Horse* comes as a result of having been cut off from a past both familiar and questionable and to awake suddenly in a strange and alien place, Santa Fe, New Mexico, during Fiesta, with no room in which to stay but a prospect of money which might assuage the loss of everything else.

Both of these novels have been adapted as motion pictures, but awareness of the film versions will inevitably prove misleading since the story-lines were drastically changed for the screen. *In a Lonely Place* (Columbia, 1950) starred Humphrey Bogart as Dix Steele and Gloria Grahame as Laurel Gray and was directed by Nicholas Ray. A still from the film is on the cover of the paperback reissue. Yet the film story is so different from the novel as to have no real connection. The book is a study in subjectivism and insanity, filled with a nightmarish atmosphere at times more real than reality. The Laurel Gray character, when first we meet her in the book, remains one of the truly original creations in mystery fiction. "He didn't move," we are told of Dix Steele's reaction. "He stood and watched her, his mouth still open. She walked like a model, swaying her small buttocks. She had exquisite legs. She knew he was watching her and she didn't care. She expected it."[1] The film in its own way is an admirable *tour de force,* but it is not the novel, and, for those who haven't read it, the novel is an experience which perhaps ought not to be missed.

Even better, in my opinion, is *Ride the Pink Horse.* Here again, the film starring Robert Montgomery and Wanda Hendrix and directed by Montgomery, like *In a Lonely Place,* is in the *film noir* style, but it cannot, because of the nature of film and the era in which it was made—*Ride the Pink Horse* was released by Universal in 1947—approach the complexity of the novel nor hope to encompass its probing, unsettling themes of disillusionment and, above all, the clash of cultures. As in the best of Harvey Fergusson's fiction, another author who dealt with the antinomies and conflicts inherent in New Mexican culture, the Santa Fe setting of *Ride the Pink Horse* brings together Anglo-Americans, Mexican-Americans, and Native Americans. The two most memorable characters in this novel are Native Americans, the merry-go-round operator, a mixed blood whom the protagonist calls Pancho, and Pila, an Indian girl. They come, in fact, to have more reality for Sailor, the protagonist, than he has for himself. "She was there," he reflects about Pila. "She existed. He was the one without existence, the dream figure wandering in this dreadful nightmare."[2]

Erle Stanley Gardner: The Case of the Real Perry Mason (1978) is Dorothy B. Hughes' first book in fifteen years and her first attempt at biography. There is no question that Gardner is a man deserving of a biography. He led an unusual life, one filled with extraordinary achievements, but somehow all we get of Gardner in Hughes' biography are the externals; the man no more comes to life than do most of the characters in his many novels. According to the latest figures, Hughes informs us, Gardner's eighty-two Perry Mason books in all editions have sold more than 300,000,000 copies. This is an impressive number, to be sure, and it may even be unique, although the late Agatha Christie probably isn't too far behind. Yet a biographer, and beyond this a critic of Hughes' stature, to say nothing of her talent as a novelist, should not confuse sales figures with literary quality, an error which the late Frank Gruber was continually prone to commit in his adulatory *Zane Grey: A Biography* (1970). In Gruber's case, he had been hired by Zane Grey, Inc., to write the "official" biography and his familiarity with Grey's novels was so slight that on the few occasions when he did refer to a particular plot he got it wrong. This is pardonable, I suppose, insofar as the biography he wrote was intended as a sales tool and an exercise, on behalf of Grey's heirs, in self-congratulatory chest-thumping. Hughes was asked to write her biography not by Gardner's estate but by Leonard Hughes — no relation — of William Morrow, Gardner's publisher. Despite the evidence to the contrary, Hughes states unequivocally that Gardner's last book, *The Case of the Postponed Murder,* published posthumously in 1973, "was as sharp and spunky as if it was the first book in the series."[3] Hughes rejects completely the rather widely held opinion that Gardner's work underwent a gradual decline, especially after 1945, and she attests "as the years went on, and I began to hear of his work being taken for granted and even sloughed off by certain critics, I climbed staunchly on my soapbox. I never missed an opportunity in my critiques to point out his importance as a writer."[4]

It has become an accepted convention among critics of detective fiction *not* to reveal a murderer's identity in their assessments of a particular novel. I think in terms of book reviews of current detective fiction this convention ought to be respected; but if, instead of writing a review, a critic is attempting to evaluate a subject's importance as a writer, which objective Hughes gave herself, there is no need to be bound by this convention. In the first place, Gardner himself claimed that his finest attribute was his ability to plot a detective story; and, in the second place, if plot is to be given the preference over character which he gave it, then how can an author be critically evaluated without at least examining some of his plots? Hughes chose to remain tacit on this. I believe it to have been a mistake. It does, however, explain why only Gardner's own opinions of his books and his sales figures are discussed.

Hughes quotes Gardner as remarking about his book, *The Case of the Counterfeit Eye* (1935), that it has a "fast-moving story, an unusual plot development, a semblance of reality, and a touch of driving characterization. If I have done this, what more can the bastards ask?"[5] I hope, without declaring myself to be too much of a bastard, that there is one more thing I would ask and which is all too often lacking in detective stories: plausibility. In *The Case of the Counterfeit Eye,* Mason's client wears a glass eye. He has a number of different glass eyes for the various times of day and one that is blood-shot for when he is hungover. The blood-shot eye is stolen and a substitute of a cheaper kind is left in its place. When the unscrupulous money-lender, Hartley Basset, is found murdered, the missing glass eye is in his hand. An eyewitness claims to have seen a man run from the murder room, his face hidden by a make-shift mask consisting of a sheet of carbonpaper with two holes punched in it for the eyes. In one of the holes only an empty, gaping eye socket is visible. Now Mason's reasoning is to the point: his client would have had to be a fool so to call attention to his malady, not merely leaving his glass eye behind but punching a hole in the carbonpaper so his blank socket would be apparent! Therefore, as Mason explains in the privacy of the judge's chambers during the course of the trial, "'if some other person in that household had an artificial eye and that fact was not suspected by any of the other persons in the house, he would have gone to great lengths to have made it appear that the crime was committed by a person who had only one eye. . . .'"[6] If we were, however, to submit this case to the modern calculus of probability, it cannot but stagger credulity.

For example, what is the probability that one would draw from an ordinary deck of playing cards two cards both of which would be red? If we use a formula in which "h" is equal to the datum that an ordinary deck consists of 26 red cards and 26 black cards and "p" stands for the equivalent that "the first card is red" and "q" for the equivalent that "the second card is red," then "$(p \text{ and } q)/h$" is the chance that both are red, "p/h" is the chance that the first is red, and "$q/(p \text{ and } h)$" is the chance that the second is red, given that the first is red. Thus "p/h" = ½ and "$q/(p \text{ and } h)$" = 25/51. In terms of the calculus of probability, the chance that both would be red is ½ x 25/51. When this formula is applied to a structured card game such as poker, the calculus of probability indicates that one will be dealt at least one pair in every two hands, that one will receive two pair once in every twenty-one hands, and that one may expect to be dealt a straight flush once in every 65,000 hands. When it comes then to *The Case of the Counterfeit Eye,* if, at the time the book was written, it was likely that out of a population of 70,000,000 American males there were as many as 100,000 who possessed glass eyes which fit perfectly due to 5% or less socket damage when the eye loss occurred, the reader can use this same formula to determine just what would be the chance of two such persons being involved in the same place at the same time.

I bring up the point because Gardner objected vociferously and repeatedly that too many detective stories were filled with utter improbabilities. When he saw that *The Saturday Evening Post* had purchased Agatha Christie's *The Body in the Library* (1942) to be serialized prior to book publication, he became "particularly interested in it because I saw she had got herself into such a position that, to my mind, there was no *logical* way out. But then she starts her chapter of explanation—oh, my God! But the point is the *Post* bought this story. More and more readers are reading Agatha Christie. The same is true of about half a dozen other writers whose stuff is full of improbabilities."[7] It ought to be pointed out, however, in Gardner's defense that improbability is not so persistently frustrating in his fiction as it is in stories by Ellery Queen, Agatha Christie, and a good many others. Most often the improbabilities in his fiction have to do with time laws which Gardner invariably subjected to the exigencies of fast pacing. "Erle violated time laws over and again—when he felt that hewing to the fact would slow down his story," Hughes wrote. His editors, she added, never "let him get by with it, even if, as a usual thing, he ignored their findings."[8] This is a serious fault. Take *The Bigger They Come* (1939), the first of the Bertha Cool/Donald Lam novels Gardner wrote under his A.A. Fair pseudonym. In an incredible time sequence Donald Lam listens to Alma Hunter's story at the agency office. He then goes to lunch with Alma, after which they go together to Sandra Birks' apartment. Donald has a talk with Sandra's brother Bleetie (who turns out to be the missing man Donald has been hired to find, only in disguise). Donald then talks to Sandra and gets some photographs from her before he returns to the office. Upon his arrival at the office, he notes the time, because Bertha is out to lunch. All of this has been accomplished in fifty-five minutes! Even in 1939, it was not possible to get around Los Angeles that quickly.

To me implausibilities and impossible timetables are, however, still short-comings in fiction of any kind. They should not be over-looked or discounted in any author merely because of sales volume. The fact of the matter is that Gardner at times in the beginning took in-sufficient care in writing his books and this carelessness increased over the years. In *The Case of the Daring Divorcee* (1964), a book of 172 pages, the murderer isn't introduced until page 102 and he isn't heard of again until Mason pulls him out of the hat in the final chapter. Murderer is perhaps too exalted a word to describe a name, without anything more than that to make him even a paste-board figure, much less a character.

Gardner, however, did have virtues as a writer. He was a master of pacing, even though this was largely the result of confining himself to dialogue and one-sentence descriptive paragraphs, a technique he learned while writing for the pulps. (Pulp writers like Gardner with their immense popular influence have, in fact, affected fiction to a degree in the United States that the stylistic elegance and grace of a Henry James or even of a Scott Fitzgerald would be unthinkable in a contemporary novelist.) In the first Perry Mason novel, *The Case of the Velvet Claws* (1933), when Mason tells his client that people come to him because of what he can do for them, his client asks him just what it is he does. "He snapped out two words at her. 'I fight.'"[9] This aggressive attitude is what made Mason so extraordinary as an attorney and may account at least to some degree for his popularity. As Gardner became more and more successful, he began to alter somewhat Mason's character and the permissible means by which he could fight for his clients. During the last two decades of his life, Gardner became so entrenched with the Establishment and so enamored of the prestige he had been accorded that the early Perry Mason might as little have recognized him as he, the early Mason. The same thing, as Hughes does note, took place when Gardner upgraded the image of the police, replacing the fractious Sergeant Holcolm with the more sophisticated Lieutenant Tragg. Yet, in the final analysis what may have contributed most to Gardner's outstanding sales record might not have been the early fighting Mason or his later endorsement of the Establishment; it may well have been just the sheer volume of books he produced coupled with the expertise with which they were marketed by both Morrow and Pocket Books.

Gardner's editor and friend at William Morrow was Thayer Hobson, the president of the firm in 1933 when the first Perry Mason novel was submitted. Hughes is apparently unaware that Gardner's first novel was rejected by several publishers prior to Hobson's reading it. Gardner submitted a second book to Hobson before Hobson suggested both should be rewritten and the lawyer/detective made a series character, a fact which Hughes does mention although she seemed not to know that the name Perry Mason derived from a character in *The Seven Pearls* (Pathé, 1917), a movie serial! Nor was she apparently cognizant that it was Thayer Hobson who launched the successful Peter Field/Powder Valley Western series, writing the first three himself and then hiring a number of other writers to ghost the rest of the series. For years Gardner wrote introductions to Morrow's Triple-A Western Classics and Hobson even set up the Jefferson House division of Morrow to handle the books and protect Gardner's introductions. Each introduction meant Gardner's name on the cover of another book and added to his public exposure.

Yet, if I am befuddled by how little of Hughes' critical sensibility carried over to her biography, I am even more disappointed that, having had access to so many original documents, she still failed to show in any significant way how precisely through a joint venture between publisher and author Erle Stanley Gardner was mass-merchandised into the best-selling category. About the only conceivable excuse I might imagine for this omission would be a biographer's prerogative to concentrate on the personal life of the subject, but it is here that the book is at its sketchiest. There are several chapters devoted to naming people intimate to Gardner but unknown outside his personal circle. They are not introduced to demonstrate how they influenced Gardner's life or his work; they are just names named.

Two years before he died in 1970, Gardner married Jean Bethel *née* Agnes Walter, his principal secretary and companion for forty years. Gardner was separated from his wife *née* Natalie Talbert in 1931. They were never divorced, nor would Gardner have contemplated marriage until after her death, however lightly he may have treated divorce and remarriage in novels like *Give 'em the Ax* (1944). This was one of the curiosities about him and his peculiar relationship with Jean carried over to the scrupulous way in the Perry Mason novels he described Mason's association with Della Street. Film director Edward Dmytryk knew Gardner in the early thirties when both were living in Los Angeles. Dmytryk once recalled how he went to a party given by Gardner and his wife and, when it came time to leave, how Gardner left with the other guests since he lived by himself further on down the street.

In criticizing Hughes' biography of Gardner it might appear as if I blame her personally for writing such a long book about a popular writer and an interesting man only to leave out almost everything an inquisitive reader would want to know and have every right to expect. After all, it does seem to be a truism that once a writer has taken his final leave, should he have been fortunate enough to have excited a loyal readership during his lifetime, his life becomes even more an object of study than the books he leaves behind. But I do not know how many of the failings of Hughes' biography are to be laid at her door. There are errors, such as the remark that Raymond Chandler was a screenwriter in 1934 when he wasn't one until much later; but what book hasn't its share of minor errors? I attach little significance to them. Rather, in view of how carefully Gardner's memory is guarded by his estate, we perhaps ought to be grateful for even this much. Hughes glosses over Gardner's lingering death from cancer, and this I know from personal knowledge is as the estate wishes it to be. There was combined in Erle Stanley Gardner the contradictions of the hack writer who wrote only for money to support his extravagant, paternalistic, but wholly independent lifestyle contrasted with the ardent crusader who believed in fighting even for lost causes, the very private man almost obscured by the public image created in order to market his books. Someday I hope someone will do Gardner the honor of introducing him to us as he was. Until such a time, Hughes' biography is the best to be had.

The Expendable Man (1963) was Hughes' last work of fiction. Briefly told, it is the story of a young black intern who gives a hitch-hiking teenage girl a ride from Indio, California, to Phoenix, Arizona. Once in Phoenix, the girl is murdered. It is also found that, before she died, she had undergone an abortion. Throughout the rest of the book, two racially bigotted Phoenix cops try to tag the black intern with the murder because of his color and refuse at almost every turn to follow any clues that might lead away from him. The intern, in a desperate effort, tries to find the abortionist and the girl's lover in order to save himself from being railroaded. Sound familiar? It should, if you are acquainted with John Ball's *In the Heat of the Night* (1965) and the subsequent film version released by United Artists in 1967. The late Anthony Boucher who seems to have permanently endeared himself to mystery writers because of the constant superlatives — often undeserved — with which he celebrated their efforts declared *The Expendable Man* to be Hughes' finest novel to that time. Two years later, when he reviewed *In the Heat of the Night,* Boucher had similar high praise to bestow, predicting that Ball's protagonist would probably become one of the great fictional detectives, but there was no mention of any of the similarities between the plots of the two books. Ball's protagonist is a black policeman who becomes involved in a murder case far from home in which he is the prime suspect of a racially bigotted local cop and who must find an abortionist in order to clear himself. As for the film version, almost any motion picture in the late sixties which paid lip-service to satirizing white prejudice toward blacks would have won wide-spread endorsement, as *In the Heat of the Night* did. However, John C. Mahoney, reviewing the film for *The Hollywood Reporter,* probably was more accurate when he accused Ball and screenwriter Stirling Silliphant of creating not characters but rather clichés which have long made Southern playwrights and novelists the object of ridicule and satire.

Personally, I do not believe Hughes' novel warranted Boucher's excess of praise, but I find it to be superior to Ball's effort. Subsequently, in his series of Virgil Tibbs sequels, Ball saved himself the necessity of having to characterize much of anybody other than his black policeman who is a white man's version of a black with wholly white values. Of course the vein had to run out eventually and, when it did, Ball came up with another scheme epitomized by the appearance of *The Mystery Story* (1976) which he edited. The hard-bound edition was originally published by the University of California Press and then reprinted as a paperback by Penguin Books. There is a clique of mystery story sycophants who spend their time writing laudatory reviews of each other's books and write each other open letters published in *The Armchair Detective,* a quarterly journal once published by the University of California at San Diego which also used to sponsor an annual visit to Los Angeles/San Diego by this group to help John Ball select titles for reissue in the University's mystery story reprint series and to conduct a seminar open to the public. I happened by accident upon this group one night when it was holding a celebration it called a "Bouchercon" at the Pacifica Hotel in Los Angeles. The guest of the evening was Mrs. Anthony Boucher and as part of the ritual honoring her husband's memory there was to be a special showing, reverently attended by all these professors and scholars of the mystery story, of a chapter from *Gangbusters,* a Universal serial of 1942. In case you are wondering who is included in this group, most of the members have contributed essays to *The Mystery Story.* The dean of the University

Extension provided the Introduction and it's a hard sell all the way, filled with descriptive words (for the contributors) like "world renown," "most distinguished personalities," "dean of all mystery-story collectors," "international stature," "a reputation . . . that can hardly be surpassed," "novelist of distinction," "anthropologist of distinction," and "international fame." As if this isn't enough, there are line drawings of each of the contributors preceding their essays and more of the same hype. Ball himself contributed two essays. In "Murder at Large," which leads off the book, after a superficial overview of mystery stories, he comes to the conclusion that "probability is not an essential ingredient."[10] In his second essay, "The Ethnic Detective," despite the fact that the dean has already told the reader so in his Introduction and it has been repeated again in the credits alongside Ball's portrait, he has to inform us a third time that *In the Heat of the Night* won "both the Edgar Award in the United States and the Golden Dagger in England" and that the "film received five Academy Awards. . . ."[11]

Donald A. Yates who wrote the essay "Locked Rooms and Puzzles: A Critical Memoir" is, to put it charitably, a buffoon. Carrying the philosophy of never discussing mystery story plots to its most ridiculous extreme, Yates refused even to mention any titles so that a reader is informed that on any list of locked room mysteries "there would be at least one book each by Agatha Christie, Freeman Wills Crofts, Michael Gilbert, Harry Stephen Keeler, John Rhode, Hake Talbot, S.S. Van Dine, Edgar Wallace, and Anthony Wynne."[12] Somehow, John Dickson Carr who under his own name or writing as Carter Dickson specialized in locked room murder mysteries is not even mentioned and you can bet Yates wasn't about to give away willingly the titles to any of the books by any of the authors he did mention in case you might be sufficiently intrigued to want to read one!

The other essays, too, are mostly more of the same: lists and more lists, titles of books, mention of detectives, but never is there anything intelligent or interesting said about them. There is trivia galore, however, as for example when the reader is informed not once but twice that in the first three Dr. Fu Manchu books by Sax Rohmer the Fu and Manchu were hyphenated but not in the later books. On the cover, this purports to be "an introduction to detective-mystery fiction." It isn't that. It's a scam. Only the contributions by Robert E. Briney, a sympathetic and sensitive reader and critic of fantasy fiction, and the two essays provided by author Hillary Waugh save the book from being a total debacle.

Far more encouraging is *Dimensions of Detective Fiction* (1976) edited by Larry N. Landrum, Pat Browne, and Ray B. Browne. I have read just about every anthology of criticism about detective fiction and I continue to find that Howard Haycraft's *The Art of the Mystery Story* (1946) is the best to be had; but *Dimensions of Detective Fiction* published by Bowling Green University Popular Press is its modern counterpart. Briney in the foreword to his annotated bibliography in *The Mystery Story* suggests "reading *about* mystery fiction can be almost as habit-forming as reading the fiction itself."[13] *Dimensions of Detective Fiction* proves his case. The twenty-three essays which it contains—thirteen of them original, ten of them reprints—are more thought-provoking than much that is in Haycraft's collection and, among modern collections, inviting even to the casual reader.

Since the majority of these essays are by academics, they suffer occasionally from dullness, but this is never the case with the best of them. George Grella in an essay on what is known as the formal, or English, detective story demonstrates how it is a descendant of the comedy of manners and hence the close relationship it bears to the works of Henry James. Mick Gidley shows how much William Faulkner owed to S.S. Van Dine's detective, Philo Vance, in creating his own detectives in the Yoknapatawpha sage while Douglas G. Tallack traces the influences of the so-called "tough guy" school—Hemingway, Hammett, Chandler, Horace McCoy, and James M. Cain—on Faulkner's *Sanctuary* (1931) and his other novels from the thirties. Tallack also makes mention of that body of French literary criticism which cites Faulkner as the father of the *roman noir*, the literary equivalent of *film noir*, and quotes a reviewer in *Samedi Soir* who wrote that *"le Sanctuaire perut en son temps le comble de l'audace et de la noirceur...."*[14] In Hammett's work, Tallack finds "the style and technique are almost the subject."[15] He recognizes the fact that literary objectivity was indebted most to John B. Watson's Behaviorism and that, as Behaviorists do to this day, the objective stylists reject subjectivism in order to reduce psychological reality to only its consequences without any inquiry into motivation. Tallack also cites the *films noirs* of Fritz Lang which depict the individual as hopelessly crushed by the combination of environment and heredity. In a similarly insightful essay on Eric Ambler's spy fiction, Ronald Ambrosetti finds that "Ambler's protagonists are ... grimly reminded through tragic circumstances that human happiness is too easily subject to chance and fate."[16] Add to this George Orwell's observation that Edgar Wallace's

Establishment detectives and G.K. Chesterton's Father Brown stories are reflections of an age of totalitarian ideology—a point made in Patrick Parrinder's "George Orwell and the Detective Story"—and Elliott L. Gilbert's observation in a different essay—that "every effort made by a detective to increase the amount of good and order in any portion of society has the inevitable effect of increasing the amount of evil and disorder in the society as a whole"[17]—and you have just a sampling of the ideas, fecund and rampant, to be found in this remarkable anthology.

Perhaps the weakest essay in *Dimensions of Detective Fiction* is that devoted to the female of the species which devolves mostly into feminist carping, but this shortcoming is somewhat compensated for by consulting Michele B. Slung's anthology, *Crime on Her Mind* (1975). Slung is a member of the clique that participated in *The Mystery Story* and her essay on women in crime fiction there illustrates little more than bibliographical mania, but her membership does probably explain why Allen J. Hubin, another member of the clique, declared that *Crime on Her Mind* is a "delight" to read. This is scarcely accurate. Many of the stories which Slung included date from the Victorian and Edwardian ages and are hard-going for a modern reader. If they were not detective stories and were not about female detectives, it is unlikely that anyone would be motivated to read them. Yet, in a sense, we are fortunate that there are these added inducements since this anthology *is* well worth reading, not for delight so much as to realize the literary milieu from which our contemporary fiction has come and the truly striking changes in the image of social reality which has occurred in detective fiction since the American hard-boiled school rose to prominence. Nancy Y. Hoffman in "Mistresses of Malfeasance" in *Dimensions of Detective Fiction* comments that Anna Katherine Green's Violet Strange who made her debut in 1915 "was probably the first women detective extant, with disturbingly few successors despite the numbers of women detective writers."[18] Slung's anthology, with its comprehensive introduction, annotations, and bibliographies, not only disproves this assertion but, if an interested reader follows her advice, especially in the bibliography, there are a number of quite fascinating, little-known books waiting to be discovered, such as the two Gale Gallagher novels Will Ourseler and Margaret Scott cowrote under the Gallagher pseudonym about Gale who heads up her own agency, the Acme Investigating Bureau. There are also at the very least a dozen more of comparable quality. Slung in her anthology, therefore, achieves what every anthologist diligently should strive to do: she strikes myriad new paths for her reader in literary exploration and she manages it by creating a sense of excitement. To have that experience I do not even mind reading a story by Anna Katherine Green.

Another anthology to appear recently is *The Great American Detective* (1978) edited with an Introduction by William Kittredge and Steven M. Krauzer. Their selection of stories is impressive, including a few hard-to-find items such as "Too Many Have Lived," one of Dashiell Hammett's three Sam Spade short stories, and the stylistically fantastic "The Lake of the Left-Hand Moon" by Robert Leslie Bellem. My quarrel is with the editors' Introduction in which they assert that "social institutions such as democracy and due process are of course necessary; if they are not the most effective way of punishing the guilty, they constitute the most foolproof system for protecting the innocent."[19] There are a number of people — and I am one of them — who would disagree with that. I believe the editors of *Dimensions of Detective Fiction* come closer to the mark when they comment that the private detective hero "lives on the fringes of crime, which area is usually pictured as a somewhat dirty mirror of the moral and legal authority structure or indeed a part of it."[20] Edward Dmytryk put it so aptly in his autobiography, *It's a Hell of a Life but Not a Bad Living* (1978): "In America, as in any other country on this earth, if you're rich, you're innocent until proven guilty. If you are poor, you are guilty as hell the moment the law lays its heavy hand on your shoulder."[21] The deepest thrusts of detective fiction lie in its endeavor to mirror the rather unseemly side of human reality which, ordinarily, we would rather not acknowledge, the netherworld of corruption in which we all live, in which we are all victims, and from which there often doesn't seem to be any viable means of escape. Kittredge and Krauzer also insist that "we will even accept the role of the outlaw as justice's guardian when we are convinced beyond a doubt that a criminal needs and deserves arm-breaking or teeth-shoving."[21] There are probably also a number of people who would agree with that — but I am *not* one of them. The editors, in thinking this way, have only come to the same conclusion promoted by so much popular fiction: that individual vigilantism is the most workable solution for social problems. George Orwell perceived in this tendency the triumph of the bully over those who are weaker, an endorsement of raw and brutal power, "a love of cruelty and wickedness *for their own sakes,*"[22] that which reduces to "might is right": *vae victis.*

Finally, Chris Steinbrunner, who with Otto Penzler coedited the *Encyclopedia of Mystery and Detection* (1976), has with a new collaborator, Norman Michaels, produced in *The Films of Sherlock Holmes* (1978) *the* book about Sherlock Holmes on the screen. My book for this Citadel series, *The Films of Mae West* (1973), was the first one to break away from what had been the accepted pattern for such books: photographs, a brief plot synopsis, and block quotations from various reviews of individual films. Since this series is intended primarily for the buff, I tried to include as much background and production information on each film as I could. Steinbrunner and Michaels wisely opted to do the same thing for the Sherlock Holmes films. I say wisely because, as difficult as this might make such a book to read from cover to cover unless you are extremely interested in the subject, it serves a higher purpose, namely to provide a complete reference source.

What so many of these books do point up, however, is that notwithstanding the fact that one out of every four novels published in the English language is a mystery story no one has as yet written an objective history of detective and mystery fiction. There have been several books, such as Julian Symons' *Mortal Consequences* (1972), which argue specialized theses, but none that is sufficiently removed to be wholly dispassionate. All in all the problem with much that is written about detective fiction remains that the majority of the writers are either buffs who purposely have exposure to little other than their specialty, or academics who are trained to analyze fiction and film rather than imaginatively to enjoy them. My own interests have never been so circumscribed and much of what I have read in the genre and about it has been a consequence of books I have wanted to write rather than a voluntary inclination; yet I certainly do believe that the detective stories I have read, if they have done nothing else, have made me a very careful reader. To have had this occur is something for which I have never had any cause for regret.

The American West in Fiction

I was in Seattle, Washington, the other day and went into a brief council with Mark Hoover. He is my friend; he is an Aleut. We first met when we worked together on *Images of Indians* (PBS, 1980). Mark and I know well the words Seathl, Dwamish chief, spoke to Isaac Stevens, Governor of Washington Territory in 1854. "And when," he said, "the last red man shall have perished, and the memory of my tribe shall have become a myth among the white men, these shores will swarm with the invisible dead of my tribe, and when your children's children think themselves alone in the field, the store, the shop, upon the highway, or in the silence of the pathless woods, they will not be alone. At night when the streets of your cities and villages are silent and you think them deserted, they will throng with the returning hosts that once filled and still love this beautiful land. The white man will never be alone."[1]

Mark composed the music for *Images of Indians*. His music does not justify the belief that the last red man has perished, because the Native American is ever with us, physically and spiritually. It will not justify any tribe having become only a myth. His music instead justified Seathl's conviction that we, the white men and women, are not and cannot ever be alone in this land we now call America. We are only the latest immigrants. We are very arrogant. We do not yet realize that this land made the red men what they were and what they are; that it works its magic slowly; and that in the thousands of years which lie ahead it will not ultimately be we who remake this land: it will remake us.

That is what we said to each other in our brief council.

I

It was in 1922 that Zane Grey wrote *The Vanishing American* (1925) and that it appeared in the *Ladies' Home Journal,* a Curtis publication as were *The Saturday Evening Post* and *The Country Gentleman.* The story told of Nophaie, a full-blood Navaho brave, kidnapped when a child and educated by whites, returning to his

reservation as a young man only to find it dominated by an unscrupulous Indian agent and, still worse, a vicious missionary who uses his dogmatic beliefs to get his way. If Grey had a philosophy at all, he was a social Darwinist, a man who believed that human existence and the survival of the races are guided by the ineluctable laws of an evolutionary scheme which endorses industrial progress and endows white civilization with a natural superiority provided, however, that what Grey meant by the "heritage of the desert," the need to conquer the elements of Nature, is kept in mind. In one of Grey's Indian stories, "Blue Feather," unpublished until long after his death when it appeared in *Blue Feather and Other Stories* (1961), Grey conveyed his vision of evolutionary social history, highest to lowest: "Human being, man, Indian, savage, primitive beast."[2]

In *The Vanishing American,* Grey stripped Nophaie of his Nopah religion but also made him reject the missionary's Christianity as well, arriving instead at some nebulous patheism in which the white Christ and Nature are dual manifestations of God. Grey summed up his view of the Native American this way: "Indians were merely closer to the original animal progenitor of human beings."[3] Nophaie falls in love with the blonde-haired, blue-eyed school teacher and, so inspired by his love does he become, that he is prompted to enforce among his own people Grey's prejudice concerning the supreme importance of sexual virginity prior to marriage. Morgan, the missionary, likes to seduce young Indian maidens at his mission school. One of them, Gekin Yasha, is taught by Nophaie that "'when a white woman loves she holds herself sacred for the man who has won her.'"[4] This moral exhortation doesn't do Gekin Yasha much good. She is seduced by Morgan, becomes pregnant, returns to the reservation and marries an Indian, only to pay the price in Zane Grey's West that often is paid by those who indulge in sexual intercourse outside of marriage, no matter what the circumstances: she dies.

In the magazine version, Nophaie, as part of his dramatic betrayal of himself and his people, comments: "'Let the Indians marry white women and Indian girls marry white men. It would make for a more virile race . . . absorbed by the race that has destroyed him. Red blood into white! It means the white race will gain and the Indian

On the set of *The Vanishing American* (Paramount, 1925) with Lois Wilson on the left, Richard Dix on the right, and director George B. Seitz in white shirt. Photo courtesy of the Museum of Modern Art.

vanish....'"⁵ And so Grey furthered a notion which had come to replace James Fenimore Cooper's division of Native Americans into either villains or noble savages; Nophaie is a *romantic* savage who wants to vanish for the betterment of the white race. "'Examples of the white man's better ways would inevitably follow association,'" he says.⁶ The magazine version ended with Nophaie and the yellow hair in each other's arms, about to achieve Grey's synthesis of "red blood into white." But this ending, to say nothing of Grey's treatment of Christian missionaries, caused such a furor at the *Ladies' Home Journal,* what with thousands upon thousands of angry letters of protest, that Harper's refused to publish the magazine serial as a book until Grey changed the ending. This he did. In the book version he had Nophaie fatally shot and, dying, he murmurs "'vanishing ... vanishing ... vanishing.'"⁷ No doubt this was a preferable ending to the story for Grey's many white readers.

Grey had stepped up his production to get more money from the magazines and, hence, Harper's was building up a backlog of novels, willing to publish usually two a year whereas Grey was writing three and sometimes four a year. Since Paramount Pictures frequently filmed Grey's books when they were still in magazine serial form, for the motion picture version of *The Vanishing American* (Paramount, 1925) Lucien Hubbard, who did the adaptation, borrowed a portion from the first chapter of *The Thundering Herd* (1925) and some from "Blue Feather." In this way the film could have a Prologue in which it could be shown visually how the Indians had preyed on each other, one tribe wiping out another, albeit weaker, tribe until at last the culmination of evolution had been reached, the white man had arrived in the New World and with his coming signaled to all Native Americans who might have survived the evolutionary struggle thus far that the time had come for them to vanish. The film also adopted the new ending Grey had provided for the book version.

Nor was this all of it. After the unhappy experience with *The Vanishing American,* all Curtis publications adopted an editorial policy prohibiting authors of Western stories and serials from characterizing Native Americans in their fiction. Indians could be present, but, if they were, they were either minor characters or renegades on the war path. The far-reaching effects of this decision can be seen in a number of the serials which ran in *The Saturday Evening Post* and which were sub-sequently made into films: Ernest Haycox' *Bugles in the Afternoon* in 1943 and *Canyon Passage* in 1945, Luke Short's *Ambush* in 1948, Alan

LeMay's *The Searchers* in 1954 and *The Unforgiven* in 1957, many of James Warner Bellah's stories about Fort Starke (four of which were used to comprise John Ford's Cavalry trilogy), Will Cook's *Comanche Captives* from 1959 which was filmed under the title *Two Rode Together* (Columbia, 1961). I could go on, but the point is just this: when the Indians were not characterized in the original stories, it would be absurd to expect that they would somehow come to be differently characterized in the films based on those stories. Editors were telling Western writers to tell lies if they expected to be published, and so Western writers were telling lies.

I will admit that some of those writing Western fiction during these years probably didn't know anything about Western history; or, if they did, they held history in the same contempt that so many Americans do today. They probably comforted themselves with the notion that deceit had nothing to do with it; their only objective was to entertain, to spin a good yarn, to tell an interesting story. The moral issue of the responsibility any artist has to be the conscience of his culture either didn't appeal to them or didn't occur to them. In the words of one of Will Cook's characters in *Comanche Captives* concerning the manner in which he deceives his feeble-minded wife, words which John Ford personally believed (as he once told me) and so made sure they were also in the screenplay: "'. . . If I can give her comfort in a lie, then I guess God won't kick me out of heaven for it.'"[8]

But for one of the writers whom I have named above I can tell the reader it wasn't this way. When he died, Ernest Haycox' library was transferred *en masse* to the Special Collections division of the University of Oregon Library at Eugene. His widow, Jill Marie Haycox, made it a provision of the bequest that the books of her late husband be kept in a room all to itself and so it was possible for me some time ago to go through them volume by volume. Haycox once commented — and Jill Marie Haycox confirmed it to me — that he never read Western fiction. He didn't want to "borrow" something from what others had written. When he read about the American West, he read its history; and he assembled what still is an excellent library on a complex subject. He knew the story that in the most cursory fashion I am about to relate. It is recounted, much of it, in books to be found in his library.

In 1855 James Lupton, a self-proclaimed "Major," marched into Jacksonville, Oregon, with a group of Yreka volunteers. These men called a public meeting to sound out Oregonians on adopting a policy of exterminating the Indians. Things went so well for Lupton that he convened a second meeting on October 7 which consisted of a recitation of complaints against the Indians, the crowd becoming increasingly worked up. Thinking the time for action had come, once the meeting broke up Lupton led his company of volunteers to an old Indian village on Butte Creek, a short distance from the reservation. They found the village asleep and opened fire in the dark, killing without quarter everyone they could find. Eight men were shot, three of them aged, along with fifteen women and children. Charles Drew, quartermaster for the volunteers, declared the action admirably executed and only regretted that a larger number of Indians had not been killed.

"The Rogues struck back in reprisal," Stephen Dow Beckham wrote in his fine book on the subject, *Requiem for a People: The Rogue Indians and the Frontiersman* (1971), citing in his footnotes many of the basic sources Haycox had in his personal library. "Too many memories of past wrongs and injustices, too many deaths from sickness, starvation, and murder had occurred for them to trust the white men again.... At dawn on October 9 the settlers living along the river between Gold Hill and Vannoy's Ferry near Grants Pass began another workday. The actions of Lupton's volunteers were unknown to them. The Rogues, pushing down river toward the wilderness in the coast mountains, first struck the Jacob B. Wagner ranch, where they murdered Wagner's wife and daughter and left the body of Miss Sarah Pellett, a temperance lecturer on her way to Jacksonville, in the smoldering ruins."[9]

And so the Rogue War of 1855–1856 began. There were approximately 9,500 of these essentially peaceful Rogue country peoples in 1851; after the war and their removal to the Siletz reservation, there were only some 2,000.

If many of the settlers at the time didn't know about Lupton and his volunteers, neither did most of the readers of Ernest Haycox' *Canyon Passage.* Every time one of Haycox' white characters sees a Rogue, there is uneasiness; the outbreak, which occupies the final chapters of the novel and brings all the dramatic situations to a climax, is in this sense wholly predictable. All the reader sees are the atrocities committed by the Rogues against characters he has come to know and some of whom he has even come to like. There is a motivation provided for this uprising. Honey Bragg, one of Haycox' villains, sets off the hostilities when he attempts to rape and murder two Indian squaws. However, there is a very important difference between such an action—an isolated villainy—and the collective activities of Lupton and his volunteers to exterminate the Rogues; and, lest it be overlooked, Lupton had the endorsement of a majority of the Oregonians in Jacksonville. These warring Rogues were fighting for their very survival, not seeking revenge for the actions of only one evil white man.

Canyon Passage (Universal, 1946) was filmed after the novel had been serialized in *The Saturday Evening Post* and had appeared in book form. "The world premiere was to have national importance," Jill Marie Haycox recalled in her Introduction to a reissue of the novel in 1979. "The newspaper stories and radio announcements went to all parts of the U.S. There was a tie-in with the NBC radio show 'People Are Funny' giving *Canyon Passage* additional publicity. Wayne Morse, colorful Senator from Oregon, lauded the picture from the floor of the Senate. The *Congressional Record* for that day bears his entire speech which was sent out over the wires and printed by hundreds of newpapers throughout the country.... Hollywood distributors arranged for a showing of the film in Washington, D.C., for Oregon members of Congress—Senators, Representatives, and their families."[10]

The world premiere itself was held in Portland, Oregon and a number of Universal stars attended the occasion. After receiving his honorary Doctor of Literature degree from Lewis & Clark College, Haycox rode in a parade in an open convertible. According to D'Arcy McNickle's *The Indian Tribes of the United States: Ethnic and Cultural Survival* published by the London Institute of Race Relations in 1962, there were in 1946 approximately 82 Tututni and 79 Umpqua descendants of the original Rogue tribes. The decision was made to film *Canyon Passage* in Oregon to add significantly to its authenticity, but the Indians playing Rogues were not Rogues. They were Yakimas from the Yakima reserve in the State of Washington. Many of them, in Jill Marie Haycox' words, "moved into Portland" for the premiere, "using the park blocks, close to the downtown area, for their encampment. They added a lot of color with their tepees, spotted ponies, and baled hay."[11]

Of course, this whole idea of American history as a Wild West show began in the nineteenth century. Americans are so accustomed to lies in this way, it was no surprise at all to me that Robert Altman, who once told me that in all of his films he's just parodying the Greatest Show on Earth—the United States—should have titled one of his better pictures *Buffalo Bill and the Indians, or Sitting Bull's History Lesson*

(United Artists, 1976). Or, as George Orwell put it in *1984* (1949), "day by day and almost minute by minute the past was brought up to date. In this way every prediction made by the Party could be shown by documentary evidence to have been correct; nor was any item of news, or any expression of opinion, which conflicted with the needs of the moment, ever allowed to remain on record. All history was a palimpsest, scraped clean and reinscribed exactly as often as was necessary."[12]

If as Count Joseph de Maistre wrote in the nineteenth century ". . . *le véritable vainqueur, comme le véritable vaincu, c'est celui croit l'être,*"[13] then it is the same with historical personalities and the events of history; they are whatever we today wish them to have been: there is no historical reality. In socialist countries, we call this phenomenon propaganda; in the United Stated, we call it entertainment.

II

I have found it convenient to make a distinction regarding the types of Western fiction. I divide Western novels and stories into two general categories, the formulary Western and the historical reconstruction. Between these two, there is a third, partial category which draws something from each and that is the romantic historical reconstruction. Because it is the most familiar, I should like to comment first on formulary Western fiction.

Frederick D. Glidden who, as Luke Short, wrote some of the finest formulary Westerns managed to do it in such a way that the Western setting is almost irrelevant. This is borne out in the posthumous tribute Glidden paid Ernest Haycox. ". . . My favorite Haycox yarns don't lean on a known time or place," Glidden wrote. "In these stories, I suspect Haycox made his own geography, named his own towns and mountains and rivers; he peopled them with tough and abrasive characters whose only law was their self-will."[14] The world of the formulary Western is, therefore, a world of total make-believe; what charm it has is derived from the fact that it can never intersect with the real world.

Once this premise is accepted, it then becomes possible to approach critically each formulary Western and, by reading an author's Western stories, you can reconstruct the various make-believe worlds uniquely true for particular authors, where they are similar to those of others, where different. You are also free to speculate about innovations and who influenced whom, never forgetting that while the terrain may have a Western appearance, the topography is imaginary and the characters components of a ritualized, conventionalized, and collective fantasy whose sole function is to divert us from our lives and never to touch in any way the depths of the soul. As movie cowboy Hoot Gibson once put it to me, "People like Westerns because they always know who's gonna win." Then he smiled, a bit sadly, because he had had a bitter and hard time of it. "But," he added, "it ain't that way in life." The formulary Western during its halcyon days was popular with readers because they always knew how it would come out.

C.G. Jung in his *Zwei Schriften über analytische Psychologie* [Two Essays on Analytical Psychology] (1967) described what he called the *mana-personality,* an archetype of the collective unconscious, "a being filled with an occult, conjuring capacity, or mana, and endowed with magical skills and powers."[15] In the chapter Jung devoted to this phenomenon, he felt compelled to warn that "one can only alter his attitude in an effort to impede being naively possessed by an archetype that forces him to play a role at the cost of his humanity. Possession by an archetype makes a man into a purely collective figure, after the fashion of a mask, behind which his humanity can no longer develop but rather increasingly atrophies. One must remain conscious of the danger of falling beneath the dominant of the mana-personality. The danger consists not merely in the fact that one person assumes the mask of a father figure but that that person can fall victim to the same mask when it's worn by another person. In this sense, master and pupil are one and the same."[16] Expressed in other words and applied to the subject at hand, if we believe in the existence of Western heroes, we will frequently attempt to emulate these Western heroes. However, when we do this, when we emulate in our own lives the values we have projected onto Western heroes, we, as they, become collective figures; our humanity atrophies. The development of the formulary Western in the twentieth century would seem to bear this out.

The *mana* of the formulary Western is the psychic force of self-will and the *mana* of the formulary Western hero is his virtuous and triumphantly superior self-will. In the enactment of this ritualized, violent competitiveness between degrees of self-willedness from Owen Wister's *The Virginian* (1902) to George G. Gilman's more recent *Edge* series the heroine must become as dehumanized and as convinced of the efficacy of violence as the only solution to social frustration as is the hero. Accepting the Virginian as a hero requires of Molly Stark Wood that she condone the Virginian's placing property before friendship by his participation in the execution of his friend Steve and that in order for the Virginian to maintain his status as a hero in the community he must shoot and kill Trampas. The Virginian set the tone for the formulary Western hero. He might be a gunfighter like Lassiter in Zane Grey's *Riders of the Purple Sage* (1912) or an Easterner forced by necessity into violence like Jack Hare in Grey's *The Heritage of the Desert* (1910) or like John Shefford in Grey's *The Rainbow Trail* (1915), but in any case the heroine is required to endorse the hero's violence as when Jane Withersteen in *Riders of the Purple Sage* exclaims: "'Roll the stone! . . . Lassiter, I love you!'"[17] — when rolling the stone means that the principal villain and all his minions will be destroyed beneath a rock slide.

Charles Alden Seltzer in *The Range Boss* (1917) had his hero inform the heroine, an Easterner who inherits a ranch, "'You'll shape up real Western — give you time. . . . You'll be ready to take your own part, without depending on laws to do it for you — laws that don't reach far enough.'"[18] Such a hero has to have *some* kind of motivation and in a later novel, *Square Deal Sanderson* (1922), Seltzer spelled it out rather succinctly when we learn that Sanderson was "deliberately and unwarrantedly going to the Double A to interfere, to throw himself into a fight with persons with whom he had no previous acquaintance, for no other reason than that his chivalrous instincts had prompted him."[19] Engaging in such a contest means that Sanderson must and will vanquish the villain.

Seltzer drew Western heroes who were grim, quiet, powerful men, thus initiating a convention since embellished by dozens of other writers and perhaps most significantly by Ernest Haycox, Luke Short, Norman A. Fox, Wayne D. Overholser, and Louis L'Amour. Within the rigid boundaries set by the formulary Western plot, there are nonetheless a wide assortment of acceptable variations. Max Brand, one of eighteen pen names used by Frederick Faust, made his first appearance as a Western writer with *The Untamed* (1919). Faust was disgusted by the actual physical West and avoided, whenever possible, even driving through it. He made his heroes and locales mythological and, therefore, timeless. He preferred in his hundreds of novels to employ one basic plot structure — pursuit and capture — with one variation: delayed revelation; and within this structure he projected his two most basic myths: the son in search of an illustrious father and a warrior who has an Achilles' heel. Faust's advice to young writers was to read a story half way through and imagine how it comes out. Then come up with a new beginning for the new conclusion and you have a new story.

He wanted to write better fiction than formulary Westerns, but when, as in *Destry Rides Again* (1930), he attempted to write a more sophisticated novel — actually a rewrite of Odysseus' return to Ithaca from *The Odyssey* — his agent warned him that he was writing too well; he must concentrate less on characterization, more on story. In this context "more story" meant more action.

Dane Coolidge in *Hidden Water* (1910) was the first to my knowledge to introduce the theme of the two heroines into formulary Westerns, although James Fenimore Cooper had been fond of it in the previous century. In this plot the hero must choose between the two heroines at the end of the story. Ernest Haycox was also fond of this plot ingredient. However, no matter where you find it in Haycox' fiction, the reason behind the selection is always identical. "'We're exactly the same kind of people,'" heroine Diana Castle says in Haycox' *Alder Gulch* (1941), speaking about herself and hero Jeff Pierce. "'It is all or nothing with each of us.'"[20] In Luke Short's first hardbound Western novel, *The Feud at Single Shot* (1936), hero Dave Turner tells heroine Dorsey Hammond that the only way the world gives a man what belongs to him is if he is willing to fight and die for it. By the end of the novel, after a number of villains have been dispatched by Turner, he remarks to Dorsey: "'It was pretty bloody.'" Dorsey, however, has become a convert. "'But,'" she responds, "'if a man doesn't fight for what he has and loves, people will take them away from him.'"[21] In *Brand of Empire* (1940), Short refined this perspective to the point that after hero Pete Yard shoots and kills heroine Chris Mellish's brother, Chris not only tells Yard that she forgives him but, if he will promise to stay with her, she'll never even think about it again. In Short's *Ride the Man Down* (1942), taking over the two heroines theme from Haycox, Celia Evarts is drawn to hero Will Ballard because she, as opposed to the other heroine, Lottie Priest, admires Ballard for the violence by which he must live in order to protect her property. She doesn't object in the least when Ballard must shoot and kill her fiancé. In contrast to Ballard and his ascendant *mana,* there is a weak man named Kennedy with virtually no *mana* at all and, therefore, there is a difference in the kind of woman he has: "She was a plain drudge of a girl, Will saw, probably the only kind of woman Kennedy could attract."[22] From this it is only a short step to Louis L'Amour's *Hondo* (1953) where Angie Lowe takes Hondo for her second husband and her son Johnny accepts Hondo as a second father despite the fact that it was Hondo who killed Angie's first husband and Johnny's real father.

Hondo's *mana* is obviously the more powerful and the more desirable.

A novel nearly as influential as Wister's *The Virginian* in the development of the formulary Western was Dashiell Hammett's *Red Harvest* (1929) in which there is so much killing that the characters, in Hammett's words, become "blood simple." Eugene Cunningham, whom critic W.H. Hutchinson once described as "one of the greatest lapidaries who ever polished a 'horse opera' for public consumption,"[23] transposed Hammett's plot into a Western setting in *Riders of the Night* (1922) in which, in the course of the novel, some seventy villains are killed. In *Buckaroo* (1933) Cunningham expanded this number of villains who "needed" killing to 300!

While in *Riders of the Night* Cunningham, too, resorted to the theme of the two heroines, he did something else slightly more original: he introduced a trio of gunfighters named Sandrock Tom, Three Rivers, and Happy Jack to whom he gave the sobriquet the "Three Mesquiteers." Cunningham employed another trio in *Buckaroo* and so it was left to William Colt MacDonald to pick up on this idea and fashion a different trio which he called the "Three Mesquiteers," beginning with *Law of the Forty-fives* (1933). MacDonald's trio of Tucson Smith, Stony Brooke, and Lullaby Joslin appeared in some ten novels and some fifty-two "B" Western films. MacDonald's pattern for his novels was identical with Cunningham's and he invariably had his trio riding into a community intimidated by a master villain and his gang, a situation which, in Tucson Smith's words in *Law of the Forty-fives,* called upon the Mesquiteers to "employ the only law effective in this sort of case—gun law."[24]

However indigenous violence may have been in formulary Westerns prior to Cunningham and MacDonald, never before had it been present in such abundance nor had the death of a human being been treated with quite their attitude of casual indifference. They did their work well; so well, in fact, that it would be extremely unlikely these days for a formulary Western writer to treat the death of a human being any other way. MacDonald's Mesquiteer novels consist of one chapter after another of blood-letting until the final chapter in which the master villain himself is destroyed. This plot structure has become almost a sub-genre with formulary Western fiction, but even when it isn't used, the moral posture embodied in it is all pervasive. In Norman A. Fox' *Silent in the Saddle* (1945), Fox' hero Brad Seldon reflects after a shoot-out that he will never know "a moment's regret for that killing"[25] and in Louis L'Amour's *To Tame a Land* (1955) hero Rye Tyler says that "for once I didn't feel bad about a shooting."[26]

The idea of a Western story as an occasion for killing has become self-propagating. A. Leslie Scott, under his Bradford Scott pseudonym, wrote nearly 125 entries in his Walt Slade, Texas Ranger series in which Slade, joined by his friends Estevan (whose dialogue is generally confined to "my blade thirsts") and Sheriff Gene Putnam, battles it out with a master villain and his minions, killing and blood-letting. Currently this tradition is being carried on principally by British writers, among them J.T. Edson (whose American publishers guarantee the reader at least twelve thrilling killings per book) and Terry Harknett. Harknett's career began with his novelization of Sergio Leone's *A Fistful of Dollars* (United Artists, 1967) after which, under the pen name George G. Gilman, he created the *Edge* series of *Blut und Boden* Western fiction as well as co-authoring the *Apache* series with Laurence James under the *nom de plume* William M. James. Gordon D. Shirreffs has continued the tradition among American writers, particularly in his Lee Kershaw saga. Typically in this series, the end of the book finds Kershaw alone because everyone else has been killed.

All of which brings me to a further observation about the *mana-personality*. The stronger the hero's *mana*—his self-willedness, his ability to kill better than anyone else, his inhumanity, his indifference to human life—the greater the dehumanization of the heroine. Once killing becomes wholesale, as it has become increasingly in formulary Western fiction, the traditional heroine must either vanish completely or be transformed herself into a blood-letter. Jack Slade's girl friend in the Bradford Scott series is named Jerry Nolan. She operates the Deuces Up dance hall and Slade likes her best when she wears tights; he sees her only when driven by carnal desire and, otherwise, she has no function and really no existence. For Shirreff's Lee Kershaw, although Kershaw has a different female companion in each adventure, the woman will engage in cold-blooded killing right along with Kershaw. When in Shirreffs' *The Marauders* (1977) the woman is smashed in the face with a rifle butt by the master villain and her thigh ripped into by a shark, when in short she is dying, all she can think of is having sexual congress with Kershaw one last time and all Kershaw can feel about her after he humps her and after she dies is that "she was only a woman and a half-breed Yaqui at that."[27]

There is an inevitable progression from this to the porno–Westerns which, since 1979, have proven such a bonanza for publishers. In the porno–Westerns, women are stripped of their clothing and their souls, reduced to physical objects capable of producing detumescence in the heroes following their bouts of incredible carnage and slaughter. These series are written by several authors but published under house names like Jake Logan or Tabor Evans. In *Slocum's Revenge* (1979) by Jake Logan — to take a single instance — Slocum's (play on words?) price for returning a deed to a property owned by a beautiful young Spanish virgin is to have a night with her and the ecstasy and repeated orgasms she experiences are recounted in graphic detail. Jake Logan is billed on the cover as "the hottest best-selling Western author since Louis L'Amour," but there is nothing Western about this series save the manner of dress. All such series are merely pornography in a period setting and the logical development of the lying which began innocently enough in Wister and before him in the Dime Novels. What it illustrates is a story completely under the dominant of the *mana-personality*. Men and women have been denied all possibility of *humanitas,* to use Cicero's Latin, the word closest to my meaning. They are purely collective figures indulging in orgies of sexuality and violence. Slocum and his brethren use women insensately and sometimes brutally before casually moving on to their next conquest; but let me invoke Tolstoy's warning in the scene in *War and Peace* (1869) where Napoleon surveys the battlefield at Borodino: *Quos vult perdere — dementat.*[28]

If the tradition of the Western hero as a loner was given much of its initial impetus by Owen Wister, so also was the idea of a family Western. Wister was primarily a short story writer and, from the beginning, he populated his West with characters who are bound together by common experiences and emotional ties, including the Virginian, Lin McLean, and Scipio LeMoyne. Indeed, one of Wister's story collections was titled *Members of the Family* (1911). B.M. Bower was the first to follow Wister in this direction, beginning with her first novel, *Chip of the Flying U* (1906). Although she continued writing Western fiction for almost forty years, she included regularly among her output yet another adventure with Chip or others from the Flying U whom she had come to refer to collectively as "The Happy Family." Clarence E. Mulford similarly in *Bar-20* (1907) began his saga of the Bar-20 outfit held together by ties of friendship and mutual commitment, including Hopalong Cassidy, Red Connors, Johnny Nelson, Buck Peters, Tex Ewalt, and, later, Mesquite Jenkins. The Bar-20 saga proved so popular that with *Corson of the JC* (1927) Mulford launched a second saga with a different set of characters.

The groundwork was thus well laid for Janice Holt Giles when she began her own saga with *The Kentuckians* (1953), tracing the settlement of the American frontier through four generations of a Kentucky family that eventually moves West. Although scarcely in a class with Giles, Louis L'Amour subsequently created three separate series of sagas having to do with large families who migrate West. What Giles and L'Amour and several others have most in common is that they have united the formerly loose conclaves of individuals in Wister, Bower, and Mulford into family units bound by blood ties. In *Bar-20 Three* (1921), for example, Mulford has Cassidy and Connors come to the aid of Johnny Nelson when he is beset by villains; at the conclusion of *Mojave Crossing* (1964) L'Amour has Tell Sackett saved from torture and death by Nolan Sackett, a distant relative and up until then in the employ of the villains.

The unifying spirit behind these family-oriented formulary Westerns is the same which Ralph Brauer in his excellent book *The Horse, The Gun, and The Piece of Property: Changing Images of the TV Western* (1975) discerned in the plethora of family and community Westerns which figured so prominently on television in the sixties and seventies. "Seth Adams [of *Wagon Train*]," Brauer wrote, "and Gil Favor [of *Rawhide*] and John Kennedy ask not what you can do for truth, justice, and morality . . . but rather ask what can you do for the trail crew, the wagon train, the organization, the country?"[29] Or, in a word, what can you do for the family? Although there is a degree of individual initiative permitted in the family-oriented Westerns, the fact remains that their major significance in the history of the formulary Western is the emphasis they place on collectivism as opposed to isolated individualism, their repudiation of individual freedom for cooperation within a community, their rejection of the Native American notion that each man must seek his own vision, for which they substitute the overwhelming white American desire for social conformity, the search for that feeling of consensus which has so long preoccupied and eluded white Americans. If you look objectively at the formulary Western, I believe you cannot help but agree with La Rochefoucauld's observation in his *Reflexions Morales* (1678): *"Nos vertus ne sont, le plus souvent, que des vices déguises."*[30]

III

In what space remains to me I cannot survey historical reconstructions or romantic historical reconstructions even as cursorily as I have

dealt with formulary Westerns, but what might be done is to select a
theme and contrast the varying ways it has been treated in the two
respective modes. One such theme, surely, is that of the captivity novel.
Among novels which focus on the abduction of whites by Comanches
during the middle of the nineteenth century, Alan LeMay's *The
Searchers* comes to mind as does Will Cook's *Comanche Captives* but
also Benjamin Capps' *A Woman of the People* (1966) and Matthew
Braun's *Black Fox* (1972). The first two are romantic historical
reconstructions. It was a trend in the fifties to introduce anti-hero
elements into even formulary Westerns, but generally this trend
manifested itself most often in romantic historical reconstructions. It
was usually accomplished, as in *The Searchers* and *Comanche Captives,*
by splitting the traditional formulary hero into two distinct characters.
Alan LeMay did it by splitting his hero into Amos Edwards, a dark
figure, and Mart Pauley, a young man adopted as a boy by the Edwards
family. Will Cook did it by splitting his hero into Jim Gary, a lieutenant in the U.S. Cavalry, and Guthrie McCabe, sheriff of Oldham
County, Texas. Now in calling this a trend I do not wish to imply that
it originated in the fifties. It had been done with Indians as early as
James Fenimore Cooper's *The Last of the Mohicans* (1826) with
Chingachgook and Magua, and film director Delmer Daves preferred
to resort to this splitting device in films like *Broken Arrow* (20th-Fox,
1950) between Cochise and Geronimo—in this case his source was
Elliott Arnold's novel *Blood Brother* (1947)—and, in a film Daves wrote
himself, *Drumbeat* (Warner's, 1954) between Captain Jack and
Mannik. In the fifties the real novelty was in splitting the white heroes.

In *The Searchers,* Amos Edwards' two nieces are taken captive by
the Comanches. One of them is raped and killed. The other, Debbie,
is apparently still alive and for nearly six years Amos and Mart search
for her. LeMay's Comanches are savages and it is their unredeemably
savage spirit which comes to influence the conduct of both Amos and
Mart in their quest. LeMay did not find both sides in the conflict
equally savage; nor was he the least sympathetic with the Comanches,
whatever momentary lip-service he gave to the fact that they were
fighting to protect their sacred lands. The whites, Amos and Mart,
become almost superhuman during the course of their heroic undertaking. Amos, however, is obviously intent on killing Debbie because
of the humiliation she has experienced by being made the wife of a
Comanche war chief. In this he is frustrated and, ironically, he dies at
the hands of a Comanche squaw. Mart finds Debbie and, together, they

find their once innocent love again—or, at least, the reader is led to believe they do.

In *Comanche Captives,* McCabe is hired by the U.S. Cavalry to bring back white captives from among the Comanches. He is accompanied on this mission by Jim Gary. All the white captives these two discover have been transformed into brutish animals as a result of their captivity and the one adolescent boy McCabe does bring back commits a vicious murder and is hanged by the outraged whites. Jim Gary rescues Janice Tremain, the niece of a U.S. Senator, who for five years has been the captive wife of Stone Calf. Gary kills Stone Calf, but he finds he must reject Janice because "he was a prudish man who wanted all women pure, until they were married at least."[31] This wasn't so much a consideration for Mart Pauley as for men generally on the frontier where there were so few women, virgins or otherwise. McCabe for his part is saved from Amos Edwards' fate by being enslaved by the Comanches and he is only rescued by Jim Gary once he has learned the value of friendship and the virtue of community spirit.

Both of these novels, as I have mentioned, appeared in *The Saturday Evening Post* and so it could not be expected that the Comanches would be humanly characterized. Yet, it isn't this deficiency alone which makes them romantic historical reconstructions; this comes about chiefly because of their reliance on heroes. A hero, as a villain, isn't really human, and can never be human. When the characters in a story are not human, it cannot claim to be literary art in quite the sense that was once the case. "The ancients have left us examples of epic poems in which the heroes provide the entire interest of the story," Tolstoy wrote, "and we are still unable to accustom ourselves to the fact that for our epoch history of that sort is meaningless."[32]

In the historical reconstruction the hero is replaced by a human being, a person of flesh and blood, while the structure has been expanded to encompass far greater complexity. "No longer confident of the inevitability of its own history, or the 'American way of life,'" Lawrence W. Towner wrote in his Introduction to the reissue of D'Arcy McNickle's fine historical reconstruction, *The Surrounded* (1936), "the America of the 1970s may be more sympathetic to other peoples and their cultures than it was, or at least more understanding of other peoples who may seem also to have lost their way."[33]

Both Capps and Braun knew a great deal more about Comanches than did LeMay or Cook. This may have been due to the circumstance that the history of the American West has come to be written more conscientiously than it used to be, but it is also probably due to the fact that these authors cared enough about historical reality to discover it for themselves and in the process recreate it for their readers. Their books are proof that it is possible to produce fiction that is stirring and entertaining and notwithstanding historically accurate. In *A Woman of the People,* Helen Morrison and her younger sister, Katy, are made captives of the Mutsani Comanches in 1854. The entire story is told from Helen Morrison's point of view and for all of it she remains living with the Comanches. We see her grow to womanhood among them, learn their customs and language, marry Burning Hand and bear him a child, and we see the beautiful and touching relationship between them. Because the Comanches can be characterized, because there is an absence of heroes and a corresponding presence of human beings, *everyone is humanized. A Woman of the People* transcends mere fiction and becomes literature.

Capps was not concerned with arguing racial superiorities or cultural supremacy; instead his novel shows us how and why the Comanches were different. The same is true for Braun's *Black Fox.* The Black Fox of the title is Britt Johnson, a freed black from the South. When the Comanches and Kiowas stage a joint raid in 1860 to drive the white-eyes from their sacred lands and take captives, Black Fox, whom the whites regard as an uppity nigger, volunteers to negotiate to get the captives back, not the least motivated because his own family is among the captives. Braun deftly characterizes Running Dog and Santana among the Kiowas, Little Buffalo among the Comanches, showing us at the same time all the minute and yet quite distinct differences between these two peoples, just as he characterizes Black Fox and his relations within his family and among the whites, the whites themselves, and the multitude of ways in which various individuals perceive each other. Britt comes to realize that "'the strong fight the strong for the right to harness the meek to the plow.'"[34] His greatest conflict is induced by Running Dog, his friend among the Kiowas, who cannot understand why Black Fox should prefer to live among the whites where he is subject to the most demeaning treatment when he might live in freedom and dignity among the Kiowas. Each of the central characters is a fully rounded human being and so, from this perspective, we are better able to understand the suffering and personal travail in which each must live and somehow find his own way within his community and within himself.

If the question is put to me, would I replace the romantic West with the historical West, my answer would be an unequivocal yes. I would also suggest that we must learn enough Western American history to know what is romance, and what is not. Western fiction has only surpassed being a minor literature in those instances where it has addressed actual human experience and real human conflicts. Unlike the characters in Orwell's *1984*, we cannot persist in constantly rewriting our history to suit the fashion of the moment, as if history were nothing more than the handmaiden of wish-fulfillment. The primary task of Western American fiction, as of all art, is the same (to paraphrase Dr. Samuel Johnson) as it has always been: to prepare us better to understand life, or, at least, better to endure it. To fall victim to romantic illusions, to dehumanize ourselves through the dominant of the *mana-personality,* and therefore to become wholly uncritical in our acceptance of what amounts to self-serving lies can only assure us that finally we shall do neither.

It may seem that I have unfairly singled out Ernest Haycox for criticism in what I have had to say. I did not do so, however, without knowing at the same time that he was ultimately a champion of the historical reconstruction and that, had he lived longer, he would have fulfilled the promise of the new direction he took in the last years of his life. "I could not write some of the stories I wrote five years ago," he once confessed. "I wish I could, since I enjoyed them so much. But my fingers will not trace the same patterns — and it would be foolish for me to try to force them into the old patterns."[35] There are writers of Western fiction — some of whom I have named; others, such as Elmer Kelton, whom I have not — who know, as Haycox did, in the depths of their souls that the past does have something to teach us if we are willing to learn it, and that the Western novel is the ideal literary form through which our American past can be evoked vividly and painfully — painfully, because it was mostly painful. The story of the American West is not romance. It is tragedy. Yet, even in tragedy, as writers since Aeschylus have known, there can be human nobility.

The Westerner Returns

Among the great mysteries in book publishing is why Jenni Calder's *There Must Be a Lone Ranger* (1974) has been reissued. There isn't only an error on every page; there is some kind of error in practically every paragraph. Some of them may be forgiven because the author is an English woman without access to primary sources. For example, the manner in which copyright information is blurred or often ignored by British paperback publishers (American paperback houses are only a little better) makes it understandable that she should feel W.C. Tuttle, a veteran Western writer from the twenties and thirties, should be ranked with T.V. Olsen as one of the best currently writing Westerns. It is a bit more difficult, however, to explain why she has Sitting Bull dying at Wounded Knee when he wasn't even there, and at least a hundred similar inaccuracies. The reissue of the book can only be explained by the one thing Jenni Calder got right. "At regular intervals," she wrote, "the demise of the Western is announced . . . but . . . the Western myth is . . . invulnerable."[1] Why should this be so? It may be true that the Western film is in a bad way these days, but Westerns are cautiously re-emerging on the small screen and Western literature at last is winning an unexpected but certainly deserved recognition. The explanation of this invulnerability is perhaps best given by C.L. Sonnichsen in his new book, *From Hopalong to Hud: Thoughts on Western Fiction* (1978). Sonnichsen, senior editor of *The Journal of Arizona History* and past president of the Western Writers of America, is what one so often looks for in a literary historian but all too rarely finds: a man of encyclopedic knowledge with wide reading who pays attention to accuracy and yet is articulate, stimulating, entertaining . . . and, rarer still, a man with a reverence for his subject. Sonnichsen has no private campaigns, fixed ideas, or dogmatic judgments which he intends to compel his reader to accept. In short, although he holds a doctorate from Harvard, he possesses what few academics ever have: a respect for his reader's intelligence. He writes as

211

a friend of Western American literature and he does so in such a fashion
that his compassion is always evident.

"I suggest," Sonnichsen has said, trying to explain the vitality of
the memory of the American West, "...we want to have roots in
ancient times like other peoples, but we don't stay in one place long
enough to grow them. We move about freely, and some of us live on
wheels. Many of us know nothing about our own grandfathers. Pride
of family is denied to all but a few of us. Pride of race has to be built.
Any group with a thousand year history has these things provided, but
the American is a newcomer and not yet completely at home in his vast
country. All he has is the mythical West, and he needs it desperately."[2]
To this Sonnichsen also attached a warning: "A nation which does not
believe in its own heritage is in real danger."[3]

Sonnichsen's book is not so much a study of Western American
literature as it is an attempt to look "at the Western novel, much of it
on the popular level and much of it contemporary, in an effort to reach
some valid conclusions about where we the people have been, where
we are, and where we are going as revealed in our fiction."[4] He makes
a notable effort to resist the academic division of Western fiction into
"literature" and "trash." "So many novels fall into the gray area
between," he has observed, "so much that is said of the one applies to
the other, so necessary is the understanding of one to the comprehen-
sion of the other that the student finally gives up and works both sides
of the street simultaneously."[5]

Due to his vast reading, Sonnichsen has discovered what few have
realized: there are many more significant differences between Western
films and Western fiction than there are similarities. In the sixth
chapter, from which the book draws its title, Sonnichsen traces the
history and development of the Westerner who in fiction has been
anything but the heroic stereotype of the movies: he might rather be—
as the fictional Hopalong Cassidy—very nearly an alcoholic; he is
usually a troubled man, a darkening figure who is capable only at
singular moments of rising above man's common estate.

The "Wyatt Earp Syndrome" is the term Sonnichsen has given to
that trend, beginning in the late twenties, to mythologize the gunman
who presumably tamed Tombstone (and which was later perpetuated
by movies and television). At the root of this trend to glorify the
gunfighter, Sonnichsen discovered that repulsive tendency in our own
time to adulate the one-man vigilante committee. In films this
character has often been portrayed by Clint Eastwood, in or out of

Western garb, while in fiction he has prospered in the popular writings of the American blood and soil school of fascist gunfighters. Mickey Spillane's Mike Hammer has his Western counterparts in George Gilman's Edge, John Benteen's Fargo, and Jack Slade's Lassiter, killers all whose escapades fill whole series of books. Gordon D. Shirreffs also belongs to this school, as does Forrest Carter in novels such as *The Vengeance Trail of Josey Wales* (1976). It is only a step beyond this to the highly sexualized men and women fornicating their way through another group of Western adventures, which Sonnichsen surveys in his final chapter, "Sex on the Lone Prairie." It is Sonnichsen's overriding intention to make us more cognizant of the good and bad in Western fiction, as we become equally aware of the good and bad in American society reflected in these stories.

From Hopalong to Hud is a vital step we should all take to disenthrall ourselves from our stereotypical notions of the American West so that we can optimally realize that, at its finest, the Western remains an adventure story set in open country, so open and so free as once it was, and which presents us with the possibility of men and women behaving in accordance with a way of life that stubbornly resists the contagions and corruptions of our modern technocracy. The Western, ideally, answers not only the question of how it was, but also how it might have become; how it is that, starting out so full of hope and promise, we came to realize so little of that hope and promise. I have read many books about the Western over the years, but none before this one which I could recommend without serious reservation.

A renewed interest in Western fiction has also become evident in the American publishing industry. The Aeonian Press, which recently has been reissuing the works of Clarence E. Mulford, who created Hopalong Cassidy, and a contemporary of Mulford's, Charles Alden Seltzer, in cloth-bound editions for collectors and libraries, has been able to interest Pocket Books in reprinting for the mass market at least the later Seltzer titles, beginning with *Arizona Jim* (1939) reissued in July, 1978. An even more ambitious, book-store-oriented project has been launched by the Gregg Press division of G.K. Hall & Company, similar to its reissue series of science fiction classics in hardbound format. The initial reissues, comprising fifteen titles of varying quality artistically, are handsomely bound with dust jackets. It is the Gregg Press' intention to make these reissues an annual event.

The initial titles are: *The Girl of the Golden West* (1925) by David Belasco, *The Untamed* (1919) by Max Brand, *The War Chief* (1927) and *Apache Devil* (1933) by Edgar Rice Burroughs, *Wolf Song* (1927), *Blood of the Conquerors* (1921), and *In Those Days* (1929) by Harvey Fergusson, *The Border Trumpet* (1939) and *Bugles in the Afternoon* (1944) by Ernest Haycox, *Hondo* (1953) by Louis L'Amour, *The Searchers* (1954) and *The Unforgiven* (1957) by Alan LeMay, *Early Americana and Other Stories* (1936) by Conrad Richter, *Butcher's Crossing* (1960) by John Williams, and *From Where the Sun Now Stands* (1959) by Will Henry.

If any one of these books could be cited as required reading for every American, it is Will Henry's *From Where the Sun Now Stands*. As Betty Rosenberg wrote in her Introduction to this novel, prior to its appearance "the information . . . for realistic and honest novelization of the Indian wars was available. Lacking was a novel-reading audience willing to accept tragedy in place of romance. Such an acceptance would force the reader to recognize that Indian cultures and ways of life are sophisticated realities and their destruction wanton evil; that the invaders' Manifest Destiny was a blatant hypocrisy, an excuse to cover theft of land and commercial exploitation; that missionary activities were a tool of subjugation; that the imposition of an Anglo culture upon the Indians was an unwelcome curse."[6] The subject of Will Henry's exceptional historical novel is the war against the Nez Perce Indians in 1877 and their virtual extermination, a tribe with a long tradition of peace and friendliness toward the white man, who in their terrible passage from Idaho through Montana to reach the Canadian border, in which attempt they failed, not one white woman or child was harmed because, in the words of the Indian narrator of the novel, "we had lived too long as brothers of the white man. Even in our last hours, we could not kill and mutilate his loved ones."[7]

Much of Western American literature over the last thirty years has come gradually to embody the spirit of dissent. It is increasingly carrying on the tradition of Henry David Thoreau and, if it sometimes still retains the character of a morality play, the depiction of evil is not so stereotyped as one might think who is only casually familiar with it. The novel set in the nineteenth-century West may present the reader with a critique of historical events, or, even more commonly, an alternative to what life has now become since Manifest Destiny has totally triumphed. What the white man had to teach the red man was the necessity for conformity. By enslaving the Indian in the white man's economic system, the land and Nature were henceforth no longer to be respected; harmony with the natural elements was to be replaced by an aggressive spirit which raped, ravaged, and left the land in ruins. Concrete and steel were destined to replace the trees and flowers and the war between the cattlemen and the dirt farmers for possession of the "sea of grass" produced the Dust Bowl.

It is worth noting that eight of these novels, or more than half, focus on some aspect of the Indian wars. Will Henry has reconstructed the Nez Perce way of life. Edgar Rice Burroughs, more familiar to most readers for his fantasy novels about Tarzan and life on Mars, managed in *The War Chief* and *Apache Devil* to recreate the Apache way of life, using as his point of view character Shoz-Dijiji, the Black Bear, a white ostensibly adopted by Geronimo while still an infant. *The War Chief* was run first serially in *Argosy All-Story Weekly* in 1927 before it was published in book form by A.C. McClurg & Co. In the 1890s Burroughs had served with B Troop, 7th Regiment, U.S. Cavalry in Arizona, stationed at Fort Grant. Just ten years after Geronimo's surrender, he visited the sites of the Apache wars. The Apaches rarely were named after animals, but Burroughs makes Shoz-Dijiji's name-taking credible, as he does the ritual character of Apache life.

Apache Devil was serialized in *Argosy All-Story Weekly* in 1928 but not published in book form until 1933, and then under the Edgar Rice Burroughs, Inc. imprint. The main outline of events surrounding the Apache wars are sedulously accurate and the historical characters include Geronimo, Cochise, Mangas Colorado, Natchez (Naiche), Nanay, Juh (Whoa), General Crook and General Miles—the same General Miles who figures in the Nez Perce campaign.

When Ray Bradbury declared Burroughs to be the most influential author of this century, he had in mind the Tarzan and science fiction books which have been translated into fifty-six languages, selling over twenty-five million copies. These two novels, unlike most of what he wrote, unlike even Burroughs' other Western novels, were not particularly popular. Editors rejected them because they were "too historical." Yet they may well constitute whatever claim is made for him as a serious novelist. It is more commonplace now than it was in 1927 to write as Burroughs did in *The War Chief:* "To have said: 'He is an Indian. He stands in the way of our acquisition of his valuable possessions. Therefore, having no power to enforce his rights and being in our way, we will destroy him,' would have been no more ruthless than the policy we adopted and cloaked with hypocrisy. It would have had the redeeming quality of honesty, and would have been a policy that the Apache could have understood and admired."[8]

The Apache wars, unlike the Nez Perce campaign, were more episodic and Burroughs had no choice but to be episodic in his treatment of them. *Apache Devil* is a much weaker novel than *The War Chief,* not because it is even more episodic—which it is—but because Burroughs insisted on infusing into his narrative a formulary white villain and his gang and an imperiled rancher's daughter. Perhaps, as I suspect, Burroughs was fearful that his readers would recoil when in *Apache Devil* Shoz-Dijiji gives his argument for war against the "white eyes": "'They wish us to live in their way which is not a good way for the Apache to live. If we do not wish to, they send soldiers and arrest us. Thus we are prisoners and slaves. Shoz-Dijiji cannot be happy either as a prisoner or as a slave, and so he prefers the war trail and death to these things.'"[9] It is one of the ironies in Western American fiction, in its struggle to escape the formulae imposed upon it by editors and the reading public's taste, that the voices which inspired the American Revolution came to be embodied not in the victors but in the vanquished in the Western states, and in the Indians.

According to C.L. Sonnichsen in the chapter devoted to the treatment afforded the Indians of the Southwest in over 200 novels, "the trouble with most such reconstructions is that the authors can't possibly get inside an Indian, and they inevitably make him heroic in white man's terms."[10] This is unfortunately what Burroughs did with Shoz-Dijiji, aided by having made the Black Bear white to begin with and so free to find socially acceptable requited love with a white woman. But none of these shortcomings detracts significantly from the impressive authenticity with which he presented the external features and the internal rituals by which the Apaches lived.

There must be *some* formulary conventions in fiction. W. Somerset Maugham once said that all stories properly end in death or marriage. In *From Where the Sun Now Stands,* a title derived from Chief Joseph's statement, "From where the sun now stands, I will fight no more forever," Will Henry understood the Nez Perce way well enough to observe that "when an Indian is discouraged he is like a sick dog; all the strength goes out of him in one day."[11] It was Chief Joseph who realized what it was the white man wanted because "to pen up the Indian in a small place was to destroy his spirit, to break his heart, to kill him."[12] Nor did General Sherman mince his words about his military objective in the Sioux campaign: "We must act with vindictive earnestness against the Sioux, even to their extermination, men, women, and children. Nothing less will reach the root of the case."[13]

These are words well worth savoring perhaps amid all the righteous declarations in Washington and in the news media concerning the long-standing American commitment to human rights which, apparently, the rest of the world is to accept without question. That commitment, as reflected in our literature about the Westward expansion, depends on human rights being defined as synonymous with the American middle-class way of life which, of course, is scarcely valid. "'They want the Apaches to live as the white-eyed men live,'" Shoz-Dijiji remarks in *Apache Devil*. "'The Apache cannot live as the white-eyed men live. They would not be happy. They would sicken and die.'"[14] Edgar Rice Burroughs and Will Henry, three decades apart, confronted with a story that must logically end in death—not the death of an individual but of a people, of an entire way of life, and, most painful of all, the death of hope on a continent that once seemed the fulfillment of all hopes—can be forgiven for permitting their point of view characters at the conclusion to find a momentary respite in love. Other American authors such as Ernest Hemingway went much farther. They stripped love from their protagonists, and finally their lives. A story set in the West somehow continues to resist this total indulgence in despair. And, I believe, there is a reason for this. The Western story so infrequently abandons itself to complete negation because, beyond telling a story of adventure, it continues in its effort to envision alternatives to what now predominates as the American way of life, projected into the past but still interconnected with the present.

Probably no author better symbolizes the attempt to transcend formula in the Western story than did Ernest Haycox. Beginning in the late thirties, he tried writing historical novels rather than the Western serials with which he had begun. He was especially at his best in his cavalry novels, *The Border Trumpet* and *Bugles in the Afternoon*. Not even James Warner Bellah could rival Haycox when it came to complexity and diversity of point of view, although neither, consistent with the mandate to ignore completely the Indian point of view in the thirties and forties, ever dared to characterize the Native American's perception of what was happening. *The Border Trumpet* is set at Camp Grant, soon to become Fort Grant, and, although essentially a romance, the central conflict is the effort to subdue Antone, an Apache renegade, and his band of warriors. Betty Rosenberg in her Introduction to *From Where the Sun Now Stands* seems to have had a legitimate perspective. The Indian cannot be characterized if the romance is to be retained, and Haycox preferred romance. Yet, even so, the voice of dissent can be heard, as when Al Hazel, a scout, tells Lieutenant Tom Benteen, Haycox' protagonist, pointing at a smoke signal: "'Someday those things won't show against the sky. Then it will be a different country. I don't take much to your kind of civilization, Tom. Put a man in a town, in a house, give him a steady job and let him worry about his pay check—and he ain't a natural man any more. The Lord never meant us to live that way.'"[15]

It may be the real tragedy of American history that, given a nearly limitless wilderness, all that Manifest Destiny came to mean was the enslavement of the whole population in an economic system and proposed lifestyle that measures all values against material possessions. I am reminded of a comment a Navajo chieftain made to C.G. Jung which he quoted in his essay, "The Spiritual Problem of Modern Man," first published in 1928. "Once," Jung wrote, "when we were talking confidentially about the white man, he said to me: 'We don't understand the whites. They are always wanting something, always restless, always looking for something. What is it? We don't know. We can't understand them. They have such sharp noses, such thin, cruel lips, such lines in their faces. We think they are all crazy.' My friend had recognized, without being able to name it, the Aryan bird of prey with his insatiable lust to lord it in every land, even those that concern him not at all."[16]

Each volume in this Gregg Press reissue series has an introduction, some by scholars like that to *Hondo* which borders on the inarticulate if not illiterate, but most of them are adequate and a few, like Betty Rosenberg's, worthy of the novel which it precedes. This last is also true of Jill Marie Haycox' Introduction to *The Border Trumpet,* filled as it is with reminiscences of her late husband, and that of Ernest Haycox, Jr., to *Bugles in the Afternoon.* The latter provides us with a portrait of what Haycox' life as a writer was like, as seen through the eyes of his son growing up in Portland, Oregon, where Haycox spent most of his life. "'It seemed reasonable,'" Haycox once told his son, "'. . . that a fellow who writes about the West ought to be able to live in it.'"[17]

In a letter to his editor Ray Everitt at Little, Brown on July 14, 1943, Haycox explained the difficulties he had had in trying to be impartial about the Custer massacre at Little Big Horn. "This whole Custer thing is not in the hands of scholars," he wrote. "It is in the hands of partisans who started with a conviction and thereafter spent years hunting for facts to justify their view."[18] The Introduction to this reissue will tell the reader none of the controversy which initially surrounded *Bugles in*

John Wayne as Hondo Lane with his dog Sam from *Hondo* (Warner's, 1953). Photo courtesy of Warner Bros.–Batjac Pictures.

the Afternoon, but that was long ago and even Colonel W.A. Graham whom Haycox singled out for his objectivity in writing of the battle praised Haycox' novel as the finest fictional rendering we have had of the military rivalries and follies which precipitated the massacre — massacres being where the whites lose, as opposed to campaigns. *Bugles in the Afternoon* is a subtle and effective mixture of fiction with historical accuracy. Haycox' depiction is still one of the best we have of General George Armstrong Custer whose fascination as a cult figure has not diminished for Americans in the more than thirty years since Haycox wrote about him.

Louis L'Amour's novelization of James Edward Grant's screenplay for *Hondo* (Warner's 1953) was published as a Fawcett original paperback in 1953 and it remains one of his better novels. The hero, Hondo Lane, is self-reliant, capable without being excessively aggressive, sufficient unto himself without surrendering to greed. "'There's no word in the Apache language for lie,'" he tells Angie Lowe who has been deserted by her husband and lives with her young son in the midst of Indian territory, "'and they been lied to.'"[19] Hondo is presumably able to bridge the white and red cultures because he has lived five years among the Apaches and he possesses an independence of perspective as well as of character. This is symbolized in his relationship with his dog. "'That's a strange dog you have,'" Angie observes. "'I don't have him,'" Hondo replies. "She was puzzled. 'But the two of you are together!' 'He stays with me,'" Hondo answers.[20] L'Amour's conception of the relationships between men and women, such a dominant theme in his fiction, is but a variation of this, brought about by the fact that every man and every woman is a separate individual, best together when they are heading in the same direction.

Many of the novels in this group exist also in motion picture versions. The screenplay for *Hondo,* based on a L'Amour short story, was intended as a vehicle for John Wayne. The notion embodied in the screenplay and L'Amour's novelization of it of a white man bringing civilization to a wild land in a nation long nursed by Western films, just as a similar paternalism can be found informing nearly all television Westerns, is not a convention so deeply imbedded in Western American literature. In the best of it there are no John Wayne figures, no Hondo Lanes, and it is frequently evident that the civilization introduced into the wilderness is more savage, more cruel, and more self-destructive than anything in the natural order. In the film, as in the novelization of the film, Hondo Lane appears to admire the Indian ways (as they are somewhat fancifully conceived), but no doubt is left that they are things strictly belonging to the past.

Both Alan LeMay's *The Searchers* and *The Unforgiven* enjoy the status among some critics of being semi-classics in Western American fiction. They were written at the end of a career which had begun with LeMay writing formulary Western fiction and which led to Hollywood where he worked for years as a screenwriter, eventually even producing and directing a few mediocre Western films. These two novels, if inherently weak in characterization, are strong in atmosphere and nearly models of slick magazine plot construction. Both are captivity novels, although *The Unforgiven* is one in reverse. The hostiles in *The Unforgiven* are the Kiowas and LeMay leaves no room to doubt their utter savagery. Indeed, so effective are his descriptions of Kiowa atrocities that it will be a rare reader who can resist the call to arms. LeMay stresses that the Kiowas are unlike many Indian tribes; they "raided for glory, loot, and sport."[22] This circumstance leaves moot any question of a conflict in human rights when it comes to dispossessing the Indians of their territory. What do property rights matter anyway when, as LeMay observes, "...the vast areas the Horse Indians required, in order to live by the hunt, could not much longer be held against a race that fed a thousand people upon land the Wild Tribes needed to feed one."[23] Rachel Zachary, adopted by the Zachary family as an infant, is suspected by their neighbors and even by them of being a Kiowa. She is compared with Seth, the most vicious of the Kiowa warriors, who is a white raised by the Indians. Thus LeMay sought to illustrate that savagery derives from culture, not race, and certainly not from human nature. If red and white are taken to be racial terms, Rachel is no more red than Seth is white. Added to this are the suspenseful siege of the Zachary sod hut which occupies the last third of the novel and LeMay's fastidious reconstruction of what pioneer life was like raising cattle on a small ranch in Texas in 1875. The Indians pose a substantial threat to what the small ranchers want to do and there is no ambiguity about this struggle: the Indians are hopelessly to be contemned, the hard-working, self-sacrificing white pioneers their obvious moral superiors. It may be ironic but it is nonetheless valid to contrast how persuasive a novel like *The Unforgiven* can be compared with the emotions evoked by *From Where the Sun Now Stands*.

Ever since Zane Grey published *The Rainbow Trail* in 1915, searchers and wanderers have come to play a significant role in stories set in the West. This ought not be too surprising since it is a theme with a sustaining attraction for American readers, one which to my mind offers the greatest literary potential and which, insofar as he was almost exclusively preoccupied with its spiritual dimension, may go a long way toward explaining the popularity among American readers of an European author like Hermann Hesse. Alan LeMay's *The Searchers* is probably the best novel he wrote. It possesses a graphic sense of place, as does *The Unforgiven,* but even more so it etches deeply the feats of human endurance which LeMay tended most to admire in the American spirit. Yet, notwithstanding, the novel has little depth of character and motivation is likely to be summed up in a sentence—as when the reader is perfunctorily told: "Amos was—had always been—in love with his brother's wife."[24] The novel revolves around Amos Edwards' quest for his young niece, Debbie, taken into captivity by the Comanches when she was eleven after they had brutally murdered her family. Debbie's adopted brother Mart Pauley accompanies Amos in this search. LeMay knew much about the externals of Comanche life, but, regrettably, he knew little of them as men and so, despite all the detail, they remain essentially incomprehensible savages.

Both of these LeMay novels inspired films. *The Unforgiven* (United Artists, 1960) was rather disappointingly brought to the screen by John Huston, although it probably deserves its reputation as one of the most vicious anti–Indian films ever made. *The Searchers* (Warner's, 1956), on the other hand, may readily be John Ford's most stunningly beautiful Western due, in large part, to the lyrical manner in which he had the camera capture the changes in season to mark the passage of time. However nothing better illustrates the difference between the conventions of Western fiction and Western films than to examine how Frank S. Nugent's script and Ford's direction altered many of the basic premises of LeMay's novel, beginning with the fact that Amos Edwards was changed to Ethan Edwards and, since it was John Wayne portraying him, he could not be killed as he was in the novel but instead was transformed into the John Wayne Western persona.

LeMay avoided flagrant mythmaking or idealized heroism; what heroism there was came from personal tenacity in a struggle with the land and human obstacles. The late Conrad Richter had a similar orientation, but with some rather important differences. Compelled to leave the East and settle in New Mexico in 1928 for reasons of his wife's health, Richter was inspired as a result of his subsequent experiences to write the nine short stories in *Early Americana* between 1934 and 1936. They preceded his novel *The Sea of Grass* (1937) by only a year and prompted his historical novels about pioneering for which he has been praised. It never occurred to LeMay that his pioneers were intruders in Indian lands and to Richter, if the Indians counted at all, they served primarily as an impediment to progress and the settling of the West. In "Smoke over the Prairie," one of the longer stories in *Early Americana* and a sort of preliminary sketch for *The Sea of Grass,* Vance

Rutherford is an advance man for the railroad. Frank Gant, a sheep rancher, owner of a cartage company, and proprietor of a "rude empire" in land, resists the railroad in its attempt to gain right-of-way across his domain. Rutherford elopes with Gant's daughter and, by the end of the story, Gant is killed when a locomotive collides with the buggy in which he is riding. But before that happens, Rutherford has a chance to tell him what is happening: "'Mr. Gant, you've been a pioneer in this country. You've had to deal with savages and outlaws, but those days are nearly over. The territory is on the threshold of prosperity. A flood of people are coming with the railroad. Schools and churches will spring up everywhere. It's going to be an empire, the Southwestern empire, sir.'"25

Richter belongs to that group of writers about the American West who must rarely have questioned the ultimate value of the spread of civilization and who found it inevitable and perhaps preferable to the wilderness. Certainly he was unlike a number of nineteenth-century American authors from Thoreau to Twain who had many serious reservations. William A. Bloodworth in his Introduction to *Early Americana*, after commenting on the way Richter slighted "the ethnic diversity of the Southwest," went on to observe that Richter's "heroes are not the men in buckskin, the yearners for wilderness and freedom; they are the builders of families and communities.... His allegiance in the stories is to the Anglo-Saxon pioneer...."26 Obviously that same large segment of middle-class America that endorsed paternalistic Western series like *Gunsmoke* and *Bonanza* or soap operas like *Little House on the Prairie* and *How the West Was Won* was sympathetic with Richter's view that it is best not to question too much the benefits of industrial progress precisely because it is the main thrust of the American way.

It was not for Richter to perceive in that progress the seeds of human regression. That vision was often left to writers like John Williams in novels such as *Butcher's Crossing*. It is unfortunate that for so long a time publishers and reviewers have insisted on lumping all books with a Western setting into a single category. In this way a novel like *Butcher's Crossing* can too easily be overlooked. Will Andrews, much as John Shefford in Zane Grey's *The Rainbow Trail*, comes from the East in the hope of finding an alternative way of life in the West. Yet by 1960 so many perspectives had changed that it was possible to show how Andrews found not at all what Shefford found. Andrews discovers that the land can be brutal and more savage than the buffalo

hunter whom he finances. Rather than seeking Fay Larkin in a
sequestered valley as Shefford does, Andrews and his group locate a lost
buffalo herd which they summarily slaughter for the hides. Only winter
comes before they can vacate the valley. One of the party goes insane
and finds God. Another barely makes it through to spring and then
only to get kicked fatally in the head by a horse. Miller, the buffalo
hunter, has been wounded so deeply by the land that he can only take
out his revenge by trying to destroy whatever lives on it. *Butcher's
Crossing* is a powerful novel and one that deserves wider recognition
which its reissue may provide for it.

   The Untamed which Max Brand published in 1919 was his first
Western. It was made into a film that same year starring Tom Mix and
was filmed twice more, once in 1931 with George O'Brien and again in
1955 with Tyrone Power. Since its super hero is Whistling Dan Barry,
I supposed Ken Maynard's programmer *Whistlin' Dan* (Tiffany, 1931)
can be regarded as an unofficial derivation. It is among those of Brand's
potboilers which have sold in excess of a million copies. But for all that
it is a poor novel with a contrived and fantastic plot and a super hero
who joins that trend in Western fiction which for many years prevented
any of it from being taken seriously. Whatever its historical importance, I doubt if *The Untamed* can appeal much to the same audience
that can enjoy Will Henry or Conrad Richter.

   Another curiosity is *The Girl of the Golden West*, a novelization
by David Belasco of his successful but now extremely dated 1904 stage
play. Nonetheless, it inspired one of Puccini's lesser operas and four
different motion picture versions, the last and most fanciful of which
was made by M-G-M in 1938 and starred Jeanette MacDonald as the
Girl. It is a sentimental, highly melodramatic, altogether far-fetched
story of the triumph of true love between the Girl and her bandit lover
who must finally go East to find happiness.

   Of greater interest is Harvey Fergusson. He has been "re-
discovered" with some regularity by critics just about every ten years
and yet his stylish novels about New Mexico have been more out of
print than in. Fergusson's lyrical prose informed by the gentlest irony,
his nearness to and respect for the land, his closeness to the ethnic
environment in which he was raised, of Native American and Mexican-
American, combined with his perception of the Anglo-American
temperament which began invading northern New Mexico just before
the Civil War. Born at Albuquerque, New Mexico, in 1890, Fergusson
was one of four children, all of whom became writers. His brother,

Francis Fergusson, professor and critic, is best known for *The Idea of a Theatre* (1949), among the best books of criticism of the drama. Erna Fergusson and Lina Fergusson Browne both became historians. Harvey Fergusson left New Mexico in 1912 at the age of twenty-two. By the time of his death at eighty-one, living in Berkeley, California, he had written fourteen books. His last novel, *The Conquest of Don Pedro,* published in 1954, has been reissued by the University of New Mexico Press. What Fergusson subtitled "A Trilogy of the Santa Fe Trail" has been reprinted by the Gregg Press.

Blood of the Conquerors was written first but, chronologically, it should be read last. It appeared in 1921 and deals with modern Albuquerque during the dispossession of the Mexican *ricos,* proud and once rich families following the course, under persistent Anglo-American pressure, that the New Mexican Indians had been forced to follow earlier. "It is the typical Southwestern town of the end of the frontier period," Fergusson later described the setting, "when all the booms were over and all the battles fought, when the free wealth of the wilderness all had been either squandered or hoarded and men had to learn the difficult and cunning technique of taking things away from each other without the aid of firearms."[27] The story, briefly told, is how Ramon Delcasar, by attending law school so he can master the principles of the Anglo-American legal system through which the land has been dispossessed from its rightful owners, achieves success. But then he quits. Just why he does, why he has to, is what makes Fergusson's novel even more poignant today than when he wrote it.

Lawrence Clark Powell in *Southwestern Classics* (1971) quotes the late J. Frank Dobie from a letter. "I had occasion," Dobie wrote Powell, "last night to look for something in Harvey Fergusson's *Wolf Song,* which I rate above Guthrie's *The Big Sky,* as a novel of the mountain men. It is easily among the best half dozen novels of the West, in my estimation. Willa Cather, Conrad Richter, nor anyone else has equalled Fergusson in the swiftness, economy, and prose rhythm of chapter one in *Wolf Song.*"[28] With the possible exception of *The Conquest of Don Pedro, Wolf Song* is the best novel Fergusson ever wrote, true to its setting in antebellum New Mexico and irresistible by virtue of its enchanting style. Although published in 1927, it begins the trilogy.

In Those Days, dating from 1929, bridges the center. Robert Jayson is the protagonist, a man who comes to New Mexico, becomes a prosperous merchant, and who winds up in penury. Perhaps Fergusson was too close to his source. He based much of his narrative on the memoir left by Franz Huning, his maternal grandfather, who did become a successful merchant in New Mexico. Lina Fergusson Browne published this original memoir in 1973 under the title *Trader on the Santa Fe Trail*. Fergusson's *The Conquest of Don Pedro* is a better fictional rendering of the same materials, and it is only in his final book that Fergusson at last had the courage to let his protagonist quit and become a wanderer, to change himself when time made change inescapable, but to retain his integrity. "The pioneering past has now been diligently debunked," Fergusson once reflected, "but as surely as the flavor of the reality has been recaptured the quality of the heroic has been lost. I sought to unite them because it seemed to me the heroism of the pioneer life was genuine and had its value."[29]

If Fergusson was right and it did, then we as Americans cannot afford to move too much farther ahead without evaluating again our collective national past, our roots as a people, and re-examine the basic premises on which our civilization has come to rest. Western American literature can help us do this and, therefore, I think the Gregg Press is to be congratulated for its efforts. I question the wisdom of reissuing several of these books in expensive cloth editions when they are currently available in paperback, yet many of them are well worth reading for the first time, and some warrant re-reading. The best of them, especially the novels by Fergusson, Henry, Williams, Burroughs, and Haycox can be far more rewarding and spiritually more profitable than many of the flashy titles presently gracing the best-seller lists.

Eugene Manlove Rhodes:
An Appreciation

If I envied the favored few
That lightly loitered their light lives through,
I said no word as I watched them go,
But I set my teeth, and I hoed my row.
                        Eugene Manlove Rhodes[1]

The parents of Eugene Manlove Rhodes—Hinman Rhodes and Julia Mae Manlove—first met in Schuyler County, Illinois. Julia was a vivacious, energetic woman with a reputation for being an excellent rider. As befitted the daughter of a prosperous family, she attended Lombard College at Galesburg, Illinois. In July, 1866, brevetted with the rank of colonel, Hinman Rhodes joined the influx of other Union Army veterans entering Nebraska Territory. He purchased numerous town lots at Tecumseh and became a partner in a general mercantile business, Rhodes & Tingle. He and Julia were married on March 5, 1868. Eugene was born in a double log cabin at Tecumseh on January 7, 1869. It was two weeks after his mother's twenty-sixth birthday. Nebraska had become a state and Hinman was away from home at the time serving his first term in the newly formed state legislature.

In 1871, during the elder Rhodes' second term in the legislature, the firm of Rhodes & Tingle failed. Rather than dodge the debts of the defunct partnership, the colonel's attitude was summed up in a homily of that day, "I pay for what I break." It took Hinman Rhodes years to pay out what was owed. His son was profoundly impressed by this attitude and it became his own standard for measuring himself and for distinguishing friends and enemies alike. It also made him something of an anachronism among Americans in this century.

The family next tried dry farming near Beatrice, Nebraska, where the only fecundity was human—a second son, Clarence, was born—whereas two years of drought, grasshoppers, cyclones, and what was termed "The Crash of '73" resulted in another economic failure. It was during this ordeal that Gene suffered a permanent eye injury. He saw a harvest hand remove a glass eye in order to wash it and tried to do the same with his own.

Hinman Rhodes moved his family to Cherokee, Kansas, where he went on the road selling sewing machines while Julia opened a dressmaking shop. It was from the latter that the family derived the major part of its income. A daughter, Helen, was born here, before the family moved on again, this time to Columbus, Kansas, where in 1880 the elder Rhodes went into the lumber business. However, he was persistently troubled by back injuries engendered during his years in the Army and he also suffered from asthma. Gene apparently inherited a propensity for respiratory illness from his father. He suffered his life long from asthma which, in later years, became aggravated by chronic bronchitis. He had also been born with a speech impediment. He could not pronounce the letter "g" and he had so much difficulty with the letter "r" that it came out sounding more as if it were "th." "It is impossible to reproduce in type his exact enunciation," Agnes Morley Cleaveland recalled in *No Life for a Lady* (1941), "but strangers often mistook his 'Rhodes' for 'Thodes.' One day, so his mother related, three strangers rode into his horse camp and asked for Mr. Rhodes. 'I'm Thodes,' Gene politely informed them. 'But it is *Rhodes* we want to see,' the visitors insisted. Gene regarded them for an instant in silence and then turned and bellowed to a comrade some distance away, 'Hey, Pete, come over here and tell these sons-of-guns what my name is and find out what they want.'"[2]

Julia Rhodes was a strong-willed woman. In Columbus it was once more her millinery business which supported the family. The last formal schooling Gene was to have occurred while the family lived in Cherokee. Henceforth, until he decided to enter a university, what education he received came first from his mother who taught him at home and then, because he was a voracious reader, from the books in the family library which included novels by Dickens, Scott, and Cooper, poetry by Longfellow, Tennyson, Byron, Burns, and Poe, and of course Shakespeare and the King James Bible.

It has been the tendency among Rhodes' biographers to stress the influence his father had upon him as well as the men he met while attaining his majority. Yet, I should not want to pass over so quickly the influence of his mother or, perhaps better said, Rhodes' reaction to his mother and his attitude toward women in general. Agnes Morley

Cleaveland recalled one summer she spent in Los Angeles while Rhodes, who was by then married, was also there by himself visiting his mother who was living on the outskirts of Pasadena. "I had an automobile but Gene hadn't, so I would call for him and deliver him back home after our expedition, whatever it might be, was over. He had been long enough in a conventional setting to feel that he should express regret at this reversal of roles, until I reminded him that our cattle-country code held it to be the highest form of compliment to allow every fellow to do what the situation demanded of him and to assume that he wanted to do it. Gene gave in, until the night we went to a Hollywood Bowl pageant. It was after one o'clock when we drew up to his door. He started to protest at allowing me to make the long drive home at that hour of the morning. 'Don't weaken, pardner,' I admonished. He watched me drive away, and I knew that my insistence on going alone was giving him a bout with his double code."[3]

Bernard DeVoto commented in an essay on Rhodes' inability to draw young female characters from life. His heroines, when he did include one, are in DeVoto's words "incredible, and the attitude in which they are approached, the lush and trepidant veneration, the tropical breathlessness in the presence of mysterious, mysteriously fine, and infrangibly virginal female flesh makes one wonder why an artist who could differentiate the colors of grasses under a five-miles-distant wind never bothered to observe what a woman looks like. They are distillations of sweetness and exist merely to stimulate the hero to precariously gallant behavior, usually on occasions when good sense in a woman would have made it impossible, and to reward him when the complications have been worked out."[4] Rhodes himself confessed in a letter to historian Walter Prescott Webb that "there was no 'star' system on the range. Also, few women and vague in my stories — because they are just so in my memories." In a subsequent letter to Webb, Rhodes observed that "Sir Walter Scott's novels . . . just about ruined me."[5] Combined with his idealization of his father, Rhodes no doubt derived from Scott much of his idea of a hero, but with this idealization of a father-hero went inevitably the idealization of womanhood. He preferred — to place the matter in the context of the contrast between women which Scott used in *Waverly* (1814) — a Rose Bradwardine to a Flora Mac-Ivor. "It is," DeVoto concluded about Rhodes' fictional females, "only when they have reached middle age, when he can read from their hands and faces what life in the desert had cost them, that they are human or even credible."[6]

It was possibly for reasons of health that Hinman Rhodes decided to move to New Mexico. The colonel, now fifty-four, went first, taking only Gene with him. The year was 1881. "I came to New Mexico the year that Billy the Kid was killed," Gene Rhodes later remarked.[7]

During his early years in New Mexico, Hinman Rhodes worked as a miner. On one occasion he accepted a temporary job in Old Mexico, leaving Gene in charge of the family which had taken residence in an adobe house in Engle. At times Gene would accompany his father on local jobs; at other times he would work by himself for such prospectors as "Uncle Ben" Teagarten, a man in his high seventies, and Preston G. Lewis, a Virginian who bore a striking resemblance to graven images of Jove. Later, in his fiction, Gene's father came to serve as the model for the character, John Wesley Pringle; Teagarten as Ben Teagardner and Pres Lewis, called by his right name, appeared as themselves. Gene also worked as a swamper for a freight rig and he saw a herd of cattle watered at gun point at the Rincon railroad pens. These experiences he incorporated decades later in what I regard as his finest novel, *The Trusty Knaves* (1934). Notwithstanding his various jobs, Gene worked mostly for the Bar Cross, although his employment by the spread was scarcely sequential, and it was this outfit in his subsequent fiction which came to represent the best he had known of the final days of the free range in a lonesome land.

Hinman Rhodes was granted a monthly pension of $12.50 for his Civil War disability. He filed on an eighty-acre homestead at the head of Cottonwood Canyon in the San Andrés Mountains. Gene was seventeen by now and he helped his father erect a two-room cabin with a rock fireplace. The colonel embarked on a career as a stockman, although on a small scale. To help meet expenses Gene worked for the Bar Cross as a wrangler. He smoked cigarettes rolled from Blackwell's Genuine Bull Durham Tobacco. Each four ounce sack contained two coupons; four coupons bought any paperback title in Munro's Library of Popular Novels. The list included, among others, titles by Conan Doyle, Wilkie Collins, Alexandre Dumas, Robert Louis Stevenson, Jules Verne, and Anthony Trollope. It was probably at this time that Rhodes first discovered Stevenson's fiction, an author for whom he would always retain a special attachment.

The Santa Fe "Ring," a group headed by attorney Thomas B. Catron, had conspired to gain economic and political control of New Mexico Territory. W.G. Ritch, a "Ring" member, had been appointed acting governor under Lew Wallace during the final phase of the

Lincoln County War. It was Ritch who had refused to pay Pat Garrett, then sheriff of Lincoln County, a $500 reward for capturing Billy the Kid and he tried to avoid payment again after the Kid broke jail and Garrett ambushed him at the Maxwell home at Fort Sumner. In 1887 Ritch filed a contest of Hinman Rhodes' homestead which precipitated a lengthy legal battle.

In 1888 the colonel's pension was raised to $25 a month and it was then that Gene approached him to borrow $50 so he might enter the University of the Pacific, a Methodist institution in San Jose, California. Just what influence the fact that Rhodes' family was Methodist may have had on Gene's selection of this school cannot be said with certitude, but he did attend for almost two years, earning the remainder of his expenses himself and confined, during the school year, to a diet consisting almost exclusively of oatmeal. His course work included Latin, Greek, geography, mathematics, mythology, and ancient history. Later when this became blended with his desultory reading over the years and was combined with his customary setting of New Mexico peopled by the men he had known there, the style of his fiction emerged, an aggregate so peculiar to him, a Westerner writing about the West in prose informed by classical references, snatches of poetry and homespun doggerel, a profound familiarity with the Bible and its splendid, fabulous imagery. Rhodes' first literary efforts occurred while he was an underclassman and were published in the school's newspaper. His earliest predilection was for poetry. In an autobiographical non–Western story, "The Torch," published in 1908 in *Out West,* Rhodes had one of the characters express what must have been his own feelings about his college years. "'I was there two years, the happiest of my life. Not one care, not one unhappy moment. I had attained my majority at thirteen. At least, I have done a man's work ever since. I had never known any boys. Just rough men. I had my youth in one deep, priceless draught.'"[8]

Hinman Rhodes in 1889 entered his application for the position of agent at the Mescalero Indian reservation. This agency had been a central pawn in the Lincoln County War and the victors of that struggle, Catron, John H. Riley, and Colonel William L. Rynerson among them, had retained political control of valuable government subsidies such as the Mescalero beef contract. Catron, Riley, and Rynerson owned the Tularosa ranch adjacent to the agency and had customarily filled the beef contracts with inferior livestock. They opposed Hinman Rhodes' appointment and, once he had secured it and tried to institute honest business practices at the agency, they sought his removal. In 1890 Hinman Rhodes lost his homestead contest with W.H. Ritch and in August, 1891, he lost his position at the agency. Gene, who had now returned from school, was so infuriated by this contretemps that he aligned his political sympathies with the Democratic machine which stood in opposition to the Republican "Ring." The leaders of the Democratic machine were Albert Bacon Fall and Oliver Milton Lee. Gene had first met the latter in 1885 when he had worked briefly for the Bar W near Carrizozo. When New Mexico achieved statehood in 1912, Fall changed parties, becoming a Republican so he could join Thomas B. Catron in the U.S. Senate. Fall later resigned his Senate seat to become Secretary of the Interior in the Harding Administration only to find himself embroiled in the Teapot Dome and Elk Hill scandals. He was accused, convicted, and finally sentenced to prison for accepting a bribe of $100,000 from the Sinclair Oil Company to allow clandestine oil exploration on federal and Indian lands. Despite all the evidence to the contrary, Gene remained convinced of Fall's innocence and "sided" him until the end.

Gene himself in late 1892 filed on a homestead, about six miles north of what had been his father's homestead, located in the bottom lands of what became known as Rhodes' Canyon. Here he built a two-room *jacal* and set up a large horse corral. There was a spring on this eighty acres and control of it, along with some illegal fencing, gave Gene possession of fifty sections of the Public Domain. He took care of the cattle owned by his parents and he worked at odd jobs to supplement his income, including bronc busting. Then he turned around and leased his ranch to the Bar Cross, three years while Cole Railston was ramrod, two while Carroll McCombs had the job. "Gene never claimed to be a top-hand," Railston said of him years afterward, "but he was an all-around good hand. I never knew him to carry a pistol. Next to cowboying and reading, he liked poker and a fight. He was not a trouble-maker, far from it, but no one stepped on his toes or rode his pet horse. I never knew a man to throw Gene in a wrestling match. He was a real good bronc rider."[9]

In April, 1895, Bill Doolin entered New Mexico and the bad man hid out at Rhodes' ranch. He also managed to save Rhodes' life when Rhodes was in danger of being stomped to death by a wild horse. This episode inspired the basic plot of *The Trusty Knaves*.

The Rhodes family moved to Mesilla where Gene's brother, Clarence, walked three miles a day to the state college located at Las

Cruces. Clarence earned $12.50 a month doing janitorial work at the college while attending classes in mining engineering. Gene, when he was in town, audited courses in English and history, but most of his time was spent in poker games, often with card sharps and they ended as frequently as not in bouts of fisticuffs.

Colonel Albert J. Fountain was a Santa Fe "Ring" Republican. He had been appointed Billy the Kid's defense attorney at his trial at Mesilla. Since the "Ring" wanted the Kid dead, the trial concluded with predictable results. In 1896, with A.B. Fall and Thomas B. Catron locked in a political contest to dominate the Territory, Oliver Milton Lee and William McNew, two Fall cronies, were indicted for brand changing and cattle stealing. Fountain attended the court session at which these indictments were handed down. A.B. Fall ostensibly feared Fountain's political power. Shortly after the trial, Colonel Fountain and his nine-year-old son Henry disappeared in the area around White Sands. Lee was widely suspected of having been behind their murders. Governor W.T. Thornton, Catron's law partner during the time of the Lincoln County War, hired Pat Garrett to hunt down and capture Lee. Garrett's *modus operandi* in his manhunt for Billy the Kid had been to shoot from ambush and by this means he dispatched not only the Kid but also Tom O'Folliard and Charlie Bowdre who rode with the Kid. Chances were rather good that Lee would never be brought to trial. However, the case dragged on for two years and despite having had Garrett installed as sheriff of Doña Ana County in order to make any killing from ambush Garrett might do official and legal it seemed as if nothing was going to happen. McNew, to escape assassination, surrendered himself and was safely in custody at Las Cruces, outside Garrett's jurisdiction. In July, 1898, Garrett led a posse to ambush Lee and James Gililland. The latter had by now also been charged with the Fountain murders although no bodies had ever been found. Garrett and the posse opened fire on the building in which the fugitives were presumably asleep. But Lee and Gililland were able to turn the tables. Deputy Sheriff Kent Kearney was mortally wounded and Garrett and the others, to their humiliation, were compelled to walk away with their hands held high in the air. Lee and Gililland then kept on the prod, seeking shelter occasionally at Rhodes' secluded ranch. Rhodes bunked with them much of the time except when he worked sporadically for Charles J. Graham whose ranch served as a listening post for Garrett's pursuit activities.

Clarence in the meantime graduated from college and secured

employment as a mining engineer working in Old Mexico. The family sold the Mesilla home. Gene's mother and sister moved to Pasadena. Colonel Rhodes remained in New Mexico for another two years, living with friends and intermittantly with Gene at his ranch before he, too, went to California. In 1896 Gene had his first poem published in a commercial magazine, *Land of Sunshine* edited by C.F. Lummis. Henceforth, Gene continued to submit poems and Lummis continued to publish them.

The Lee and Gililland case persisted for another two and a half years before Rhodes negotiated their voluntary surrender to George Curry, then sheriff of Otero County. The county was named after Miguel A. Otero who had succeeded Thornton as territorial governor. Otero was at loggerheads with Catron and the "Ring" and it seemed an auspicious time to end the matter if Lee and Gililland could only avoid Garrett. During the Lincoln County War, Curry had backed Garrett's election as sheriff of Lincoln County. Billy the Kid had even spent a night at Curry's place without Curry's knowing who he was until after he had left. Later, Curry would join the Rough Riders. As would be the case with A.B. Fall, Curry switched parties from Democrat to Republican. This move permitted President Theodore Roosevelt to appoint Curry governor in 1907. It was from Curry a year later that Garrett, down on his luck, would borrow $50 and he still had the check on his person when he was murdered from ambush. The surrender of Lee and Gililland proved a success even though Garrett was himself on the same train as Rhodes and the two fugitives and recognized none of them.

Oliver Milton Lee was an expert cowman and a man who loved horses. He was fastidious in his dress and in his person; and he was wont to read the Greek and Latin classics in their original languages. Rhodes used him as the model for Kit Foy, a character in his short novel *The Desire of the Moth* (1920). In the novel Kit Foy is engaged to marry Stella Vorhis. However, Foy is framed for a murder by Matthew Lisner, a sheriff running for re-election. John Wesley Pringle, who had made his debut in Rhodes' first novel, *Good Men and True* (1910), saves the day by effectively scheming to have the sheriff exposed by his own men. When Kit and Stella are reunited at the end, Pringle, an old man, "bent and kissed her hands — lest, looking into his eyes, she should read in the book of his life one long, long chapter — that bore her name."[10] *The Desire of the Moth* was serialized in *The Saturday Evening Post* in 1916 and it was filmed by Universal in 1917 with Monroe Salsbury cast as Kit Foy. Lest one might think that the crooked sheriff in the story was based on Pat Garrett, it must be noted that Rhodes made a hero of Garrett, and by name, in a subsequent book, *Pasó por Aquí* (1927), which ran serially in the *Post* in 1926. And he went even further. In 1927 in response to the appearance of Walter Nobel Burns' *The Saga of Billy the Kid* (1926), Rhodes published an article in *Sunset* magazine titled "In Defense of Pat Garrett." In it he repeated the common belief that the Kid and Garrett had been on friendly terms during the Kid's rustling days and that the Kid never should have been sentenced to hang, "not unless they hanged several others at the same time."[11] "I wonder if you can believe," he added, with regard to the Kid, "that my deepest feeling for him is pity for his hard fate?"[12]

Billie Wilson was a young desperado who had been captured with Billy the Kid when Garrett and his posse ambushed the Kid at Stinking Springs, killing the unarmed Charlie Bowdre in the process. Wilson and the Kid were taken in shackles to the prison at Santa Fe. Wilson later escaped, making his way eventually to Texas where he married under an assumed name, started a family, and became a customs inspector near Langtry. When Garrett learned of Wilson's reform, he notified him that he would use his influence to gain for him a presidential pardon. Installed as sheriff of Doña Ana County during the Lee case, Garrett managed to entice Governor Thornton and other prominent New Mexicans to join him in securing a pardon which was granted by President Grover Cleveland.

Charles A. Siringo, a range detective who retired to write rather successfully about the Old West, became friends with Rhodes in later years. Rhodes even encouraged his publisher Houghton Mifflin to publish one of Siringo's books. Siringo happened to be in New Mexico at the time of Garrett's pursuit of the Kid and he included a highly imaginative account of the Kid's life and escapades in his early book, *A Texas Cowboy* (1885). For most of the details about the Kid, Siringo cribbed from the book Ash Upson ghosted for Pat Garrett about the Kid's early years and his capture, escape, and death. Upson was an itinerant journalist and one of Garrett's cronies. However, Siringo did include one apocryphal anecdote about the Kid the origin of which seems to lie with him exclusively. "A man," he wrote, "now a highly respected citizen of White Oaks, was lying at the point of death in Fort Sumner, without friends or money, and a stranger, when the Kid, who had just come into town from one of his raids, went to his rescue, on hearing of his helpless condition; the sick man had been placed in an old out-house on a pile of sheep skins. The Kid hired a team and hauled him to Las Vegas, a distance of over a hundred miles, himself, where he could receive care and medical aid. He also paid the doctor and board bills for a month, besides putting a few dollars in money in the sick man's hand as he bid him good bye."[13]

I do not believe there is a word of truth in this anecdote; but it is the kind of incident that particularly appealed to Rhodes' romantic sense of the Old West which had vanished, as did Garrett's action on behalf of Billie Wilson. Rhodes may have opposed Garrett in the Lee case, but he would never judge a man all of a piece. *Pasó por Aquí* is commonly considered to be Rhodes' finest Western story. In this judgment I cannot concur. For me, the principal charm of the story lies in the two long soliloquys given to the Mexican-American, Monte, whose border English would serve to inspire numerous other Western writers, not least of all Clarence E. Mulford who had created the Bar-20 saga and in his character El Toro in a different series of books was the most obvious in his imitation. For the basic plot of *Pasó por Aquí* Rhodes appears to have combined Siringo's anecdote about the Kid with the true incident of Billie Wilson's pardon. Ross McEwen, in Rhodes' story, holds up a bank in rather daring fashion and is pursued by a posse. He throws away the paper money rather than face capture. After changing horses, he finally is compelled to ride a steer for several miles before the steer, too, plays out. McEwen comes upon a Mexican-American family suffering from diphtheria and nurses it through the illness, even though this activity exposes him to arrest. Pat Garrett is among those who are on McEwen's trail and he is sufficiently impressed with what McEwen has done — he finds the Mexican-American family's rancho by means of McEwen's signal fire — that, although cognizant of McEwen's real identity, he manages to provide him with a safe-conduct out of the Territory.

I think James K. Folsom is correct in *The American Western Novel* (1966) when he views much of Rhodes' fiction, and *Pasó por Aquí* in particular, as nostalgia, "a lament for the old times."[14] There is no conventional romance in this story, as there isn't in much that Rhodes wrote, but Rhodes did introduce an Eastern nurse into *Pasó por Aquí*, Jay Hollister, who works at the hospital at Alamogordo and who hates the West. She is not made to change her mind, neither through love for a cowboy nor because her Eastern values are found to be ineffectual. Instead, her values remain unassailable in the face of the Western values illustrated by McEwen, Garrett, and Monte. It is Monte's second soliloquy to the nurse which closes the story. "'And thees fellow, too, thees redhead,'" he says of McEwen, "'he pass this way, "pasó por aquí" . . . and he mek here good and not weeked. But, before that—I am not God!'" "'And him the sheriff!'" Nurse Hollister objects, realizing that Garrett has let a wanted man escape. "'Why they could impeach him for that. They could throw him out of office.'" "'But who weel tell?'" Monte responds. "'We are all decent people.'"[14]

Folsom in his critique of Rhodes recognized that Rhodes' *aficionados* have at times been too extravagant in their praise of his fiction, that there are manifest flaws which spoil much of his work. "At times," Folsom wrote, "when his adherence to the conventions of 'slick' writing trips him up, he can be one of the most maddening of writers. His stories are marred by an annoying coincidental quality in which someone invariably happens along just at the right moment to hear the villains plotting their crimes, which they do explicitly and at great length. . . . Even his often beautifully conceived dialogue deteriorates far too much into the tedious smartness which passes for wit among the devotees of the slick magazines. When Rhodes is at his best, however, these faults are only those of detail, which may mar but do not destroy the real quality of his fiction."[15] Folsom saw, aptly, that Rhodes' major contribution to Western fiction was in his presentation of a cowboy hero, a man who "is both insightful and active" and with "a certain distrust of the forms by which less gifted mortals operate; for he believes that he is better able to resolve problems on his own than by the conventional methods used by ordinary men."[16] *Pasó por Aquí* was not brought to the screen until almost two decades after Rhodes' death, titled *Four Faces West* (United Artists, 1948). It was produced by Harry Sherman, the man who had brought Clarence E. Mulford's Hopalong Cassidy to the screen portrayed by William Boyd. The formula of the cinematic Western had been too simplified by that time for a story of the subtle tensions between supposed Eastern and Western values to hold much interest for the audience. In fact, Sherman himself had once described his successful formula for Westerns in these terms: open big, forget the middle, and come to a furious finish. No story by Rhodes could be reshaped to embody that philosophy and *Pasó por Aquí*, as written, is ultimately unfilmable.

To reflect on Rhodes' notions of a Western hero have not taken me too far afield. Just how he came to conceive of that hero in his fiction was a direct consequence of what happened to Rhodes once he left New Mexico. It was in California that Julia Rhodes made the acquaintance of a trained nurse in her thirties, Emma Antoinette Davison, who told Julia about her younger sister, May Davison Purple, back home in Apalachin, New York. May had been married to Fred Purple. He had been walking one day with his brother along a railroad track when the two men were surprised to find a train bearing down on them. Fred pushed his younger brother to safety but was himself killed. Now May was a widow with two small children. Julia showed Emma some of the poetry Gene had been writing for *Land of Sunshine* and Emma took some of these poems back East with her when she returned to Apalachin to nurse May during a bout of diphtheria. May was so impressed by the poems that she wrote Gene a highly complimentary letter. After a long wait, she received a twenty-page reply. A correspondence began between them and in July, 1899, Gene went East. He went as a cow puncher, literally using a prod to keep steers in cattle cars from reclining so that they would not be trampled underfoot by the others. He also managed to get in a fist fight on the way and so he was somewhat battered when he and May met for the first time.

"A quiet, medium-sized man whose blond hair and moustache, he always insisted, were mouse-colored," May later wrote of him in *The Hired Man on Horseback: My Story of Eugene Manlove Rhodes* (1938). "Blue eyes, a face richly sunburned. . . . A man of strange contradictions, gentle and dreamy, who wrote exquisite poetry and had a superfine taste in literature, yet, in the twinkling of an eye, could be metamorphosed into incarnate rage. . . . He had been in a big fight, and one ear was a bit torn off, his face bruised. He wore a cheap light suit. . . . We kissed each other, a bit timidly I'll allow, and hand in hand we paced slowly up the hill to the house."[17]

It was the custom of the time that the youngest daughter generally was expected to remain with her parents to care for them in their old age. May and her two children lived on her parents' farm. After spending less than a month in Apalachin, Rhodes proposed. Four days after the wedding, Rhodes, who was penniless, left May and her children in Apalachin and returned to New Mexico in order to earn enough money to bring them West. He was finally able to do so half a year later.

The marriage was a strange one by all accounts, including that of May Davison Rhodes herself. By inclination and nurture, she was too strongly attached to her parents and, conversely, totally unprepared for the lonely and to her mind brooding way of life in Tularosa, much less the isolation up at Rhodes' ranch. Although his parents now lived in California, Rhodes continued to tend their livestock, having merged their brand with his own, and he usually sent them most of what income he made selling or trading their brand. When the Rhodes family had lived at Mesilla, Rhodes had briefly taught school at Eagle Creek. The class to which he had been assigned had a reputation for unruliness. May recalled that "when Gene took his place at the teacher's desk, he pulled his six-shooter from the band of his pants, rapped smartly on the desk with it, and announced, 'The school will now come to order.' It did."[18] With May in New Mexico and now pregnant, Rhodes hoped to supplement his income and applied for a teacher's certificate. It was denied him on the grounds of his moral character.

May became so disconsolate with the way of life and so filled with yearning for her parents and some kind of economic stability that Rhodes was finally forced to mortgage his ranch to Oliver Milton Lee for $250 on a one-year note at twelve per cent interest so he could send May, her sons Jack and Fred, and the son they had had together, Alan Hinman Rhodes, back East. Alan had been named after Alan Breck in Stevenson's *Kidnapped* (1886). It was said in Tularosa and Alamogordo that May had flatly told Gene that if he ever wanted to see his son again it would have to be in Apalachin.

In January, 1902, Rhodes had published his first short story in *Out West* magazine. Spurred on by financial desperation and encouraged by May's unwavering belief in his ability as a storyteller, Rhodes published eight more stories in *Out West* that year and in 1903. These stories brought him to the attention of Henry Wallace Phillips whose Western stories featuring such characters as Red Saunders and Agamemnon Jones appeared regularly in such major magazines as *McClure's* and *The Saturday Evening Post*. Somehow Phillips was able to persuade Rhodes to send him raw material for plots, scenes, and characters and then Phillips would work the elements into stories which he would publish under his name and for which Rhodes received neither credit nor remuneration. Eventually, however, Phillips did agree to give Rhodes a co-author credit on several short stories published in *The Saturday Evening Post*. The collaboration may have taught Rhodes something about commercial writing for the slick magazines. It certainly did make his name familiar to the editors at the *Post* which was to remain the principal outlet for his fiction throughout his literary career.

Emerson Hough, who had once practiced law at White Oaks before returning East to write, hired Pat Garrett in 1904 to take him on a tour of various areas in New Mexico so he could gather material for a book he was working on, *The Story of the Outlaw* (1907). The two encountered Rhodes and Hough encouraged Gene to continue writing. Rhodes at the time would write out his stories in a scarcely legible long-hand and then send them East for May to type. George Davison, his brother-in-law, would try to place the stories with a number of magazines. In a letter Rhodes wrote to George Davison in 1905, he told of having met Agnes Morley Cleaveland for the first time. She was already an established writer and her fiction was bringing her two cents a word. Rhodes expressed the hope that he might do as well.

Finally, in 1906, Rhodes decided to leave New Mexico and come to Apalachin to live with May, May's parents, and the children. He asked his long-time friend, Hiram Yoast, who would figure prominently as a character in "The Line of Least Resistance," a serial published by *The Saturday Evening Post* in 1910, to round up what cattle and horses were at his ranch, both with his brand and that of his parents, and deliver them to S.E. Renick of Engle. Julia was paid only $15 for almost 150 head of cattle! That year the colonel's pension was increased to $40 a month and in November he was admitted to the Veterans' Home at Sawtelle, California. Julia had visited Gene briefly when he and May had been living together at Tularosa. Her response to the marriage was to censure her son. "'Why did Gene have to marry a widow with two children?'" she had confronted May. "'I took care of them before I met your son and I can do it again,'" May had responded.[19] Doubtless Julia regretted having been the occasion for the two having met. At the same time, Gene had a similarly hostile relationship with May's mother, although he did establish a strong bond with May's father, a man who was in his seventieth year when Rhodes arrived to join them on the farm. Jack and Fred Purple began calling themselves by Gene's surname, to which May objected vociferously. Rhodes, for his part, made no attempt to adopt them.

Hinman Rhodes died in December, 1907. A year and a month later, in February, 1909, a second child was born to Gene and May, named Barbara after Barbara Grant in Stevenson's *David Balfour* (1893). She lived only twenty months and her death left Rhodes so deeply anguished that even twenty years later mention of her name could bring tears to his eyes.

Following Barbara's death, Rhodes moved his family into a rented house where they lived for two years before he himself bought a farm in Apalachin atop Mutton Hill which had a house on it with fourteen rooms. One of the reasons he could afford to do this was that Rhodes was now writing regularly and being relatively well paid. *Good Men and True* had been readily accepted for serialization by *The Saturday Evening Post*. In a way, given the character of John Wesley Pringle who figured so prominently in it, the short novel was Rhodes' memoriam to his father. It is also permeated with a profound nostalgia for New Mexico's landscape, a characteristic which almost all of Rhodes' fiction possesses from the time of his self-imposed exile in the East.

Rhodes' writing habits had become even more preposterous than had been those of Balzac. He first sketched out each story in his head, complete as to characters and sequence of incidents. Then, after this gestation period which might require months or even years, he began to write down the story, usually under the impetus of financial need, revising his longhand script repeatedly, until finally May would type it. Then he would revise the typescript, going through as many as eleven drafts. Once the story was published, he would rewrite it again before moving on to a new story. The occurrence of a death in the family could incapacitate him for months, as happened in the case of his father and of Barbara, but it might also happen after the death of even a casual acquaintance. During the day, Rhodes would both work his own farm and help out May's father on his farm. At night, he would write. As early as December, 1907, Rhodes reported to George Davison that he had earned $1,747 from writing stories that year and that he had spent all of it. "And again—to write stories one needs some ease—and *rest* when you are worn out. Otherwise," he lamented, "I can see my finish. . . . Tonight for instance, I am very tired. Can hardly write legibly. But I must write at night or not at all."[20]

Agnes Morley Cleaveland had read some of Rhodes' stories in *Out West* magazine and it had been she who recommended him to her editor at *Munsey's*, Bob Davis. Davis liked Rhodes' fiction but he objected to what he felt—correctly—to be an essayist quality in much of it. Mrs. Cleaveland stopped to visit with Gene and his family on a trip East. She had not seen her own son, who was Alan's age, for the last six months. She perplexed May Rhodes upon leaving by saying, "'My children will venerate me as one of the pioneer mothers.'"[21]

Wayne Brazel shot Pat Garrett in the back on a lonely road in New Mexico in 1908 while Garrett was relieving himself. A.B. Fall assisted in Brazel's defense. Although Garrett had scarcely been in a position to threaten any one, Brazel was acquitted on the grounds of self-defense! Thanks to his new prominence as a consequence of his stories in the *Post,* many New Mexicans wrote to Rhodes, including Fall who commented in a letter that everyone had been afraid that Garrett "was going to kill someone and a sigh of relief went up when he was finally killed."

As late as 1934, and despite *Pasó por Aquí* and his article in Garrett's defense, Rhodes summed up his attitude toward the sometime lawman: "It is only fair to say that Garrett was a better man in Billy the Kid's time than in my day. Being made sheriff with the definite object of killing a man — for big pay — is not good for character. Neither is unlimited legend. He disintegrates."[22]

In August, 1910, *Good Men and True* was published in a cloth edition by Henry Holt & Company. In October of that year, after reading the book himself, Holt sent Rhodes a personal letter. "You overflow with ideas to a very enviable extent," he observed, "and put more of them into your conversations than almost any human being but yourself would be able to do. Now what I want to take the liberty of doing, is to call your attention to the old saw — and there was never a sounder one — that *Art is selection,* which in your case of course would involve selecting the people from whom your wit and ideas should flow, and selecting from the ideas themselves only the best. You are to be envied and congratulated on your power in producing these good things, but if you give only the best, the total effect will be better than if you gave with great freedom, and your reputation of course will then be gauged by your best and not by your average."[23] I do not think that Rhodes ever benefitted from this advice. He was convinced in his viscera that every Westerner was a complete individual, totally unlike another, except that his heroes were united by the code he projected into them. Easterners, by contrast, were conformists and tended to be too much alike to be interesting. Rhodes was also intent on making his villains engaging conversationalists. If there was one plot mechanism which most appealed to him, it was that of the detective story, and, although the reader might know the identity of the villain before most of the characters, much of the emphasis is on how the villain is discovered and his schemes exposed.

In 1913, May's father died and her mother moved in with them. This could not have been altogether pleasant for Gene. When the war broke out in Europe, Rhodes did not see the conflict as endangering the United States in any way and he had deep reservations about the colonial policies of both Germany and Great Britain. Once the *Lusitania* was sunk, however, and Fred Purple having missed the draft enlisted on his own, Gene lost his impartiality. He threw himself into farming with monomaniacal diligence, convinced that this, more than anything else he might do, would help achieve final victory. He wrote only one propaganda piece, for the Binghampton *Press,* and otherwise nothing at all. Even his letter writing diminished.

Gene was strickened with influenza in 1919. It was the first major organic illness of his fifty years. His heart became enlarged and this condition would continue to plague him for the rest of his life, finally bringing on his death. His asthma worsened. In November of that year, *The Saturday Evening Post* purchased the serial he had been at work on, *Stepsons of Light,* published as a book first in 1921. Dedicated to May Davison Rhodes, Gene felt this story to be his favorite. In a little Prologue to the cloth edition, Rhodes reflected that "today we dimly perceive that the history of America is the story of the pioneer. . . . They went West for food. What they did there was to work; if you require a monument—take a good look."[24] All of Rhodes' optimism and his romantic attachment to his vision of the West had at last found a voice. Basically, *Stepsons of Light* is the story of how three greedy men kill Adam Forbes to gain his gold claim and try to blame it on Johnny Dines and how Johnny, triumphantly, through the informality of a frontier court is able to prove his innocence and their guilt. The story is somewhat marred by the interpolation of a long essay on realism and pessimism in literature with Rhodes' position being made clear. "It is the business of the realist to preach how man is mastered by circumstances; it is the business of a man to prove that he will be damned first."[25] This sermon was unnecessary. It is articulated by the action of the plot. Aunt Peg, a character in the story, feels that "'the people who care for other things more than they do for money are slowly crowded out by the people who care more for money than for anything else.'"[26] Rhodes' plot, however, contradicts this. It demonstrates the moral superiority of the West in that those who care most for money do *not* succeed. Yet, he could not withhold an occasional critical observation which was informed by that very realism which he condemned. "In Doña Ana County taxes were high and life was cheap. Since the Civil War, Doña Ana had been bedeviled by the rule of professional politicians."[27]

Johnny Dines is no less chivalrous—or, perhaps, just plain stupid is the word—than is Jeff Bransford in *The Little Eohippus* (1912). Bransford breaks jail and escapes, pursued by a posse, rather than allow the heroine to soil herself by appearing in court and establishing his innocence. Dines would rather lose his life than involve a woman in his struggle. Such was Rhodes' romanticism. Even the victim, however, is given a eulogy. "'He did many things amiss,'" old Pete Harkey says of Adam Forbes; "'he took wrong turnings. But he was never too proud to turn back, to admit a mistake, or to right his wrongdoing. He paid for what he broke.'"[28] The villains in *Stepsons of Light* make the same mistake the villain Lake makes in *The Little Eohippus,* "of failing to reckon with the masterless men, who dwell without the wall."[29] Johnny Dines had come to Jeff Bransford's aid in *The Little Eohippus.* Charlie See comes to Johnny's aid in *Stepsons of Light,* but, as John Wesley Pringle before him, he must ride off at the end, leaving Johnny and the heroine behind, "for at the world's edge some must fare alone; through all their dreams one unforgotten face—laughing, and dear, and lost."[30]

It would be a mistake, however, to think that most of Rhodes' magazine serials ended with the heroine and the hero embracing. Nothing could be further from the truth, although Rhodes had it to his credit to be the first to publish a ranch romance in a slick magazine. Owen Wister began the tradition of the ranch romance, this most for-mulary ingredient of what was to become the formulary Western, in *The Virginian* (1902), but only the novel ends in marriage; the parts of this novel which Wister published first in magazines as short stories do not contain the romance. In Rhodes' first *Post* serial, *Good Men and True,* Jeff Bransford is taken prisoner by the villain and there is no heroine in the story. It wasn't until "The Line of Least Resistance" was serialized in the *Post* in 1910 that Rhodes introduced a romance as a uni-fying plot ingredient. "The Line of Least Resistance" was never publish-ed in book form. *The Desire of the Moth* continues the tradition, as do *The Little Eohippus,* published in cloth in 1914 by Henry Holt & Company under the title *Bransford in Arcadia, or The Little Eohippus,* and *Stepsons of Light.* But in his best longer fiction, from *Pasó por Aquí* through *The Trusty Knaves,* Rhodes eschews romance complete-ly. Far more important in all of his longer fictions, including even the ranch romances, is the role played by friendship. "The Line of Least Resistance," for example, has the obligatory—for that time—"savage redskins" as its menace, but what is enduring about it is neither the romance nor the battle with the Indians, rather the friendship between Don Kennedy and Hiram Yoast which brings the story to life and sus-tains its interest. As Bret Harte and Owen Wister before him, Rhodes used many of the same characters in a number of stories of varying lengths. This applies not only to major characters, such as Jeff

Bransford and John Wesley Pringle, but even minor ones, such as Spinal Maginnis and Travis the dwarf who appear in *Stepsons of Light* and return in *The Proud Sheriff* (1935) or the minor villain, MacGregor, one of Bransford's jailers in *Good Men and True,* who is the central character in the first of the four long short stories which Rhodes rather ineptly tried to weave together into a novel he titled *West Is West* (1917).

The money which Rhodes realized from his sale of *Stepsons of Light* to the *Post* enabled him to purchase a train ticket to Los Angeles where he hoped to spend Christmas with his mother whom he had not seen since 1911. Although the impression is not evident because of the hiatus between visits, Rhodes actually remained closely attached to Julia. He also opined that he might sell some of his stories to motion picture companies. And then, as May herself admitted, "we had some good times before we had another of those 'vacations' which Gene said made our marriage so successful."[31] Before he left, Gene deeded his share of the Mutton Hill farm to Jack and Alan. Following his discharge, Fred Purple had decided that he was no farmer. He moved to West Virginia. Jack married and deeded back his share. This left only Alan who got himself a job in Binghampton and returned just on weekends. May and her mother moved back to the Davison farm where May started a poultry and egg business to supplement what Gene might send her. It had been Rhodes' original intention to spend six months in California and then return to New Mexico for a visit in preparation for writing another magazine serial. It was not to be. His stay in California stretched out to three years during which time he wrote virtually nothing, although he did sell several properties to motion picture producing companies. As early as 1914 Universal had purchased *The Little Eohippus* and "The Line of Least Resistance" and had filmed them as two-reelers. I have already mentioned that *The Desire of the Moth* was filmed in 1917. Now, with Rhodes in Hollywood, remake rights were negotiated as well as new contracts. *Bransford in Arcadia; or, The Little Eohippus* (Universal-Eclair, 1914) was remade as a feature film titled *Sure Fire* (Universal, 1921) directed by John Ford and starring Hoot Gibson. *The Desire of the Moth* was remade as *The Wallop* (Universal, 1921) directed by John Ford with Harry Carey in the lead, cast as John Wesley Pringle. Carey also starred in *West Is West* (Universal, 1920) directed by Val Paul. When Carey's contract with Universal expired, he signed a new one with Robertson-Cole Productions and starred in *Good Men and True* (Robertson-Cole, 1922) directed by Val Paul who had followed him from Universal. The same company also filmed *Stepsons of Light* under the title *The Mysterious Witness* (Robertson-Cole, 1923) starring Robert Gordon with his character name changed from Johnny Dines to Johnny Brant.

Pay for the rights to these properties was good for the time—about $2,500 apiece—but nothing compared to what purchase prices would later become. Rhodes had brought his personal library with him and he moved into a woodshed, actually more a shack, behind the quarters his mother rented. Julia Rhodes and three other women all rented rooms from the owner of the house, Fanny Duvall. The youngest was Rhodes' age, the others all in their seventies. All of them, including Julia, were avid followers of Mary Baker Eddy whose teachings preoccupied all of their waking hours and all of their conversation. Little wonder, Rhodes was relieved by the prospect of going on automobile outings with Agnes Morley Cleaveland.

While *The Wallop* was in production, Harry Carey wrote to Rhodes. "I am busily engaged in filming your 'Desire of the Moth' which the Universal made four or five years ago with Monroe Salsbury in the part of Foy, but after carefully conning the said Mr. S's script and then re-reading your novel, I was wot you call 'im?, sort of nonplussed. I couldn't find a danged bit of similarity in the two tales and thereupon, moreover, and Whereas I being a great admirer of your literature (for that's just what it is) I girded up my loins and set about really making your story as I thought you would like to have it made. But I am not playing the part of Chris Foy. I do not like the name Foy, for I was once stuck on a chorus girl that worked for Eddie Foy. John Wesley Pringle is my kind of man. I mean the kind of 'Outwester' I like to play. He smells of greasewood smoke and Bull Durham instead of tan-bark and bill-posting paste. Now to the point. Jack Ford, my director, and myself want you to come out to the studio the day we do the saloon sequence where they frame up Foy. We think you ought to come and indulge in a medicine talk about this picture and some future ones. I want you to meet a couple of people anyhow."[31]

Rhodes' time in the East had changed him in some ways—at least externally. Robert Martin, who first came to New Mexico at nineteen and who two years later was running the 7TX round-up wagon, knew Rhodes during the time he lived in the area. "Gene liked the girls to chat with and put life into but no familiarities," Martin later told W.H. Hutchinson, Rhodes' principal biographer. "He could, would, and did ride any horse no matter how vicious if you don't count the times he was thrown. It took him a long time sometimes to pay his bills but he always did. His word was good in all the graver and more important things in life. . . . Cheerful, big-hearted, as unpredictable as the wind, and tomorrow would always take care of itself. Cared little for clothes and I never saw him with a suit on."[32] Tied to a plow and to his writing desk for years in the East, Rhodes came after a time to accept Eastern dress codes. Even though he might be in casual Southern California, when Gene showed up at Universal to visit with Harry Carey and John Ford on the set he wore a starched shirt, a necktie, and an armband. Indeed, this is how he continued to dress for the rest of his days, although he also usually wore a suitcoat.

For the cloth editions of his magazine serials, Rhodes switched from Henry Holt & Company to the H.K. Fly Company for publication of *West Is West* in 1917. His contract with this firm proved a financial debacle that would plague him for more than a decade after he signed it. Fly refused to send Gene royalty reports. Fly then secured rights to the books Henry Holt & Company had previously published. In the period before the paperback revolution, cheap, hard-bound reprint editions were the principal after-market for books and leading the field was Grosset & Dunlap. Fly licensed Grosset & Dunlap to publish the reprint editions and then refused to furnish Rhodes with any statements or royalties from the reprint editions. Somewhat in desperation, Rhodes turned to the Boston firm of Houghton Mifflin to issue the cloth edition of *Stepsons of Light*. Houghton Mifflin offered him a 5% royalty on all copies sold. The book retailed at $2 which meant Rhodes earned 10¢ a copy. The Grosset & Dunlap reprint contract ordinarily called for a 2¢ royalty on each copy sold. Henceforth, Rhodes was better off, with Houghton Mifflin, than he had been with his previous publishers and he was paid regularly on future reprint editions.

Henry Herbert Knibbs first met Rhodes when Knibbs was working for the B.R.P. Railway in New York state. He had always wanted to write Western fiction and Rhodes readily became his mentor. Knibbs based the character of his outlaw leader, "The Spider," in *The Ridin' Kid from Powder River* (1919) on Rhodes' physical appearance. Rhodes was anything but pleased. By the time Rhodes arrived in Los Angeles, Knibbs was living there, too, and they rekindled their friendship. In an effort to assuage Rhodes' hurt feelings (as well as to pay tribute to Harry Carey who had played a character named "Cheyenne Harry" in a number of his Universal Westerns), Knibbs based his character

Cheyenne Hastings in *Partners of Chance* (1921) on Rhodes, making him a cheerful wanderer of the plains and deserts, a man always with a song on his breath, and a man—very much as Rhodes—who dislikes violence of any kind.

Robert Martin had confided to William A. Keleher when the latter was at work on *The Fabulous Frontier* (1945) that "the keystone of Gene's character was his love of justice and fairplay and for these he would fight any time—he was a medium sized man—140 to 150—about 5 feet 7, full of nervous energy, restless, busy at all times—loved to do hard work—a tireless reader—coffee drinker thru the day and night—smoked cigarettes constantly—poker playing fiend—always broke, drank no liquor of any kind—while I drank whiskey and chewed tobacco—for years we were much together in camp on the range...."[33] This is very much the portrait Knibbs provided of Rhodes in *Partners of Chance*. Yet, as Jim Tully, a writer whom Rhodes came to know in Southern California, said of him: "Eugene Manlove Rhodes is greater than anything he ever created and he is more human than any of his fiction cowboys."[34]

Rhodes' health unquestionably improved in the sunny climate and by the summer of 1922 he was able to play semipro baseball. However, it was also that summer that his shack behind the Duvall home caught fire. In trying to save his beloved set of Robert Louis Stevenson's works, he was badly burned around the shoulders as the roof collapsed on him. This loss, combined with May's complaining missives from Apalachin about her hard row attempting to make it alone, brought Rhodes to the brink of nervous exhaustion. He had had women friends during these years, some of them very close, but given Rhodes' personality and what to some, more cynical than he was, must seem excessive prudery, all such friendships remained strictly platonic. Harry Carey, out of friendship, bought several properties from Rhodes for possible screen adaptation so that Gene, once more penniless, would have train fare to go back East. Carey and his wife Olive escorted Rhodes to the train depot on the day of his departure.

Gene made one stop on the way, in Denver, to visit with William MacLeod Raine, an Englishman who had won a considerable reputation as an author of formulary Western fiction. "We talked the moon down and the sun up," Raine later recalled. "At midnight, my wife ceased being a hostess and left us alone. All thru Rhodes' talk as in his writings ran his passionate belief in the little people whose strength and courage and fortitude were the backbone of the country. In the small hours we cooked ham, eggs, and coffee. Before the first faint streaks of dawn had come into the sky, my car was high in the hills heading for the Continental Divide. Reluctantly, when the crotches in the range became purple lakes, we turned homeward and arrived there a pair of truant penitents with a mess of trout for a peace offering. More than anybody else I know, he was my kind of Westerner — generous, fearless, tough as ironwood, gentle yet as violently explosive as powder at any injustice to the poor or oppressed."[35]

Four days after his return to Apalachin, the farm on Mutton Hill was sold and Rhodes resumed being a farmer on May's parents' farm. Ill health began once again to plague him inexorably. May, too, had become sickly and May's mother was now a hopeless invalid. When Julia died of a cerebral embolism in January, 1924, Gene could not get away so Clarence had to come up from Mexico to settle her estate. Rhodes would spend his spare time ranting over what he felt were the follies of American fiction and literary criticism. He resented Albert Bacon Fall's condemnation in the press and supported his battle to stay out of prison. More significantly, from 1919 when he had published *Stepsons of Light* until early 1925, when he finally submitted *Once in the Saddle* to *The Saturday Evening Post,* Rhodes had written nothing of consequence. Another year passed before *Pasó por Aquí* appeared in the *Post.* Houghton Mifflin combined both magazine serials in a single volume titled *Once in the Saddle* (1927).

Although he did not see many motion pictures, Rhodes did attend *The Covered Wagon* (Paramount, 1923), based on the novel by the same title by Emerson Hough, and he thought it a fine film. Hough died shortly after the film was released and Rhodes launched a campaign to protect Hough's literary reputation when it came under attack in the *International Book Review.* The book in question was Hough's final novel, *North of 36* (1923), which Rhodes refused to recognize as embodying a highly romantic and unrealistic view of the West. On the contrary, Rhodes took the position that Hough's view was in fact a truthful one, that indeed *North of 36* was one of the three best Western novels ever written. However, it must be remembered that Rhodes' own taste in Western fiction was such that he felt B.M. Bower, George Patullo, and H.H. Knibbs were among that select company who wrote "short stories where people on paper act like people and horses do...."[36]

These years must have been particularly anguished ones for Rhodes. In what he did write, he seems to have been driven more than ever to project his idealized view of Westerners. He might have scraps of paper all over his desk with notes scrawled on them, bits of story, incidents, snatches of dialogue; he might have extremely detailed maps of New Mexico which he could consult constantly when describing topography in his fiction; but what glowed inside of him was no longer mere memories of what had been and the people he had known. Instead, his fiction was now the product of a vision, of a way of life — however much of it might in reality be imaginary — that he desperately preferred to the life he was living and the way of life with which he was surrounded.

As early as *The Little Eohippus,* Rhodes had included two chapters in which Jeff Bransford, disguised as Tom West, goes East to New York to continue his courtship of Ellinor Hoffman. In *Copper Streak Trail* (1922) Pete Johnson, in order to get to the bottom of the villainy which has resulted in his partner Stanley Mitchell's being imprisoned on a fraudulent charge, has got to go East, to New York state, where he encounters Mitchell's crooked cousin, a lawyer named Oscar, Stanley's fiancée, the local schoolteacher, and Stanley's rich Uncle McClintock who has disinherited Stanley because he wants to marry the schoolteacher, Mary Selden. In Arizona, Pete and Stanley have discovered a rich copper deposit, but it will need capital before it can be worked effectively. C. Mayer Zurich, the rich and unscrupulous storekeeper in Cobre, Arizona intends to jump the claim. He has been in the employ of Oscar Mitchell, making life difficult for Stanley, but Zurich is a Western villain; the true polecats are the Easterners, Oscar and his assistant, Joe Pelman. "'Necessity doesn't make me a crook,'" Pelman confesses to Oscar. "'I'm crooked by nature. I like crookedness. . . . That's why I'm with you.'"[37] Once matters have been settled in the East, Johnson returns to Arizona. Stanley is released. Joined by two loyal friends, Pete and Stanley head out to protect their claim. Zurich and his men are in pursuit, intent on jumping it as soon as they are led to the spot by the rightful owners. However, fate intervenes. Young Bobby Carr, the ten-year-old son of the freighter working for Pete and Stanley, has been lost while searching for some horses and the four set out to find him. This leaves the claim unattended, but, when they return, with Bobby safe, all they find at the claim is a note insisting that it be called the "Bobby Carr Mine" and in which Zurich and his men inform Pete: "We did not know about the boy, or we would have helped, of course. Only for him you had beat us. So this squares that up!"[38] Once Oscar tries to grab the mine for himself, he is foiled by

Zurich. Westerners may be villains, but they are still decent human beings. Rhodes' negative attitude toward the East is to be found in his characters and what happens to them; in words, the worst he permitted himself to say was that in Apalachin "there are no traditions—and no ballads."[39] In *Once in the Saddle,* one of Rhodes' most poorly constructed stories, Pliny Mullins wants to found a township in New Mexico away from the unfair dealings of a capitalistic mine-owner and human exploiter so that "'them little kids I seen will have homes and a white man's chance.'"[40] When Malloch, the mine-owner, questions Pliny about his motives, he jeers: "'Just principle? The square deal, the great tradition—all that sort of rot? High-minded redresser of wrong, dispenser of justice?'" "'Just that kind of rot exactly,'" Pliny tells him.[41]

At this time Rhodes began corresponding with Walter Prescott Webb. "Yes," Rhodes admitted in a letter to Webb, "what you say about making my books hard to read is probably quite true and, next to the fact that there are few women in the yarns, explains why they don't sell."[42] He also insisted that, "while denounced as a weird romance, my yarns are founded solidly upon remembered facts—not the action, often imaginary, but the people, codes, traditions."[43] His highest esteem he reserved for Andy Adams, but he added to his list of truthtellers Will James, Owen Wister, Peter B. Kyne, and even William MacLeod Raine and Jackson Gregory, while he condemned Zane Grey, Charles Alden Seltzer, and Mulford as the three worst writers of Western fiction.

More and more the ideas of code and tradition came to preoccupy Rhodes. In a letter to Vincent Starrett he confessed that "I took real men for my models, yes, and by heck I did a good job in showing them as they were. But I *did not* write about other *real men within my knowledge* whose lives were disgusting and shameful. I like a good horse better than a balky horse or a runaway horse or a man-killing horse—or a horse with the botts or blind staggers. And I like a man who works and jokes and lends better than I do one who cheats at cards. To make it brief—the best men I know are the most interesting to me—the men who pay their debts—and they are the ones I write about. Most people nowadays prefer to write about bootleggers and bootlickers."[44] It is probably for this reason that, given Rhodes' ambivalent attitude toward the real Pat Garrett, when he made him a character in his short novel it was an idealized image. The tone of Rhodes' letters during the last decade of his life, particularly those in which he addressed Western fiction, indicates that increasingly for him the West, as he viewed it, constituted an alternative to the present reality. It was a preferable way of life. "We knew only too many who were without charm or interest," he observed. "But the silly ephemeral fashion of the day gives acclaim only to stories about Minus People. Most of our successful novels are case histories of sick souls — neither more nor less. I like Plus People."[45] Western fiction, for Rhodes, had become a refuge, a retreat, a philosophical and moral statement, even an *ideological* statement which is why his work was never able to rise above the level of the historical romance. He was not interested in the total reality embodied in a true historical reconstruction.

May's mother died in April, 1925. Now May had no reason to remain in Apalachin. Rhodes wanted to return to New Mexico. "It wrung my heart unutterably to leave my beloved homeland," May later remarked, "but I had told Gene that when Mother and Father were gone he could do the deciding on our future home."[46] Oddly enough, Rhodes chose to settle in Santa Fe, a place outside his traditional haunts and one where it proved expensive to live. Mary Austin resided there and Rhodes accused her of trying to set up a literary papacy. In September, 1927 Gene and May moved, this time to Alamogordo, where they rented a small house just across the street from Oliver Milton Lee's residence. Rhodes and Lee visited a great deal and, when they were together, the usually taciturn Lee was heard frequently laughing. Rhodes spent much time playing poker to all hours of the morning, or playing pool. A local druggist recalled that he met Rhodes one night at ten o'clock coming out of the pool room. "'I'll bet my wife will scold when I get home,'" he said. "'I came down this morning to get meat for dinner and I'm just making it back.'"[47]

Soon after his parents settled in Alamogordo Alan joined them. When in June, 1928 Alan decided to return to Apalachin for a visit, May went with him. Her eyes were bothering her increasingly and she began to fear blindness. While she was gone, Gene suffered a nearly fatal heart attack. His code of chivalry prevented him from saying anything about it until she returned, but he realized that his days were numbered.

Albert Bacon Fall lived on his Tres Rios ranch, outside of Three Rivers itself, still embroiled in the fight to stay out of prison. Susan McSween, who had bought a ranch in this area and who had begun raising cattle with the small herd John Chisum had given her at the end of the Lincoln County War, had sold out to Fall and gone to live at

White Oaks, by then virtually a ghost town. Fall, aware that Rhodes was on hard times, offered to let Gene and May live on the old McSween ranch, part of his holdings which had once comprised a million acres. There was no rent and they were permitted to buy all of their groceries on credit from the Fall store in Three Rivers without ever a bill being sent to them. Gene and May lived in what was known as the Rock House until the property passed out of Fall's hands in November, 1929.

Rhodes then bought a small three-acre spread with a ramshackle house that it took him two months to make habitable. In the summer of 1930, Gene and May went to San Diego to find suitable quarters. Having located a place, they returned to New Mexico so Gene could write a serial for the *Post* which would earn them enough money to buy it. Harrison Leusler, a field editor for Houghton Mifflin, persuaded Rhodes to write a book in collaboration with Clement Hightower about the old days and the old timers in New Mexico. Rhodes worked on and off on this book until his death, at which time it was far from complete. In fact, what little of it was publishable May incorporated in her biography of her husband. Rhodes wrote a short story for *The Saturday Evening Post*, "Maid Most Dear," the first fiction the magazine had published of his since 1926. He also wrote five sets of verses. Included in the latter was his long poem, "The Hired Man on Horseback." J. Frank Dobie later commented on the poem in his *Guide to Life and Literature of the Southwest* (1952) that it is imbued with a "passionate fidelity to his own decent kind of men, with power to ennoble the reader, and with the form necessary to all beautiful composition. This is the sole and solitary piece of poetry to be found in all the myriads of rhymes classed as 'cowboy poetry.'"[48] The serial on which Rhodes was at work was *The Trusty Knaves* and he persisted working and reworking, writing and rewriting from July, 1930 until February, 1931. The *Post* bought it for $7,500. Gene and May could now afford to move to California.

H.H. Knibbs had never really been a Westerner. Much of what he felt to be true about the West, he had learned from Rhodes. In *Partners of Chance,* he remarked that "in direct and effectual kindliness, without obviously expressed sympathy, the Westerner is peculiarly supreme."[49] Now *son maître* expressed the same sentiment in *The Trusty Knaves,* only far more eloquently. "A thousand handsomely printed books have said, not casually, but shrieking and beating their breasts, that life in the Western half of the United States has been all sodden misery, drab and coarse and low. . . . If these books tell the truth, then any and all my stories are shameless lies. What I remember is generosity, laughter, courage, and kindness. Kindness most of all; kindness from evil men and worthless men, as well as from good men."[50] At the center of this novel is the town of Target, rather obviously a surrogate for Engle. The Establishment, consisting of a lawyer, a judge, a sheriff, a town marshal, and an unsuccessful rancher and his men decide to rob the bank. Bill Hawkins, who is actually the outlaw Bill Doolin, has staked out the bank for himself; but, when he learns of the plan of the town's leading citizens to rob it, he sets about to thwart the attempt. There is no violence in the story. It can almost be called a comedy with dramatic overtones, a comedy of Western manners. Rhodes deplored the apathy of really good men who "'never do much of anything — not when it's risky. . . . Always fussing about the rules, stopping for Sunday and advice of counsel. Then, they foster a brutal prejudice against guessing, good men do. Worst of all, they wonder does it pay. That's fatal — that last.'"[51] Rhodes obviously agreed with Jumbo Wilkins, a character in William MacLeod Rain's *Oh, You Tex* (1920), who believes that in the West a man makes his own luck. "'Some folks are born with two strikes against them. . . . That's nonsense,'" one of Rhodes' characters reflects in *The Trusty Knaves*. "'That's doin' the baby act. It's not luck; it's the man. Every time.'"[52] Perhaps what I personally like so much about Rhodes' fiction are his sentiments. During his lifetime, among a select coterie of readers and critics, Rhodes was regarded as the doyen of authors of Western fiction. Yet, why was he not commercially more successful? Ira Kent of Houghton Mifflin put the matter rather succinctly in a letter written in 1927. "You have been urgent with us in the matter of getting your work to market," he told Rhodes. "Now I propose to be a little urgent with you about that part of the work that must precede sales, namely, the writing of books. A fairly even flow of production is one of the greatest aids in building up the market for an author. Your books have come too infrequently and at too long intervals."[53]

California, as Rhodes saw it, was only to be a respite from the winds and dust of New Mexico. He intended to live part of the year in California and part in New Mexico. The home in Palm Beach, between La Jolla and San Diego, was gray in color with a eucalyptus tree spread over it and a western exposure to the rolling surf. It was purchased on a Trust Deed, with no money down and monthly installments of $18.53, including interest. What Rhodes did there was to work; he worked harder and, I think, more concentratedly than he had at any time in his life. He wrote letters and he wrote on the old timers book and he wrote fiction. *Beyond the Desert* (1934) and *The Proud Sheriff* came out of these years, albeit the latter was too short to be published as a book until H.H. Knibbs agreed to write a long introduction to flesh it out to the required length.

Rhodes continued to spend money easily. Although the country was in the grip of the Depression, Rhodes at least earned enough to get by; but as always he was improvident. When he sent *Beyond the Desert* off to the *Post* and the *Post* rejected it, regarding it as overwritten and the pace too leisurely, Rhodes wired back that the editors could revamp the story any way that was wanted, only he had to have money. The *Post* sent him a hundred dollars. The story was cut by a fourth before the *Post* would publish it. *The Proud Sheriff* encountered similar editorial obstacles and is also thinly plotted. In it, young Otey Beach is framed for a murder he did not commit and Sheriff Spinal Maginnis sets about to find the true culprit. *Beyond the Desert* is the story of three conspirators who want to seize Bud Copeland's ranch because it has the only useable water on it that the railroad needs in order to build a spur line. The villains prove no match for the imposing good and decent men who join with Bud to save his spread. Sam Travis, Rhodes' good-hearted dwarf, is probably the most memorable character in *The Proud Sheriff*. In *Beyond the Desert* that distinction goes to Lithpin Tham, a man of questionable past who joins with the decent men and about whom it is remarked that "fanciful fellows, one or two, had been troubled, once or twice, with an uneasy guess that but for this ludicrous handicap of speech, better folk might have been kinder to Sam Clark, and that life as Sam Clark might have been different, and easier, than life as Lithpin Tham."[54] It was an imperfection about which Rhodes could write from first-hand knowledge. Notwithstanding, this was not the way Western fiction was currently being written for the slick magazines where the emphasis was increasingly on violence and action.

"I would have you note that no man is killed in *The Trusty Knaves,*" Rhodes wrote to Bernard Devoto in 1933. "I lived like that for twenty-five years — among folks who would shoot if forced to, but who would rather laugh."[55] Rhodes went so far as to refuse an opportunity to review Eugene Cunningham's *Buckaroo* (1933), a copy of which was sent to him by Houghton Mifflin which was also Cunningham's publisher. Rhodes claimed his reason for demurring was that he was not paid for writing reviews. In 1934 he even wrote in a letter to Cunningham that he could not really judge his novel. I suspect the real reason for Rhodes' reticence was that Cunningham was one of the originators of the *Blut und Boden* school of Western fiction—300 characters are killed off in the course of *Buckaroo*—and this, doubtless, offended Rhodes' sensibility at the same time as it reminded him of how out of joint he had become with the times.

"He grew steadily weaker and often had to sit up all night to ease the pain in his heart," May recorded.[56] His last day came on June 27, 1934. "After I was in bed he came in and said, 'What do you think you did?' I said, 'What did I do?' He said, 'You wrapped the book I was going to autograph for Maurice Walsh in the morning and addressed it to the motion picture man.' I said: 'Never mind. I'll fix it in the morning.' He said, 'No, I want it fixed now.' He untied the knots, changed the book, rewrapped, and addressed it. It lay on the table in the morning, and he so utterly dead. He came to bed at one o'clock and had a succession of heart spasms until morning. Nothing could ease him. He died in my arms at half-past six in the morning...."[57]

May saw to it that Gene was buried in New Mexico, in Rhodes' Canyon, about two miles up from his old homestead claim. Robert Martin was present at the burial, joining May and Hiram Yoast and various others. At a public ceremony on May 18, 1941, an official marker was placed on Rhodes' grave. Elizabeth Garrett, blind daughter of Pat Garrett, was in attendance and spoke of her father's friendship with Rhodes. The inscription read:

> Pasó por Aquí
> Eugene Manlove Rhodes
> Jan. 19, 1869—June 27, 1934

Little over a decade later, the grave site fell within the limits of the White Sands Proving Ground and visits to it henceforth were to be made only under government sanction. Soon after Rhodes' death, May returned to the family farm in Apalachin to live with Alan and his wife. She was blind, or nearly so, when in 1945 she dictated a letter to William A. Keleher objecting to his portrait of Rhodes in *The Fabulous Frontier*.

"While the incidents of Gene Rhodes' life were as vividly realistic as those of any modern novel," H.H. Knibbs said of him, "intellectually and at heart he was a romantic."[58] Rhodes usually chose for his villains the kinds of men who, historically, did exploit the West, in

Bernard DeVoto's words "the speculators, the bankers and manipulators, the mortgagees and monopolists, all the operators of the machinery by which the East systematically plundered its captive province...."[59] Rhodes' heroines may be impossible and his heroes often too good to be true and his plots too contrived; yet he did portray outlawry accurately as disorganized class struggle, men in their confusion trying to survive among all the land-grabbers and Eastern capitalists preying upon them. This was the very soul of his literary vision, this and those unforgettable characters with a snatch of doggeral or poetry on their lips, men who laugh a lot. He wrote romantic Western fiction for an ideological reason: he wanted to prove something to his readers. In the end, all an author can give you is himself. With Rhodes, as with his characters, you either like him at once, or you do not. There does not seem to be a middle path.

Dane Coolidge: Western Writer

Dane Coolidge went to explore Death Valley for the first time in 1916. He hired an old desert rat and erstwhile prospector as his guide. His name was Henry L. Smith but he was known to all and sundry as Smitty. Were you to have come across Coolidge at the time in one of the numerous canyons in the foothills of the Furnace range, you would have found a man of medium height looking somewhat older than his forty-odd years because of the Prince Albert moustache and beard, a man with sunken cheeks graced by high but scarcely protuberant cheekbones, a Roman nose, intense eyes capable of expressing a sensitive inner sadness, ears set far back on his head. He would likely be wearing a high, three-peaked Stetson with narrow brim and, if it were cool enough, a corduroy jacket over his khaki shirt, a one-color neckerchief, and khaki pants tucked into calf-high boots with heels low enough to be suitable for walking and yet high enough for riding.

During that first visit Coolidge asked Smitty many questions about the mining discoveries that had been made in Death Valley. He had otherwise been silent on the subject with everyone else because he had learned that "the only way to know anything about these mining discoveries is to go to just one man. If you go to two, what you know is reduced by half. Go to three and you don't know anything."[1]

Coolidge customarily traveled with his wife in the summer months but he returned alone to Death Valley for a second trip of exploration in 1918 in the dead of winter. This time Coolidge's guide was a man named Shorty Harris and for the first three days, as they traveled together, Shorty said practically nothing. It was bitterly cold on the high ground so the two headed down toward the floor of the Valley, putting in at Surveyors' Well where they laid over for a day. "In the old shack by the well a clutter of rough-paper magazines had been left by a former occupant," Coolidge later recalled, "and Shorty was looking them over with his heat-blurred eyes when he suddenly hurled one to the floor.

Dane Coolidge, called "Big Beard" by the Seri Indians, in his regular attire when roughing it. Photo courtesy of Nancy Coolidge Coulter.

"'What the hell is the matter with this feller?' he howled. 'Here's a story about old Panamint, and he has it out on the plain! On a plain, mind ye, when everybody knows it's clear up on top of a mountain!'

"'Oh, never mind that,' I said. 'He's a good writer—I know him—and he just wanted to use the name. So he took a town down on the desert and changed the name to Panamint.'

"'But he has the dommed town in the bottom of Death Valley—on the other side of the mountains!'

"'Poetic license! All our best writers do it. Geography means nothing to them.'

"'But he's got a parson here—the parson of Panamint—and there never was a preacher in the camp!'

"Shorty was all het up, shaken out of his three days' silence, and he went on to tell me what an old timer he was."[2]

The author who had raised Shorty's ire was Peter B. Kyne. His story, "The Parson of Panamint," had been filmed two years previously by Paramount Pictures, starring Dustin Farnum who had also played Owen Wister's The Virginian. Kyne's story would be filmed twice more, once in 1922 and again a year after Dane Coolidge died. It was a tale of the imaginary West, of people and places that, historically, never had existed. Dane Coolidge was a different kind of Western writer than Kyne and what made him most different was his fidelity to the geography of the West. Coolidge might, after his fashion, romanticize the events of Western history, but he wrote of the physical places of the West from first-hand knowledge. He took the effort personally to seek out the terrain in which he would set his stories. Where he could not ride, he walked. He observed the flora and fauna of each region with greater perspicacity than—in view of many of his fictional characters—he ever did the men and women who chose to live on these Western lands and who survived the experience to tell about it. Also unlike Kyne, none of his stories or novels was ever adapted for the screen. He tried. Coolidge wrote at least five motion picture scenarios, but none was produced.

He was born in Natick, Massachusetts, on March 24, 1873. He was a descendant of the extensive Coolidge family which traces its ancestry to John Coolidge who settled at Watertown in 1630. "I can claim direct descent from John Alden and Priscilla," he once wrote. "But as my parents moved to Riverside, California, when I was four years of age and was turned loose to grow up with jack-rabbits, I knew nothing of either John Coolidge or John Alden until I was nearly forty years old. My early life was spent on the orange ranch of my father or in hunting and trapping in the mountains. I soon became the boy naturalist of the town, digging out coyotes and robbing eagles' nests, and at the age of twenty-one when I entered Stanford University I obtained a position as field collector, working on mammals and reptiles."[3]

Coolidge graduated from Stanford with an A.B. degree in 1898. The next year he went to Harvard for a year of post-graduate study. That first position as field collector was held during the summer of 1895. During the summer of 1896 Coolidge went to work for the British Museum in the same capacity in Baja, California, and Mexico. The guide was Gumserindo Romero who could outrun a mule on open ground and who was one of the few vaqueros in the country who could rope wild cattle in the brush. Coolidge photographed him and reproduced the plate many years later in his book, *Old California Cowboys* (1939). During the summer of 1897 he went again to Baja, California, this time for the U.S. Biological Survey, collecting live animals, birds, and reptiles for the U.S. National Zoological Park. In 1899 he was field collector in Arizona and California for the Bronx branch of the New York Zoological Park. After he left Harvard in 1900, Coolidge went to Europe where he worked as field collector for the U.S. National Museum in Italy and France, the second American ever to have done so. When he returned to the United States, he took up wild life photography, especially desert forms. This training as a naturalist never deserted Coolidge and often, once he came to write Western fiction, he would make dramatic use of wild life to lend a special overtone to a particular event. "...And," he wrote in *Lorenzo the Magnificent* (1925) where the natural habits of toads are used to parallel the pleasure of the characters at the rain following a long drought, "that night in the solemn stillness that followed the storm Jason heard the joyous croaking of toads. For a year, for two years, they had been encysted in the lakebeds; boring down as the mud dried above them until at last the earth set, holding them prisoners until the next rain. Now the flood had set them free, soaking down to their mud-cased holes and softening the iron-hard ground; and all night, transported with joy, they swam in circles about the lake, raising their voices in a chorus of delight."[4] Conversely, Coolidge was too well-versed in the flora and fauna of the Western regions to indulge ever in such fantasies about rattlesnakes as can be found in novels written by such contemporaries as Charles Alden Seltzer in *The Two Gun Man* (1911) or Clarence E. Mulford in *Hopalong Cassidy Returns* (1924). In Coolidge's *Snake Bit Jones* (1936) Jones gets his name from having been bit by a rattlesnake. He keeps one, called Hungry Bill, as a pet, but finally shoots it because it dares to bite him in the toe of his thick boot.

On July 30, 1906, Dane, who had been christened Daniel, married Mary Elizabeth Burroughs Roberts at Berkeley, California. His mother, Sophia Upham Whittemore Coolidge, had died of tuberculosis, as had his two sisters. Dane and his younger brother, Herbert, had been raised in an all-male household by his father, Francis Coolidge. Mary was forty-five when she married Coolidge and she had not wanted to originally. It was a second marriage for her, a first for him, and she felt Dane deserved to be able to have children. She was a member of the California State Board of Education and a Professor of Sociology at Mills College. The daughter of Isaac Phillips Roberts, Professor Emeritus and Dean of the College of Agriculture at Cornell University, for years before she met Coolidge Mary had been writing and engaged in social and economic research with special emphasis on women's rights. Prior to their marriage, all Dane had written was a few animal stories published in David Starr Jordan's *True Tales of Birds and Beasts* (1902), a book used as supplementary reading in elementary schools. Mary Coolidge's practical sensibility, her professionalism, her independent spirit, her self-confidence obviously came to exert some influence on Dane and he would occasionally invent heroines with precisely these attibutes rather than the wooden, demure, unsure damsels in need of being rescued by a stalwart hero which populated so much Western fiction at the time. Under her married name, Mary Coolidge wrote *Why Women Are So* (1912) and produced a notable book on the social life, religion, arts, and crafts of the Southwest Indians in *Rain-Makers: Indians of Arizona and New Mexico* (1929). With Dane, she co-authored *The Navajo Indian* (1930) and *The Last of the Seris* (1939). Dane always called Mary, Lady. When they first went to study the Seri Indians in 1932, they dubbed her Lady Red Hat and called Dane Big Beard.

After their marriage, the Coolidges moved into a home in Berkeley that they named Dwight Way End, the last house on a hill with almost two acres of grounds and a view of the Bay and the city of San Francisco. Dane liked to garden and he had long, curving terraces planted with China lilies and many-colored irises. Mary's father came to live with them in the twenties following his retirement. It was then that he and Dane split the garden in half because he disagreed adamantly with Dane's horticultural theories. By that time the routine of these two very methodical people was firmly established. Mary arose very early and would light a fire and make breakfast in their modern kitchen. Dane would rise at eight. After breakfast, he would work in his garden until lunch time, plotting out his stories. In the afternoon, he would retire to a small alcove behind their bedroom and write. His daily quota was two thousand words. Over the years until his death on August 8, 1940, with this regimen Coolidge wrote thirty-six Western novels and some one hundred short stories and short novels for magazine publication as well as five books of biography and reminiscence. The Coolidges did not observe Christmas in a traditional way, but instead would hang out Navajo rugs on the front porch which ran on two sides of their home and was covered by a roof. The two even collaborated on a little chapbook titled *Navajo Rugs* (1933). Dane did his writing at a small, mahogany desk with numerous pigeon holes for manuscripts and a few shelves for books. Mary would prepare dinner when she returned from her day at Mills College and it was served at six. Two or three nights a week the Coolidges would entertain, usually artists and literary people. Mary was a singer and played the piano while Dane played the cello. No matter what might be going on, about eight or eight-thirty Dane would leave the room to wash and dry the dishes in the kitchen. Then he would return to his writing room where he would work until eleven. In the summers, when school was out, they would travel, either camping or staying with friends. Initially, Dane posed as a photographer and would take pictures while, actually, he was collecting stories and data he could use in his fiction. Because Mary was greatly interested in Indians, they made friends with numerous tribes and would often sojourn on reservations. Coolidge wrote down all of his experiences and reflections meticulously in notebooks which were donated to the Bancroft Library after his death. He went on his first round-up at Pinal, Arizona, in 1903, prior to his marriage, and his notebooks were so detailed that he could recall the experiences he had with vividness years later when he published them in his book *Arizona Cowboys* (1938). His semi-autobiographical accounts of cowboy life and what I regard as his best book of reminiscences, *Death Valley Prospectors* (1937), were all illustrated by his own photographs.

Coolidge was not an historian; he was a romantic. His weakest book was *Fighting Men of the West* (1932). Most of what he wrote in it about such frontier personalities as John Chisum, Billy the Kid, Clay Allison, and Charles Goodnight was based on hearsay and is scarcely reliable. "The time to write history is when the subject is still alive, or is survived by men who knew him," Coolidge wrote in his Introduction to the book. "That is why these stories of Fighting Men of the West are offered for what they are worth. To claim they are exactly true is going too far, but they approximate the truth."[5] All too often the approximation was wide of the mark.

I define a formulary Western as one which possesses a hero, a heroine, and one or more villains defeated by the hero before he is usually united at the end with the heroine. By this definition, with only one exception all the Western novels that Coolidge wrote, beginning with *Hidden Water* (1910) and concluding with the post-humous *Bear Paw* (1941), were formulary. The exception is probably Coolidge's most disappointing novel, *Gringo Gold* (1939), based on the life and death of the legendary California bandit Joaquin Murieta. This was one of Coolidge's attempts at what I term a romantic historical reconstruction, a novel which deals with actual historical events or personalities, albeit in a highly fanciful and romantic fashion, in which what happens does so for an ideological reason, in order to prove an author's point of view as opposed to a more impartial treatment. However, having accepted the self-imposition of the broad conventions of the formulary Western, Coolidge nonetheless managed to vary these ingredients according to his own very individual inclination. Prior to writing *Hidden Water,* Coolidge had gone among the cowboys in the Southwest, first alone, and then accompanied by Mary, several times. Yet he could remark about himself, as later he did in *Texas Cowboys* (1937), "with far more justification than Charley Russell, the Western artist, I can say I am not a cowboy."[6] Nor were Coolidge's heroes very often cowboys. They might be middle-aged ranchmen like Lorenzo de Vega in *Lorenzo the Magnificent* or Charley Barr in *Bear Paw.* They might be illiterate prospectors like John Calhoun in *Wunpost* (1920), mustangers like Johnny Lightfoot in *Horse-Ketchum of Death Valley* (1930) or Mace Bowman in *Long Rope* (1935), or even a train robber like Sycamore Brown in *The Fighting Fool* (1918). Coolidge generally eschewed violence in his heroes. They seldom engage in physical heroics of any kind. Sometimes as Clayton Hawks in *The Scalp-Lock* (1924) the hero shoots the villain from ambush, an action in this case approved by the heroine, Mary Blossom. "'You've always taken care of me,'" she tells Clay after he admits the deed.[7] For Coolidge's heroes, competition with the villain is a game, and one they delight in playing. As in Snake Bit Jones' conflict with villain George Hathaway, "it was better to get a horse on Hathaway than to win the whole saloon."[8] His heroes inevitably win, and almost always they win through cunning. There are occasional exceptions to this, such as Bill Enright in *Gun-Smoke* (1928). However, even here, it is a matter of degree and the hero, known for most of the book only as Gun-smoke, kills three men but only when absolutely forced to do so. This attitude, of course, stood in direct opposition to the incessant gun-play in most of Clarence E. Mulford's Bar-20 stories and was definitely out of the main stream by the time Eugene Cunningham could dispatch some seventy villains in *Riders of the Night* (1932). "...A new school of writers has given us a bloodier West," Coolidge once reflected. "If this crime wave of fiction continues, someone is liable to believe these boys—they may even believe themselves. The net result, up to date, is a division among our readers. Some are game to swallow anything, even the myth that, in those days, to kill a man was considered a huge joke. The other and wiser class is developing a wearied cynicism concerning everything they read about the West."[9] Coolidge's one effort at a novel in which constant killing was the main focus, *Gringo Gold*, may be such a disappointment precisely because his heart was not in it. Yet, as Owen Ulph pointed out in an essay, "Dane Coolidge: An Appreciation," it was this double vision which might explain "why the forty-five books he published between 1910 and 1940 have remained out of print and why their author is virtually unknown today. Coolidge's insistence upon authenticity and his uncompromising disregard for conventionality undermined the marketability of his 'westerns,' while his inventive disposition rendered his works of nonfiction academically suspect."[10]

I have said that Coolidge sometimes liked to incorporate certain of Mary Coolidge's qualities in his heroines. This was natural enough. Bertrand Russell once remarked that men learn about women from their wives, whereas women learn about women from other women. Yet, Coolidge was anything but consistent. His heroines generally are at their strongest when they are wearing men's clothing and this strength is conceived as being definitely masculine in character. They also tend to become petty or contrary shortly after being introduced and thus are able to remain emotionally aloof or estranged from the hero until the reconciliation at the end. In Zane Grey's Western fiction, the romance between the hero and the heroine is usually central to the plot. This is true of Coolidge's stories only about half the time. He could write a novel such as *Sheriff Killer* (1932) where the romance is so secondary as almost to be irrelevant; yet, conversely, he produced in *Silver Hat* (1934) a true romantic idyll in which the heroine, Lady Grace also known as Slender Woman, so called by the Indians, is unique because "never before among the White People had they seen a woman so fair—so slender and supple, so glad-eyed and friendly, so gifted with the beauty of the Sun."[11] *Silver Hat* was published nearly twenty years after Zane Grey's *Wildfire* began running as a serial in *The Country Gentlemen*. In the latter, Lucy Bostil, the heroine, is kidnapped and villain Joel Creech intends to make good on his threat to strip her naked, tie her on a horse, and send her to her death amid the flames of a forest fire, while the hero, Lin Slone, races to her rescue. In *Silver Hat,* Lady Grace, the daughter of a British lord, is lured by an evil Hopi, Harold Chasing Butterflies, to visit his village, only for her to be beset by Hopis on the way, stripped naked, and thrust into a cactus. Milton Buckmaster, known as Silver Hat, races to save her, wraps her in a blanket, and the reader is told "there was a quick ecstasy of pain as he raised her to the saddle and lept swiftly up behind her."[12] Lady Grace is kidnapped a second time by the Hopis. When Silver Hat rescues her again, they flee until they come to the Colorado River. He cannot swim; she can. Lady Grace gives Silver Hat the courage to attempt the rapids. They are successful, clinging to a log, and find themselves beached in a box canyon accessible only from the water when the river is low. "'It will be hard, I know, for I am naturally willful,'" Slender Woman confesses to Silver Hat, "'but as long as we are lost here together I shall try to do what you say.'"[13] Their idyll turns out to be a rustler's paradise and once the river is down they are threatened by rustlers. The only way out is to try the river again, this time in a small boat. "'If we overturn in the rapids I will swim beside you and support you till we reach the boat. Only trust me . . . as I trust you on land,'" she assures Silver Hat.[14] Later on, when their lives are in danger again, Lady Grace observes: "'A man isn't everything. . . . Now see what a woman can do!'"

With the exception of *Gringo Gold,* all of Coolidge's novels end with a romantic clinch. What's more, for every strong heroine Coolidge might draw in a particular book, he could turn right around and create a heroine like Johnsie Blood in *Gun-Smoke* who, when the hero mangles two fingers in a shoot-out crippling him for life, responds: "'. . . Just think what you did for me! Is that too much — for a finger?'"[16] And then there is Salome Lockhardt in *Bear Paw* who, while still married to the villain, declares that for hero Mark Trumbull, who wants to steal her from her husband, "'all I dream of now is a little home, with him, and I'll work my fingers to the bone.'"[17]

Some of Coolidge's heroes — and Mark Trumbull is decidely among them — are not as Puritanical as most of the heroes in formulary Westerns, even in fiction written subsequently by Ernest Haycox and Luke Short. In this, Coolidge was something of a throw-back to Owen Wister whose Virginian is not above having sexual relations with a woman toward whom he has no matrimonial aspirations. Only rarely, as in *Silver Hat,* did Coolidge show a strong man and a strong woman *together.* More often, a strong heroine for Coolidge required a weak or confused hero, and part of the purpose of the narrative rhythm is to demonstrate to him just how much he needs the heroine in order to make his way in the world effectively. In *Hidden Water,* Rufus Hardy goes so far as figuratively to surrender his gun to the heroine, Lucy Ware, for whom he works on the Dos S ranch. This is something, by way of contrast, that Lassiter, the mysterious gunfighter in Zane Grey's *Riders of the Purple Sage* (1912), adamantly refuses to do when heroine Jane Witersteen wants to take his guns away from him.

Hidden Water, however, is a seminal novel in another sense. It is the earliest instance I have encountered in formulary Westerns in which the theme of the two heroines is employed. This theme requires that hero Rufus Hardy choose between Lucy Ware and Kitty Bonnair. A good deal of ideology and value judgment can be incorporated into a plot employing this theme, prescribing which virtues a woman should possess if she is to be a heroine suitable for the hero. It is a theme that came to dominate nearly all of Ernest Haycox' novels and a good many of those of Luke Short, Louis L'Amour, and others.

Unlike many of his contemporaries, Coolidge did not physically stereotype his villains, but in common with many other Western writers his villains are often businessmen whose capital sin is greed. In this, he was seldom as perceptive and hortatory as were Eugene Manlove Rhodes, William MacLeod Raine, or even Zane Grey when it came to graphically characterizing the exploitation of the Western states by Eastern money. For Coolidge, the presence of evil characters was a dramatic necessity, nothing more; they exist solely to bring about conflict and, as such, inspire none of the animosity villains can generate in the Western fiction of other authors. To quote an old Spanish proverb of which Coolidge was fond: *"la peor cuña es la del mismo palo"* [the best wedge is one made of the same wood].[18] Coolidge's villain will devise schemes and his hero will devise counter-schemes; and so it goes, a momentary triumph for the villain, a counter-triumph for the hero, until the final play which, of course, the hero always wins, sometimes with and sometimes without the assistance of the heroine. Winning is intrinsic for the hero in a formulary Western, but Coolidge, as many of his contemporaries, would always provide his hero with a few wins between the beginning and the end of a novel, off-setting the temporary gains of the villain. It wasn't until the end of the thirties in the fiction of Ernest Haycox, and even more in that of Luke Short, that a plot was devised in which the hero would consistently lose again and again until the very last chapter when, suddenly, at the last moment, the tables turn and the hero triumphs.

To a surprising degree, in view of his prolificacy, Coolidge was lacking in the art of plot invention. Nearly all of his characters were based on someone he had met and, with an aggravating consistency, they recur in various incarnations, although viewed perhaps from a slightly different perspective. Cutthroat Bill made his first appearance in "The Man from Cherrycow," a short story from 1911, and re-emerges as Cutthroat Charley in *Gun-Smoke.* With the same equanimity,

Coolidge would repeat major plot conflicts from one book to the next, identical in many details but for a slight alteration in names or setting, such as Black Hat, the sheepman run off by the Grahams and Tewkesburys during the Pleasant Valley War as described in *Arizona Cowboys* who inspired the idea of the Mormon sheepman in *Hidden Water*, the Texas cattlemen in *Lorenzo the Magnificent,* and the rustlers of stolen Mexican cattle in *Bear Paw. The Fighting Fool* is based on the capture of Chacon, a ruthless Mexican bandit, who in history was pursued by Captain Burton C. Mossman of the Arizona Rangers, here told from the viewpoint of three train robbers; *Sheriff Killer* is essentially the same story, only this time told from the viewpoint of the Arizona Rangers. Death Valley Scotty was used as a model by Coolidge as early as *Rimrock Jones* (1917), the novel Coolidge wrote following his first trip to Death Valley and his first encounter with Scotty. The plot, basically, has to do with claim jumping, mining speculation, and stock manipulation. It contains Coolidge's first use of the "apex law," the legal stipulation that the mine located on the highest ground takes precedence over any and all claims on the same vein, even if discovered and developed prior to the strike on higher ground. There is a see-saw back and forth between Rimrock and New York financier Whitney H. Stoddard who initially capitalizes Jones and then wants the entire mine for himself. This plot, or a variation of it, recurs in *Shadow Mountain* (1919), *Lost Wagons* (1923), *Snake Bit Jones,* and elements of it predominate in the plots of *Wunpost* (1920) and *The Trail of Gold* (1937). The story of Colonel Bill Greene's discovery in Mexico of the famous Capote copper mine was also woven into these novels as well as providing elements which are central to the plots of *The Desert Trail* (1915), *Wolf's Candle* (1935), and *Rawhide Johnny* (1936). Added to the backdrop of claim jumping and stock speculation in the East and West alike, Coolidge also included events and scenes of carnage drawn from Mexico's revolutionary history in the rivalry between Diaz and Madera. *Yaqui Drums* (1940), a relatively late book, incorporates the fighting between the Yaquis and the Federales to be found in *The Desert Trail* and *Wolf's Candle* without, however, the mining aspects of those plots. The time-frame of *Yaqui Drums* is 1918. Although the Mexican general the Yaquis are fighting — Butcher Maldonado — was based on Governor Yzábal of Sonora, his character name is actually taken from the model for Pluma Blanca, the Yaqui chief in the story, based on Juan Maldonado Tetabiate who led the Yaquis in revolt in 1887. Coolidge more than once would shuffle historical models and events in this fashion. *War Paint* (1929), based on the Lincoln County War, is set in the early 1880s, but when he came to use this plot again, in *Bloody Head* (1940), he combined the story of Colonel Charles Goodnight's efforts to bring Texas cattle into New Mexico in 1867 with Pat Garrett's pursuit of Billy the Kid in 1881. The two periods do not mix well and the novel is among Coolidge's most disappointing efforts. Martin Hockaway is based on John Chisum and the literary character is the same as Coolidge described Chisum as having been in *Fighting Men of the West:* a cattle thief on a grand scale. Pat Garrett and Colonel Dudley are the only participants in the Lincoln County War who retain their real names. Comparing Red Ryan, the character based on the Kid, with Garrett, Coolidge concluded that "Pat and Red had worked side by side in the old days and regarded each other as friends. Each man was a killer, as cold as a stone, but the cards said Garrett would win. He had the law behind him, had lived a hard life, and in every way he was *hard*."[19]

Dusty Rhodes is a character who appears briefly in *Wunpost* and he reappears, just as briefly with the same name, in *Snake Bit Jones;* but this was not an attempt to include recurring characters in his stories the way, for example, that Clarence E. Mulford did with the original members of the Bar-20 crew in his novels or B.M. Bower did with the Flying U punchers in many of her novels and stories. Very few of Coolidge's novels have much to do with ranching and cowboying, although one of the earliest, and one of his best, does: *Bat Wing Bowles* (1914). "'To the young man seeking adventure I could give no better advice than to get a moderate sized hat, a pair of overalls and a horse and strike out into the cow country,'" Coolidge told a newspaper reporter at the time the novel appeared. "'If he has the nerve with which I have endowed Bat Wing Bowles he will win out, if he hasn't he will get adventures anyway.'"[20] The plot tells of Sam Houghton, a New Yorker who meets Dixie May Lee of Chula Vista, Arizona at a New York train terminal. He falls in love with her, follows her home, and manages to become a cowboy working on her father's Bat Wing ranch.

In the course of his annual travels in the summer months, Coolidge went over the ground in which his novels and stories are set many times. Yet he could never evoke them vividly, as could Zane Grey whose Death Valley novel *Wanderer of the Wasteland* (1922) literally makes Death Valley itself a character in the story, so capturing it in its many moods and hues that it is unforgettable. Similarly, the compelling sense of fantasy which imbues Grey's characters and their almost superhuman conflicts, a quality he shared with Max Brand who knew virtually nothing of the physical, geographical, and historical West, is entirely absent in Coolidge's fiction.

Despite Mary Coolidge's interest in Native American cultures and Dane Coolidge's collaboration with her on at least two books, he personally distrusted Indians. In his fiction, when Indians are not portrayed as villains and savages, they are contemned for their laziness. Coolidge did not find it the least remarkable in describing the Cherry-cow Company in *Texas Cowboys* that the company was permitted to raise its cattle on the San Carlos reserve and pay rental to government bureaucrats intended for the Apaches but which they never received; and he even sympathized with the opprobrium with which the Company regarded the Apaches for stealing a steer when they needed meat. The only Indian Coolidge liked on the San Carlos reserve was Chief Bylas who had completely submitted to the white man and had taken up farming. "'Me work!'" Coolidge quoted the chief as saying. "I shook hands with this honest Indian who was not afraid to work...."[21] In *The Fighting Fool,* Coolidge drew a white man married to an Indian woman named Desert Willow. But she is a white man's Indian. "'I do not like these Indian boys,'" she tells the white hero about her people. "'Those young men have all been to school. They have learned to read and write and speak good English, but when they come home they forget. They will not talk in English nor follow the white man's ways. They are lazy — they will not make nice houses when they know how to — I do not like that. Some boys are trained for carpenters, some for mechanics, some for gardeners and farmers — now there they are, catching rock-rats!'"[22] A *mestizo,* or mixed-blood, like Quick Murrah in *Gun-Smoke!* is invariably lacking in "all those sentiments of chivalry and of respect for a good woman which you will find in the lowest white" since once "his half-Indian nature had been stirred to the depths — he was dangerous as a rabid wolf."[23] Only two of Coolidge's heroes are white men who consciously choose to live among the Indians, Milton Buckmaster known as Silver Hat in the novel of that title and Miles Gilpin in *Under the Sun* (1926) who is captured by Navajos and eventually is adopted by the medicine man, Nahtahlish, and called Bajo Sol because of his bravery. Bajo Sol falls in love with the daughter of Chief Many Horses, known both by her home-name Debeth Lahgaigee [Little White Sheep] and, because she is something of an amazon, by her war-name Yil Quaba [She Who Goes To War]. In time, they marry only to be separated during the time when Kit Carson led the round-up of the Navajo nation, placing it on a reservation at Bosque Redondo. Gilpin is made translator by the Army for the period of captivity, but once the Navajos are released he sets out to find Debeth and, when he does, he decides to remain permanently with his adopted people.

With the possible exception of the Navajos, Coolidge might have been disinclined to grant Native Americans the integrity of separate and unique cultures, but this Anglo-American parochialism did not apply to Spanish-Americans. Coolidge was wont to balance every portrait of a cruel Mexican with a character of the same nationality who possessed a number of admirable qualities. He had a remarkably intimate grasp of Mexican customs and culture, particularly among the *ricos,* and an idiomatic if somewhat halting knowledge of Spanish. He was on as firm ground here as he was when it came to the flora of the Southwestern states which he could identify in English, Latin, and Spanish. Cruz Pizano, a local leader of revolutionists, is described in *Wolf's Candle* as "a devil in human form, and his grinning face was not among the dead."[24] In *Yaqui Drums,* the story opens with the hero a soldier of fortune working for Pizano. Yet, in *Lorenzo the Magnificent,* Don Lorenzo perceives the Anglo-American way as "nothing but lawyers, and officers of the law, and papers which robbed poor men of their rights...."[25] When Coolidge came to retell the legendary life of Joaquin Murieta in *Gringo Gold,* his sympathies were almost entirely with the dispossessed and disenfranchised Spanish-American population.

Although Coolidge probably would never have admitted it, the author who perhaps influenced him the most was Zane Grey and some of his best novels share settings and plot elements with some of Grey's finest fiction. *The Fighting Danites* (1934) is set in Utah in 1877, thirty years after the Mormons first came to Salt Lake. Brigham Young himself is a character and the novel is one of Coolidge's more notable attempts at a romantic historical reconstruction. In common with Grey, Coolidge condemned the Mormons for the practice of polygamy and, as in Grey's *The Rainbow Trail* (1915), much of *The Fighting Danites* is concerned with the hero's effort to rescue Deseret, a Gentile woman, whom the villain, Bishop Lot Drake, wants to force to become his wife. In *The Rainbow Trail,* John Shefford is searching for Fay Larkin, a Gentile who was taken away from Lassiter and Jane Withersteen in the hidden canyon in which they found themselves at the end of *Riders of the Purple Sage* and who has been raised to be a good Mormon and a sealed wife. Among those who help Shefford in his quest is Joe Lake, a Mormon who cannot endorse all that has occurred in Mormon history although still one of the faithful. In *The Fighting Danites,* Lieutenant Zachary Tarrant of the U.S. Cavalry is assisted in his search for Deseret, a child captured at the time of the Mountain Meadows Massacre who has been raised to be a Mormon, by Jake Lingo, a Mormon who has the gift of prophecy and who can foresee events which will happen in the story by virtue of his visionary powers. Coolidge's view of the Massacre is that initially it was the Paiutes who attacked the immigrant wagon train of Gentiles but were beaten back, many of them having been killed, including two chiefs. Next the Mormons, disguised as Indians, took up the battle for three days during which the immigrants were without water. The Mormon militia then waved a flag of truce and, gaining access to the embattled camp with this ruse, shot down the defenseless men and women leaving behind only the children whom they adopted. Deseret confesses to Tarrant that Bishop Drake personally killed her mother. Drake is eventually brought to stand trial for his crimes by Tarrant. Although Brigham Young escapes a similar fate by shrewdly excommunicating Drake before his capture and blaming him for the Massacre, Coolidge did not want his reader to be deceived. "He it was," he wrote of Young, "and men like him, who made the church what it was—a curse on all that fair land. . . ."[26] Ammon Clark, the leader of the Danites, Bishop Drake's fighting men, is killed in battle with Kuchene and his Navajo warriors. Before he dies, Clark asks to have his beard shaved off because Joseph Smith had prophesied that he would not die as long as he wore it. The act makes the prophecy a lie. Yet, Jake Lingo's power of prophecy and vision are held to be true as demonstrated by episodes in the narrative.

Coolidge seems to have been ambivalent about mysticism, but he is somewhat unique in having included mystical powers as themes in some of his novels. In *Under the Sun,* Nahtahlish, the medicine man, has the power of prophecy and can foretell the future. Coolidge might reflect generally on the Navajos that "kindly as they were in their home life and with their children, there was sleeping beneath the surface the volcanic nature of the Indian, with its terrible capacity for hate."[27] Notwithstanding, when it comes to the medicine man, the hero, Miles Gilpin, "in his presence felt abased; and his smile was so kindly that it seemed to convey a blessing upon everyone who crossed his path. In his wild life as a hunter and trapper Gilpin had never met a man whom he loved more devotedly—and Nahtahlish had made him his son."[28]

In *Arizona Cowboys,* Coolidge described how Apache Leap

outside Pinal, Arizona, got its name. He used Pinal as his setting for *Silver and Gold* (1919). The hero, Denver Russell, has been to a fortune-teller named Mother Trigedgo and she made a prophecy about how he would find two treasures, one of silver and one of gold in the shadow of a place of death, how he would fall in love with a beautiful woman but how he must beware how he reveals his affection or he will lose her, and how he will meet his death at the hands of his dearest friend. Russell is preoccupied with this prophecy throughout the entire story and much of what he does is done so as to escape the mortal threat it contains. The heroine is Drusilla Hill, daughter of the local storekeeper, who has ambitions to become an opera singer. Fortunately for the match between them, Russell loves opera and has a phonograph and numerous recordings which he plays up at his mine overlooking Pinal during the hours of twilight and early dark. The hold Mother Trigedgo's prophecy has upon him isn't broken until Drusilla goes to her and comes back with a corrected interpretation—one which will allow Russell to marry his dearest friend.

Russell's love of opera is not an isolated incident. Compared, for example, to the illiterate cowboys who comprise Clarence E. Mulford's Bar-20 punchers, including Hopalong Cassidy, many of Coolidge's characters are highly cultured. In *Shadow Mountain,* the hero, Wiley Holman, at one point holds a learned conversation with Colonel Huff, who is hiding in a canyon in Death Valley, about Socrates' dialogue with Lamprocles, his son, as recorded in the *Memorabilia* of Xenophon which the colonel had studied exhaustively in the original Greek until the volume was stolen by an improvident camp robber.

Sometimes, as in *Long Rope,* Coolidge would rework an entire Zane Grey plot after his own fashion—in this case that of Grey's *Wildfire*—and a theme of which both were inordinately fond was the idea of a feud as the central conflict in a story. Coolidge's *The Man-Killers* (1921) is based on the Graham-Tewksbury feud with elements added from the Canfield-McCoy feud combined with the theme from *Romeo and Juliet* of star-crossed lovers—albeit with a happy ending! The idyllic period that hero Hall McIvor and heroine Allfair spend in a mountain hide-out was, it would appear, only a rehearsal for the longer idyll contained in *Silver Hat.* A feud is also the central conflict in *Horse-Ketchum of Death Valley.*

Only in *Gringo Gold,* and then only because of the nature of the legend itself, did Coolidge forego a happy ending. Yet, however many times in his fiction Coolidge's beleaguered prospectors might win out against all the forces of money and power marshaled against them, when he came to narrate his version of the life of Colonel Bill Greene in *Fighting Men of the West,* Coolidge did record that "Greene lost Cananea, he lost the last of his stock, he lost everything he had except the land and cattle which he had deeded over to his wife. He became a changed man, living on at the scene of his former grandeur but unable to get a fresh start. In 1911 he was badly injured in a runaway and the doctors told him he would die."[29] It is regrettable that in so much of his fiction he could never bring himself to tell of the many tragedies and failures that occurred in the West, and the mettle and character of men and women who, having lost all that they had held dear, managed to survive, to maintain their integrity; and, conversely, how the land and the hardship often were too much, the odds too great.

The Depression affected Coolidge, as it affected every author. With diminished sales, he increased his output. Formerly, he might write a novel a year, sometimes every other year. By the late thirties, he was producing as many as three novels a year and added to these were his nonfiction books based on the scrupulous notes he had made over the years. He might recycle his plots from one book to the next, but only rarely did he take one of the novelettes he had written for the pulps and rewrite it. *Comanche Chaser* (1938) was a rare exception, the expansion of a story written originally in 1927. However, since it is one of his more interesting novels, the story of Boone Helms' pursuit of Comanche war chief Espejo who has kidnapped the heroine, Luz Hautcoeur, perhaps he should have done so more frequently.

In his personal life, Coolidge remained a member of the American Society of Mammalogists, the Authors League of America, and the California Writers Club. He might not have had children of his own, but for thirty-five years he was a director of the San Francisco Boys' Club. In his last years, he probably felt himself to be written out. More often he would sit on the roofed porch and tell stories to his nephew Coit Coolidge and Coit's wife Nancy, who were close friends. He made no effort to see his work safeguarded, after the fashion that Zane Grey's sons promoted his works after his death and even added to them. He died in a diabetic coma and there is some question if he was not indeed aware of his condition. Mary survived him by five years. She died on April 13, 1945. Coit Coolidge became Dane Coolidge's literary executor and, although the paperback revolution was by then in full swing, he made little effort to market his uncle's fiction in the new medium. *Bear*

Paw and *Fighting Men of the Frontier* are among the very few Coolidge titles which were reprinted in the decade or so following his death. This is unfortunate when you reflect that *The New York Times Book Review* commented in its review of *Hell's Hip Pocket* (1938): "Again Dane Coolidge has given us a lively, gripping, and well written tale of the Old West. There are gunfighting and excitement aplenty in it.... No other man in the field today writes better Western tales than Dane Coolidge."[30]

At his finest, Coolidge wrote with a definite grace and had a somewhat leisurely pace all but lost to formulary Western fiction after World War II. His longer fictions are usually set over a period of years and possess a charming sense of *temps en passant,* a visual sensation in which the characters seem to pass in and out of the narrative, in which events happen, in which time may pass but the permanent frame is always the immutable idea of a distinct geographical place.

Coolidge did experiment in an effort to expand the scope of the formulary Western. Of course, the broader this scope, the greater the sense of humanity infused into the expansion, the more significant becomes the potential of Western fiction to desert completely all of the formulary conventions which for so long have both nurtured and imprisoned it. Viewed in this context, several of Dane Coolidge's novels represent steps—even if small and sometimes very tenuous steps—away from all formulae and ideology and toward a Western American literature informed by a vision which unites historical accuracy with an impassioned concern for the human estate.

Fran Striker and the Lone Ranger

It was while I was still engaged as the special film consultant for *Images of Indians* (PBS, 1980), a series devoted to showing how the American motion picture industry has over the years completely misrepresented and distorted Native American peoples, that I received a telephone call from Phil Lucas, the Crow-Choctaw co-producer of the series. He wanted to introduce me on the telephone to Rob Thompson, a screenwriter who had just been hired by Sir Lew Grade, the British financier and film producer, to prepare the screenplay for a new multi-million dollar picture about the Lone Ranger. Thompson's most notable screen credit was *Hearts of the West* (M-G-M/United Artists, 1975), a somewhat satirical treatment of the conventions of the cinematic Western. Thompson, as yet, knew very little about the Lone Ranger and wondered what, if anything, I could tell him.

My response was to comment that the Lone Ranger was one of the most successfully manufactured commercial myths about the American West conceived in the twentieth century, but beyond this, and perhaps even more to the point given our present work at hand, the Hollywood stereotypes of Native Americans, never once in all the theatrical, radio, or television productions about the Lone Ranger and his faithful companion, Tonto, had I ever found anything derogatory toward Native Americans in the way Tonto was portrayed. I thought this was very significant and I still do. Moreover, whether the Lone Ranger and Tonto were a commercial myth or not, in the depiction of their friendship, in their mutual inter-dependence and reliance on each other in the wilderness, far more than Natty Bumppo and Chingachgook in James Fenimore Cooper's Leatherstocking Saga, they represented what D.H. Lawrence in his *Studies in Classic American Literature* (1923) described as the nucleus of a human relationship that in literary history, before Cooper's time, had sadly not existed, "a stark, stripped human relationship of two men, deeper than the deeps of sex. Deeper than property, deeper than fatherhood, deeper than marriage,

277

deeper than love. So deep that it is loveless. The stark, loveless, wordless union of two men who have come to the bottom of themselves."[1] That, Thompson assured me before he rang off, was what he hoped to capture in his screenplay. Unfortunately, he did not, but then the fault was not his alone; there were too many problems with the production, beginning with the fact that the actor chosen to play the Lone Ranger had to have his voice dubbed throughout the film. Yet, it is this notion of friendship, as opposed to everything else about the Lone Ranger, which makes him culturally and psychologically of tremendous consequence: the fact that the Lone Ranger *is not alone.* American Western fiction, as American fiction generally, can be characterized on the basis of its preponderance of loners, men, and in a few cases women, who are separated by circumstances from everybody. Real friendship is seldom found. For the Lone Ranger, almost from the very start, it has been otherwise.

The Lone Ranger was created at radio station WXYZ in Detroit, Michigan in the latter days of 1932 during the nadir of the Great Depression. He was created out of an effort to save the station which had cancelled its CBS franchise and was in dire financial straits. WXYZ was owned by John H. King, *né* Kunsky, formerly a movie theatre owner, and George W. Trendle. It was Trendle who came up with the idea of a Western drama for youngsters featuring a hero that would be a composite of Robin Hood and the character created by Johnston McCulley which Douglas Fairbanks brought to the screen in *The Mark of Zorro* (United Artists, 1920). After several conferences with his staff, Trendle telephoned Fran Striker. Striker, born in 1903, was a free-lance writer from Buffalo, New York. He had done a radio series titled *Warner Lester, Manhunter* which had been broadcast by WXYZ. Striker had never been farther West than Buffalo at the time Trendle contacted him and all that he knew of the West he had learned from a great-uncle who had once served drinks to Mark Twain and Bret Harte across a bar in Washoe County, Nevada.

Striker's first script had to be revised fifteen times before Trendle was willing to give it a trial broadcast. Trendle insisted that the Ranger must be an Easterner who was educated and who possessed a character so stern as to be prohibitive of laughter. Following the trial broadcast, Trendle waited until Striker had a backlog of twenty-four scripts before the Lone Ranger made his official debut. Striker found that he needed someone for the Ranger to talk to and so, from this necessity, he created the Ranger's close friend, Tonto, who made his debut in the tenth

Robert Livingston as the Lone Ranger, Chief Thundercloud as Tonto, and Duncan Renaldo in a scene from *The Lone Ranger Rides Again* (Republic, 1939). Photo courtesy Eddie Brandt's Saturday Matinee.

script. In Spanish, *tonto* denotes a fool or a blockhead. Striker was unaware of this. What he had in mind was that region of Arizona which Zane Grey had evoked so vividly in *Under the Tonto Rim* (1926). For Striker, Tonto was a region and, since the character was assigned no tribe or nation, the regional appellation might well speak for his origin.

On January 30, 1933, six weeks after Trendle had first come up with the idea, the program went on the air over WXYZ and seven other stations in the Michigan area. The cast was chosen from WXYZ's stock company. After six episodes, the role of the Ranger was given to George Stenius, who later changed his name to George Seaton and eventually became a film director at Paramount. Stenius played the Ranger for three months until he was replaced by Earle W. Graser who continued in the role until his death at thirty-two on April 8, 1941, the result of an automobile crash. Graser was replaced by the show's first narrator in

1933, Brace Beemer. Beemer played the Ranger on radio until the program was dropped in 1954.

How popular was the Lone Ranger? On May 16, 1933, the Ranger announced that he would give away a free popgun to the first 300 youngsters who wrote in for it. On May 18, the Ranger stated firmly that the supply of popguns had been exhausted. On May 20, he had to beg his listeners not to write in, and there was a slightly hysterical note in his voice. When the avalanche of listener mail stopped at last, WXYZ counted 24,905 letters. It was a record which, according to the Detroit post office, had been exceeded only by political commentator Father Coughlin after a nationwide broadcast. The Lone Ranger was still scarcely audible outside the state of Michigan.

This popular reaction encouraged Trendle to attempt another demonstration of the program's effectiveness before trying to sell it to a sponsor. In July, 1933, the Detroit Department of Recreation promised that the Lone Ranger would appear during the school field day on Belle Island. And appear he did, masked and on a white stallion. The police had been prepared to handle a crowd of 20,000 — the most that Belle Island could comfortably accommodate — but 70,000 showed up. The situation became so chaotic that the police had to appeal to the Ranger to help restore order. It would be many years before he dared to make another personal appearance.

Trendle sold sponsorship of the program to the makers of Silvercup Bread. The first sponsored broadcast was on November 27, 1933. A month later the program was extended to WGN in Chicago. Another month and WOR in Newark was added. WXYZ, WGN, and WOR then became the nucleus of the Mutual Broadcasting System which was formed that same year. By 1939, the Lone Ranger was heard on 140 stations, including Newfoundland, Ontario, Hawaii, and New Zealand. Roughly half of these broadcasts were "live" and half via transcription. The Lone Ranger shows were broadcast three times a night three nights a week. The first broadcast was at 7:30 EST and went to Detroit and the East. The second was at 7:30 CST and went to Chicago. The third was at 7:30 PST and went to the West Coast. The same cast played all three shows and tried to maintain the same level of dramatic intensity.

In October, 1935 Trendle founded the Lone Ranger Safety Club. The Ranger, on the air, told children to go to their neighborhood grocer and get an application card for the Club. The Club card read: "I solemnly promise: 1.) Not to cross any street except at regular crossings and to first look both ways. 2.) Not to play in the streets. 3.) To always tell the truth." In all, there were ten such promises. Typical of that curious Yankee ingenuity whereby an ethical way of life is somehow inextricably bound up with buying someone's manufactured product, a child could, in addition to an official notification of membership in the Club and a private code, earn a Lone Ranger badge by performing a single good deed. That good deed was to persuade three neighbors who did not use Silvercup Bread, or, later, Bond Bread (when Bond took over from Silvercup), to promise to buy it regularly on their next trip to the food store. A good deed, therefore, was being a good American consumer and consuming precisely those products which good American heroes told you to consume, and to enlist others in conforming to the American way by also consuming those products.

Buck Jones, a popular movie cowboy during the twenties and thirties, had formed the Buck Jones Rangers early in his screen career. His movie horse was named Silver. Jones brought a law suit against Trendle for the unlicensed use of his horse's name in calling the Lone Ranger's horse Silver. Trendle was hardly above borrowing anything he might need better to put across his property. The idea of using Rossini's "William Tell Overture" as the Lone Ranger's theme music he took from the opening credits of *The Devil Horse* (Mascot, 1932), a theatrical serial in which the thundering hoofs of a wild stallion were heard in accompaniment to this rousing music as, on the screen, the stallion charged into the range of the camera. It was even more effective when used only aurally over the radio to announce the Lone Ranger's arrival. Jones lost his suit on the grounds that you cannot copyright a horse's name. However, as a consequence of this litigation, in January, 1935 Trendle incorporated the program independently. This liberated all the more the commercial dynamism of his creation. By December, 1935, 475,574 Lone Ranger badges had been distributed for getting neighbors to buy the sponsor's bread; by 1940 this number exceeded two million.

A contract was signed with Republic Pictures for two Western chapter plays to be produced using the Lone Ranger and Tonto. *The Lone Ranger* (Republic, 1938) directed by William Witney and John English was produced in twelve chapters at a negative cost of $285,000 and, upon release, it had a domestic gross in the United States and Canada of $1,150,000. The literary rights contract called for a payment of $18,750 to be made to Lone Ranger, Inc., plus 10% of the worldwide gross above $390,000. The contract also called for a feature version, to be edited from the serial, which was released as *Hi-Yo Silver* (Republic, 1940). A second serial, titled *The Lone Ranger Rides Again* (Republic, 1939), employing the same two directors, was produced at a negative cost of $325,000 with a domestic gross of $1,250,000. This time sale of literary rights called for $40,000 against 10% of the worldwide gross with no minimal figure to be recouped first and with no provision for a feature version. Also by contract Fran Striker was given editorial supervision over story content in both chapter plays.

By 1939 the Lone Ranger was earning half a million dollars a year. King Features had begun a Lone Ranger syndicated comic strip. Manufacturers, wanting to get in on a good thing, were employing the Lone Ranger as trademark on novelty items. Also, by 1939, the seemingly indefatigable Fran Striker was single-handedly writing 156 Lone Ranger radio scripts a year, 365 Lone Ranger cartoon strips, besides producing a regular series of book-length stories about the character and his supervisory work on the Republic chapter plays. Striker regarded the Lone Ranger as his private trust, in part, he claimed, because of his three Ranger-worshipping children at home; but, no less truthfully although he did not say so, he was so protective because the Lone Ranger was making him a personal fortune and he wasn't about to permit anyone to tamper with the property. It is probably worth noting that during all its years on radio, the Lone Ranger missed only two programs—both in 1945: the day President Franklin D. Roosevelt died and the day the Empire of Japan capitulated.

The first book about the Lone Ranger to appear was *The Lone Ranger and His Horse Silver* (1935). This was what was known in those days as a Big Little Book, a book somewhat smaller in dimensions than a modern paperback with heavy cardboard covers and very thick pulp paper pages. No author's credit was given, but we know that Striker wrote it. The next year Striker began writing an entire series of Lone Ranger books published by Grosset & Dunlap and *The Lone Ranger* (1936) was the first in what would prove before Striker was finished an eighteen volume series detailing the Ranger's various adventures. The claim was made in *The Lone Ranger and His Horse Silver* that Tonto was a half-breed. Striker simply incorporated that entire book in the second and third chapters of *The Lone Ranger*, so it is not surprising to find him making the same claim in the subsequent novel; but this was to be the last time that he did so. Henceforth, Tonto became a full-blood Native American, although he continued to speak cigar store

Indianese. How the Lone Ranger and Tonto first met was described by Striker in *The Lone Ranger and the Gold Robbery* (1939). In *The Lone Ranger and Tonto* (1940), Striker revealed that Tonto's horse was named Scout and was slightly smaller than Silver. The first mention of the Lone Ranger's silver mine, used by the Ranger to support himself and, after smelting, to supply the silver ore from which he could make the silver tips of his cartridges, came in *The Lone Ranger at the Haunted Gulch* (1941).

The first Lone Ranger magazines were published in 1937 by the Trojan Publishing Corporation of Chicago and contained many of Fran Striker's subsequent novels in pre-book form. Later Dell Comics began publishing its series of Lone Ranger comic strips in comic book form and then finally launched a series of original comic book stories.

The Lone Ranger began on television in its first season on September 15, 1949. In all, 221 Lone Ranger episodes were produced. The first series of episodes featured Clayton Moore as the Lone Ranger and Jay Silverheels as Tonto. The second series of fifty-two episodes starred John Hart as the Ranger but retained Silverheels as Tonto. Clayton Moore returned to the role then for all the remaining television episodes and he and Silverheels also appeared in the two color feature motion pictures, *The Lone Ranger* (Warner's, 1956) directed by Stuart Heisler and *The Lone Ranger and The Lost City of Gold* (United Artists, 1958) directed by Lesley Selander. On September 10, 1966 a half-hour animated Lone Ranger series began on CBS, but it proved short-lived, with a total of only twenty-six episodes.

One certainly need not approach Fran Striker's first novel, *The Lone Ranger*, armed with the paraphernalia of a literary critic. It is not literature, nor was it intended to be; it is rather what is called popular culture. If my reader is a young person, let me frankly admit to you that you do not need any more justification for reading this book than I had when I first read it, which was to read an interesting story. I grew up in a small town in the Midwest, a town so small that it had no book store and what books were to be had were carried by a stationery store. It became very cold in the winter and, occasionally, upon my way home from school in the early-dark afternoons I would stop in at this store and let my eyes run along the titles of the Lone Ranger books. The store had all the volumes in the Grosset & Dunlap series, and they were arranged in order, right below the Hardy Boys and Tom Swift, and right above Nancy Drew and the Bobbsey Twins. We did not have a television — and so I only knew of the Lone Ranger from having listened to Brace Beemer portray him on the radio. I hadn't seen the motion picture versions and so the images I had of the Lone Ranger and Tonto were ones I had created in my own imagination. I can tell you this. Images which you yourself imagine stay with you longer than any which are manufactured for you now by television.

However, in retrospect, when first I read this book it was an unfortunate view of the Old West to which I was being introduced and I cannot say that I wholly profited from it. For that reason I must urge caution to you. The West was *not* a wild place where greedy and vicious men were always preying upon innocent ranchers and townspeople who could only really be saved by the likes of the Lone Ranger and Tonto. This is instead a very fanciful, even a fantastic, vision of the Old West created expressly to make money. That is to be remembered when reading this book. This is not to say that you ought not to enjoy *The Lone Ranger,* but only that in life, since human beings are what they are, there wasn't and could not have been a Lone Ranger and Tonto. It is an ideal world which has been created for your benefit. Yet, there is something else, something with which I began this introductory note, and that is the relationship between the Ranger and Tonto, between a white American and a Native American. This kind of friendship, prior to this century, was not really possible between the majority of white Americans and Native Americans because they did not understand each other and, not understanding each other, found it difficult to accept each other. Yet, this lack of understanding and this lack of friendship between the two, each one of them today as fully American as the other, can change. We who are white Americans can learn much from the Native American; he has much to teach us; and, for his part, he has always wanted our friendship. It is this very ideal of friendship, embodied in this story, which *is* a possibility.

Notwithstanding, such a possibility should not preclude being realistic about *The Lone Ranger.* By denying Tonto any tribe or nation, Striker could make him over completely into a *white man's Indian* whose allegiances and sympathies are all with the white men who would take possession of all the land, who would kill the buffalo to starve the Indians to death, who would engage in a genocidal slaughter of Native Americans on a massive scale. Moreover, Striker in his text refers to Native Americans as "wild redskins," "savages," "red devils," and "benighted Injuns." When one of the villains, Spig—perhaps a word derived from the slang for Mexican, "spic"—is accused of having Indian blood in him, he becomes violent in his denial of the charge.

Beyond this, Striker as an Easterner knew nothing of the behavior of wild horses and the description of Silver's capture and taming is the sheerest fantasy, as absurd in its way as the query from the property department, once *The Legend of the Lone Ranger* (Universal, 1981) was in pre-production, if a pair of "identical" pinto horses could be acquired for Tonto and his double! Nor did Striker know anything about the behavior of the Plains buffalos; they would seldom stampede when one or more of their number were shot down, which is precisely why they were such easy hunting. White marksmen who kept themselves concealed behind a blind could decimate an entire herd.

I have said *The Lone Ranger* should be regarded as an example of popular culture. What this means is that the novel contains nothing to which objection might be raised by readers contemporary with its publication, and nothing that might cause such a reader to question the values which emerge from the events being described. White men are all good or all bad. Only the villains are greedy. The Sioux Indians are sub-human. By definition, everything that the good white men do or want to do must itself be good or lead only to good. Everything that the villains do or want to do must itself be evil and lead only to evil. By identifying with the good white Americans and the white man's Indian, it is possible actually to believe that anything such men do must be good. Growing up thinking about oneself and other white Americans in such self-righteous terms only further reinforced that immature naiveté about which Americans tend to be so uniquely proud, however delusional and destructive it ultimately may be. Indeed, it is this posture which constitutes the basic source of that American arrogance which has perpetually insisted upon conformity to the American way of thinking and feeling everywhere in the world (depending, of course, on the varying currents of that way of thinking and feeling at a particular moment in time), the spirit that so zealously sought to destroy Native American culture and religion and very nearly succeeded, that attacked, pillaged, and ravaged the wilderness, that exploited whatever and whomever it encountered in order to make ever more money while declaring that every action was ordained and blessed in the name of the bleeding, expiring body of its white god.

Colton J. Glencoe in *The Lone Ranger* is the conspiring minion of Eastern money. However, it is "bad" Eastern money that he represents, whereas Dave Walton, chief engineer of the railroad track-laying project, and Henry Danvers, Dave's employer, represent "good" Eastern money. As an Easterner himself, Striker could write glibly about "the hour when men and steel should have bound the wilderness finally to the world of commerce"[1] as the Lone Ranger was giving away badges for getting people to buy Silvercup Bread. Striker liked to include old timers in his radio scripts and in his books, such as Old Clem in *The Lone Ranger,* but at one point the Lone Ranger rather uncharitably calls Clem an old fool. Kate Stevens, the stereotypcial "girl" to be found in any ranch romance formulary Western, somewhat surprisingly is Striker's most developed character in *The Lone Ranger.* The author has her riding side-saddle, which the majority of women did in the West in contrast to the Hollywood penchant for putting females in tight pants straddling horses, although the Lone Ranger thinks of her as nothing more than a child and, typically, after he rescues her from the Sioux and she throws her arms around him and kisses him, the Ranger is embarrassed.

There is, when it comes to the plot, very little that is original in *The Lone Ranger.* Almost every scene appears to have been lifted from two novels by Zane Grey, *The U.P. Trail* (1918), which similarly is set against the background of the building of the transcontinental railroad, and *The Border Legion* (1916) which has the villain abduct the heroine from the arms of the hero. For his scenes of Sioux village life and practices, Striker seems to have been most indebted to James Fenimore Cooper's *The Last of the Mohicans* (1826) and, as Cooper, he describes an instance of Indian torture as "'a scene which might have been copied from the infernal regions.'"[2] The burning of heretics over the centuries or the gassing of Jews in this century scarcely seem more exemplary forms of the white man's behavior.

The last broadcast of the Lone Ranger on radio was aired on September 3, 1954, the 2,956th episode. Also in 1954, Jack Wrather purchased Lone Ranger, Inc., from George W. Trendle, reputedly for $2,000,000. Fran Striker, despite the change in ownership, remained associated with the Lone Ranger property, although *The Lone Ranger on the Red Butte Trail* (1956) would be the last novel he wrote about him. Striker died in 1962, victim of a head-on automobile collision. At the time, he was still living in Buffalo. All that you might miss in this, Striker's early novel about the Lone Ranger, is what became his characteristic ending, the sudden thundering of hoofs and the hearty cry of "Hi-Yo! Silver! Awaaaay!"

Luke Short and the Western

Luke Short was the pseudonym adopted by Frederick Dilley Glidden. It was under this name that he published virtually all his Western fiction. It was the *nom de plume* chosen for him by his agent when a publisher complained that his real name sounded "too phony." Only after he had established the pseudonym did Glidden discover that there actually had been a nineteenth-century Western gunman and gambler by that name. It was, in its way, characteristic of Glidden's approach to the American West. The backcover hype of a Dell paperback reprint in 1978 of *The Man on the Blue* (1937) declared that "his novels, which have sold in the tens of millions, are renowned for their historic authenticity, and the true raw violence that typified the conquest of our last frontier." While it is a fact that Glidden's novels sold over thirty million copies during his lifetime, it is not true that they are historically authentic. The kind of raw violence depicted in them is not so much typical of the conquest of the frontier as it is typical of Glidden's highly romantic and always stylish formulary Western fiction. It was a convention in the pulp fiction market, where he began, and he retained it in all that he wrote subsequently, even after the pulps themselves had ceased to exist.

Brian Garfield was only one of a number of aspiring authors whom Glidden helped during the difficult years of apprenticeship. "When I was a kid trying to write short stories," Garfield confided in a letter, "Fred would read them and criticize them for me. He was extraordinarily patient and helpful. Thanks to him I finally got something published. If it hadn't been for him, I might have ended up in another line of work. In any case the piece of advice he gave me that stands out most vividly in my memory—to this day, and he told me this twenty-five years ago—was this: 'A Western story is no good if it relies on its Western trappings. It works, as a story, only if it's a story that can be lifted out of its setting. If the characters and plot would work equally well in a modern setting, or in ancient Rome, or some far-off future planet in space, *then* you've got a good story. But if you depend on devices — gunfights and the like — then you haven't got a story.' I think his own work bears out that advice. He wrote about the West because he lived there and he knew the people but essentially he wasn't a 'Western' writer, he was simply a slick-magazine storyteller and his yarns mostly would have worked just as well (in terms of human conflict and drama) in some other setting. In a few cases he relied on history for his plots — *And the Wind Blows Free;* it was his favorite among his novels — but mostly he just spun yarns. He spun 'em damn well. But he didn't really chronicle the West. Will Henry does that. . . . Fred wrote for a living."[1]

Frederick Glidden was born November 19, 1908 in Kewanee, Illinois. He decided on a career as a newspaperman and entered the School of Journalism at the University of Missouri from which he graduated with a Bachelor's degree in 1930. While still an undergraduate, he wrote a stage play titled "Retraction" which won a prize from the University's Dramatic Arts Club and was even published by the University in its series of Dramatic Prize Plays. Following graduation, Glidden worked for a number of newspapers, but no position lasted for very long. The Depression years were not a particularly auspicious time to embark on a career, but there was more to it than that. "I've read or heard that all newspapermen are disappointed writers," he later recalled, "but in me you behold a writer who is a disappointed newspaperman. I've been fired from more newspapers than I like to remember, even if I could. . . . There was an allergy about me that affected city editors in strange ways, causing them to point to the doorway, request me to pass through it, and tell me never to darken it again. Subsequently, I discovered that the allergy did not affect magazine and book editors, and that if I stayed 2,000 miles away from them I was safe — which might explain my living in the West."[2]

Glidden proceeded to wander throughout the Western regions of the United States and Canada. He found various employment and for a time he worked as an archeologist's assistant. For two years he trapped in Northern Canada. Once he became a successful writer, he claimed that he put many of these experiences to good use in his magazine serials. Because such claims became fashionable, especially in creating the public personae of such writers as Jack London and Ernest Hemingway, it is not surprising that Glidden should make such a claim, although he never took it to the preposterous lengths Louis L'Amour would later. Mostly, I suspect, what appealed to Glidden about his life during these years was the self-reliance it required. He once wrote to his mother that "all the glamor of dog teams, hunting, snow and snow shoes, living with a rifle, etc., turns out to be hard punishing work. But there is a joy and complete satisfaction in doing hard manual labor until you are so tired at night that you could drop; when every smoke tastes so good you'd like to eat it; when every meal no matter how bad it is tastes better than the previous one; and when you get that sense of completely fitting into the scheme of things. All that supplants the glamor and romance, but it's better. If you spent a year living that way, you'd never, never be content to go back to an apartment in a city and live through the thousand daily irritations of living by a clock, talking when you'd rather be silent, shaving when you'd like to look like a bum, taking exercise as a medicine (not as a pleasure), haggling over money and all the rest of it. If you had the courage of your convictions after such a year, you'd note mentally, 'To hell with it!' and come back here for good."[3]

On June 18, 1934, Glidden married Florence Elder in Grand Junction, Colorado. He began to write pulp fiction while living in Pojoaque, outside Santa Fe, and by November had acquired Marguerite E. Harper as his New York literary agent. It was Harper who gave him his pseudonym and who persuaded him to set his stories, not in the Far North as he had been, but in the Old West. Ernest Haycox was probably the author who exerted the greatest influence on Glidden during his years of apprenticeship. "Some twenty-nine years ago," he wrote in 1963, "newly married and lacking any kind of job, let alone the newspaper job I wanted, I decided I'd write for the Western pulp magazines. Their contents seemed simple-minded to the point of idiocy; their stories appeared easy to write if you could complete a sentence. I studied them with a secret contempt since I'd graduated from Zane Grey at the age of twelve. Then I hacked out Western pulp stories that sold. I wasn't much of a slick-magazine reader either, but, since I was committed and aspiring, I thought I should study the work of my peers. LeMay was admirable, Rhodes maddening but unique, and Bellah, then as now, inimitable. Reading them all, it was inevitable I should come across a *Collier's* serial by a new-to-me writer named Ernest Haycox. It was the third installment, as I recall it. I hated to be suckered into the middle of a cliff-hanger, but I told myself this was work. Work? Before I'd read a dozen paragraphs, I knew I was into something special. When I was finished, I went up to my wife, took the book she was reading from her hands and ordered—not told—her to read the Haycox yarn. From that day on, we were hooked; I not only hunted up the previous installments of that particular story in our town's library, but started to track down more Haycox. ...Why were his writings so special? ...Pick up one of the best of his stories, and before you are ten pages into it, a mood has been established. There is menace here, he tells you by indirection. ...There is trouble ahead. Big trouble. But those ten pages have left you with something else besides. You are in a new and somehow fearsome country; in its harshness or darkness, there is a promise of cruelty. You have entered an unfriendly country with a man who has a grim past which he has conquered and who is heading into an even grimmer future."[4]

Glidden, from the start it would seem, made a conscious effort to imitate the *early* Haycox. During his years as a writer, Haycox tried to expand and, finally, to transcend the conventions of the formulary Western. This Glidden did not do. He satisfied himself with polishing and perfecting his own variations of the formulary plot structures that he developed. When Haycox departed from the slick-magazine markets, Glidden easily came to dominate them in Haycox' stead, writing much the same kinds of stories for those markets that Haycox had been writing. Perhaps Glidden knew his own limitations better than Haycox recognized his. In any case, he set himself limits and never sought to change the kind of Western fiction he wrote. Unlike Louis L'Amour, Glidden insisted upon rewriting and revising all of his professional life. When Jove Books posthumously issued a Luke Short novel in 1980 titled *A Man Could Get Killed,* the publisher claimed that this was the first time in print of "the last great novel by the king of the Western." It was not Short's last novel, but rather a more polished draft of *The Primrose Try* (1967) which Glidden's widow had mistaken for a hitherto unpublished manuscript. Although the publication caused some consternation for a brief time between Bantam Books, which owned publication rights to *The Primrose Try,* and Jove Books, the situation did make it possible, by making a comparison of the two texts, to discern just how much care Glidden did take with his fiction. Few formulary fiction writers have taken as much, and the majority of them have taken considerably less. Yet, this care had to do principally with the fluidity of the prose and the aptness of the description. The plot is hopelessly hackneyed. The villains are Big Dad Herrington and his right-hand gunman, Seeley Carnes, and a crooked Indian agent named Con Brayton. Deputy U.S. Marshal Sam Kennery, to get the goods on this trio, has to go undercover, pretending to be an outlaw. Sam falls in love at first sight with the heroine, Tenney Payne, who works as a waitress at the hotel where the villains are staying. Sam's objective is to get someone to confess the truth, that the villains murdered the state's star witness against them. At the end, Sam shoots Big Dad and arrests Brayton. Carnes tries to gun Sam at the hotel, using Tenney as a shield. Sam tells her to drop and, when she does and he is given a clear target, he nails Carnes. This leaves Brayton in custody who is conveniently tricked into confessing when he is threatened with having Carnes—whom he does not know is dead—put in the same cell with him.

If you are inclined to accept Northrup Frye's definition of romance in *Anatomy of Criticism: Four Essays* (1957), formulary Western fiction can be classified as a variety of romance. "The essential difference between novel and romance lies in the conception of characterization," Frye wrote. "The romancer does not attempt to create 'real people' so much as stylized figures which expand into psychological archetypes. It is in the romance that we find Jung's libido, anima, and shadow reflected in the hero, heroine, and villain respectively. That is why the romance so often radiates a glow of subjective intensity that the novel lacks, and why a suggestion of allegory is constantly creeping around its fringes."[5] I would not venture to speculate what Henry James might have thought of formulary Westerns, but, after all, he did praise Owen Wister's *The Virginian* (1902) which is really the prototype for the conventions of all the formulary Westerns written since. "There is an old-fashioned distinction between the novel of character and the novel of incident," James observed in "The Art of Fiction" (1884), "which must have cost many a smile to the intending fabulist who was keen about his work. It appears to me as little to the point as the equally celebrated distinction between the novel and the romance—to answer as little to any reality. There are bad novels and good novels, as there are bad pictures and good pictures; but that is the only distinction in which I see anything. . . ."[6] I accept Frye's distinction between the novel and the romance, but I do so in a Jacobin spirit, which is to say in terms of how well the work is executed, be it novel or romance. Frederick Glidden wrote his formulary Westerns without conceit. He did not pretend, as his paperback publishers may have claimed and as Louis L'Amour later would about his own formulary Western fiction, that he was somehow writing exciting chapters directly from Western American history. Glidden knew what he was writing and he did not feel it necessary either to apologize for it or to insist that it was something else.

Lon Chaney, Jr. (left), and Randolph Scott confront each other in *Albuquerque* (Paramount, 1947), based on a novel by Luke Short. Photo courtesy of Eddie Brandt's Saturday Matinee.

Notwithstanding, beyond its being an action story, formulary Western fiction also embodies a moral view of the world and an ethical code of heroic conduct. Just because it is labeled escapist, I do not think formulary Western fiction should be excused or excluded from a critical examination of its moral vision and the fundamental assumptions it makes about human behavior and human motivations. *"Etenim omnes artes,"* Cicero wrote in *Pro Archia Poeta, "quae ad humanitatem pertinent, habent quoddam commune vinculum et quasi cognatione quadam inter se continentur"* (Truly all the arts which are pertinent to humanity have to a certain extent common bonds between them and are all but continuously related.)[7] To the extent that the formulary Western purports to have human relevance, it cannot be divorced from the critical standards which apply to every form of art. I do not think it is possible to separate Luke Short's mythical West from Frederick Glidden's moral vision. They are, I believe, all of a piece.

In Glidden's first published novel, *The Feud at Single Shot* (1935), the hero informs the heroine that the only way the world gives a man what belongs to him is if he is willing to fight and die for it. In the ensuing thirty years between that book and the final Luke Short novel, *Trouble Country* (1976), Glidden himself may have become somewhat disillusioned about life; he may have become frustrated with writing Western fiction because he had frankly wearied of it, although he could write nothing else with the same guaranteed success; the character of his heroes may have changed as they, and he, lost some of their cocksureness; but principal among the themes in Short's fiction which did not change was the view of life as a struggle. "The facts were plain enough and always had been," he observed in *Savage Range* (1938); "you fought your whole life if you wanted to live."[8] In *The Man from Two Rivers* (1974) it is written about the hero Hobe Carew that "he'd faced big odds against him before, and had beaten them. As a matter of fact, he liked them, always had, and he supposed always would. This land was his. Someday he'd be on it again and he'd stay on it."[9]

From the very beginning, Luke Short's fiction, much as that of Haycox' in the thirties, conceived of the Old West as being constantly in a volatile colloidal state, a group of armed, unstable, and potentially violent camps and partisans needing only the proper catalyst before exploding into rampant confusion; and into the very midst of this tense, electric environment rides the Short hero, isolated and alone. In his tribute to Haycox, Glidden remarked on the powerful sense of mood which Haycox could conjure, but he could not create tension and suspense as Glidden could when making use of this plot situation. Haycox might have all the ingredients, as he did when writing *Sundown Jim* (1938), but he could not achieve the taut atmosphere of imminent disaster which is to be found in such Luke Short books as *Savage Range* and *Sunset Graze* (1942). The reason for this, I suspect, has to do with the Haycox hero as opposed to the Short hero. The Haycox hero, as the Short hero, is grim and taciturn, but in addition he is also somewhat smug. A reader is never in doubt that, confronted by a brutal antagonist, the Haycox hero will be readily victorious. Short's heroes are more vulnerable; frequently they are duped; occasionally they will lose a fistfight or even be beaten nearly to death. Haycox' heroes are generally in control. Short's heroes very often are not—until the closing pages. Beyond this, Glidden himself became more circumspect, more cautious about certitude as he grew older. In *Saddle by Starlight* (1952), which was serialized in *Collier's,* the heroine tells Sam Holley, the hero, that what she dislikes about Sam is "'You're so damned sure of yourself!'"[10] By the time of *The Whip* (1956), the hero has begun to have some doubts, but not enough to prevent the heroine, Carrie Bentall, from objecting to Will Gannon's use of violence to pay back violence. "'You're so sure of yourself,'" Carrie tells Will. By the time Glidden came to write *The Some-Day Country* (1964), the hero's self-doubt almost overwhelms his self-will. "For the first time in his life Lieutenant Milham wondered if he had the stuff of which an officer was made."[11] As Robert L. Gale concluded in his study, *Luke Short* (1981), "the image of Frederick Dilley Glidden which I have gradually developed in my mind after a close reading of his half a hundred gripping novels is one of a pragmatist (not in any sense an abstract philosopher), a stoic, a lover of nature, a male chauvinist (but a chivalric, gentle, level-headed, humorous one), and most importantly a man whom life did not make more sure of himself as time went on but instead more tentative in drawing conclusions. A majority of Short's generalized statements appear well before the midpoint of his writing career. The last dozen novels seem less assertive in this regard, more tentative."[12]

Glidden always made everything—characters, dialogue, setting, incident—subservient to plot. When it all meshes, the results can be thrilling; but too often the plot can so overshadow character as to make it all seem improbable, thereby destroying the credibility of the narrative. For example, in an early short story, "The Marshal of Vengeance," published in *Dime Western* in July, 1937, Bill Combs is the hero. He has returned to Apache Tanks under an assumed name to revenge his father who was swindled out of his mine by the Ophir outfit. A man named Craig was the head of the Ophir outfit at the time and at the end of the story Combs confronts Craig. All of a sudden, Craig reveals that he is not the right man. It was his brother who did the swindling and he is now dead. He is currently in charge of his brother's mine and he confesses that for the last two years "'I've been hunting the whole West for a man by the name of Bill Combs. I wanted to settle with him for the injustice that had been done him. All the gold that's been taken out of the Ophir is waiting for him. I've kept only a superintendent's wages.'"[13] Granted, this plot twist makes for a different outcome than just another showdown in which the hero guns the villain and wins the girl, but the revelation comes too capriciously and is wholly inconsistent with all the prior incidents in the story. Similarly, in *Fiddlefoot* (1946), serialized in *The Saturday Evening Post,* the hero, Frank Chess, returns to his home range just shortly before his stepfather and owner of the Sabre spread is murdered. Frank promises his stepfather's crew that he will retain them on the ranch. However, the exigencies of the plot require that the old crew leave the ranch so that the villain, Rhino Hulst, can run stolen horses on Sabre. The hero, whom we are supposed to admire for his loyalty to certain values, makes no effort to keep the old crew despite his promise and despite the fact that he only learns later of Rhino's scheme. Then, after getting rid of the crew and never telling the reader where the crew went, four of them are conveniently brought back at the end to assist Frank in the clean-up of Rhino and his gang.

In *Raw Land* (1940), which was serialized in *Western Story Magazine* as *Gunsmoke Graze,* Will Danning is the hero. He rides into the town of Yellow Jacket and proceeds to purchase the Pitchfork spread. Will wants the ranch because it is secluded and he intends to hide his friend Murray Broome there. Murray used to be Will's employer before—according to Broome—he was framed for gunning down old Senator Mason. Milt Barron is the name by which Murray now goes, having lost weight and presently posing as Will's foreman. Broome is convinced that if he can stay in hiding for a year the reform party will be elected and he will be cleared of all charges. Formerly, Broome had owned a ranch and a newspaper. It was at the ranch that he had hired Will when Will was down on his luck and over the next five years a friendship grew between the two men that has now prompted Will to spend all the money he was able to save in order to buy the Pitchfork. This plot, too, depends on delayed revelation. Broome is at first presented sympathetically, to justify Will's friendship and self-sacrifice, but then he must be shown to have actually murdered the senator and he even goes in league with another villain to get rid of Will so the two can exploit the copper deposits which only they know exist on Pitchfork. To bring off the conflicts which such duplicity would require in Broome's character, and still to make that character credible to a reader, is beyond Short's creative ability.

In style, Glidden owed more to the laconic economy of Ernest Hemingway and Dashiell Hammett than he did to Haycox' imagistic, sometimes florid prose. And, like Hemingway's protagonists, Short's heroes must perform, for the heroines, for the society in which they live, most of all for themselves and their own sense of self-esteem. In the novels Glidden wrote between 1935 and the middle fifties, the story itself is almost always the proving-ground for the heroes. By the time he came to write *Saddle by Starlight,* he used a hero who had already proven himself before the story opens. In *King Colt* (1938) the heroine tells hero Johnny Hendry: "'Maybe I will marry you some day, Johnny—after you've proved you're worth it.'"[14] While Johnny is in the course of proving himself, the reader is expected blithely to accept it when Johnny beats up a man later found to be innocent with "blows hard and savage, merciless, countless" because, like Johnny's supporters looking on, one is supposed to "understand Johnny's part of it."[15] In *High Vermillion* (1948) the reader is similarly required to view with equanimity hero Larkin Moffat beating villain Bill Taff until he "was formless, inert, a sodden lump of flesh underneath the red muck that covered every part of him."[16] In *The Stalkers* (1973) we follow hero Deputy U.S. Marshal Tim Sefton into a cell after a tough has called him a son-of-a-bitch and are supposed to approve while he slaps the man around until his "nose and lips were bleeding" and "as, his arms crossed against his breast, he tried to hug and shrink into himself."[17] After the mid-fifties until his last novels, the Short hero was frequently more of a bully than any of the villains. I will grant that in *The Stalkers* Short avoided the usual ranch romance ending with the hero in the heroine's arms, but the reason the heroine rejects Sefton is not because he is a bully but because his job is very dangerous and he is unwilling to quit for her sake. We are expected to admire Sefton all the more for his sacrifice to the sense of duty and contemn the heroine for her weakness and inability to recognize the hero's obvious virtues. There is throughout Short's fiction this same veneer of surface pugnacity. Another contrast between Short's heroes and Ernest Haycox' heroes is that they have no insides and Short's heroes are not even falsely introspective the way Haycox' heroes are at times. They are bluff, virile, vigorous fighting machines and the reader is expected to be seduced into not asking any questions about what motivates them because they never ask any questions. They butt and push their way forward; they are stubborn, determined, persistent. In an aside in *First Campaign* (1965), Glidden might admit "whenever fate offered you a choice, it was between two bad things, never between a good or a bad thing."[18] But this reserve never is allowed to debilitate the hero from doing what he must do.

Although both Owen Wister in *Lin McLean* (1897) and Rex Beach in *The Spoilers* (1905) toyed with the notion of two heroines, it was Dane Coolidge in *Hidden Water* (1910) who devised a plot in which the hero had to choose between two heroines and in which the choice itself is a major conflict in the story. Ernest Haycox made use of the theme of the two heroines in *Free Grass* (1929) and then continued to employ it repeatedly in subsequent novels such as *Whispering Range* (1931), *Man in the Saddle* (1938), *The Border Trumpet* (1939), *Saddle and Ride* (1940), *Rim of the Desert* (1941), *Canyon Passage* (1945), and *Long Storm* (1946). It was surely a cliché already by the time Short borrowed it and yet, apparently, he could not perceive that it imparts a regrettable sameness to the plots of all the novels in which it is found since he would use it over and over again. Of course, Glidden had his own version of this theme. In Haycox' novels employing this theme, the hero chooses the heroine who is most like him. In Short's *Hard Money* (1940), when hero Phil Seay comes to choose between Sharon Bonal and Vannie Shore, Vannie has told him that they are two of a kind. Only this is not a hint. Seay rejects her for Sharon in part because Vannie has lived with a man without being married to him. In *Ramrod* (1943), hero Dave Nash chooses Rose Leland over Connie Dickason because Connie suffers from such excessive ambition that it causes her to stoop to deceit. In *Paper Sheriff* (1966), some progress has been made from the days of *Bold Rider* (1939), *Brand of Empire* (1940), and *Ramrod* in that the hero is married to one of the heroines, Callie Hoad, and in requited love with the other heroine, Jen Truro. There is very little difference in the sketchy character details between Connie Dickason in *Ramrod* and Callie Hoad in *Paper Sheriff.* As a consequence, it is not surprising when Callie, as Connie, indulges her personal ambition at the expense of the man she ostensibly loves. The reader, however, is given no idea why Callie cannot love; it is simply something that must be accepted about her so the plot may proceed and Callie can align herself with the forces opposing hero Reese Branham.

In one of the early novels, like *Bold Rider* or *The Man on the Blue,* the Short hero might be an outlaw. Later, as in *Ramrod* or *High Vermillion,* the hero is man on a lower social plane due to some difficulty in his past, but all of these circumstances notwithstanding the Short hero is always upwardly mobile. After *Saddle by Starlight,* the Short hero is customarily a man well established in the community. Yet, in all cases, the hero is better off in a strictly materialistic sense at the end of the story than he was at the beginning. This is so because

Luke Short's West reflects the astringent moral rigor of Calvinism's implacable God. The Short hero is a hero by virtue of divine grace. He
may bring about the fall of villains and their schemes, but in so doing
he is only the instrument of an immutable predestination. "As God by
the effectual working of his call to the elect perfects the salvation to
which by his eternal plan he has destined them," John Calvin wrote in
the *Institutes of the Christian Religion* (1536–1559), "so he has his
judgments against the reprobate, by which he executes his plan for
them. What of those, then, whom he created for dishonor in life and
destruction in death, to become the instruments of his wrath and examples of his severity? . . . The supreme Judge . . . makes way for his
predestination when he leaves in blindness those whom he has once
condemned and deprived of participation in his light."[19] I am not
about to say that *only* Luke Short's West embodies the notions of
Calvinist Christianity, because I think they inform the vast majority of
formulary Westerns. But unquestionably *Paper Sheriff* illustrates to
very good effect both the tenet of predestination and that of divine
grace. The genuine Hoads in the story—that is, those not related by
marriage—are wicked beyond hope of reclamation. Reese Branham is
married to a Hoad due to a youthful fall from the path of righteousness.
Fortunately there was no issue from the sin: the child was lost by miscar-
riage. Branham's punishment is that he must live for a time as Callie's
husband, although divine grace will ultimately separate him from her
because Reese, unlike Callie who is damned, is predestined to be one
of the elect.

In the sixties, Glidden drew weary of the traditional conflict of a
villain scheming to take away property belonging to the hero or to
someone close to the hero, so in novels like *First Campaign* and *Paper
Sheriff* he resorted to the plot of the "inverted" detective story in a
Western setting. R. Austin Freeman initiated this kind of back-telling
in detective fiction where the reader sees the crime committed in the
first half of the story and then follows Freeman's detective, Dr.
Thorndyke, in the second half as he reconstructs the crime and lays bare
all the subterfuges used by the murderer to avoid discovery. No doubt
a story told in this manner can generate great excitement and Short was
able to do precisely that. However, beyond this, and parallel to it, there
is the fascination a reader inevitably feels when—in Calvin's words—he
sees "the wicked bring upon themselves the just destruction to which
they are destined."[20] Because the destruction is both just and predestined, a reader is not supposed to object to the violent means by

which it is achieved. In *Debt of Honor* (1967), hero Reeves Cable explains how it is in the West to heroine, Beth Fanning, a girl from the East. "'. . . A man is dead who deserved to die,'" he remarks. "'If you're to blame any, I'm to blame a lot.' 'Then it's on your conscience too?' Beth asked. 'Not even for a second,' Reeves said flatly. 'He dug his own grave. We gave him a choice to make and he chose to be a hungry, selfish, crooked fool.'"²¹

The Gliddens became the parents of two sons and a daughter, James, born in 1940, Kate in 1941, and Daniel in 1942. I have had dealings only with Kate, but she is a great credit to her father and to have been a good parent is no little accomplishment in any man's life. Shortly after Fred Glidden began to have success publishing Western fiction in the pulps, his brother Jonathan, older by a year, tried his own hand at it, writing under the pseudonym Peter Dawson. In 1940, Jonathan won a Western manuscript contest sponsored by Dodd, Mead with a novel published the next year as *The Crimson Horseshoe* (1941). Among the novels that Jonathan wrote prior to entering the Air Force Intelligence during World War II, *The Stagline Feud* (1941) and *Gunsmoke Graze* (1942) stand out as the equal of anything his brother had published up to that time, although they are also strictly formulary Westerns and make effective use of the Luke Short idea of an isolated hero fighting back in isolation against a hostile environment. Jonathan wrote nothing during his four years in the Air Force and, when he did resume writing with *High Country* (1947), the special magic which he had once shared with his brother was oddly absent from his fiction, although he did eventually manage to move from writing stories and serials for *Western Story Magazine,* such as the short novel *Lost Homestead* in the April 5, 1941 issue, to *Renegade Canyon* (1949) which was serialized in *The Saturday Evening Post.* His plotting became more than occasionally flawed and far more seriously than was ever the case with his brother. In *Trail Boss* (1943), Jonathan had one outlaw remark to another about a third: "'He was a good man and he went sudden, which is as it should be with us all.'"²² When Jonathan died suddenly and unexpectedly in 1957, Fred was profoundly affected. Then in April, 1960 his eldest son James was accidentally drowned at Princeton, and he was even more mortally shaken.

Unlike Jonathan, Fred did not stop writing during the war, although he worked for a year in Washington, D.C. for the Office of Strategic Services before returning in October, 1944 to the Pojoaque Valley. The *Post* began serializing his novels with *Blood on the Moon*

(1941) and *Ride the Man Down* (1942) and henceforth frequently the *Post* or *Collier's* would purchase serial rights and beginning with *Ramrod* (United Artists, 1947) several of his novels were made the basis for motion pictures. The same year *Ramrod* was released, Glidden and his family moved to Aspen, Colorado. "Fred's work habits were steady," H.N. Swanson, his Hollywood agent, once recalled. "He dictated to a secretary because he had very serious eye trouble most of his life. One year he had three eye operations for cataracts and detached retinas. He actually did his writing in three different homes—in Colorado Springs, in Wickenbur, Arizona, and in Aspen, Colorado. He probably did most of his writing in Aspen, where he had a large corner office on the third floor of the Elks Building. . . . He was a civic-minded person, was on the city council and had much influence in the affairs of Aspen. . . . In an average month he was able to produce fifty thousand words in spite of severe eye trouble. And in spite of the 'winter pile-up' he liked Aspen; it had everything valuable to him— hunting, fishing, skiing and skating. And it was close to Denver, where the public library had excellent files on the early West."[23]

Much more money was paid by the slick magazines than an author could hope to make on hardbound book sales for Western fiction. This was changed by the paperback revolution. In March, 1951 Fred began his association with Dell Books to reissue some of his older and out-of-print Western novels and in June, 1956 he signed a contract with Bantam Books which guaranteed him $15,000 for each new Western he would write. When *The Saturday Evening Post* rejected *Play a Lone Hand* (1951), Marguerite Harper turned around and sold the serial rights to *Collier's*. In the summer of 1953 Glidden made a trip to Canada to observe uranium mining and presumably Communist-inspired labor unions. The trip was made at the behest of a new editor at *Collier's* who was convinced that Westerns with a contemporary setting would prove even more popular with the reading public than those set in the last century. In 1954 he researched uranium mining in Utah in the company of a multi-millionaire, but the literary results provided little that was new, except updating the typical plot of the formulary Western to contemporary times. Yet, one of these novels, *Rimrock* (1954), remains one of Fred's better efforts. Four films had been made in the forties based on his fiction, of which perhaps only *Albuquerque* (Paramount, 1948) based on *Dead Freight for Piute* (1940) was as notable as its source. Of the five films made in the fifties based on Luke Short novels, none was particularly memorable. Too often the corners were rounded on the rough-hewn and violent characters and the suspense of an isolated hero surrounded by danger was mitigated too much to be effective. In fact, *Station West* (RKO, 1948), based on the novel by the same title published the previous year, even went so far as to make the heroine in the novel the chief villain in the film, a *femme fatale* in the best *film noir* tradition.

Already in the early fifties, Glidden no longer really wanted to write Western fiction, but every attempt he made to write something else — and there were several of them — was unsuccessful whereas now in paperback his Western novels were beginning to sell in the millions. Throughout the decade Marguerite Harper tried ceaselessly to encourage Glidden and to spur him on, but without much effect. He only published six new novels in the entire decade and a similar number in the next. A Dutch firm allegedly pirated two of his books and an American writing in England began to plagiarize his novels. In both cases, legal action was brought but without fruitful results. By the sixties, the slick magazine market had all but vanished, having been replaced — so it was said — by television. Half of the six novels Fred wrote in the 1960s were serialized, but in *The New York Daily News*.

Insofar as the formulary Western is a variety of romance, it would perhaps be worthwhile to reflect that its origin actually had nothing indigenous to do with the American West. Rather it was inherited from the ancient Greeks. In Classical Antiquity, romance was divided into three stages. The first, the *agon,* means a conflict of some sort. The second stage is the *pathos,* the life-and-death struggle. The third and final stage is the *anagnorisis,* the recognition. There is an optional middle term which, when present, proves pivotal in determining whether the story is merely formulary or a romantic historical reconstruction and this is the *sparagmos,* the mangling. The Perseus myth, in simple form, without the later embellishments of Ovid and Apollodorus, well illustrates the stages of the romance. There is a helpless old king whose kingdom is menaced by a devouring sea monster. Each year an innocent victim is offered to the sea monster in propitiation until, finally, the choice has fallen on the king's beautiful daughter. At this juncture the hero, Perseus, comes on the scene, kills the sea monster, and thus rescues the princess. In due course he marries her and inherits the kingdom. The *agon* is the conflict between the people of the kingdom and the sea monster. As in most Classical romances, the princess is motherless and her father impotent to save her life. The *pathos* is Perseus' struggle with the sea monster in which the monster dies. If the stage of the *sparagmos* is added to the telling, Perseus is badly mangled during the death-struggle. The *anagnorisis* is the recognition that the sea monster *had to be killed*, not propitiated, in order for the kingdom to enjoy true happiness, peace, and prosperity.

In the romantic historical reconstruction, the hero often dies as a result of the *sparagmos*. Since Luke Short wrote only formulary Westerns, this never happens and the heroes are always ultimately triumphant. However, in the majority of novels prior to *First Campaign*, there is a *sparagmos* episode. In *Raiders of the Rimrock* (1939), hero Tim Enever is wounded and must carry on in spite of his wound. In *Raw Land*, hero Will Danning is shot in the leg and yet must persist. The hero in *Coroner Creek* (1946) is named Chris Danning — no relation — and he must continue the battle even though his right hand is mashed under the boot heel of one of the villains. In *Summer of the Smoke* (1958) hero Keefe Calhoun is wounded by being stuck in the right leg by an Apache lance. In *First Claim* (1960) hero Giff Ballew is wounded when trying to escape from a crooked deputy sheriff. Even in such a late novel as *The Outrider* (1972), Short would revert to this device when hero Will Christie is badly beaten by toughs and must be nursed back to health by the heroine, a prototypical incident which already occurs in Owen Wister's *The Virginian*.

If in the first two decades of his literary career as a writer of Western fiction, Fred Glidden had been influenced by Ernest Haycox, the same influence can be cited probably for the shift in direction which Fred took beginning with *First Campaign*. What originally had appealed to Fred about Ernest Haycox' West was that it was strictly a product of Haycox' imagination. Haycox named all his towns and rivers and districts, and they were of no known place or topography. In the mid-forties all this changed. Haycox set his stories in actual locations in the West and even, upon occasion, would include actual historical personalities among his characters. *First Campaign* was the first Luke Short novel set in Primrose, a town presumably in Colorado. Primrose is the state capital. The action centers here or in nearby Junction City, a large mining town. Fred even had elaborate maps of Primrose and hoped to create an epic saga around this setting in a series of books. The novel, accordingly, is longer than most of his and he refused to reduce it on the basis of its having epic proportions. This it does not have, but a number of characters introduced here were to become standard fixtures in later novels about Primrose, most particularly the crooked mine owner, Burley Hammond; the corrupt newspaper editor, Red Macandy; fat Dave Hardy whose Miner's Rest saloon in Junction City is the headquarters for much skullduggery; and Louis Selby and his daughter Louise who own the Primrose Hotel. There is also a greater awareness of social and economic conditions than had been the case in any Luke Short novel hitherto with the possible exception of *And the Wind Blows Free* (1945), as for example in this description of the miners as "men without any possessions except what they had in their pockets, homeless and womanless and rootless, many of them strangers in a foreign land. They came in to find a few hours of blessed oblivion in stinking, lice-ridden blankets."[24]

Perhaps it had been Fred's hope that a television series would be inspired by the Primrose novels, but, if that were the case, it did not happen. He returned to the imaginary West in his last books, although in *The Outrider* he produced a Primrose novel with all the names changed, yet in which all the general descriptions remain the same. His sight became worse and further surgery hindered rather than helped his condition. In the early seventies, he augmented dictation with writing with soft pencil on legal-sized tablets. Good times or bad, Fred worked at his writing. In November, 1974 he was diagnosed as having terminal cancer of the throat. He underwent radiation treatment and chemotherapy in Denver, but his body continued to waste away until it was less than half his usual 160 pounds. He died on August 18, 1975 at the Aspen Valley Hospital and his ashes were subsequently interred at the Aspen Grove Cemetery.

"I knew him best in the late 1950s when I was a teenager," Brian Garfield wrote to me. "He was a big guy with the wide shoulders and lean frame of the cowboy heroes he wrote about; he looked the part. . . . Mainly what I remember about him is the quiet amiability of his personality. He was very much like the Gary Cooper sort of Western character: humorous, soft-spoken, often bemused and amused. He took things as they came. I don't think he saw himself as an important lit'ry figure, ever, even though he was looked up to (by most of the other Western writers) as the king of the hill after Haycox' death. . . . Nor did he think of himself as a hack; don't misunderstand. He was a craftsman and he took pride in his craft but he thought of it as a rather ordinary way to make a living and didn't think he was anything very special. . . . His later years were marred by tragedy and illness: you probably know that his son died in a boating accident at Princeton, after which Fred became much more subdued than he'd ever been theretofore; then his eyesight began to give out on him. The last time I saw him, in Aspen, he was much more taciturn and less genial than he'd been in earlier years, although he wasn't bad-tempered at all, simply withdrawn, more introspective."[25]

In 1969 he was the recipient of the Levi Strauss Golden Saddleman award and the year he died he received the Western Heritage Award from the National Cowboy Hall of Fame in which the citation read: "For his achievement, through his high calibre writing, in bringing wider public attention to the Western story and for his role in establishing a Western tradition which has since become a model for Western writers." I am doubtless too critical of Luke Short's fiction to endorse completely the sentiment that, in terms of Frederick Glidden's romantic treatment of the West, his work should be regarded as a model of its kind for a new generation of Western writers; but I cannot overlook the fact, nor would I wish to, that Frederick Glidden was much of the time a very effective storyteller. Although his world-view must be approached with a cautious reserve, his fiction can bring pleasure to a reader. I am inclined to ask more of the Western novel than Frederick Glidden ever brought to it, but at the same time I will not deny that I have enjoyed his novels more than those of most formulary writers and his craftmanship, unwillingness to repeat himself ever, his professionalism remain admirable.

There are unforgettable scenes in his best novels. The scene which opens *Station West* comes to mind, when Lieutenant John Haven arrives in South Pass City in civilian dress during the heart of a bitter winter. The special knowledge of freighting and the harrowing scene of the giant ore wagons hauling ore down the side of a steep cliff in *Dead Freight for Piute* also stays with me, as do the blizzard scenes from *Barren Land Showdown* (1940), or the interview between the hero and an old Apache renegade at the beginning of *Coroner Creek,* or the scenes of a typical mining town and the intimate knowledge of frontier mining true of *Hard Money* (1938). Then, in a more technical sense, there are novels which satisfy strictly in terms of the way they are plotted — *Savage Range, Sunset Graze, Ramrod* — where the story never lets up until the final page and one is fascinated by the sharply aggressive attitude of all the characters, each working intensely for his or her own ends, well-made plots which bring their own sense of a unified aesthetic experience. Finally, there is *And the Wind Blows Free,* Fred Glidden's most ambitious Western novel and the only one he wrote with a first-person narrator. "I had discovered, perhaps too soon," the narrator reflects in the course of the story, "that not all questions were answerable, that justice was not immutable and that the lives of real people, unlike the lives of people in my childhood stories, had little direction and were handled by an indifferent author. The real life stories had no logical beginnings; they lagged and stumbled and reversed their morals, and ended either too abruptly or not cleanly and decisively."[26] The scenes of the terrific snow storm in this novel and the freezing to death of thousands of cattle are among the finest in all Western American literature. I cannot say with certainty why Fred Glidden did not continue in the direction he took in *And the Wind Blows Free,* but I suspect he did not feel the market for this kind of Western fiction was sufficiently strong.

The final years of his literary life were spent under the shadow of Louis L'Amour's ever-growing popularity. Already in his pulp novels of the late forties, L'Amour had amended the Haycox/Short formula of the odd-man-out hero in a hostile environment. The L'Amour hero might be alone at the beginning of the story, but before too long one and then another character would join in with him in his battle against the villains. In late Luke Short novels the impact of Louis L'Amour's West is readily discernible. In *The Man from Two Rivers,* the hero is joined first by the heroine and then by a group of independent-minded, fighting nesters and ranchers to combat the *manqué* villain, land-grabbing Lew Seely. So formidable does this fighting combination become that the villain is deserted by his crew and finally is shot to death by his own hired killer. In *Trouble Country* hero Sam Dana, a fiddlefoot, returns to the Bar-D to battle his wicked, cattle-stealing half-brother for control. So many eventually join forces with Sam that by the end of the story Walt is the one who is alone, isolated, fighting against all odds. It was a reversal from the Luke Short formula of earlier years, yet not everything is changed. Sam still has to choose among two heroines, straight-laced Sistie Cable and Rita, Walt's estranged wife. Notwithstanding, here, too, time has wrought its effect and while, formerly, a Short hero would choose a virgin over a sexually experienced woman, it is Rita who wins Sam's favor.

For me, there are degrees of aesthetic delight and if, in the final analysis, Luke Short's West is too often found to be lacking—to use Cicero's word—in *humanitas,* it would still be erroneous for me therefore to conclude that his stories are not—again to call upon Cicero—*ad humanitatem pertinent.*

Louis L'Amour's Western Fiction

> It is this by which we measure a man,
> by what he does in his life, by what
> he creates to leave behind.
> Louis L'Amour[1]

When Louis L'Amour died from lung cancer on June 10, 1988, he was the most decorated author in the history of American letters. The years spent being a familiar figure at Republican party fund-raisers paid off in big dividends. In 1983 he was the first American novelist ever to be awarded a Special National Gold medal by the United States Congress for lifetime literary achievement and in 1984 President Reagan awarded him the Medal of Freedom, the highest civilian honor in the nation. L'Amour for decades had merchandised himself as much, and even more, than his Western fiction with a success enjoyed by no one since Ned Buntline had made Buffalo Bill Cody a figure of international prominence.

Movie cowboy Tim McCoy, who knew Buffalo Bill, recalled him as once saying that so much had been written about him and his various exploits that he no longer knew himself what was true and what may have been exaggeration. L'Amour had no such publicist as Buntline; instead, he was the principal source of information about his past. In a letter quoted in the Gregg Press' reprint edition of L'Amour's *Kilkenny* (1954), L'Amour claimed to have been taught to use a six-shooter by Bill Tilghman, a frontier lawman noted for having captured Bill Doolin and who was shot to death in 1924 at the age of seventy-one by a drunken Prohibition agent when Tilghman was city marshal at Cromwell, Oklahoma.

L'Amour never gave out the date of his birth, but he did give the year as 1908 and the place as Jamestown, North Dakota. There is evidence to suggest that his actual name was Louis Dearborn LaMoore. The main source for biographical information are the brief sketches which L'Amour supplied and periodically revised on the back page of his paperback novels published from 1958 by Bantam Books. He contended that he ran away from home at fifteen and for at least two decades traveled throughout the world having the kinds of adventures he would later describe in his fiction. Among the jobs he said he had were those of ranch hand, merchant seaman, roustabout for a traveling circus, fruit picker, ship loader, and lumberjack. He recalled being very athletic, bicycling through Italy, Hungary, and India, fighting as he traveled, eventually becoming a professional boxer. Depending on which one of those sketches you might read, L'Amour won anywhere from fifty-one to fifty-eight of fifty-nine bouts. While in Macao in 1927, L'Amour claimed he heard a story about a sunken ship and was determined to be the first one to salvage the money left in the captain's safe. He was first and, afterwards, went to live a Bohemian life in Paris. Wearying finally of being a drifter and loner for so long, L'Amour said he returned to the United States in the late thirties and turned to writing fiction for pulp magazines, turning out mysteries and detective stories, adventure tales, sports stories, and Westerns. His first book was a collection of verse titled *Smoke from This Altar* (1939), printed in a very limited edition by a publisher in Oklahoma City. During the Second World War, L'Amour served in a Tank Destroyer unit and in the Transportation Corps. It was not until after the war that he came to specialize in writing formulary Western fiction for the pulp markets, much of it copyrighted initially by the individual publications for twenty-eight years — as specified by the old Copyright Act — but never renewed by L'Amour himself when the time came to renew all those old copyrights in his own name for another twenty-eight years. Even stories he published in a slick magazine like *The Saturday Evening Post* were forgotten. For example, the short story, "Booty for a Badman," a Tell Sackett story originally published by the *Post* on July 30, 1960, was renewed by the new *Saturday Evening Post* because L'Amour never asked for a reversion of copyright and was *serialized* over two issues beginning in September, 1988. However, it is due to his carelessness in protecting his copyrights that so much of L'Amour's early pulp fiction, including novels and stories he subsequently reworked into paperback novels, was reissued by L'Amour himself in an effort to impede any success Carroll & Graf might have when this New York publisher began issuing his Public Domain fiction in the 1980s, a situation which has outlasted him.

"The cowards didn't go," L'Amour remarked as we sat across from each other in the summer of 1980 on the patio behind his large,

Spanish-style home on the corner of Sunset Boulevard and Loring Avenue in Los Angeles. "It was inevitable that the Indian way of life should cease. And look at what replaced it! Where there was wilderness, there are now hospitals and schools."

"And what of the buffalo?" I asked him.

"They had outlived their usefulness," he replied confidently. "It was necessary that they be killed. Now there are farms throughout that whole area, farms that grow food to feed one third of the world. It's a matter of progress. The Indians didn't own the lands they occupied. Many of the tribes, in fact, had only recently occupied certain regions before the white man arrived. The Indians took the land from others, the cliff dwellers, for example. And the white man took the land from the Indians. It wasn't the Indians' to claim or to sell. It went to the strongest. The white men were stronger. There's nothing more stupid, in my opinion, than to talk about paying the Indians for the land. It was never theirs to sell."

The garden beyond the patio was neatly manicured, a truly Wordsworthian garden, Nature cut back, trimmed and controlled. A seemingly endless stream of cars swished past on Sunset and the sky was tinted by a reddish-brown smog. Maybe in this setting, it was easy to believe — as the Germans used to put it — that *"die Weltgeschichte ist die Weltgericht"* (world history is the judgment of history).[2]

"My favorite tree," L'Amour continued, "is the white aspen. For me, it is the most beautiful tree in all Nature. I saw a terrible thing on a recent trip I took. I climbed to the top of this hill and I could see white aspen covering an adjacent hill. But growing around the bottoms of those white aspens was scrub oak. Scrub oak is short, tough. It will choke the life out of the white aspens. That's the way it is in Nature."

L'Amour then took me on a tour of that part of the house in which he worked, the library with its ten thousand volumes stored in gigantic bookcases which could swing out into the room only to reveal a second built-in bookcase of a similar dimension, all of them filled from top to bottom with books, most of them pertaining to some aspect of the American West.

"I use these books in my research," L'Amour explained. "Every incident in any story I write is authentic and usually based either on something I personally experienced or something that happened in history. And over here," he said, moving toward a map case in the hall way, "are my maps." He pulled open a drawer to show a thick pile of topographical maps. Handing me one to study, he pointed out the extensive detail in the cartography. "When I say there is a rock in the road in one of my books, my readers know that if they go to that spot and look they'll find that rock."

"There is one thing that continues to trouble me about your books," I said.

"And what is that?"

"Well, take *Last Stand at Papago Wells*. After an Indian attack, according to the story, only five characters have been killed, but one of the surviving characters counts six corpses."

"I'll have to go back and count them again," L'Amour said, and smiled. "But, you know, I don't think the people who read my books would really care."

It was a curious remark and very much at odds with the impression he had been trying to give me when showing me his library and his detailed maps. Even the way he dressed, with the striped cowboy shirt, the silver belt buckle, the Western boots and rawhide neckpiece was intended to give one the impression that he was a man who had stepped out of the last century into this.

"If you want to know about the way the West was, and if you want to know about me," he said with emphasis, "you're going to have to read my books, as many of them as you can. It'll become clearer to you that way, rather than by anything I might tell you here today."

In the entry for Louis L'Amour in *Twentieth Century Western Writers* (1982), Michael T. Marsden pointed out that "Louis L'Amour is without question the best-selling Western writer of all time. With sales of his books in excess of 100,000,000 copies, he has eclipsed even the most prolific Zane Grey. The impact of L'Amour's popular fiction about the American West upon the American imagination is incalculable."[3] I have no argument that L'Amour's total sales have probably surpassed every other author of Western fiction in the history of the genre. Indeed, at the time of his death his sales had topped 200,000,000. What I would question is the degree and extent of his effect "upon the American imagination." His Western fiction is strictly formulary and frequently, although not always, features the ranch romance plot where the hero and the heroine are to marry at the end once the villains have been defeated. Not only is there nothing really new in the basic structures of his stories, even L'Amour's social Darwinism, which came to characterize his later fiction, was scarcely original and was never dramatized in other media the way it was in works based on Zane Grey's fiction.

More than two decades ago I was in the audience in a large motion picture palace in Detroit, Michigan where I saw *The Vanishing American* (Paramount, 1925) for the first time. The film was based, in part, on Grey's novel by the same title, but the Prologue with which the film opens was derived from a short novel not published in book form until 1961, *Blue Feather*. The story narrates how the more physically adept Nopah Indians systematically destroy a nation of cliff dwellers known as the Sheboyahs. The Prologue of *The Vanishing American* begins with a title card quoting Herbert Spencer's *First Principles* (1864) to the effect that human societies so function that the weaker must give way to the stronger and that it is always the fittest who survive. A mighty theatre organ accompanied the grandeur of the screen images showing the great stage of the world which will outlast the pageant of history as one technologically superior race after another rises to destroy a technologically inferior race. History progresses before the viewer's eyes from cavemen to basket weavers to cliff dwellers to Indians. When the Indians sweep down majestically to destroy the cliff dwellers, the high priest of the cliff dwellers utters a curse. "May Paya the Father drive you into darkness, as you drive us!" the title card reads. "May he send a stronger race to grind you into the dust and scatter you through the four worlds of lamentation." This stronger race first appears in the guise of Spanish explorers but even they soon give way before the irresistible onslaught of the Anglo-Americans.

Spencer had been among the foremost philosophers to develop a popular and comprehensive theory of social evolution in advance of Charles Darwin's theory of biological evolution. Spencer regarded societies and civilizations as organisms subject to definite laws; in fact, it was he who coined the phrase "survival of the fittest." His ideas, accepted tepidly if at all by the British intelligentsia of his time, were more immediately and fervently embraced by its American counterpart. "I am an ultra and thoroughgoing American," Edward Livingston Youmans, founder in 1872 of *Popular Science Monthly*, wrote to Herbert Spencer. "I believe there is great work to be done here for civilization. What we want are ideas — large, organizing ideas — and I believe there is no other man whose thoughts are so valuable to our needs as yours are."[4]

Spencer believed that human beings were put to a decisive test by Nature. "If they are sufficiently complete to live, they *do* live, and it is well they should live," he wrote in *Social Statics* (1864). "If they are not sufficiently complete to live, they die, and it is best they should die."⁵ It was a pseudo-scientific transformation of John Calvin's theology in which mankind is divided into the elect, who are saved by the grace of God, and the reprobates, who are damned by God's withholding of His grace, a transformation whereby Nature became as implacable as the image of Calvin's God.

Following the publication of Darwin's scientific findings, Spencer's philosophy was combined with, and was presumably even justified by, biological evidence. "Let it be understood," William Graham Sumner wrote, "that we cannot go outside this alternative: liberty, inequality, survival of the fittest; not-liberty, equality, survival of the unfittest. The former carries society forward and favors all its best members; the latter carries society downwards and favors all its worst members."⁶ Theodore Roosevelt embraced social Darwinism as a political philosophy and he believed that "in this world the nation that has trained itself to a career of unwarlike and isolated ease is bound, in the end, to go down before other nations which have not lost the manly and adventurous qualities."⁷ Richard Hofstadter concluded in *Social Darwinism in American Thought* (1959) that "the virtues that Spencer and Sumner preached — personal providence, family loyalty and family responsibility, hard work, careful management, and proud self-sufficiency — were middle-class virtues. There is a certain touching irony in the thought that, while writers like these preached slow change and urged men to adapt to the environment, the very millionaires whom they took to be the 'fittest' in the struggle for existence were transforming the environment with incredible rapidity and rendering the values of the Spencers and Sumners of this world constantly less and less fit for survival."⁸

Carlton Jackson in *Zane Grey* (1973) spent some time tracing the Darwinian influences which affected Grey's conception of the American West. "When Darwinists made these points in the early part of the twentieth century," he concluded, concerning Grey's belief in the survival of the fittest and the predatory character of Nature, "the rural and small-town middle classes usually charged them with error about human nature and atheism. Yet when Zane Grey said the same things in less formal language the middle classes regarded him as a man of great common sense and insight."⁹ With the passing of the years, American thinkers and historians have inclined to give little credence to social Darwinism, tending on the whole to agree with Morris R. Cohen who wrote in *The Meaning of Human History* (1947) that "the last stage of anything is not necessarily the best. Thus we must reject the . . . Spencerian evolutionary [philosophy] for [its] failure to deal seriously with the natural and tragic evil in the course of human events. The jaunty and atrociously optimistic belief in the inevitability of progress involves an obtuseness to the natural and social calamities which crowd the pages of history, e.g., the great plagues, or the barbaric destruction of Greek, Roman, and Saracen civilizations."[10] A careful examination of Louis L'Amour's Western fiction reveals that he came to embrace the tenets of social Darwinism only after he became successful, that in his early Western fiction the positions he held were exactly the opposite of those he espoused later.

Very early in his career as a pulp writer, in the period just prior to the outbreak of the Second World War, L'Amour created a series character named Pongo Jim Mayo, the master of a tramp steamer in Far Eastern waters, in L'Amour's words "an Irish-American who had served his first years at sea sailing out of Liverpool and along the west coast of Africa's Pongo River, where he picked up his nickname. He's a character I created from having gotten to know men just like him while I was a seaman in my yondering days." After the war, when L'Amour began to specialize in Western fiction, he wrote most frequently under the pseudonym Jim Mayo, taken from this early fictional creation. One of L'Amour's earliest series characters in his Western fiction was the gunfighter, Lance Kilkenny, who figured in two of his early pulp novels. "The Rider of Lost Creek" appeared under the Jim Mayo byline in *West* in April, 1947. It was expanded slightly when it reappeared as a Bantam original paperback in 1976. L'Amour in all his Western novels had actually a very limited number of plots which he would use over and over again and, of course, borrowed incidents and episodes from this story or that for re-use. The method he developed in writing for the pulps — a single draft, composed quickly and never re-read not even for typographical errors much less errors in construction — would remain his method of composition until the end of his life.

The Rider of Lost Creek employs what I would call L'Amour's range war plot. The first chapter is given over to establishing Lance Kilkenny's mode of operation: that he is the fastest gun in the West, that once there is a gunfight he leaves the district right after it is over, and that very little is known about him, even what he looks like. One day some time back Mort Davis saved Kilkenny's life after he was shot up and now Davis has sent out word that he needs Kilkenny's help. Mort has filed a claim on a water hole near Lost Creek in the Live Oak country. The district is dominated by two wealthy cattlemen, Webb

Steele and Chet Lord, and both are at loggerheads, claiming for himself the water hole which Davis occupies. There is a master villain, Royal Barnes, who is masquerading as an Easterner. He has a secret cabin in Apple Canyon just above the saloon operated by heroine Nita Riordan and her bodyguard, Jaime Brigo. Barnes is responsible for stirring up the trouble between Steele and Lord, figuring they will kill each other off so he can claim both their ranches. There is also a mad-dog killer loose in the district and there have been a number of murders over the years. Barnes is not the murderer, but rather Steve Lord, Chet Lord's crazy son. Kilkenny enters the fracas, meets and falls in reciprocal love with Nita at first sight, and then works to get Steele and Lord to realize that they are but pawns in a bigger game. The Brockman brothers, Abel and Cain, are among the renegades working for Barnes. Lance manages to gun Abel while only knocking Cain unconscious. Cain seeks revenge against Lance in a fistfight in which he is beaten into submission. As many of L'Amour's heroes, Lance's prowess is due to his having done some boxing in the past. There are the typical L'Amour errors of construction in the book. In one scene a scarred puncher is a Lord rider for his first piece of dialogue and the next time he speaks he is identified as a Steele hand! As is the case with most of L'Amour's heroes — and as he claimed about himself — Lance is a self-created man. When Nita inquires about his parents, Lance asks "'Does it matter? No man is anything but what he makes of himself, I suspect, although no doubt the inheritance is there. It is what he does with what he was given that matters. . . .'"[11] There is also the most common L'Amour theme of all, the new home theme, as we are told that for Kilkenny "it was the longing of a lonely man for a home, a fireside, for the nearness of a woman and the laughter of children. For someone to work for, to protect, someone to belong to, and some place where you fitted in."[12] Chet Lord tells Kilkenny the sad truth about his son when he is dying of natural causes. Steve Lord is killed by a hidden spring gun when trying to enter Barnes' secret cabin and Kilkenny goes up against Barnes despite raw hands from the fight with Cain Brockman. Lance kills Barnes but is wounded and Nita helps nurse him back to health. At the end, Lance rides off to think things out, to determine if he dares to marry in view of his reputation as a gunfighter.

In the Author's Note prefacing the reissue of "A Man Called Trent," L'Amour commented that "such people as Jared Tetlow in this story were all too familiar."[13] Apparently, L'Amour did not re-read the novel before he submitted it for republication since Jared Tetlow is not the villain in this story, but rather in the final novel in the Kilkenny series, *Kilkenny,* first published as an Ace original paperback in 1954. Because L'Amour re-worked "A Man Called Trent" into *The Mountain Valley War,* published by Bantam in 1978—the reissue of "A Man Called Trent" in its original form did not occur until 1986—it is instructive, I think, to go into some detail concerning the plot of the original in order to contrast it with the rewrite. The basic story is the one variation L'Amour contrived for the range war plot. As it stands, "A Man Called Trent" is one of the two or three really fine formulary Westerns L'Amour would ever write. It appeared in the same pulp, *West,* as had "The Rider of Lost Creek," only later in the year, in December, 1947. It is set in New Mexico, but all of the places and names came from L'Amour's imagination. The novel opens to a nester named Dick Moffitt lying dead where he was killed by King Bill Hale's riders. Sally Crane, who is sixteen and was adopted by Moffitt, and Moffitt's fourteen-year-old son Jack witnessed the murder from hiding and then went to the cabin owned by a man named Trent for safety. Kilkenny has taken the name of Trent, hoping to escape his reputation as a gunfighter. King Bill Hale has decided that he wants the graze in the high country for his cattle and to get it he must drive out the nesters. Cub Hale, King Bill's son, is a killer who has been running rough-shod ever since he became old enough to carry a gun. Heroine Nita Riordan owns the Crystal Palace in Cedar Bluff where she is protected by her half-Yaqui bodyguard, Jaime Brigo. King Bill Hale wants Nita to marry him, but she is holding out for Lance, hoping eventually he will overcome his scruples about leaving her a young widow. Kilkenny joins forces with the other nesters. When a storekeeper in Cedar Bluff refuses to sell supplies to the nesters, Kilkenny tells him: "'This is America, an' here the people always win. Maybe not at first, but they always win in the end.'"[14] This is a theme which would figure prominently in all of L'Amour's subsequent Western fiction. In L'Amour's West, the people always do win. But they do not win by themselves. They win because the L'Amour hero shows them the way and because they can work with the L'Amour hero. The most interesting group among the nesters is the Hatfield clan, headed up by Parson Hatfield. The Hatfields are from Kentucky and obviously constituted the germinal idea from which, later, the Sacketts would grow. Lance makes an attempt to restore peace by confronting King Bill Hale at Hale's saloon in town. The attempt results in a bloody fistfight in which King Bill is left in a heap on the floor. It is known that King Bill has been planning a celebration in Cedar Bluff to mark his first ten years in the district and, after this beating, he decides to import a professional prize fighter named Tombull Turner to go up against Kilkenny in the ring. Lance accepts the challenge because it will provide the only chance for him to communicate with officials from Santa Fe who have been invited to attend. Kilkenny "knew how men of all sorts and kinds admire a fighting man. The Santa Fe officials, especially if one of them was Halloran, would be no exception. He would be going into the fight as the underdog. Hale wanted him whipped, but King Bill's power was destroying his shrewdness."[15]

A wagon with four of the nesters has left for the nearby town of Blazer to get supplies denied to them in Cedar Bluff and Kilkenny hopes, by taking a wagon directly across the Smoky Desert, to reach Blazer at the same time or a little ahead of them. Some of the best descriptive writing L'Amour would ever do is to be found in his handling of the trek across this wasteland. When Kilkenny arrives in Blazer, a tough named Gaddis is seen to enter a saloon wearing Jody Miller's gun. Jody Miller was a nester with the first wagon. While the nesters with Lance purchase supplies, Kilkenny enters the saloon and begins a conversation with Gaddis, claiming that he recognizes him from the gun he is wearing. He calls Gaddis Jody Miller and recalls where he first saw him. "'Miller stopped off in Santa Fe to see some folks at the fort there an' to talk to Halloran and Wallace. Seems they was old friends of his.'"[16] The bluff works. It throws the renegades in the saloon off balance and several of them are gunned down in the ensuing fight. Afterwards, when Kilkenny comes upon the first wagon, he finds that two of the nesters are dead and two are badly wounded. Once back at the Hatfield place, Kilkenny insists that his way is best. He wants to fight Turner and talk to Halloran during the bout. In the meantime, Lance also learns that Cain Brockman has arrived in Cedar Bluff, determined to kill him. Lance goes into Cedar Bluff and manages to persuade Cain to hold off until after the fight. The fight takes place and Lance does talk to Halloran from the ring between clinches and body blows. Lance wins and Halloran warns King Bill that if Kilkenny's charges are true, King Bill will be tried and hanged. This is the beginning of the end for King Bill. Some of his hands, seeing the writing on the wall, run off with a herd of his cattle and Cub Hale takes off after them with some hardcases still loyal to the brand. In despair, King Bill shoots himself. When Cub and the hardcases return, Cub sends the hardcases into town to kidnap Nita, but Lance outwits them and they are captured. The final confrontation is the shoot-out between Cub and Lance in which Cub is finished off.

In L'Amour's rewrite, all of the bad traits of the later L'Amour are unfortunately in evidence. To begin with, there is the strident L'Amour rhetoric. On the way to the Hatfield place, Lance now tells young Sally Crane and Jack Moffitt that "'the Hatfields know who they are, they know what they believe in, and their kind will last. Other kinds of people will come and go. The glib and confident, and whiners and complainers, and the people without loyalty, they will disappear, but the Hatfields will still be here plowing the land, planting crops, doing the hard work of the world because it is here to be done. Consider yourself fortunate to know them.'"[17] The reader, however, is never told if the youngsters are suitably impressed.

The first Dell Books paperbacks provided maps on the back cover which a reader could consult while reading the story, whether it be a detective story, a Western, or some other kind of fiction. L'Amour during his final decade adapted this idea to his own purposes, providing maps at the beginning of his novels to show a reader where the action supposedly took place. Since no such places could be found in New Mexico, L'Amour changed the location of the story to a "remote corner of southwestern Idaho."[18] The name Smoky Desert was retained, but it was said to be only a local and not very well known designation for some rough lands. A footnote about actual boxing matches in the nineteenth century was added to provide a flavor of authenticity to Kilkenny's fight with Turner. Worst of all, L'Amour destroyed the credibility of the entire plot. When Kilkenny enters the saloon in Blazer and confronts Gaddis and the other renegades with the story about Jody Miller supposedly knowing Halloran at the state capital, it is no longer a ploy but an actual statement of fact. Hence, when Lance bends Halloran's ear during the boxing match, King Bill tries to throw Halloran off by calling Jody Miller "trash" only for Halloran to reply: "'Jody Miller . . . was married to my sister. He was as likely a young man as I know. And as honest.'"[19] This remark makes the whole fight sequence and the entire conclusion to the novel superfluous. All that was needed to happen was for Jody Miller's widow to come to town to see her brother, or even just to write Halloran a letter, and King Bill Hale's reign of terror would have been over before it had really begun!

The Kilkenny trilogy was concluded with *Kilkenny,* first published by Ace and then in a new Bantam edition in 1983 when the copyright held by Ace Books reverted to L'Amour. The plot of *Kilkenny* was essentially the same range war plot variation as that to be found in "A Man Called Trent" with one difference: instead of the villain's being a rancher indigenous to the district, as was King Bill Hale, Jared Tetlow with his giant herds of cattle comes to the district intent on driving out all the other ranchers so he can carve out an empire for himself. Included among these ranchers is heroine Nita Riordan with her faithful bodyguard Jaime Brigo, still hoping that Lance Kilkenny will come to her. She is what the Romans called *univera*, as are most L'Amour heroines, since "her childhood training, her father, all her background conditioned her to love for one man only."[20] Lance has homesteaded in the district, again using the name Trent in order to elude his reputation. This is early L'Amour, when he was against the big ranchers, before the Sacketts who would become empire builders themselves with L'Amour's total endorsement. "Kilkenny's sympathies were with the small ranchers, the men who were building homes rather than empires. For one man to grow so large as Tetlow meant many men must remain small or have nothing. The proper level lay between the two extremes, and this was the American way."[21] Kilkenny joins forces with the small ranchers and townspeople opposing Tetlow's take-over. We learn one more thing, in the process, about Nita and Lance: "It was not like her to question his judgment."[22] This time her loyalty is rewarded and Lance, once Tetlow is jailed and charged with murder, his herds dispersed, and his gunmen killed off, rides off with her to his sequestered homestead. Cain Brockman is also in the cast of characters. He had been talked out of a confrontation with Lance in "A Man Called Trent" and now the two are friends and allies. In a brief résumé of the previous Kilkenny stories, none of which had appeared outside the pages of pulp magazines at the time *Kilkenny* was first published as a paperback novel, the events in the Live Oak country are recounted followed by those in "the cedar breaks of New Mexico where Kilkenny had been trying to establish a home."[23] Even though the new Bantam edition of *Kilkenny* appeared five years *after* the reworked *The Mountain Valley War* where the location had been changed to Idaho, L'Amour made no effort to alter this minuscule reference to the earlier story so as to be consistent. Also his counting is off here, as it is in *Last Stand at Papago Wells* (1957). A gunman starts out with three men accompanying him, only for two to be shot, and then walks "out on the street with his two remaining men."[24]

Kilkenny was published under L'Amour's own byline, whereas the previous novels had originally been stories by Jim Mayo. "The Trail to Crazy Man" was published under the pseudonym Jim Mayo in *West* in July, 1948 and was later expanded into a paperback original by Louis L'Amour first published by Ace Books in 1954 with the title *Crossfire Trail*. It belongs to the second major plot group: the hidden wealth plot. The hero, Rafe Caradec, has been shanghaied and escapes from the ship after beating the skipper's "face into a gory pulp."[25] The Ernest Haycox hero, as the Luke Short hero, is a man alone against all the odds. It was never so for the L'Amour hero. Even if at the beginning of the story the hero is alone, rapidly along the way he picks up sympathizers who join him in his battle. In Rafe's case, Tex Brisco, one of the men who escapes with him, decides to side him in his effort to ride to Painted Rock, a town in Wyoming, where he intends to save the ranch belonging to Charles Rodney, a man they befriended aboard ship but who died as a result of a number of beatings. Obviously L'Amour was influenced somewhat by Zane Grey's *The Border Legion* (1916) since the two principal villains who want possession of the Rodney ranch because of the oil to be found on it, Bruce Barkow and Dan Shute, bear more than a little resemblance to Kells and Gulden in Grey's novel. Rodney's wife has died in the interim and his daughter, the heroine, Ann, is in love with Barkow, or at least she thinks she is until Rafe arrives on the scene. Rafe announces that "'I promised her father I'd take care of her, and I will, whether she likes it or not!'"[26] Rafe goes up against Trigger Boyne, a gunslick in the employ of Barkow and Shute, and he walks so swiftly toward him that Boyne is rattled. Rafe guns him and, right after, turns and shoots another killer hidden in an upper story room. Rafe is brought to trial and Barkow figures it will be Caradec's finish since the judge is on his side. In a bit of gratuitous history, a trait that would become increasingly commonplace in L'Amour's fiction, Rafe asks that Ann be empaneled on the jury and reminds the judge that "'women served on juries in Laramie in eighteen seventy, and one was servin' as justice of the peace that year.'"[27]

"Showdown Trail," published in *Giant Western* in Winter, 1948 as by Jim Mayo was expanded to form the novel *The Tall Stranger*, first published by Fawcett in 1957 and was adapted for the screen that same year as *The Tall Stranger* (Allied Artists, 1957). A few scenes were added when L'Amour expanded "A Man Called Trent" into *The Mountain Valley War*, but in most cases his expansions of pulp novels into original paperbacks required little more than verbal padding. Here is how "Showdown Trail" opens: "With slow, ponderously rhythmical steps, the oxen moved, each step a pause and an effort, each movement a deadening drag. Fine white dust hung in a sifting cloud above the wagon train, caking the nostrils of the animals and men, blanketing the lean sides of oxen and horses, dusting with a thin film the clothing of men and women."[28] Here is how it was expanded in *The Tall Stranger:* "With slow, ponderously rhythmical steps the oxen moved, each step a pause and an effort, each movement a deadening drag. Fine white dust hung in a sifting cloud above the wagon train, caking the nostrils of animals and men, blanketing the sides of oxen and horses, dusting a thin film over men and women. And the miles stretched on before them, endless and timeless."[29]

In *The Tall Stranger,* Rock Bannon is the hero. The story is a variety of L'Amour's waylaid wagon train plot. Bannon had been found on the trail with two bullet wounds and has been nursed back to health by the heroine, Sharon Crockett, who with her father is among a group of settlers who have formed a wagon train to get to California. The villain is Morton Harper who convinces the people in the wagon train to take a short cut, despite Bannon's counsel against it, and once he leads them to Indian Writing, he persuades most of the settlers to remain right there and homestead. The area the settlers choose for their town site is on Hardy Bishop's range. Hardy adopted Rock as his son after Rock's parents were killed by Kaw Indians and Rock tries his best to maintain the peace. In this he fails because it is Harper's plan to get the settlers and the Bishop riders to kill each other off so he can have the valley for himself. Ultimately, Bannon succeeds in upsetting Harper's plans and Harper attempts to make a getaway, kidnapping Sharon in the process. Bannon trails them and one of L'Amour's strongest attributes as a Western writer could be exercised in a situation where he was describing a man on the trail replete with appropriate kaleidoscopic details. "The country grew rougher, but he shifted from draw to draw, cut across a flat, barren plateau of scattered rocks and rabbit grass, traversed a lava flow, black and ugly, to skirt a towering rust red cliff. A notch in the cliff ahead seemed to indicate a point of entry, so he guided the stallion among the boulders. A lizard darted from under the stallion's hoofs, and overhead a buzzard wheeled in wide, lonely circles."[30] When Rock catches up with the fugitive, Harper gets the drop on him. Rock resorts to the cigarette trick. He rolls a cigarette and then lights a match, all the time talking with Harper. He lets the match burn down to his fingers, distracting Harper's attention just long enough for him to reach for his gun and shoot Harper. It would not be the last time in L'Amour's fiction that a hero would use the cigarette trick to get out of a tight spot. Then Bannon tells Sharon of Harper, "'At the wrong time he was too filled with hate to even accomplish a satisfactory killin'.'"³¹

"The Rider of the Ruby Hills" was first published under the Jim Mayo pseudonym in *West* in September, 1949 and was not expanded to a paperback novel until it appeared as *Where the Long Grass Grows* from Bantam in 1976, although in its original pulp version it served as the basis for the film *Treasure of the Ruby Hills* (United Artists, 1955). It employs L'Amour's basic range war plot. The hero is Ross Haney who is twenty-seven, broke, but armed with two six guns and a Winchester. He rides into the district and feels that "it was a good country, a country where a man could live and grow, and where if he was lucky, he might have sons to grow tall and straight beside him."³² The two big ranches are the RR—owned by Chalk Reynolds—and the Box N—owned by Walt Pogue. There is a persistent rivalry between them, actually instigated by the master villain, Star Levitt, who is using the occasion to rustle from both men and who intends to see that they kill each other off so he can claim both their spreads. He has blackmailed the heroine, Sherry Vernon, into agreeing to marry him because of information he has about her brother and in the meantime is using her ranch to hide opium that he has been smuggling across the border. "'There's an old law, Rio,'" Haney tells his horse, "'that only the strong survive. . . . Those ranches belong to men who were strong, and some of them still are. They were strong enough to take them from other men, from smaller men, weaker men.'"³³ Ross is alone when he arrives but soon he has managed to gather a number of allies in his cause. There is a typical element of bad construction which L'Amour did not alter when he came to reprint the original story: a key scene is set in the hotel restaurant which is interrupted and when the reader comes back to this setting it is said to be in the saloon across the street. Ross eventually exposes Levitt and Levitt goes into hiding. When Ross came into the district, he was aware of a hidden grotto where there were wild cattle. Near the end of the story, he takes Sherry to this grotto only to be confronted by Levitt. Levitt has the drop on Ross but Sherry distracts Levitt just enough to allow Ross to draw and kill him.

"The Trail to Peach Meadow Canyon" was published under the Jim Mayo name in *Giant Western* in October, 1949 and was substantially expanded subsequently to form *Son of a Wanted Man* (1984) in which episodes, only peripherally related to the main plot, were added featuring Borden Chantry and Tyrel Sackett who first meet in the novel *Borden Chantry* (1978). Tyrel Sackett was introduced in *The Daybreakers* (1960), a novel set in the years following the Civil War. Tell Sackett, the eldest of the brothers, is off in Dakota Territory fighting Indians. Tyrel, his older brother Orrin, their younger brothers Bob and Joe, and their pipe-smoking mother all want to head West from their home in Tennessee. This novel is narrated in the first person by Tyrel, permitting L'Amour to employ his loosely episodic mode of plotting which he used regularly in the Sackett saga and in which what keeps the story moving is a constant series of emergencies, dangers, and plot complications, none of which is necessarily even related to the central plot. In commenting on his pulp stories, L'Amour observed that "the essentials demanded by our editors were action and color, but, above all, one had to tell a story with a beginning, a middle, and an end. And the story had to move."[34] The way in which L'Amour assured that all of his stories moved was precisely to introduce a new plot complication every thousand words or so. What is somewhat different in the Sackett books is that these plot complications can often taken a reader rather far afield from the main story, bound to the central plot by the device of the first person narrator and the focus on his various experiences. *The Daybreakers* for its central plot employs a variation of the range war plot: Jonathan Pritts has organized a gang of renegades and proceeds to New Mexico, intent on taking Don Luis' Spanish land grant away from him and keeping it for himself. In this he is foiled ultimately by Tyrel Sackett who has fallen in love with the heroine, Drusilla, Don Luis Alvarado's daughter. At one point when Tyrel is surrounded by some of Pritts' renegades, one of them holding a rifle on him, Tyrel uses the cigarette trick although he does not normally smoke, the match burning down to his fingers a sufficient distraction to allow him to draw his gun and kill the renegade. In one of the longer, loosely related episodes Tyrel rides off with another character to prospect for gold in Montana. Once at the mining camp, Tyrel becomes aware of the fact that Martin Brady, the local saloon owner, and his two henchmen have been preying upon the prospectors, taking their gold in gambling and whiskey and ambushing them if they try to leave the district with their gold. Sackett confronts Brady in a showdown and in strident L'Amour rhetoric informs him of what the score is: "'Brady, this country is growing up. Folks are moving in and they want schools, churches, and quiet towns where they can walk in the streets of an evening.' . . . Right then I felt sorry for Martin Brady, although his kind would outlast my kind because people have a greater tolerance for evil than for violence. If crooked gambling, thieving, and robbing are covered over, folks will tolerate it longer than outright violence, even when the violence may be cleansing."[35] All in all, about three years elapse before Tyrel finally manages to run off Pritts and settle down with Drusilla on the land grant. In the interim, Ma and the rest of the family have come West to New Mexico and although New Mexico would not achieve statehood until 1912 Tyrel remarks that "already they were talking about Orrin for the United States Senate. . ."[36]

Some of L'Amour's early pulp fiction were detective stories, later reprinted in *The Hills of Homicide* (1983). *Borden Chantry* is a Western with a detective story plot. Joe Sackett, now grown to manhood, arrives in the nameless town were Chantry is the town marshal and is murdered. The story is the narrative of Chantry's successful investigation, tracking a serial murderer in which Sackett's murder is only his latest depredation. Unfortunately, a detective story requires extremely careful plotting, too painstaking and detailed to be well suited for L'Amour's one draft, no rewrite approach and all manner of ridiculous inconsistencies emerge. The focus is constantly on Chantry so the reader is dismayed when Chantry discovers a .52 calibre rifle used by the murderer only for it to drop from sight without explanation when Chantry crosses the street to the hotel as is also the case when Chantry, during the denouement, suddenly relates how he investigated the death of the previous marshal and recalls a talk he had with the local doctor although, in the time frame the reader is given, there would have been no opportunity for him to have done either.

"The Trail to Peach Meadow Canyon" is actually the shortest of the seven pulp novels which L'Amour later reprinted and, therefore, was most in need of additional sub-plots and padding. However, instead of admitting what he had done, simply recycling his pulp fiction in a paperback format where it could continue to earn him money, L'Amour had to claim that "pleased as I was about how I brought the characters and their adventures to life in the pages of the magazines, I still wanted the reader to know more about my people and why they did what they did."[37] If that had indeed been L'Amour's intention, it did not happen in any of the expanded versions. In "The Trail to Peach Meadow Canyon," young Mike Bastian is the adopted son of outlaw leader Ben Curry. As such, it is a variety of the initiation into manhood

plot. Mike has been raised, ever since he was orphaned, to take over
Ben's criminal operations once Ben decides to retire. His big choice is
whether to become a criminal or not. In the course of the story, Mike
learns that Ben has long been secretly married and has two daughters,
the younger of which Mike meets and the two fall in requited love at
first sight. Her name is Drusilla. There is a mutiny in Ben's gang,
several of the toughs wanting to take it over themselves, and Mike finds
himself in the company of Drusilla on the trail of an outlaw named
Ducrow who has kidnapped Ben's older daughter, Julie. Mike and
Ducrow shoot it out in sequestered Peach Meadow Canyon after which
they return to Ben's hideout only to learn that he and his loyal followers
have stood off the mutiny and now Ben can retire with his swag. Mike
and Dru decide to take up cattle ranching in Peach Meadow
Canyon.

In expanding this pulp novel into *Son of a Wanted Man*, L'Amour
commented that "I was able to follow in more detail what happened
to the various groups of outlaws operating out of their canyon hideout
and bring them into contact with two law officers of the time and area,
Tyrel Sackett and Borden Chantry, neither of whom is aware that they
are distantly related."[38] *That* story L'Amour intended to narrate
elsewhere. What his additions came down to in reality was that a
splinter group of outlaws breaks off and intends to rob the bank in the
still nameless city where Borden Chantry has now become sheriff.
Sackett and Chantry put their heads together, figure out what is going
to happen, and foil the outlaws in a street fight. In introducing a little
extraneous history lesson into this story, L'Amour, misspelling
McSween's name, has Ben Curry remark: "'Take Billy now, I knew him
as a youngster. Not a bad kid, but in Lincoln County them days you
took sides. You had to. Billy took the right side, too. Tunstall and
Maqueen were good men, and then of the whole two hundred or so
involved in that fight Billy was the only one ever brought to trial.'"[39]

"Showdown on the Hogback" published under the name Jim
Mayo in *Giant Western* in August, 1950 was reworked as an Ace
original paperback titled *Showdown at Yellow Butte* (1953). The story
is basically the variation on the range war plot already employed in "A
Man Called Trent" and which would be re-used many times in the
future, including in *The Daybreakers*. In *Showdown at Yellow Butte*,
the town is called Mustang and the normal situation is "a killing every
day...."[40] Clay Allison is playing poker at the Morrison House.
Supposedly he has "killed thirty men" and Black Jack Ketchum is in

town sleeping off a drunk. The hero is Captain Tom Kedrick, a soldier of fortune as increasingly L'Amour's heroes would become. He has been sent for by a friend, John Gunter, who is in partnership with Colonel Loren Keith and Alton Burwick. Burwick is the true brains behind the scheme. He is described as a "a strange, fat, and dirty man . . . a thing of evil, of corruption. There was some foul thing within him, something cold and vicious as a striking snake."[41] The heroine is Consuelo Duane, Gunter's niece, who lent her uncle the money to buy into Burwick's scheme. She becomes rapidly disillusioned with what is happening. Burwick has laid claim to the ranches and farms in the district and he wants Kedrick to lead his men against these squatters and drive them out within ten days. Kedrick, as Lance Kilkenny in similar circumstances, soon realizes that "it was a fight between a bunch of hard-working men against the company, made up largely of outsiders, seeking to profit from the work of local people."[42] Kedrick switches sides and leads the local people successfully against Burwick's renegades. After the defeat of his men, Burwick vanishes. It turns out — absurdly! — that in the past he was a white renegade who led an Indian attack on a wagon train while wearing a suit of armor which impressed the Indians enough that they followed him. Added to the range war plot is the hidden wealth plot: it seems that a gold shipment that Burwick wanted had been buried somewhere in the district and for this reason he wanted all of the local people forced off their land.

It would seem, surveying L'Amour's pulp fiction objectively, that he was already burned out on the Western story, even though the years of fame, wealth, and tremendous sales figures were still before him. "Riders of the Dawn" was published under the name Louis L'Amour in *Giant Western* in June, 1951. It was later expanded to form *Silver Canyon*, published as an original paperback by Avalon Books in 1956. It is again a combination of the range war plot with the hidden wealth plot. It is narrated in the first person by Matt Sabre — the Mathurin Sabre who is featured in short stories such as "Ride, You Tonto Riders!" published in *New Western Magazine* in August, 1949 and "The Marshal of Painted Rock" from *Triple Western Magazine* in February, 1953, published four years later. The "Painted Rock" in the latter short story, incidentally, is not the same Painted Rock as in "The Trail to Crazy Man." Matt's name in the pulp novel is spelled Mathieu Sabre and it is said that he was once marshal of Mobeetie and that he is known as the Mogollon gunfighter. Matt rides into Hattan's Point and discovers that the district is in the midst of a range war. Rud Maclaren of the Bar M and Jim Pinder of the CP outfit both want the water located on the Two Bar, a ranch owned by a man named Ball. The heroine is Olga Maclaren, Rud's daughter, and Matt falls in love with her at first sight. A man named Morgan Park is the master villain and secretly behind all the trouble. He considers himself engaged to Olga and has actually discovered silver on Maclaren's land. He hopes that Maclaren and Pinder will kill off each other so he can lay claim to the Bar M. Matt joins forces with Ball and is soon aided by the Benaras, six dead-shots — another early rehearsal of the Sacketts. Matt sees in the district "a country where I plan to stay and grow my children. . . ."[43] He realizes that fighting is necessary for there to be peace. "'The murderers, cheats, and swindlers must be stamped out before the honest citizens can have peace,'" he comments.[44] He hires a man named Mullvaney who teaches him how to box so when he goes up against Morgan he is able to win the fight. Jack Slade appears briefly in the story and even has a bit of dialogue with Matt when Sabre comes to his campfire to borrow a horse. By the end, Morgan is killed by an Indian and the crooked lawyer working with him is exposed by Matt in a trial scene similar to that found in "The Trail to Crazy Man."

L'Amour could see that the pulp markets were disappearing and that if he was to survive and prosper he would have to make the transition to original paperback Westerns. *Westward the Tide* (1950) was his first attempt, a longer novel than any he had written so far, but one which no American paperback publisher apparently wanted since it was ultimately brought out by World's Work, a British paperback publisher which also published some mystery titles and science fiction pulp novels around the same time. The book did not have general distribution in the United States until it was published, unaltered, by Bantam Books in February, 1977. *Westward the Tide* utilizes the waylaid wagon train plot. The hero is gunfighter Matt Bardoul. He meets the heroine, Jacquine Coyle, on the stage to Deadwood and is so attracted to her that he decides to join in the venture supposedly headed up by her father, Brian Coyle, and a man named Clive Massey who turns out to be a notorious Civil War renegade leader by the name of Sim Boyne. There is a problem in dating the time period of the novel. Early on it is stated that "not much over two years ago Custer had made his fateful ride. . ."[45] This would put the year at 1878. Yet, later in the text, Captain Gordon Sharp of the U.S. Cavalry says "'this is 1877. . . .'"[46] Moreover, Jacquine Coyle is said to be familiar with the name "Billy the Kid," although he was not really known at all outside Lincoln County in either 1877 or 1878. However, the most interesting aspect about L'Amour's first paperback novel is its ideology which is totally at odds with what he came later to believe and which he did not excise when he republished the book almost three decades later. First, there is the conservation theme. "In the short view," L'Amour wrote, "there was much good in this westward trek, but in the long view it was a mad rush of greed and rapine, the lust of men who ripped the wealth from the land and then deserted it. . . . Like a young man who inherits a fortune the people of the country were spending their birthright in a wild orgy of finance and greed, heedless of the years to come."[47] L'Amour was even more outspoken in his defense of the Indians. "'The white man came and the beaver are gone, the buffalo are going,'" Matt remarks. "'The white man cuts the timber along the streams so the rain rushes unchecked into the streams and causes floods that formerly the roots and brush held back. Already, in some places, he is putting too much stock on the grass, over-grazing the country.'"[48] In contrast to the white men are the Indians. "'In all recorded history,'" Matt continues, "'there is no more tragic epitaph to a beaten, dying people who have been robbed of their birthright than that uttered by Spotted Tail when he said, "The land is full of white men; our game is all gone, and we have come upon great trouble."'"[49]

A wagon train is being organized of well-to-do settlers and their families and is being led by Coyle and Massey, headed to the Big Horns where ostensibly gold has been discovered and these settlers can both mine gold and build a town. Each has to buy into the venture and pack into wagons all that will be needed to found such a town once they arrive. Massey's ultimate intention is to seize the wagon train, once it is safe to do so, kill off those who resist, enslave the others to build him a town, then kill them, giving the women to his renegades as a reward. Accordingly, Massey does not want Matt along. He hires a professional gunfighter to go up against Matt before they pull out, but Matt walks so fast in the gunfighter's direction that he is unnerved and humiliated and finally forced to leave town. It is a ploy that Tyrel Sackett and other L'Amour heroes will use in future books. On the trail Matt beats up one of Massey's riders, explaining that he is so good with his fists because— as Lance Kilkenny before him—he studied boxing "'with an Englishmen I met in New Orleans, name of Jem Mace.'"[50] Matt is a believer in the use of violence. "'There are Indians here,'" he tells Jacquine, "'and white renegades that are worse. These men are savage, they understand only the law of force, and if one is to live in such a country one must be prepared to protect those one loves and the things one lives by.'"[51] L'Amour carried over the new home theme from his pulp stories. "'I'm a man who knows what he wants,'" Matt insists, "'a home, a ranch, time to work without strain, and time to love.'"[52] It is an ambition that L'Amour himself would achieve in his life. Matt is a self-educated gunfighter, quoting Schopenhauer and explaining that "'around these campfires I've heard men discuss questions of philosophy in a manner that would do justice to Berkeley and Hume.'"[53]

Because it was written hurriedly, there are the typical L'Amour errors in construction. The renegades steal all the ammunition from the settlers' wagons. Matt reflects on their situation and comes to realize that "as things stood, in a prolonged battle, all the advantage lay with the renegades due to their stealing of ammunition."[54] Yet, four pages later, it turns out that Matt has known nothing about the ammunition having been stolen!

That same year L'Amour published "Guns of the Timberlands" in the September, 1950 issue of *West* under the Jim Mayo byline. The hero is Clay Bell who runs his cattle on Deep Creek range. The trees on that range provide a needed watershed. However, Jud Devitt and his loggers come to town with the intention of harvesting the Deep Creek timber. He has brought a federal judge with him to ensure his right of use to the range and he is engaged to marry the heroine, Colleen Riley. Sam Tinker, who founded the town, tells Colleen's father that there are two kinds of men, "'Them that come to build, and them that come to get rich and get out.'"[55] In L'Amour's West, of course, it is always the builders — in contrast to history — who are the big winners and it is no exception in this case. The master villain responsible for importing Jud and his loggers is the local banker, Noble Wheeler, a man who, "knowing the way of war, . . . realized both sides would lose in the end. And that, he decided as he rubbed fat hands together, was exactly as he wanted it."[56] As such, *Guns of the Timberlands,* expanded to an original paperback novel published by Jason Press in 1955 and adapted for the screen as a film by the same title in 1960 released by Warner Bros., uses the basic range war plot of *Kilkenny* and other early L'Amour books, only instead of cattle being moved onto the local range from the outside the invasion is one of Jud and his loggers.

The fifties would be a very good decade for L'Amour, with no less than nine Western films based on his fiction. However, it did not begin very auspiciously. First, there had been the problem of finding a publisher for *Westward the Tide,* and, second, there was the very sudden shrinking of L'Amour's traditional pulp markets. More or less in desperation, L'Amour accepted an offer from Doubleday & Company to write four Hopalong Cassidy novels under the house name Tex Burns. These books feature a sanitized image of Hopalong. Instead of the red-headed, hard-drinking, cigarette, cigar, and pipe-smoking roustabout Clarence E. Mulford had created, a man who began working for the Bar-20 when barely out of his teens and who aged until he was in his sixties in *Hopalong Cassidy Serves a Writ* (1941), this Hopalong was based on the image projected by William Boyd in the feature films and television series. "Clad entirely in black, from his sombrero to his ebony-hued boots, he was a striking figure—a man to attract attention anywhere. In marked contrast to his dark range clothes were his white hair, his silver spurs, and the two white bone-handled silver six-guns. . . ."[57] In L'Amour's stories, this figure clad in what Harry Sherman, the original producer of the Hopalong Cassidy theatrical films, had once called Boyd's "monkey suit" moves among ranchers and thieves without anyone laughing at his outlandish costume. His favorite horse is the white stallion, Topper. This Hoppy neither smokes nor drinks although he does chew gum. He has cold blue eyes and, despite the white hair, he is referred to as a young man. L'Amour obviously studied the original Mulford books with great care and he brought many of the characters along with Hopalong to this new series, commissioned because Mulford did not want to write any further stories. Red Connors figures prominently in the first book in the series, *Hopalong Cassidy and the Riders of High Rock* (1951), along with a less substantial portrait of Mesquite Jenkins and, in a later book, Tex Ewalt is included. L'Amour almost paraphrased Mulford in describing the Bar-20 spirit, but with an element of his own that he would employ in the Sackett saga, a series unquestionably inspired by Mulford's Bar-20 saga. In *Bar-20 Days* (1911) Mulford observed that it was "the quality of friendship which bound the units of the Bar-20 outfit into a smooth, firm whole. They were like brothers, like one man."[58] For L'Amour, the Bar-20 "had worked as a team for so long that they could easily guess what the others were doing at any given time."[59] Mulford's Hopalong was a man of violence. There is a scene in *Bar-20* (1907) in which it is said of Hopalong that "never in all his life had he felt such a desire to kill. His eyes were diamond points of accumulated fury, and those whom he faced quailed before him."[60] L'Amour, the man who had created Kilkenny and numerous other pulp heroes who were not afraid to use lethally guns or fists when necessary, now had to restrain himself to make credible a Hopalong who had a reputation for avoiding violence and gunplay whenever possible. This Hopalong would shoot a villain's gun out of his hand, rather than plug him. He tries only to wound villains when in a gun battle. When an outlaw suffers a broken leg in a skirmish, Hoppy sees to it that the man receives care and attention. When attacked by a villain during a stampede, Hoppy knocks him unconscious in order to drag him to safety. When it comes time for the big clean-up, Hopalong remarks, "'let's hope we can do it without killing.'"[61] In the final showdown with master villains, Hoppy, however, is not above shooting them down in a fair gun fight.

Basically, the prose and action in these Tex Burns books are pedestrian, but the tightness of the plotting and the consistency in matters of characters and action indicate that L'Amour was closely supervised in writing them and that here, at least, he did revise, rewrite, and polish his finished product. When I was preparing his entry for the *Encyclopedia of Frontier and Western Fiction* (1983), L'Amour objected to their being included among his works. "The situation was this," he wrote to me, "during a period after the collapse of the magazine field when all the pulps and many other publications went under, I was asked to write four Hopalong Cassidy novels. This was during the sudden boom that followed his popularity on TV. I assured the publisher that the books would not sell. The fans of Hopalong were kids and they could get all they wanted in comic books about Hopalong. Moreover, I viewed the Boyd Hopalong with some distaste. However, they preferred to believe the books would sell and I was paid a flat fee to write them. . . . Being broke I was in no position to argue. I wrote the books and they supported me during a very bad year." Once I responded that nothing in what he had said indicated that he had not written the books and that they were, therefore, among his works, L'Amour became even more adamant. "To attribute those books to me, in any sense, would not be a credit to your accuracy. The best thing I can advise, in all sincerity and good will, is to forget my connection with them. I deserve no more credit than would a president's speech-writer . . . and I have never yet seen one of them given credit. I am trying to help you keep your book honest. If you intend to list those works as mine I shall insist you also list every essay my children have written with which I helped them as well as every other document I can scrape up in which I had a hand. It would make just as much sense."[62] Yet, as bold as life, there is in these books, beyond all else, the inimitable L'Amour rhetoric: "'We need homes, schools, churches here, and we can have them, but before we can have peace we must be rid of those men who cling to the old way of doing things.'"[63]

L'Amour's big break, the one that put him firmly on the road to success, came the same year that Doubleday published the last of his Tex Burns titles, *Hopalong Cassidy, Trouble Shooter* (1952). With the short story, "The Gift of Cochise," published on July 5, 1952 by *Collier's,* Louis L'Amour under his own name broke into print in a slick magazine. In this story, Angie Lowe lives in Apache country with her seven-year-old son Jimmy and her five-year-old daughter Jane. Her husband, Ed Lowe, has gone to El Paso for supplies and he dallies there, drinking and gambling. He is not a bad man, simply an irresponsible one. Cochise comes to visit Angie in Ed's absence and is impressed by her spirit and the spirit of her son, Jimmy. He will allow Angie to wait, unmolested, for the return of her man. In a barroom brawl in El Paso, Ed Lowe steps into a gun fight between hero Ches Lane and the three Tolliver brothers, getting killed in the fracas. Ches learns that Ed has a wife and two children and heads out to pay them his respects and to see if he can be of some help. On the way there, he is surrounded by Apaches and defeats one of the warriors in a knife fight. This wins him the admiration of Cochise. When Lane finds Angie, the Apaches regard him as her man, a feeling she comes to share. The story ends with the line, "'A man could get to like it here.'"[64]

"The Gift of Cochise" was purchased by Robert Fellows and John Wayne who wanted to produce it for the screen. James Edward Grant, Wayne's favorite screenwriter, did the screenplay, with Warner Bros. financing and releasing the film. Grant changed the original plot considerably, beginning with the character of the hero, now called Hondo Lane. In the film Hondo was given a dog named Sam as a companion. John Ford acted as an unofficial adviser on the picture, wanting to do what he could to make Wayne's venture into film production a success.

L'Amour had, as yet, been unable to interest any American paperback publisher in his fiction. He got the Wayne-Fellows group to agree to let him novelize James Edward Grant's screenplay and publish it under his own name, as if it were *his* story, and he even got Wayne to allow himself to be quoted as saying that *Hondo* (1953) was the finest Western he had ever read. Fawcett published the paperback

original in the same year that the film appeared and henceforth
L'Amour always claimed that *Hondo* — when not even the title had
been his — was his first paperback novel rather than *Westward the Tide*.
Nor would this be the last time that L'Amour would novelize a
screenplay and publish it under his own name. He would again in *How
the West Was Won* (1963), based on James R. Webb's Academy
Award-winning original story and screenplay. There is no particular
dishonor for a writer to engage in hack work for the purpose of making
money. Lewis B. Patten, for example, wrote two books in the Gene
Autry series, stories about the adventures of Gene Autry supposedly
written by him, and felt no qualms about including those titles in his
bibliography. L'Amour on the other hand because he was creating as
much a legend about himself as writing Western fiction was willing to
take credit for *Hondo* but not for his Tex Burns books.

L'Amour's novelization of *Hondo* (Warner's, 1953) follows Grant's
screenplay very closely, using much of Grant's dialogue. Angie Lowe
was retained as the heroine, but Jane is removed as a character; Angie
has only her young son, Johnny. Her husband is a wicked man and he
has deserted her. Hondo, together with his dog Sam, arrives at the
Lowe ranch and stays around to help out. Later, in a fight in the desert,
Hondo kills Lowe when Lowe would steal his horse. L'Amour did add
one scene to the novel not in the screenplay, a sexual episode between
Hondo and Angie before Hondo tells her that he has killed her husband. Cochise was changed to Vittoro. L'Amour also adopted Grant's
social Darwinism and from this point on it came to characterize his view
of the Indian wars as opposed to his posture when he wrote *Westward
the Tide*. The Apaches "saw the white men endlessly coming, their
many soldiers, their many ponies, their food supply that was endless,
and their many cartridges of brass. The Apache knew his hour was past.
He knew the white men would take even this last land, but it was not
in him to buckle under. He would fight, sing his death song, and
die."[63]

One of L'Amour's other contributions to the novelization of
Grant's screenplay was to incorporate his view of marriage when he
reflected about Angie and Hondo that "this was as it should be . . . a
man and a woman working toward something, for something. Not
apart, but a team."[66] Three years hence, considering himself financially
secure at last, L'Amour himself married Katherine Elizabeth Adams
and from this union came his two children, a son, Beau, and a
daughter, Angelique. In the meantime, on the basis of the success of

Hondo as a film—more than a decade later it would inspire a short-lived television series—L'Amour began vigorously to market his pulp stories to motion picture producers. He expanded five of his pulp novels to form paperback Westerns in the fifties and wrote nine additional original titles. He did not, however, give up his Jim Mayo pseudonym at once and books such as *Utah Blaine* (1954) filmed under this title in 1957 by Columbia Pictures was first published by Ace Books as a Jim Mayo Western. *Kilkenny* was filmed as *Blackjack Ketchum, Desperado* (Columbia, 1956) the year L'Amour married.

By this time, L'Amour had forged his basic plot themes and, as the years passed and the books multiplied, he found no reason to alter what continued to work for him. *Utah Blaine* uses the range war plot. The two biggest ranches in the district are owned by men who built them up from nothing and, as the story opens, they are coveted by greedy men who came later and found the best land already taken. Utah interposes himself into this conflict and it becomes personal when one of the big ranches is left to him, which is just about what happened to Matt Sabre in *Silver Canyon*. In *Flint* (1960), the hero believes he is dying of cancer and, after having been a success during his years in the East, he returns to the West in order to die. What he encounters is the range war plot. Porter Baldwin, a crooked stock manipulator and also from the East, as Jared Tetlow in *Kilkenny* has moved into the district with a large herd of cattle and intends to force all the ranchers already in the area off their ranches so he can perpetuate a phony land scheme among would-be settlers. Similiar to Ross Haney in "The Rider of the Ruby Hills," Flint knows about a hideout in the badlands where, in this case, wild horses are trapped. In the course of the narrative, Flint learns that his condition was mis-diagnosed. He only had ulcers. As happened to Jim Gatlin in the short story "The Black Rock Coffin Makers" published in *.44 Western* in February, 1950, Flint scales a sharp V in a canyon wall to escape from a tight spot.

With the publication of *Radigan* (1958), L'Amour's American paperback publisher became Bantam Books. It was a stroke of extremely good fortune. Frederick D. Glidden was under contract to Bantam to receive a $15,000 advance for every original Luke Short novel he would write, but his production was far from what the publisher wanted. L'Amour was prepared to write two or three new books each and every year. As the years passed, Bantam came up with the idea of keeping *all* L'Amour titles continuously in print and, as his number of paperback novels progressed, this meant that very often in Western

paperback racks at least half of the available titles were books by Louis
L'Amour. The marketing strategy was quite the same, in its way, as
Jared Tetlow's scheme of overrunning the available range with his cattle
herds and it proved effective to an astonishing degree. L'Amour also
decided to merchandise himself. Most Western writers were rather
retiring men. It was not so with L'Amour. He dressed up in fancy
cowboy outfits, traveled about the country in a motor home making
personal appearances, promoting himself at every opportunity. He also
began to write his novels with topographical maps beside him. To give
but one instance. *Under the Sweetwater Rim* (1971) employs the
waylaid wagon train plot. A gang of renegades under Civil War
renegade leader Reuben Kelsey waylays a wagon train and kills
everyone in it in hopes of capturing an Army ambulance which is carrying the Army payroll. The hero is Tenadore Brian, a soldier of fortune
now a lieutenant in the U.S. Cavalry in Wyoming. He and the heroine
are aboard the ambulance but they separate from the wagon train
before the renegades attack. One of the reasons L'Amour could expand
this story to novel-length proportions is that a good part of the action
is focused on the heroine's father, Major Mark Devereaux, who leads
his company in pursuit of the renegades with parallel plotting telling
of the adventures of the hero and heroine in their efforts to elude the
renegades. Using his maps, L'Amour could write that "the head of the
Little Sweetwater was on his left and behind him; Sioux Pass was to the
right."[67] By checking the flora of the region, L'Amour was able to
describe how the hero after "cutting through a patch of ragwort and
monkey flowers, ... rounded a patch of spruce...."[68] This sort of
thing did not make the plot new or less predictable, nor did it change
the fact that as in all formulary Westerns character must always be in
the service of the plot. When Ten and Mary Devereaux are in a tight
spot one of the renegades conveniently switches sides to get them out
of it, just as at another point a prospector conveniently appears to inform the Major about how he found Reuben Kelsey's hideout by
accident.

By the end of the seventies, L'Amour grew restless. He wanted to
write longer, more historical novels and he wanted them published first
in hardbound. To put it in the words of Ruth Macken, one of the
characters in what would prove the first of these more ambitious works,
"'Nobody got anywhere in this world by simply being content.'"[69] It
is to L'Amour's credit that he did try, when he was seventy years old,
to take a new direction in his Western fiction. Unfortunately, however,

he refused to alter his methods of composition. *Bendigo Shafter*, as he titled this first effort, uses the first person narrative L'Amour had pioneered in some of his early pulp short stories and in early paperback novels such as *To Tame a Land* (1956) and which he tended to prefer in writing his Sackett saga. This technique permitted him to forego a compact plot, allowing him instead to be loosely episodic on a grand scale where all the various action episodes and plot complications introduced every thousand words or so are bound together by the simple fact that the narrator is always the center of the focus. L'Amour needed a beginning for this novel and so he went back to what happened after the events narrated in what I consider to be his finest short story, "War Party," published on June 13, 1959 in *The Saturday Evening Post*. In this story, Mrs. Miles has just buried her husband. It is narrated by her thirteen-year-old son, Bud. Mrs. Miles, together with Bud and six-year-old Jeanie, wants to continue with the wagon train on its trek. There is the familiar L'Amour rhetoric. "This was a big country needing big men and women to live in it, and there was no place out here for the frightened or the mean. The prairie and sky had a way of trimming folks down to size, or changing them to giants to whom nothing seemed impossible."[70] The story ends as Mrs. Miles leads a small group of settlers away from the main wagon train to build their homes in an ideal valley.

In *Bendigo Shafter*, the only characters retained from the short story by name are John Sampson and a man named Webb. Mrs. Miles was changed to Ruth Macken and she has only one child, twelve-year-old Bud. Cain Shafter and his wife, his younger brother, Bendigo, and their sister, Lorna, along with the guide Ethan Sackett, a distant relation to the Tennessee Sacketts, are among the pioneers who follow Mrs. Macken to settle in a valley somewhere in Wyoming. One of the charms of "War Party" is its strong heroine. *Bendigo Shafter* is late L'Amour and his view of the role to be played by women had changed and so Mrs. Macken undergoes a reduction from what Mrs. Miles had been. When Bendigo tells Ethan Sackett that he regards Mrs. Macken as the real leader among them, Ethan corrects him. "'Mrs. Macken is a thinking woman who knows her own mind,'" he says, "'but you watch and listen, Bendigo. You'll see she starts things. She opens the ball but nothing moves unless Cain says so. . . . A woman needs a man, Bendigo, even a woman like Ruth Macken. No woman, however strong, should have to stand alone. Believe me, she's a stronger woman because Cain is there and she knows he's there.'"[71] As Rye Tyler in *To*

Tame a Land and Tyrel Sackett and countless other L'Amour heroes before him, Bendigo becomes a self-educated man by voracious reading, including a standard among L'Amour heroes: Plutarch's *Lives*. From Ruth Macken and Cain, Bendigo in true L'Amour style learns "the beauty of building, and a hatred of all who destroy, of all who are heedless of the work of others."[72]

Despite the many sub-plots, complications, and accidental action episodes, *Bendigo Shafter* is divided into three major parts, the first describing the building of the settlement during the first winter, the second describing Bendigo's journey further West to secure a herd of cattle for the settlement, and the third describing Bendigo's trip east to New York in pursuit of the heroine whom he eventually finds and whom he will marry at the end in typical ranch romance fashion. Because of the hurried composition, there are the usual L'Amour errors in construction. When Bendigo returns to the settlement, he comments that "no light showed from the bench where Ruth Macken's place stood,"[73] only to comment a few pages later, following a momentary plot complication, that there "was a light at the Crofts' and one up at Macken's."[74] To his theme of social Darwinism, L'Amour had by now added another string to his bow, the concept of one-settlement culture. "The Indian, like the buffalo, would pass from the face of the land or become one with those who came, for they were all caught up with change, the inevitable change that comes to men and towns and nations. Men move across the face of the world like tides upon the sea, and when they have gone, others will come; and the weak would pass and the strong would live, for that was the way it was, and the way it would be."[75] After 1960, perhaps because he knew that a good many young people read his Western novels, L'Amour undertook to sanitize his heroes much in the way that his Hopalong Cassidy had become sanitized. There was no consistency in this. When he reprinted one of his earlier stories, the heroes were still seen drinking and smoking; but the later heroes were such as would have pleased a Ladies' Aid society. L'Amour kept insisting that his protagonists were not heroes, but they were increasingly men like Bendigo Shafter who always do the "right" thing, who not only do not drink, smoke, or curse, but who, unlike earlier heroes, do not even so much as drop their g's.

Having written *Bendigo Shafter,* all that remained was for L'Amour to find a hardbound publisher to take it on. He tried Doubleday but the firm rejected the book because L'Amour adamantly refused to revise it in accordance with what the editors there felt to be accep-

table guidelines for trade fiction. Finally, Dutton took the book on.
Prior to this, The Saturday Review Press had published some of
L'Amour's more formulary Westerns in hardbound editions, but the
relationship cooled, as it did with Dutton, and L'Amour finally was
compelled to convince Bantam Books itself to issue hardbound editions
of his "big" novels while continuing to publish as paperbacks his
regular original paperbacks and reprints. In *The Walking Drum* (1984),
L'Amour was able to tell a picaresque, episodic story set in the twelfth
century, narrated by its hero, and using the same basic structure
employed in all his formulary Westerns, including *Bendigo Shafter,*
except of course for period setting and costuming. *The Haunted Mesa*
(1987) was the last of L'Amour's "big" best sellers and in it he combined
the plot structure of the formulary Western ranch romance with science
fiction.

When it came to the Hopi religion, as set forth in *The Haunted
Mesa,* L'Amour was a fundamentalist. When the Hopis say that the
Anasazi, the ancient ones, the cliff dwellers, came from the Third
World into this one, the Fourth World, because the Third World had
become evil, that is literally what they did: they passed through a time-
warp! Erik Hokart, a retired businessman, is kidnapped by these people
from the Third World and his friend, Mike Raglan, has to go into the
Third World and get him back. In the course of the action, Mike falls
in love with Kawasi, a Third World woman, and finds allies on the
other side to assist him in his battle against the master villain, called
The Hand, and his minions. Much of the first part of the book is ver-
bose padding and, in keeping with the pulp tradition, paragraphs can
be just a single sentence. There are also the common errors in construction. At one point, Mike is being chased by a couple of Third World
people in this world. "The pickup was behind him," the reader is
told.[76] Six paragraphs later, the pickup is transformed into a car: "The
car behind him was gaining."[77] Erik's last recorded act, before he was
seized by Third World people, was to ask the owner of a restaurant
where he was dining with Kawasi if he could borrow a gun. Some time
later, in conversation with Kawasi, Mike, who used to know this of Erik,
has now forgotten it and so thinks that Erik did have a gun, "'an
automatic, I expect,'" and he asks Kawasi if Erik would be searched on
the other side.[78] All the sympathy that Matt Bardoul in *Westward the
Tide* felt for the Native American has by now not only vanished but it
has been replaced with a forceful stridency of tone. Mike instructs a
friendly policeman that "'what we must do is stop talking nonsense and

understand that what happened here was the result of a natural historical development that no man could halt or change. ...Our dreamers imagine that contact with an advanced civilization would bring enormous benefits. On the contrary, it would destroy all we have of civilization, undermining our beliefs. We would become as other primitive cultures have become, a poor, benighted people hanging about the fringes waiting for a handout.'"[79]

In *The Haunted Mesa,* as in so many L'Amour Westerns, the hero proves himself more than a match for fortune and by the end he is ready to settle down with the heroine to a life of peace and harmony—a space-quake seals off the Third World, at least for the time being. A Louis L'Amour Western is nothing if not an occasion to pretend. "I am no prophet," he once said to me, "but I would predict that I am the only Western author writing today who will still be read twenty years from now." I am even less of a prophet. I must leave the answer to that prediction to the passage of time. At the end he was able, as few any more are able, to die at his home. A few hours before he expired he was still at work, reading over his autobiography which, doubtless, will finally flesh out all of the many adventures hinted at over the years in the brief vignettes at the back of his paperback books.

Will Henry's West

Henry Wilson Allen was born on September 29, 1912, in Kansas City, Missouri. He was forty years old when he saw his first Western novel published. It was titled *No Survivors* (1950) and it was published by Random House. Allen chose the name Will Henry for his *nom de plume*. He did this primarily because he had been employed for the last nine years in the short subjects department at M-G-M — in a word, he worked on theatrical cartoons. He did not want anyone at the studio to know he was writing fiction. He also wanted a name which sounded suitably "Western."

No Survivors is an historical romance concerned with the Fetterman massacre. What is the difference between a formulary Western, one with an identifiable hero, heroine, and villain, and an historical romance? In a formulary Western, the hero triumphs at the end and usually, although not always, marries the heroine. In an historical romance, there is another option. The hero can die for his principles. This is what happens in *No Survivors*.

Allen's treatment of Native Americans is sympathetic in *No Survivors*, especially in the treatment of their conflict with the Anglo-Americans, something rather unusual for that time. This is even more the case in his next novel, *Red Blizzard* (1951), in which the protagonist is a mixed-blood employed by the U.S. Cavalry. Random House, however, did not like the novel and rejected it. Consequently, Allen offered it to Simon & Schuster which did accept it. He published it under another pseudonym, Clay Fisher. And for some time, that is the way it went. When Random House accepted a novel, it was a Will Henry; when it did not, it became a Clay Fisher.

Out of a total of fifty-six books to date, forty-six have been published first in hardbound. This is a considerable achievement for any Western writer. About two thirds of these titles have been published under the name Will Henry, the others by Clay Fisher.

Marc Jaffe, when he was Western fiction editor at Bantam Books, signed Allen, adding him to the Bantam stable which included authors such as Louis L'Amour and Luke Short. In paperback, Allen's novels to date have sold fifteen million copies. This is an impressive figure until you put it alongside L'Amour's sales, but then L'Amour was in a class by himself. Jaffe used to reassure Allen that "L'Amour is the mass, Will Henry the class." What this came down to in practice was that Bantam kept *all* of L'Amour's titles constantly in print, while reissuing authors like Allen at the rate of one title every other month and then letting that title go out of print for three or four years. Then, there is something else. L'Amour wrote strictly formulary Westerns. Not only does a reader know how the story is going to come out, but L'Amour's heroes do not ever die at the end! Allen's do not die all of the time, either, or even most of the time, but sometimes they do. That makes a difference. Another difference is that Allen's protagonists might be on occasion a young Indian brave or a Franciscan padre. For the readers of traditional formulary Westerns, such characters are simply not the stuff of which heroes are made.

Dale L. Walker, editor of *The Roundup,* the house organ of the Western Writers of America, and an author and biographer concerned with the history of the American West, in editing *Will Henry's West* (1984) has assembled an extraordinary anthology of Allen's writings. First, it is not confined to fiction. It contains a total of six stories. Two of these — "Isley's Stranger" and "The Tallest Indian in Toltepec" — won the coveted Spur Award for Best Western Short Story for the years in which they were first published. One story, "Not Wanted Dead or Alive," has never been published before. Also included is "Lapwai Winter," a short story Allen fashioned from an early section of what I regard as his finest novel, *Where the Sun Now Stands* (1960). It is a novel of particular interest to those who live in the Pacific Northwest since it is concerned with the Nez Perces' attempt to flee from this area and cross the border into Canada, an attempt in which they were unsuccessful. Walker has organized these six stories among twelve essays written by Allen on all manner of topics. He voices his opinion of the new porno-Westerns which have become something of a bonanza. The only thing Western about these books is the apparel worn by the characters; otherwise, they are simply pornography. Allen has written novelized biographies of a number of actual historical personalities, Wyatt Earp and Jesse James among them, and this aspect of his work he addresses in another of the essays. Still another is concerned with "Will Henry and the Indians"—and Allen's Indian novels, I believe, rank among his best work. His view of religion—Native American, Christian, and his own credo—occupies another essay.

Walker has provided a comprehensive chronological bibliography of Allen's complete works, plus a filmography and a guide to critical writings about Allen's fiction. Probably the most important film based on Allen's fiction was *Tom Horn* (Warner's, 1980) although many are more likely to remember *MacKenna's Gold* (Columbia, 1963), a film which Allen himself condemns. *Tom Horn* was the last film Steve McQueen finished before his death.

Walker's Introduction is by way of an appreciation so a reader cannot look to it for a critical perspective on Allen's fiction. Moreover, if by the foregoing I have given the impression that Allen never wrote a formulary Western, let me correct that. He has written a number of them, just as he has written a number of historical romances. He believes in heroes, as he makes evident in the essay, "A Time to Talk of Heroes." Now there is a profound and real difference between the heroic acts a man or woman might do in a given situation and being a *hero*. A hero is a literary convention. A hero is always a hero and, therefore, he is expected to act heroically at all times. Both formulary Westerns and historical romances always have heroes. But there is a third kind of Western fiction, a kind which depicts real flesh and blood human beings, characters who are capable of heroism and cowardice at various times, characters which embody the Gallic view that Walker himself cites in his Introduction: *"Le homme n'est ni ange ni bête."*[1]

The kind of Western fiction which features these kinds of characters I term the historical reconstruction. Allen has also written fiction in this mode. *Where the Sun Now Stands* is a paradigm of the form. How is this kind of Western story different from the others? Allen said it best himself at one point in this book. "I expect the historical Western to entertain before it educates," he wrote. "But once the history is brought into the story, then that history must not be violated. The writer may neither add to it, nor take away from it. He may use it but must honor it. Building his fictional tale around the real events never licenses the author to alter those events. There has been more historical revisionist nonsense practiced in the good name of The Western Story than in almost any other form of the American novel. History that is bent and shaped, reshaped actually, to fit any author's plotline, or political persuasion, or philosophical pitch, is the most tawdry of literary frauds. I detest it above all other wrongs in Western writing."[2]

There is much in this book, as concerns the essays, with which a reader may find cause to argue; but is that not the purpose of the essay: to inspire dialogue? I am reasonably certain that a reader will enjoy the stories; and, if you are discovering Henry Allen for the first time, you may well be inclined to read further. Above all, in bringing this book together in quite this way, Dale L. Walker has shown us once again that it is time that Western fiction, the best of it, be taken seriously and accepted for what it always has been: a vital force in American literature.

A Word After Reading
Elmer Kelton's
The Time It Never Rained

ἔστιν οὖν τραγῳδία
μίμησις πράξεως σπουδαίας καὶ
τελείας μέγεθος ἐχούσης

*(Tragedy, then, is a representation of a
progress that is serious, complete, and
filled to a magnitude....)*

Aristotle[1]

It was Dr. Samuel Johnson who said that "modern writers are the moons of literature; they shine with reflected light, with light borrowed from the ancients. Greece appears to me to be the fountain of knowledge; Rome of elegance."[2] As one who has spent a good number of years learning Latin and Greek so that I might experience the literature of those languages at first-hand, I cannot but agree with him. Moreover, the experience has a lasting effect on you. You come to expect literature, even comic literature, no matter to what lengths it might go, to have notwithstanding a serious purpose. You find yourself going to literature, as to all kinds of art, ever mindful of Horace's admonition: *"vis recte vivere: quis non?"* [does anyone not wish to live life well?] And this is what, I believe, great literature can do for us: it can show us the ways men and women, about whom the author's power of representation has made us come to care, have lived their lives and to reflect upon what it is we might be able to learn from their examples. Beyond this, being schooled in Classical literature tends to make you keenly, even painfully aware of the artificial, the pretentious, the insincere, the fraudulent, the superficial, the conventional, the crude, the decadent — all of which are so rife in the literary efforts of the modern world.

I would like to say that it was always this way, but I cannot. There is a decided difference between contemporary American culture and that of Athens in the fifth century before Christ. The artistic center of ancient Athens is to be found in the epic poems of Homer, the odes of Pindar, the tragedies of Aeschylus, Sophocles, and Euripides. By contrast, the average American at sixteen has been exposed to 18,000 hours of television with a violent murder occurring every seven minutes and what might best be termed a "heart-warming" moment every four minutes and where the predominant convention of the culture is the happy ending. This habituation to falsehood was no less true of American popular culture in the nineteenth century and, perhaps for this reason, American literature has always found itself at odds with the icons and conventions of that popular culture.

In writing about his opera-oratorio *Oedipus Rex,* Igor Stravinsky addressed the question of musical manners. "All I can say," he wrote, "is that my manners are my personal relations with my material. *Je m'en rends compte.* Through them I discover my laws."⁴ Elmer Kelton has chosen to discover his artistic center, the manners of his literary composition and his personal relationship to life, to people, and to the American land, by means of the Western story. The Western story, indeed Western American literature, has had no parallel in world literature since Antiquity. It was then that the Greek city-states were expanding into the unknown reaches of Ionia and Homer became their poet. Later, when the Romans were dreaming of empire, it was the Latin poet Vergil who dreamed aloud *"imperium sine fine dedi"* [I have given an empire without boundary].⁵ Western American literature has passed through these same stages, dreaming of fabulous heroes and their adventures, of empires, of battles, confrontations, and conquests. In the midst of it, however, because of authors such as Elmer Kelton, it has also come of age; it has matured. A handful of contemporary American authors have taken Horace to heart and have sought to examine our past on this continent— the Native American past, the Spanish-American past, the Anglo-American past—and have found in it neither what the formulary Western nor the historical romance continue to find: an opportunity to sing a paean to the virtues of one-settlement culture. Instead they have found diversity, variety, a wealth of ways in which life can be lived well; and they have also found a common spirituality, born of a soul in conflict, nurtured by a land of a thousand moods, of light and shadow in an infinite play with solitude and expanse, calm beauty and tempest, a land in which, as a powerful force of invisible dimension, change can come about as swiftly and unexpectedly as a shift in air current, the sudden congealing of clouds, the lonely wail of a bird or howl of a frightened animal in the remote darkness of a prairie night. This experience—what I would call the *American* frontier experience—is wholly and uniquely new to world literature. It is this experience which I feel is embodied in so much of what Elmer Kelton has written.

In *The Time It Never Rained,* Kelton was able to weave economic desperation into the very flesh and blood of his characters, much as Balzac did in *La Recherché de L'Absolu* (1834) and *La Cousine Bette* (1846). However, in Charlie Flagg's resistance to government subsidy one has an intimation of the hard realities of Ayn Rand's *Atlas Shrugged* (1957), albeit without Rand's flagrant rhetoric. Kelton is at all times the consummate literary artist. I think one of the reasons I regard *The Time It Never Rained* so highly is because its truths have been truths in my own life. As one who worked sixty-hour weeks in a foundry to attend a university before I traded the years of thirteen hours of sleep a week to continue henceforth to educate myself and as one who started his own business at twenty-six because I could not abide the compromises working for someone else invariably required, I can admire Charlie Flagg from my own corner; and, because bankers believed in me and what I wanted to do, I can appreciate the character of Big Emmett Rodale. There are still such human beings as these in the world and, when you encounter them, it is always a rare occasion and a welcome one. I can particularly respond to the character of Mary Flagg because once in business during a recession I had to call in an employee to tell her I could no longer afford to pay her only for her to ask me since when did I think she worked for me only because of the money I paid her. Some years later we were married, but only after I had learned from her the lesson that Charlie Flagg learned so well from Mary and which his son Tom has not learned: that only a fool ever judges a woman by a tape measure.

Kelton in this novel, as Tolstoy in *The Cossacks* (1863), has effectively created and populated a rural community; and, again as Tolstoy in *War and Peace* (1869), he has made as effective use of the spectre of drought as the Russian did of the shadow of the Napoleonic invasion. The drought is seen to touch and even shatter lives through the complex interdependent social fabric of Rio Seco—and without Tolstoy's misogyny and his heavy-handed tendency to proselytize. Kelton, it seems to me, has Jane Austin's ability to reveal character in the smallest of every-day details and Dickens' ability to penetrate into the most diverse mileaux and, thereby, allow his readers to understand better how such diversity is woven together into an enveloping tapestry. Beyond this, what makes him a great Western American novelist, indeed a great novelist, is that through it all the land itself is a character. Kelton has learned well from the masters and he has made them his own through his own uniquely Western American perspective.

It was Flaubert who proposed *"ne lisez pas comme les enfants lisent, pour vous amuser, ni comme les ambitieux lisent pour vous instruire. Mais lisez pour vivre.*"6 It is in terms of reading in order to live that, for me, the greatest significance of *The Time It Never Rained* will be found. I receive a quantity of mail each year from readers, many of whom use this opportunity to unburden their souls. Some time ago a woman wrote to me who had been married for thirty years when, one day, her husband asked her for a divorce because he wanted to marry a younger woman. The woman granted him his wish although she still loved him. When the younger woman rejected the man, he shot himself. It is rare that men kill themselves over love; usually, as in the case of Page Mauldin in this novel, it is over money. I recommended to the woman that she read *The Time It Never Rained*. I have recommended it often.

Charlie Flagg believes that the minute a man quits trying he's finished. Unlike Santiago in Ernest Hemingway's *The Old Man and the Sea* (1952), Charlie Flagg does not need to prove himself and this makes him, I believe, a healthier character. Hemingway had to go elsewhere, outside the United States, to find his artistic center. Kelton, it is evident, has never needed to do so. Charlie Flagg has helped to shape the Texas land he loves, but even more he has been shaped by it and shaped by all those who have gone before him. There was the pioneer August Schmidt and, before him, the lone Comanche brave whose defiance in the face of inevitable death becomes a guiding symbol of a way to live. Charlie learned very early from Juan Nieto the Indian and Mexican way of living with Nature. Even Charlie's view of God owes little to Christian theology. It is the Indian religion of the Great Spirit. Yet, Charlie is a true Anglo-American to the extent that he rejects the Mexican-American's stoic acceptance of Fate. He will accept nothing that places a limit on a man.

Charlie Flagg's opposition to the U.S. government's manner of dealing with the small farmer and rancher gains our sympathy. Kelton also manages to accomplish this without resorting to melodramatic pathos as Edward Abbey did when dealing with a similar theme in *Fire on the Mountain* (1962). Rio Seco is really a microcosm of what has been happening throughout this country since the latter half of the last century: the big combines continue to take over the land with the direct or indirect assistance of the federal government. The potential consequence is most terrifying, that the big combines will exploit the land until the soil itself is utterly exhausted.

In this novel, as in life, sheep and cattle are seen to mix well, despite the prejudices of the years, just as Anglo-Americans and Mexican-Americans can and do. Chuy Garcia's attitude toward the Anglo-Americans is best taken as a contrast with that of Manuel Flores'. It is in the scene of Manuel and Kathy hunting that ancient stereotypes begin to be overcome. They embody the hope of the next generation.

Elmer Kelton was born on a ranch in Andrews County, Texas. He grew to manhood associating with cattlemen and farmers, indeed himself coming from a long line of pioneers beginning with his great-grandfather who immigrated to West Texas in 1875 in a wagon with a string of horses. He began writing and publishing Western fiction in 1948 at the same time as he began holding a number of editorial positions with livestock publications. I regard all of his novels and stories as well worth reading, but for me his masterpiece is *The Time It Never Rained*. I began by quoting Aristotle because this novel is tragedy in the Sophoclean sense as Aristotle defined it in the *Poetics*. In Charlie Flagg, Kelton has given us a human being who is morally and spiritually superior to the average run of men. It has sometimes been observed that the tremendous gulf which separates us from Antiquity is demonstrated in the *Oedipus Coloneus* in which, after a lifetime of undeserved suffering, the only respite granted Oedipus is a tranquil burial. For Oedipus it is enough. He has endured and he welcomes his final peace. *The Time It Never Rained* is an American tragedy and so its ending, while no less austere than the Greek drama, is as new as the New World in which it occurs. The land abides. Having lost almost all of his holdings, Charlie Flagg retains his integrity—and he has more: he has Mary and his friendship with the determined representatives of the new generation whose values he can understand and share. He has become as the spirit of the new land itself: he does not perish. He must begin over again.

The Historians and Billy the Kid

My first knowledge of Billy the Kid came to me when I was three years old by way of a phonograph recording, "The Ballad of Billy the Kid" (Capitol 25070), sung and narrated by Tex Ritter. I really believed that Billy the Kid killed twenty-one men and that "Pat Garrett must make twenty-two." I believed it because Tex Ritter said so. I had no idea then, nor for many years after, that this "ballad" was composed by the Reverend Andrew Jenkins solely for the sake of promoting Walter Noble Burns' *The Saga of Billy the Kid* (1926) when it became a Book-of-the-Month Club selection. It was not until I had become friends with Tex Ritter that Tex told me that he had first heard of Jenkins' "ballad" from J. Frank Dobie whom Tex had met when he was a student at the University of Texas at Austin.

When I was working on *The Filming of the West* (1976), Sam Peckinpah had told me that his film *Pat Garrett and Billy the Kid* (M-G-M, 1973) was going to tell "the *real* fucking story." Of course, the film actually told me nothing at all about the historical Billy the Kid. It was only after I had completed *The Filming of the West* in 1974 and turned it in to Doubleday that a senior editor there, Harold Kuebler, gave me a copy of Leon C. Metz' *Pat Garrett: The Story of a Western Lawman* (1974) which had just been published by the University of Oklahoma Press. In reading Metz' book I was surprised to learn that it could be documented that Billy the Kid had only killed four men, all of them in life-or-death encounters. The "ballad" was wrong. Next I read a copy of Ramon F. Adams' *A Fitting Death for Billy the Kid* (1960) and it was then that I realized, to my own chagrin, that it is impossible to write film history, or literary history, or cultural history without knowing first the historical reality and by this standard alone to survey the varying degrees of deviation. Accordingly, I began a systematic study of Western American history. Western fiction, whether literary or cinematic, I was convinced, had to be evaluated in terms of how the actual history was treated.

349

When the Greenwood Press proposed that I write a book about the Kid in its bio/bibliography series, I decided to do it. Billy the Kid, it turned out, was a character perfectly suited to my purpose in this book which was, first, to narrate the actual historical events of the Lincoln County War; then to show how piece by piece the legend was created around the Kid, by historians then by fabulists and filmmakers; and finally, to demonstrate how historical reality could be used as a means to measure deviations from this standard and thus to determine the *ideological* intention of each of the deviations.

This last focus concerns what is now termed "popular culture" and it was here that I discovered one of the silliest theories that had ever been devised. Based, apparently, on techniques used by Henry Nash Smith in his book, *Virgin Land: The American West as Symbol and Myth* (1950), this theory asserts that by reading the popular fiction of a given period—or, by extension, by viewing the films of a given period—we can somehow tell what was in the minds of the audiences for which these works were intended. Not only is such a view of media communications preposterously static, it is hopelessly naive about the nature of modern media. Sam Peckinpah was not telling the real story about Billy the Kid: he was telling the Kid's story the way he wanted a viewer to see it and respond to it. He wanted to prove something with the Kid's story. In Ernest Hemingway's French in *For Whom the Bell Tolls* (1940), Peckinpah's film was designed to prove that *"nous sommes foutus. Oui. Comme toujours. Oui. C'est dommage. Oui."*[1]

"History," Quintilian stated in the first century, "is written in order to narrate, . . . not in order to give proof."[2] Yet, when it is history narrated by the popular media, then almost invariably it is history narrated in order to give proof. This is what virtually all that has been written about Billy the Kid has come to. Pat Garrett caused *The Authentic Life of Billy the Kid* (1882) to be written to prove in part that he was a fearless lawman, that the Kid was a fabulous antagonist, and, above all, that the Kid was armed the night Garrett shot him—when, in fact, the Kid was unarmed, half undressed, and Garrett himself was not certain at first whom it was he had shot, not until the body was examined.

What has consistently flawed most books published about Billy the Kid and the Lincoln County War—and three more appeared in 1986—is that they also have sought only to give proof. One author wants to prove that Billy was wicked and got what he deserved when Garrett shot him that night of July 14, 1881. The next wants to prove that Billy was essentially good and died a martyr's death. A third wants to prove that Billy was a good man who went bad. This is indeed the vital center of an American folk hero: he must be capable of having these three sides.

The only reason at this late date to write a book either about the Kid or the Lincoln County War would be to provide new information or perhaps a new interpretation based on new evidence. A book that unfortunately does neither is Robert M. Utley's *Four Fighters of Lincoln County* (1986). Utley, formerly Chief Historian and Assistant Director of the National Park Service, has written a number of books dealing with Anglo-American frontier military history. His sympathies have been traditionally on the side of the military Establishment, as opposed to the politicians back East or the Indians in the West, a stance tempered only moderately in a recent book on what Utley termed the "Indian frontier." The point is relevant because his pro-military bias permeates this book. Two of the four fighters Utley chose are General Lew Wallace, briefly governor of New Mexico, and Colonel N.A.M. Dudley, commander at Fort Stanton who decisively influenced the outcome of the Lincoln County War. The other two fighters are Alexander McSween and Billy the Kid.

Reduced to its most basic terms, the Lincoln County War was a struggle between two mercantile factions. The Murphy-Dolan store was well established. Murphy had been quartermaster with the New Mexican Volunteers during the Civil War. Afterwards, he became a civilian merchant with the beef and grain contracts for Fort Stanton and the Mescalero Indian Reservation. He was tied to T.B. Catron, head of the Sante Fe "Ring," and controlled most of the economic and political life of the Lincoln County Territory. Murphy had the courts on his side and Sheriff Brady in Lincoln enforced the law as Murphy wanted it enforced. The officers at Fort Stanton were variously in debt to the Murphy-Dolan store. The opposing faction consisted of John H. Tunstall, an English entrepreneur, Alexander McSween, a lawyer, and John Chisum, a cattle baron. Billy the Kid, whose real name was Henry McCarty, worked for Tunstall. The Murphy-Dolan faction assassinated Tunstall and wanted to do the same to McSween. The conflict culminated in a five-day pitched battle in Lincoln with McSween and his men barricaded in his house and the Murphy-Dolan forces headquartered in the Wortley House Hotel.

To illustrate Utley's bias, let a single episode suffice. On the third day of the Lincoln siege, Sheriff Peppin, on behalf of the Dolan side,

requested a car⋅⋅on from Colonel Dudley at the fort. Dudley sent a
messenger to Lincoln to advise that he could not do it. A wild shot was
fired when the soldier rode into town, probably by someone on the
Dolan side. Colonel Dudley dispatched a board of inquiry which held
its hearing at the Wortley House and interviewed only men on the
Dolan side. McSween personally was blamed. Here is how Utley
described the event: "Infuriated, Dudley sent a board of officers to
Lincoln the next day to conduct an investigation. They not only ascer-
tained that the fire had come from Regulators barricaded in the
McSween house, but they found added cause for casting them as
villains."[3] Colonel Maurice G. Fulton, who spent most of his life studying this conflict and who wrote the definitive book on it in his *History
of the Lincoln County War* (1968), put the matter this way: "Considering the officers' friendship with Dolan and his associates, and their
open hostility to the McSween faction, their findings are not surprising."[4] What the Lincoln County War does not need is another instance
of partisanship. Regrettably, this is all that Utley has provided, along
with some twenty errors contradicting documented facts and ranging
from the minor to the rather serious.

It was Pat Garrett himself who chose to view his conflict with the
Kid as a struggle between a hero and a villain. Yet, while such a
dichotomy is irrelevant to any participant in the Lincoln County War,
it nonetheless persists as the major tendency in most who have written
about the conflict. Donald R. Lavash's title for his book tells it all:
Sheriff William Brady: Tragic Hero of the Lincoln County War
(1986).

How John H. Tunstall died is thoroughly documented. On a
charge that would later be dismissed as spurious by the Grand Jury,
Sheriff Brady dispatched a posse to attach Tunstall's cattle. The attachment did not even pertain to Tunstall but rather to McSween. To head
up this posse, Brady deputized Billy Mathews, a Murphy-Dolan
employee, and with the posse rode known outlaws Jesse Evans, Billy
Morton, and Tom Hill. These last three, in advance of the posse, found
Tunstall on the road to Lincoln. When he was well within range,
Morton raised his rifle and fired, hitting Tunstall in the chest and
knocking him from his horse. Jesse Evans then rode up, dismounted,
and, snatching Tunstall's revolver, shot into the back of Tunstall's head
and then sent another bullet into Tunstall's horse. When the posse
arrived, Evans showed it Tunstall's gun, recently fired, and claimed he
was shot resisting arrest. Judge Angel, a federal investigator, after

exhaustive inquiry concluded that Tunstall "was murdered in cold blood and was not shot in attempting to resist an officer of the law."[5] Lavash insists that "Tunstall and Evans were friends,"[6] which is insupportable. In order to preserve his image of Brady, he had to omit any reference to Murphy and Dolan and what their side did. Here is his description of Tunstall's murder: "It was almost nightfall making it difficult for the posse. Moments later shots were fired. Tunstall was dead."[7] Only when known and documented facts are screened in this way can one succeed in making Brady out to be a hero. On little more than speculation by Sheriff Brady's great-grandchildren, Lavash asserts that McSween offered $500 apiece to his adherents to kill Brady. Utley wrote the Foreword to Lavash's book, praising it as "radical revisionism—no less."[8] Yet even he knew better since in his own book he noted that McSween was insolvent during the time of the conflict and that "repeatedly throughout the winter of 1877–78 he overdrew his account."[9]

However, I have saved the worst book for last. *Alias Billy the Kid: The Man Behind the Legend* (1986) by Donald Cline is the most formidable collection of fantasies and fabrications to be published about the Kid since the appearance of the Garrett book. Cline appears to be totally unfamiliar with most of what is documented about the Kid and there are almost two hundred errors of fact in his account. His tone throughout is belligerent, his text without coherent organization, his prose frequently ungrammatical. Cline, too, wanted to prove something, that the Kid was "a cowardly, petty outlaw" who has become a legend.[10] To do this, he often has to resort to his imagination. Most importantly, he failed to respect that cardinal rule of the historian once voiced so well by Fustel de Coulanges: no documents, no history. Following the Garrett account, Cline would have us believe that Henry McCarty and his older brother Joe were born in New York City. He claims to have found a birth certificate for a Michael McCarty born November 20, 1859, but he does not reproduce it, nor give the page and volume citation of where it is to be located in the Municipal Archives and Records Center. He cites three versions in newspapers concerning a murder committed by Michael McCarty who had a brother named James and expects the reader simply to overlook the discrepancies in the names. Cline follows Lavash in the fantasy that the Kid once worked for Sheriff Brady, but he departs when it comes to who offered payment to kill Brady, stating that "John Chisum offered to pay each participating man in the affair the sum total of $500 a piece [sic]."[11]

The only thing Cline does get right is that the Kid had no gun when Garrett shot him, but he has the name of one of the two deputies with Garrett wrong and attributes to the other, John W. Poe, the statement that "he never saw the pistol until Garrett returned with it from Celsa Gutierrez' room."[12] I do not know where he got that since John W. Poe wrote in his published account that "we saw a man lying stretched upon his back dead, in the middle of the room, with a six-shooter lying at his right hand and a butcher knife at his left. Upon examining the body, we found it to be that of Billy the Kid."[13] Poe covered for Garrett.

What we have in these books are instances of a new group of fabulists, making up history where they please, or trying again to prove their biases by means of it. And so the legend will continue.

Notes

Introduction

1. Pilkington, Tom, "Afterword," from Kelton, Elmer, *The Time It Never Rained* (1973; Fort Worth: Texas Christian University Press, 1984), p. 377.
2. Randisi, Robert J., "Wholly Negligible?" in *The Roundup* (February, 1985) Vol. 33, No. 2, p. 13.

Trader Horn: A Cinematograph

1. Horn, Alfred Aloysius, with Ethelreda Lewis, *Trader Horn* (New York: Simon and Schuster, 1927), p. 49.
2. *Ibid.*, pp. 67–68.   3. *Ibid.*, p. 203.   4. *Ibid.*, p. 49.
5. *Ibid.*, p. 141.   6. *Ibid.*, p. 66.
7. Riggan, Byron, "Damn the Crocodiles—Keep the Cameras Rolling," *American Heritage* (Vol. 19, No. 4), p. 42.
8. *Ibid.*, p. 103.
9. Fairfield, Lynn, "Renaldo, Convicted in Passport Case, Renews Citizenship Fight," *Movie Classic* (March, 1933), p. 29.
10. *Ibid.*, p. 29.
11. Van Dyke, W.S., *Horning into Africa* (Los Angeles: California Graphic Press, 1931), p. 146.
12. Horn, Alfred Aloysius, with Ethelreda Lewis., *op. cit.*, p. 52.
13. Van Dyke, W.S., *op. cit.*, p. 217.

Rain: A Cinematograph

1. Menard, Wilmon, *The Two Worlds of Somerset Maugham* (Los Angeles: Sherbourne Press, 1965), p. 57.
2. *Ibid.*, p. 59.
3. Maugham, W. Somerset, *The Complete Short Stories of W. Somerset Maugham* (New York: Doubleday, 1952), Volume I, p. 12.
4. *Ibid.*, p. vi.
5. Rascoe, Burton, and Groff Conklin, editors, *The Bachelor's Companion: A Smart Set Collection* (New York: Reynal and Hitchcock, 1934), pp. xl–xli.

6. Menard, Wilmon, *op. cit.*, p. 151.
7. Tuska, Jon, and Vicki Piekarski, editors, *Close-up: The Contract Director* (Metuchen: Scarecrow Press, 1976), p. 310.
8. Gargan, William, *Why Me? An Autobiography* (New York: Doubleday, 1969), p. 176.
9. *Ibid.*, p. 260.   10. *Ibid.*, pp. 151–152.
11. *Ibid.*, pp. 152.   12. *Ibid.*, pp. 152.
13. Crawford, Joan, with Jane Kesner Ardmore, *A Portrait of Joan: The Autobiography of Joan Crawford* (New York: Doubleday, 1962), p. 95.
14. *Ibid.*, p. 95.
15. Maugham, W. Somerset, *Christmas Holiday* (1939; New York: P.F. Collier and Son, n.d.), p. 314.
16. Menard, Wilmon, *op. cit.*, p. 301.
17. Maugham, W. Somerset, *The Complete Short Stories of W. Somerset Maugham*, Volume I, *op. cit.*, p. 33.
18. *Ibid.*, p. 129.   19. *Ibid.*, p. 6.
20. Maugham, W. Somerset, *The Moon and Sixpence* (1919; New York: P.F. Collier and Son, n.d.), p. 216.

Visions of Armageddon: *War of the Worlds*

1. Wells, H.G., *The Island of Dr. Moreau* in *Seven Science Fiction Novels of H.G. Wells* (New York: Dover Publications, Inc., n.d.), p. 181.
2. Wells, H.G., *The War of the Worlds* in *Seven Science Fiction Novels of H.G. Wells*, *op. cit.*, p. 309.
3. *Ibid.*, p. 311.

The American Western Cinema: 1903–Present

1. Mann, Thomas, *Der Zauberberg, Band III* in *Gesammelte Werke in zwölf Bänden* (Frankfurt am Main: S. Fischer Verlag, 1960), p. 9. In my translation it reads: "for history must be past, and the more past it is, one might say, the better for it in its aspect as history and for the storyteller, that whispering conjurer of the imperfect."
2. Quoted in Parkinson, Michael, and Clyde Jeavons, *A Pictorial History of Westerns* (London: Hamlyn Publishing Group, 1972), p. 182.
3. *Ibid.*, p. 175.
4. Quoted in O'Neal, Bill, *Encyclopedia of Western Gunfighters* (Norman: University of Oklahoma Press, 1979), p. 237.

Yakima Canutt: A Career Study

1. Goodman, Ezra, *The Fifty Year Decline and Fall of Hollywood* (New York: Simon & Schuster, 1961), p. 300.

2. Canutt, Yakima, with Oliver Drake, *Stunt Man: The Autobiography of Yakima Canutt* (New York: Walker, 1979), p. 237.

A Conversation with Dick Richards

1. Willis, Donald C., *The Films of Howard Hawks* (Metuchen: Scarecrow Press, 1975), p. 43.
2. Quoted in Rieupeyrout, Jean-Louis, *La Grande Aventure du Western: Du Far West à Hollywood* (1894–1963) (Paris: Editions du Cerf, 1971), p. 318. In my translation, it reads: "When I made *Red River,* I thought it might be possible to make an adult Western, for mature people, and not one of those about mediocre cowboys."
3. Bogdanovich, Peter, *John Ford* (Berkeley: University of California Press, 1978), p. 87.
4. French, Philip, *Westerns* (New York: Viking Press, 1974), p. 74.
5. Kitses, Jim, *Horizons West* (Bloomington: Indiana University Press, 1970), p. 168.
6. Chandler, Raymond, *The Little Sister* contained in *The Midnight Raymond Chandler* (Boston: Houghton Mifflin, 1971), pp. 356–357.

Rex Stout and the Detective Story

1. Wright, Willard Huntington, *The World's Great Detective Stories: A Chronological Anthology* (New York: Charles Scribner's Sons, 1927), p. 5.
2. *Ibid.,* p. 8.
3. Stout, Rex, *Please Pass the Guilt* (New York: Viking Press, 1973), p. 74.
4. McAleer, John J., *Rex Stout: A Biography* (Boston: Little, Brown, 1977), p. 9.
5. Anderson, David R., *Rex Stout* (New York: Frederick Ungar., 1984), p. 76.
6. Quoted in Baring-Gould, William S., *Nero Wolfe of West Thirty-Fifth Street* (New York: Viking Press, 1969), p. xii.
7. Quoted in McAleer, John J., *op. cit.,* p. 461.
8. Quoted in Baring-Gould, William S., *op. cit.,* p. vii.
9. Quoted in McAleer, John J., *op. cit.,* p. 556.
10. *Ibid.,* p. 380. 11. *Ibid.,* p. 366. 12. *Ibid.,* p. 201.
13. Stout, Rex, *A Right to Die* (New York: Viking Press, 1964), p. 47.
14. Quoted in McAleer, John J., *op. cit.,* p. 494.

It's Murder, My Sweet

1. Hughes, Dorothy B., *Ride the Pink Horse and Two Other Great Mysteries* (New York: Doubleday, n.d.), p. 193.
2. *Ibid.,* p. 82
3. Hughes, Dorothy B., *Erle Stanley Gardner: The Case of the Real Perry Mason* (New York: William Morrow and Co., 1978), p. 299.

4. *Ibid.*, p. 6.   5. *Ibid.*, p. 124.
6. Gardner, Erle Stanley, *The Case of the Counterfeit Eye* (1935; New York: Pocket Books, 1942), p. 228.
7. Quoted in Hughes, Dorothy B., *Erle Stanley Gardner: The Case of the Real Perry Mason, op. cit.*, p. 163.
8. *Ibid.*, p. 167.
9. Gardner, Erle Stanley, *The Case of the Velvet Claws* (1933) contained in *A Perry Mason Omnibus* (New York: William Morrow, n.d.), p. 5.
10. Ball, John, editor, *The Mystery Story* (1976; New York: Penguin Books, 1978), p. 24.
11. *Ibid.*, p. 158.   12. *Ibid.*, p. 202.   13. *Ibid.*, p. 365.
14. Landrum, Larry N., Pat Browne, and Ray B. Browne, editors, *Dimensions of Detective Fiction* (Bowling Green, Ohio: Bowling Green State University Popular Press, 1976), p. 249. In my translation, it reads: "*Sanctuary* appeared to be at the time the acme of audacity and darkness...."
15. *Ibid.*, p. 261.   16. *Ibid.*, p. 103.   17. *Ibid.*, p. 29.   18. *Ibid.*, p. 97.
19. Kittredge, William, and Steven M. Krauzer, *The Great American Detective* (New York: New American Library, 1978), p. xxxiv.
20. Landrum, Larry N., Pat Browne, and Ray B. Browne, editors, *op. cit.*, p. 4.
21. Dmytryk, Edward, *It's a Hell of a Life but Not a Bad Living* (New York: Times Books, 1978), p. 129.
22. Orwell, George, "Raffles and Miss Blandish," in *The Collected Essays, Journalism, and Letters of George Orwell*, Volume 3 (New York: Harcourt Brace Jovanovich, 1968), edited by Sonia Orwell and Ian Angus, p. 222.

The American West in Fiction

1. Turner, Frederick W. III, *The Portable North American Indian Reader* (New York: Viking Press, 1973), p. 253.
2. The actual quotation is from Grey, Zane, *The Vanishing American* (New York: Harper's, 1925), p. 201. "Blue Feather," however, is a story of internecine combat between the Rock Clan, a tribe of cliff-dwellers, and the Nopahs, embodying in Grey's words "the strength and cunning of a superior race." Grey, Zane, *Blue Feather and Other Stories* (New York: Harper's, 1961), p. 53.
3. Grey, Zane, *The Vanishing American, op. cit.*, p. 114.
4. *Ibid.*, p. 120.
5. Grey, Zane, "Nophaie's Redemption," in *Zane Grey's Greatest Indian Stories* (New York: Belmont Tower Books, 1975), which is actually the text of the original magazine version, p. 152.
6. Grey, Zane, *The Vanishing American, op. cit.*, p. 267.
7. *Ibid.*, p. 308.
8. Cook, Will, *Comanche Captives* (New York: Bantam Books, 1960), p. 42.
9. Beckham, Stephen Dow, *Requiem for a People: The Rogue Indians and the Frontiersman* (Norman: University of Oklahoma Press, 1971), p. 153.
10. Haycox, Ernest, *Canyon Passage* (1945; Boston: Gregg Press, 1979), reissued with an Introduction by Jill Marie Haycox, pp. vi–vii.
11. *Ibid.*, p. vii.
12. Orwell, George, *1984* (1949; New York: Signet Classics, 1961), p. 36.

13. Maistre, Joseph de, letter of September 14, 1812, quoted in Berlin, Isaiah, *The Hedgehog and the Fox: An Essay on Tolstoy's View of History* (New York: Simon & Schuster, 1953), p. 54.
14. Short, Luke (pseud. of Frederick D. Glidden), "Ernest Haycox: An Appreciation," *The Call Number*, Fall 1963–Spring, 1964 (Vol. 25, Nos. 1 and 2), p. 3.
15. Jung, C.G., *Zwei Schriften über analytische Psychologie* (Zürich: Rascher Verlag, 1964), p. 249.
16. *Ibid.*, p. 256.
17. Grey, Zane, *Riders of the Purple Sage* (New York: Harper's, 1912), p. 335.
18. Quoted by Vicki Piekarski in the article, "Seltzer, Charles Alden (1875–1942)," in the *Encyclopedia of Frontier and Western Fiction* (New York: McGraw-Hill, 1983), coedited by Jon Tuska and Vicki Piekarski, p. 319.
19. Seltzer, Charles Alden, *Square Deal Sanderson* (Chicago: A.C. McClurg, 1922), p. 23.
20. Haycox, Ernest, *Alder Gulch* (Boston: Little, Brown, 1941), p. 271.
21. Short, Luke, *The Feud at Single Shot* (1936; New York: Bantam Books, 1976), p. 212.
22. Short, Luke, *Ride the Man Down* (1942; New York: Bantam Books, 1975), p. 52.
23. Hutchinson, W.H., in his Introduction to Rhodes, Eugene Manlove, *The Proud Sheriff* (1935; Norman: University of Oklahoma Press, 1968), p. viii.
24. MacDonald, William Colt, *Law of the Forty-Fives* reprinted as *Sunrise Guns* (1933; New York: Avon Books, 1972), p. 83.
25. Fox, Norman A., *Silent in the Saddle* (1945; New York: Dell Books, n.d.), p. 63.
26. L'Amour, Louis, *To Tame a Land* (1955; Boston: Gregg Press, 1981), p. 70.
27. Shirreffs, Gordon D., *The Marauders* (Greenwich: Fawcett Publications, 1977), p. 196.
28. The quotation occurs in Ann Dunnigan's translation of Leo Tolstoy's *War and Peace* (New York: Signet Classics, 1968), p. 737. The maxim has long been the subject of learned debate. James Boswell in his *The Life of Samuel Johnson* (New York: Modern Library, n.d.), which is a reprint of Malone's sixth edition, inserts: the following footnote by Edmund Malone after the passage is rendered in the text (p. 1029) as *"Quos DEUS vult perdere, prius dementat": "*. . . Quos Deus (it should rather be *Quem Jupiter*) *vult perdere, prius dementat,* — Mr. Boswell was furnished by Mr. Richard How, of Apsley, in Bedfordshire, as communicated to that gentleman by his friend Mr. John Pitts, late Rector of Great Brickhill, in Buckinghamshire: 'Perhaps no scrap of Latin whatever has been more quoted than this. It occasionally falls even from those who are scrupulous even to pedantry in their Latinity, and will not admit a word into their compositions, which has not the sanction of the first age. The word *demento* is of no authority, either as a verb active or neuter. — After a long search for the purpose of deciding a bet, some gentlemen of Cambridge found it among the fragments of Euripides, in what edition I do not recollect, where it is given as a translation of a Greek Iambic: Ου θεος θελει απολεσαι, πρωτ' αποφρεναι. The above scrap was found in the hand-writing of a suicide of fashion, Sir D.O., some years ago, lying on the table of the room where he had destroyed himself. The suicide was a man of classical acquirements: he left no other paper behind him.'"

The Latin translation is attributed to Plutarch. In English, it would read: "Whoso a god desires utterly to destroy is broken in spirit beforehand."

29. Brauer, Ralph, with Donna Brauer, *The Horse, the Gun, and the Piece of Property: Changing Images of the TV Western* (Bowling Green, Ohio: Bowling Green State University Popular Press, 1975), p. 101.
30. La Rochefoucauld, François VI de, *Maximes* (1678; Paris: Éditions Garnier Frères, 1967), p. 7. In my translation, it reads: "Our virtues are often no more than our vices disguised."
31. Cook, Will, *op. cit.,* p. 907.
32. Tolstoy, Leo, *op. cit.,* p. 907.
33. Towner, Lawrence W., Introduction to McNickle, D'Arcy, *The Surrounded* (1936; Albuquerque: University of New Mexico Press, 1978), p. ix.
34. Braun, Matthew, *Black Fox* (1972; New York: Pocket Books, 1979), p. 181.
35. Thacher, W.F.G., *Dear W.F.G.* (Boston: Little, Brown, 1951), p. 10.

The Westerner Returns

1. Calder, Jenni, *There Must Be a Lone Ranger: The American West in Film and Reality* (1974; New York: McGraw-Hill, 1977), p. 218.
2. Sonnichsen, C.L., *From Hopalong to Hud: Thoughts on Western Fiction* (College Station: Texas A & M University Press, 1978), pp. 16–17.
3. A remark made by "Doc" Sonnichsen in conversation with the author shortly after his book appeared.
4. Sonnichsen, C.L., *op. cit.,* p. 176.
5. *Ibid.,* p. 178.
6. Rosenberg, Betty, Introduction to Henry, Will, *From Where the Sun Now Stands* (1959; Boston: Gregg Press, 1978), pp. v–vi.
7. *Ibid.,* p. 220.
8. Burroughs, Edgar Rice, *The War Chief* (1927; Boston: Gregg Press, 1978), p. 71.
9. Burroughs, Edgar Rice, *Apache Devil* (1933; Boston: Gregg Press, 1978), pp. 65–66.
10. Sonnichsen, C.L., *op. cit.,* p. 70.
11. Henry, Will, *op. cit.,* p. 132.
12. *Ibid.,* p. 23.
13. Quoted by Turner, Frederick W., III, in his Introduction to *Geronimo: His Own Story* (New York: Ballantine Books, 1971), p. 12.
14. Burroughs, Edgar Rice, *Apache Devil, op. cit.,* p. 8.
15. Haycox, Ernest, *The Border Trumpet* (1939; Boston: Gregg Press, 1978), p. 258.
16. Jung, C.G., *"Das Seelenproblem des modernen Menschen,"* contained in *Zivilisation im Übergang* (Olten und Freiburg im Breisgau: Walter-Verlag, 1974), p. 106.
17. Haycox, Ernest, Jr., in his Introduction to Haycox, Ernest, *Bugles in the Afternoon* (1944; Boston: Gregg Press, 1978), p. x.
18. Letter to Ray Everitt in the Ernest Haycox Papers in the Special Collections of the Library at the University of Oregon at Eugene, Oregon.
19. L'Amour, Louis, *Hondo* (1953; Boston: Gregg Press, 1978), p. 25.

20. *Ibid.*, p. 26.   21. *Ibid.*, p. 134.
22. LeMay, Alan, *The Unforgiven* (1957; Boston: Gregg Press, 1978), p. 188.
23. *Ibid.*, p. 188.
24. LeMay, Alan, *The Searchers* (1954; Boston: Gregg Press, 1978), p. 33.
25. Richter, Conrad, "Smoke over the Prairie," in *Early Americana and Other Stories* (1936; Boston: Gregg Press, 1978), p. 61.
26. Bloodworth, William A., Introduction to Richter, Conrad, *op. cit.*, p. ix.
27. Fergusson, Harvey, Introduction to *Followers of the Sun* (New York: Grosset & Dunlap, n.d.), p. xii.
28. Powell, Lawrence Clark, *Southwest Classics* (Los Angeles: The Ward Ritchie Press, 1974), p. 62.
29. Fergusson, Harvey, *op. cit.*, p. x.

Eugene Manlove Rhodes: An Appreciation

1. Rhodes, Eugene Manlove, "A Song of Harvest," published in *Sunset Magazine* in June, 1923, and reprinted in *The Hired Man on Horseback: My Story of Eugene Manlove Rhodes* (Boston: Houghton Mifflin, 1938), by May Davison Rhodes, p. 26.
2. Cleaveland, Agnes Morley, *No Life for a Lady* (1941; Lincoln: University of Nebraska Press, 1977), pp. 286–287.
3. *Ibid.*, pp. 282–283.
4. DeVoto, Bernard, "The Novelist of the Cattle Kingdom," in Rhodes, May Davison, *The Hired Man on Horseback: My Story of Eugene Manlove Rhodes, op. cit.*, pp. xxviii–xxix.
5. Letters from Eugene Manlove Rhodes to Walter Prescott Webb contained in Hutchinson, W.H., *A Bar Cross Man: The Life and Personal Writings of Eugene Manlove Rhodes* (Norman: University of Oklahoma Press, 1956), p. 208 and p. 263.
6. DeVoto, Bernard, "The Novelist of the Cattle Kingdom," *op. cit.*, p. xxviii.
7. Hutchinson, W.H., *A Bar Cross Man: The Life and Personal Writings of Eugene Manlove Rhodes, op. cit.*, p. 18.
8. *Ibid.*, p. 36.   9. *Ibid.*, p. 48.
10. Rhodes, Eugene Manlove, *The Desire of the Moth*, in *The Best Novels and Stories of Eugene Manlove Rhodes* (Boston: Houghton Mifflin, 1949), edited by Frank V. Dearing, p. 351.
11. Rhodes, Eugene Manlove, "In Defense of Pat Garrett," in *The Rhodes Reader: Stories of Virgins, Villains, and Varmints* (Norman: University of Oklahoma Press, 1975), p. 314.
12. *Ibid.*, 316.
13. Siringo, Charles A., *A Texas Cowboy* (1885; Lincoln: University of Nebraska Press, 1966), p. 172.
14. Rhodes, Eugene Manlove, *Pasó por Aquí* (1927; Norman: University of Oklahoma Press, 1973), pp. 126–128.
15. Folsom, James K., *The American Western Novel* (New Haven: College and University Press, 1966), p. 116.
16. *Ibid.*, p. 118.
17. Rhodes, May Davison, *The Hired Man on Horseback: My Story of Eugene Manlove Rhodes, op. cit.*, pp. 3–4.

18. *Ibid.*, p. 25.
19. Hutchinson, W.H., *A Bar Cross Man: The Life and Personal Writings of Eugene Manlove Rhodes*, op. cit., p. 75.
20. *Ibid.*, pp. 113–114.
21. Rhodes, May Davison, *The Hired Man on Horseback: My Story of Eugene Manlove Rhodes*, op. cit., p. 97.
22. Hutchinson, W.H., *A Bar Cross Man: The Life and Personal Writings of Eugene Manlove Rhodes*, op. cit., p. 124.
23. *Ibid.*, p. 125.
24. Rhodes, Eugene manlove, *Stepsons of Light* (1921; Norman: University of Oklahoma Press, 1969), pp. 10–11.
25. *Ibid.*, p. 67.   26. *Ibid.*, p. 102.   27. *Ibid.*, p. 96.   28. *Ibid.*, p. 315.
29. Rhodes, Eugene Manlove, *Bransford in Arcadia or, The Little Eohippus* (1914; Norman: University of Oklahoma Press, 1975), p. 92.
30. Rhodes, Eugene Manlove, *Stepsons of Light*, op. cit., p. 317.
31. Hutchinson, W.H., *A Bar Cross Man: The Life and Personal Writings of Eugene Manlove Rhodes*, op. cit., p. 149.
32. *Ibid.*, p. 9.
33. Keleher, William A., *The Fabulous Frontier* (1945; Albuquerque: University of New Mexico Press, 1982), p. 168.
34. Hutchinson, W.H., *A Bar Cross Man: The Life and Personal Writings of Eugene Manlove Rhodes*, op. cit., pp. 144–145.
35. *Ibid.*, pp. 148–149.   36. *Ibid.*, p. 200.
37. Rhodes, Eugene Manlove, *Copper Streak Trail* (1922; Norman: University of Oklahoma Press, 1970), p. 210.
38. *Ibid.*, p. 318.   39. *Ibid.*, p. 150.
40. Rhodes, Eugene Manlove, *Once in the Saddle* (Boston: Houghton Mifflin, 1927), p. 40.
41. *Ibid.*, p. 45.
42. Hutchinson, W.H., *A Bar Cross Man: The Life and Personal Writings of Eugene Manlove Rhodes*, op. cit., p. 208.
43. *Ibid.*, p. 208.   44. *Ibid.*, p. 268.   45. *Ibid.*, p. 294.
46. Rhodes, May Davison, *The Hired Man on Horseback: My Story of Eugene Manlove Rhodes*, op. cit., p. 146.
47. Hutchinson, W.H., *A Bar Cross Man: The Life and Personal Writings of Eugene Manlove Rhodes*, op. cit., pp. 234–235.
48. Dobie, J. Frank, *Guide to Life and Literature of the Southwest* (Dallas: Southern Methodist University Press, 1952), p. 185. Dobie, however, was not so generous when it came to Rhodes' fiction: "Rhodes was ample-natured, but he cannot be classed as great because his grasp was too often disproportionately short of the long reach. His fiction becomes increasingly dated." *Ibid.*, p. 115.
49. Knibbs, Henry Herbert, *Partners of Chance* (Boston: Houghton Mifflin, 1921), p. 100.
50. Rhodes, Eugene Manlove, *The Trusty Knaves* (1933; Norman: University of Oklahoma Press, 1971), pp. xv–xvi.
51. *Ibid.*, p. 88.   52. *Ibid.*, p. 121.
53. Hutchinson, W.H., *A Bar Cross Man: The Life and Personal Writings of Eugene Manlove Rhodes*, op. cit., p. 246.
54. Rhodes, Eugene Manlove, *Beyond the Desert* (Boston: Houghton Mifflin, 1934), pp. 38–39.

55. Hutchinson, W.H., *A Bar Cross Man: The Life and Personal Writings of Eugene Manlove Rhodes, op. cit.,* p. 344.
56. Rhodes, May Davison, *The Hired Man on Horseback: My Story of Eugene Manlove Rhodes, op. cit.,* p. 247.
57. *Ibid.,* pp. 254–255.
58. Knibbs, Henry Herbert, Introduction to Eugene Manlove Rhodes, *The Proud Sheriff* (1935; Norman: University of Oklahoma Press, 1968), pp. xxviii–xxix.
59. DeVoto, Bernard, "The Novelist of the Cattle Kingdom," *op. cit.,* p. xxxiv.

Dane Coolidge: Western Writer

1. Coolidge, Dane, *Death Valley Prospectors* (New York: Dutton, 1937), p. 132.
2. *Ibid.,* pp. 142–143.
3. Quoted from the dust jacket of the original edition of *Death Valley Prospectors.*
4. Coolidge, Dane, *Lorenzo the Magnificent* (New York: Dutton, 1925), pp. 243–244.
5. Coolidge, Dane, *Fighting Men of the West* (1932; New York: Bantam, 1952), p. ix.
6. Coolidge, Dane, *Texas Cowboys* (1937; Tucson: University of Arizona Press, 1985), p. 11.
7. Coolidge, Dane, *The Scalp-Lock* (New York: Dutton, 1924), p. 252.
8. Coolidge, Dane, *Snake-Bit Jones* (New York: Dutton, 1936), p. 127.
9. Coolidge, Dane, *Fighting Men of the West, op. cit.,* p. x.
10. Ulph, Owen, "Dane Coolidge: An Appreciation," in *Texas Cowboys, op. cit.,* p. 8.
11. Coolidge, Dane, *Silver Hat* (New York: Dutton, 1934), p. 9.
12. *Ibid.,* p. 35. 13. *Ibid.,* p. 176. 14. *Ibid.,* p. 230. 15. *Ibid.,* p. 232.
16. Coolidge, Dane, *Gun-Smoke* (New York: Dutton, 1928), p. 201.
17. Coolidge, Dane, *Bear Paw* (1941; New York: Hillman Periodicals, n.d.), p. 114.
18. Coolidge, Dane, *Lorenzo the Magnificent, op. cit.,* p. 126.
19. Coolidge, Dane, *Bloody Head* (New York: Dutton, 1940), p. 174.
20. Coolidge, Dane, quoted in "Dane Coolidge: An Appreciation" by Owen Ulph, *op. cit.,* p. 1.
21. Coolidge, Dane, *Texas Cowboys, op. cit.,* p. 160.
22. Coolidge, Dane, *The Fighting Fool* (New York: Dutton, 1918), pp. 194–195.
23. Coolidge, Dane, *Gun-Smoke, op. cit.,* p. 180.
24. Coolidge, Dane, *Wolf's Candle* (New York: Dutton, 1935), p. 214.
25. Coolidge, Dane, *Lorenzo the Magnificent op. cit.,* p. 198.
26. Coolidge, Dane, *The Fighting Danites* (New York: Dutton, 1934), p. 126.
27. Coolidge, Dane, *Under the Sun* (New York: Dutton, 1926), p. 108.
28. *Ibid.,* p. 109.
29. Coolidge, Dane, *Fighting Men of the West, op. cit.,* p. 191.
30. Quoted on the inside page opposite the title page in the original edition of *Yaqui Drums.*

Fran Striker and the Lone Ranger

1. Letter from Brian Garfield to Jon Tuska dated November 20, 1978.
2. *Ibid.,* p. 210.

Luke Short and the Western

1. Letter from Brian Garfield to Jon Tuska dated November 20, 1978.
2. Quoted by Robert E. Briney in the article, "Glidden, Frederick Dilley (1908–1975)," in the *Encyclopedia of Frontier and Western Fiction,* coedited by Jon Tuska and Vicki Piekarski, *op. cit.,* p. 118.
3. Quoted by H.N. Swanson in his Introduction to *Luke Short's Best of the West* (New York: Arbor House, 1983).
4. Short, Luke (pseud. Frederick D. Glidden), "Ernest Haycox: An Appreciation," *The Call Number, op. cit.,* p. 3.
5. Frey, Northrup, *Anatomy of Criticism: Four Essays* (Princeton: Princeton University Press, 1957), p. 304.
6. James, Henry, "The Art of Fiction," in *The Portable Henry James* (New York: Viking, 1951), edited by Morton Dauwen Zabel, pp. 404–405.
7. Cicero, *Pro Achia Poeta,* i, 2.
8. Short, Luke, *Savage Range* (1938; New York: Bantam Books, 1971), p. 10.
9. Short, Luke, *The Man from Two Rivers* (New York: Bantam Books, 1974), p. 36.
10. Short, Luke, *Saddle by Starlight* (1952; New York: Bantam Books, 1975), p. 62.
11. Short, Luke, *The Some-Day Country* (New York: Bantam Books, 1964), p. 40.
12. Gale, Robert L., *Luke Short* (Boston: Twayne Publishers, 1981), p. 150.
13. Short, Luke, *"The Marshal of Vengeance"* contained in *The Marshal of Vengeance* (New York: Lorevan Publishing Co., 1985), p. 25.
14. Short, Luke, *King Colt* (1938; New York: Dell Books, 1975), p. 30.
15. *Ibid.,* pp. 163–164.
16. Short, Luke, *High Vermillion* (1948; New York: Bantam Books, 1967), p. 49.
17. Short, Luke, *The Stalkers* (New York: Bantam Books, 1973), p. 91.
18. Quoted in Gale, Robert L., *Luke Short, op. cit.,* p. 151.
19. Calvin, John, *Institutes of the Christian Religion* (Philadelphia: Westminster Press, 1960), translated in two volumes by Ford Lewis Battles, Volume 2, pp. 978–979.
20. *Ibid.,* p. 964.
21. Short, Luke, *Debt of Honor* (New York: Bantam Books, 1967), p. 126.
22. Dawson, Peter, *Trail Boss* (New York: Dodd, Mead, 1943), p. 169.
23. Swanson, H.N., in his Introduction to *Luke Short's Best of the West, op. cit.,* pp. 13–14.
24. Short, Luke, *First Campaign* (1965; New York: Bantam Books, 1973), p. 142.
25. Letter from Brian Garfield to Jon Tuska dated November 20, 1978.
26. Short, Luke, *And the Wind Blows Free* (1945; New York: Bantam Books, 1965), p. 97.

Louis L'Amour's Western Fiction

1. L'Amour, Louis, *Bendigo Shafter* (New York: Bantam Books, 1979), p. 25.
2. Although the aphorism is attributed to German poet Friedrich Schiller, it was actually based on a familiar medieval maxim.

3. Marsden, Michael T., "L'Amour, Louis (Dearborn)," contained in *Twentieth Century Western Writers* (London: Macmillan Publishers, Ltd., 1982), edited by James Vinson, p. 473.
4. Quoted in Hofstadter, Richard, *Social Darwinism in American Thought* (1944; New York: George Braziller, 1959), p. 31.
5. Spencer, Herbert, *Social Statics* (New York: D. Appleton, 1864), pp. 414–415.
6. Quoted in Hoftstadter, Richard, *op. cit.*, p. 51.
7. *Ibid.*, p. 170.   8. *Ibid.*, p. 12.
9. Jackson, Carlton, *Zane Grey* (New York: Twayne Publishers, 1973), p. 58.
10. Cohen, Morris R., *The Meaning of Human History* (1947; La Salle, Ill.: Open Court, 1961), p. 285.
11. L'Amour, Louis, *The Rider of Lost Creek* (New York: Bantam Books, 1976), p. 118.
12. *Ibid.*, p. 120.
13. L'Amour, Louis, *The Rider of the Ruby Hills* (New York: Bantam Books, 1986), pp. 208–209.
14. *Ibid.*, p. 224.   15. *Ibid.*, p. 269.   16. *Ibid.*, p. 274.
17. L'Amour, Louis, *The Mountain Valley War* (New York: Bantam Books, 1978), p. 12.
18. *Ibid.*, p. 13.   19. *Ibid.*, p. 163.
20. L'Amour, Louis, *Kilkenny* (New York: Bantam Books, 1983), p. 58.
21. *Ibid.*, p. 21.   22. *Ibid.*, p. 81.   23. *Ibid.*, p. 22.   24. *Ibid.*, p. 103.
25. L'Amour, Louis, *The Trail to Crazy Man* (New York: Bantam Books, 1986), p. 9.
26. *Ibid.*, p. 20.   27. *Ibid.*, p. 55.
28. L'Amour, Louis, *The Rider of the Ruby Hills, op. cit.*, p. 112.
29. L'Amour, Louis, *The Tall Stranger* (1957; Boston: Gregg Press, 1981), p. 5.
30. *Ibid.*, p. 119.   31. *Ibid.*, p. 125.
32. L'Amour, Louis, *The Rider of the Ruby Hills, op. cit.*, p. 3.
33. *Ibid.*, p. 5.
34. L'Amour, Louis, *The Trail to Crazy Man, op. cit.*, p. viii.
35. L'Amour, Louis, *The Daybreakers* (New York: Bantam Books, 1960), p. 135.
36. *Ibid.*, p. 141.
37. L'Amour, Louis, *The Trail to Crazy Man, op. cit.*, p. vii.
38. L'Amour, Louis, *The Rider of the Ruby Hills, op. cit.*, p. vii.
39. L'Amour, Louis, *Son of a Wanted Man* (New York: Bantam Books, 1984), p. 161.
40. L'Amour, Louis, *Showdown at Yellow Butte* (1953; Boston: Gregg Press, 1980), p. 5.
41. *Ibid.*, p. 58.   42. *Ibid.*, p. 88.
43. L'Amour, Louis, *The Trail to Crazy Man, op. cit.*, p. 156.
44. *Ibid.*, p. 168.
45. L'Amour, Louis, *Westward the Tide* (1950; New York: Bantam Books, 1977), p. 4.
46. *Ibid.*, p. 138.   47. *Ibid.*, p. 7.   48. *Ibid.*, p. 27.
49. *Ibid.*, p. 28. L'Amour wrote to me on November 6, 1978, that "you will find in my books, incidentally, a lot of ecology before anybody was passing that term about. *Guns [of the Timberlands]* was one example; there is a bit of it in *Westward the Tide* (for your information, my first novel published in book form: in England in 1950) and I had published material on the subject more than 35 years ago."

50. *Ibid.*, p. 73. 51. *Ibid.*, p. 98. 52. *Ibid.*, p. 100.
53. *Ibid.*, p. 99. 54. *Ibid.*, p. 165.
55. L'Amour, Louis, *Guns of the Timberlands* (1955; New York: Bantam Books, 1960), p. 14.
56. *Ibid.*, p. 46.
57. Burns, Tex, pseud. for Louis L'Amour, *Hopalong Cassidy and the Riders of High Rock* (New York: Doubleday, 1951), p. 12.
58. Mulford, Clarence E., *Bar-20 Days* (Chicago: A.C. McClurg, 1911), p. 388.
59. Burns, Tex, *op. cit.*, p. 92.
60. Mulford, Clarence E., *op. cit.*, (New York: Outing, 1907), p. 188.
61. Burns, Tex, *op. cit.*, p. 145.
62. Letters from Louis L'Amour to Jon Tuska dated respectively November 7, and November 16, 1978.
63. Burns, Tex, *op. cit.*, p. 114.
64. L'Amour, Louis, *Hondo* (1953: Boston: Gregg Press, 1978), p. 132.
66. *op. cit.*, p. 133.
67. L'Amour, Louis, *Under the Sweetwater Rim* (New York: Bantam Books, 1971), p. 132.
68. *Ibid.*, p. 133.
69. L'Amour, Louis, *Bendigo Shafter*, *op. cit.*, p. 39.
70. L'Amour, Louis, *Bendigo Shafter*, *op. cit.*, p. 21.
71. L'Amour, Louis, *Bendigo Shafter*, *op. cit.*, p. 21.
72. *Ibid.*, p. 26. 73. *Ibid.*, p. 173.
74. *Ibid.*, p. 176. 75. *Ibid.*, p. 289.
76. L'Amour, Louis, *The Haunted Mesa* (New York: Bantam Books, 1987), p. 123.
77. *Ibid.*, p. 123. 78. *Ibid.*, p. 81. 79. *Ibid.*, pp. 174–175.

Will Henry's West

1. Henry, Will, *Will Henry's West* (El Paso: Texas Western Press, 1984), edited with an Introduction by Dale L. Walker, p. xix. In my translation, it reads: "The human being is neither angel nor devil."
2. *Ibid.*, pp. xx–xxi.

A Word After Reading Elmer Kelton's
The Time It Never Rained

1. Aristotle, *Poetics*, VI, 2–3.
2. Boswell, James, *The Life of Samuel Johnson*, *op. cit.*, pp. 832–833.
3. Horace, *Epistles*, I, vi, 29.
4. Igor Stravinsky in the liner notes of *Oedipus Rex* (Columbia Masterworks M-31129).
5. Vergil, *Aeneid*, I, 278–279.
6. Quoted in Lucas, F.L., *The Greatest Problem and Other Essays* (New York: Macmillan, 1961), p. 157. In my translation, it reads: "do not read as children read, in order to amuse yourself, nor as the pretentious read in order to instruct yourself. But read in order to live."

The Historians and Billy the Kid

1. Hemingway, Ernest, *For Whom the Bell Tolls* (New York: Charles Scribner's Sons, 1940), p. 428. In my translation, it reads: "We are fucked. Yes. Like Always. Yes. 'Tis a pity. Yes."
2. Quintilian, *Institutio Oratoria*, X, i, 31.
3. Utley, Robert M., *Four Fighters of Lincoln County* (Albuquerque: University of New Mexico Press, 1986), p. 45.
4. Fulton, Maurice G., *History of the Lincoln County War* (Tucson: University of Arizona Press, 1968), edited by Robert N. Mullin, p. 255.
5. *Ibid.*, p. 240.
6. Lavash, Donald R., *William Brady: Tragic Hero of the Lincoln County War* (Santa Fe, N.M.: Sunstone Press, 1986), p. 75.
7. *Ibid.*, p. 75.   8. *Ibid.*, p. 9.
9. Utley, Robert M., *op. cit.*, p. 91.
10. Cline, Donald, *Alias Billy the Kid: The Man Behind the Legend* (Santa Fe, N.M.: Sunstone Press, 1986), p. 103.
11. *Ibid.*, p. 65.   12. *Ibid.*, p. 118.
13. Poe, John W., *The Death of Billy the Kid* (Boston: Houghton Mifflin, 1933), p. 41.

Index

Aeschylus 209, 344
Anderson, G.M. (Broncho Billy) 63, 65, 66, 68, 145
Aristotle 343, 347
Autry, Gene 78, 85–86, 98, 101, 102, 103, 109, 111, 112, 133, 137, 139, 332

Barrymore, Lionel 37
Bennet, Spencer Gordon 109, 111, 117–146
Billy the Kid *see* McCarty, Henry
Booth, Edwina 19, 20, 21, 23, 92, 97, 98
Brand, Max (pseud. Frederick Faust) 200–201, 213, 224, 271

Calvin, John 298, 312
Canutt, Yakima 87–115, 142
Carey, Harry 18, 19, 20, 21, 23, 24, 26, 62, 65, 66, 67, 74, 77, 90, 97, 98, 245, 246, 247, 248
Carey, Olive Fuller Golden 19, 23, 24, 90–91, 92, 248
Chandler, Raymond 154, 155–156, 157, 158, 184, 187
Chisum, John 252, 264, 270, 351, 353
Christie, Agatha 165, 181
Cicero 204, 292, 305
Coolidge, Dane 201, 259–276, 297
Crawford, Joan 35, 37, 38, 39–40, 42, 43, 44, 46
Cunningham, Eugene 202, 255–256, 265

Dmytryk, Edward 156, 157, 183, 189

Eagels, Jeanne 36, 37, 44, 46
Elliott, Bill (Gordon) 109, 111, 112, 138, 139, 141, 144, 145–146

Faulkner, William 129, 187
Ford, John 60, 61, 62, 65, 66, 67, 70, 71, 73, 75, 77, 78, 85, 104, 105, 106, 107, 114, 148, 149, 152, 195, 222, 245, 247, 331

Gardner, Erle Stanley 165, 174, 178, 179, 180, 181, 182, 183, 184
Garrett, Pat 231, 233, 234, 235, 236, 237, 239, 241–242, 256, 270, 349, 350, 352, 353, 354
Gibson, Hoot 61, 65, 66, 67, 69, 73, 74, 92, 93, 98, 127, 128, 245
The Great Train Robbery (Edison, 1903) 62, 63, 66, 83
Grey, Zane 68, 69, 73–74, 98, 179, 191–194, 200, 221, 223, 251, 266, 267, 268, 270, 272–273, 275, 279, 286, 289, 310, 311, 312, 319
Griffith, D.W. 37, 63, 65, 66, 67–68, 79

Hammett, Dashiell 164, 187, 189, 202
Hart, William S. 65, 68–70, 71, 122

Hawks, Howard 76, 77, 148, 149,
  152, 172
Haycox, Ernest 194, 195, 196, 197,
  198, 200, 201, 209, 214, 217–219,
  226, 267, 268, 289–290, 293–294,
  295, 296, 297, 302, 303, 319
Hemingway, Ernest 288, 295, 296,
  346, 350
Henry, Will (pseud. Henry Wilson
  Allen) 8, 214, 215, 216, 217, 224,
  226, 288–289, 339–342
High Noon (United Artists,
  1952) 61–62, 76, 77, 79
Horace 343, 344
Horn, Alfred Aloysuis 15, 16, 17,
  18, 19, 25
Huston, Walter 38, 40, 43, 45

Johnson, Samuel 209, 343
Jones, Buck 62, 65, 66, 67, 71, 72,
  73, 74, 96, 123, 127, 130, 131,
  135, 137, 139, 146, 281
Jung, C.G. 199, 218, 291

Kelton, Elmer 10–11, 85, 209,
  343–347

Laemmle, Carl 64, 65–66, 67, 69,
  79, 90
L'Amour, Louis 9, 200, 201, 203,
  204, 205, 214, 220, 268, 288,
  290, 291, 307–338, 340
The Last of the Mohicans (Cooper)
  26, 206, 286
The Last of the Mohicans (Mascot,
  1932) 20, 97, 98
LeMay, Alan 206–207, 214,
  220–222, 289
Levine, Nat 89, 90, 91, 92, 93, 94,
  96–97, 98, 99, 100, 101, 102, 103,
  131, 133
Lewis, Ethelreda 16, 17, 19, 25
The Lone Ranger Rides Again
  (Republic, 1939) 109–110, 141,
  279, 282
Lyons, Cliff 2, 93, 134

McCarty, Henry (Billy the Kid) 11,
  230, 231, 233, 234, 235, 236,
  264, 270, 324, 326, 349–354
McCoy, Tim 61, 65, 69, 74, 78, 79,
  96, 98, 126, 127, 130, 135, 137,
  138, 140, 145, 307
Maugham, W. Somerset 3, 29, 30,
  31, 32, 33, 34, 35, 36, 37, 38,
  42, 43, 44, 45, 46, 47, 216
Maynard, Ken 2, 61, 65, 66, 67,
  69, 71, 73, 74, 75, 87, 94, 99,
  101, 102, 127, 131, 133–134, 135,
  137, 145, 224
Milestone, Lewis 35, 37, 38, 39, 40,
  41, 42, 44, 46, 47
Mix, Tom 62, 65, 66, 67, 68, 69,
  71, 72–73, 74, 87, 95, 127, 129,
  224
Mulford, Clarence E. 68, 70, 204,
  205, 213, 236, 237, 262, 265,
  270, 274, 329

Orwell, George (pseud. Earl
  Blair) 187–188, 189, 198, 209

Pal, George 49, 51, 52, 54, 55, 57,
  58
Peckinpah, Sam 76, 81, 82, 349,
  350

Quintilian 350

Rain (United Artists, 1932) 3–4, 36,
  37, 38, 39, 40, 41, 43, 44, 45
Renaldo, Duncan 3, 19, 21–23, 24,
  98, 140, 142, 279
Rhodes, Eugene Manlove 169,
  227–257, 268, 289
Rogers, Roy 109, 111, 112

Short, Luke (pseud. Frederick D. Glidden) 1, 194, 198, 200, 201, 267, 268, 287–305, 319, 333, 340
Sophocles 344, 347
Stagecoach (United Artists, 1939) 70, 72, 75, 104, 105, 107, 108
Stewart, Peggy 111, 114, 142–143
Stout, Rex 163–175

The Time It Never Rained (Kelton) 10–11, 85, 343–347
Tolstoy, Leo 204, 207, 345
Trader Horn (M-G-M, 1930) 15, 16, 17, 19, 21, 22, 24–26, 92

Van Dyke, W.S. (Woody) II 18, 19, 23, 26, 27, 79
The Vanishing Legion (Mascot, 1931) 20, 92, 94, 97
Vergil 344

War of the Worlds (Paramount, 1953) 49–58
Wayne, John 2, 61, 62, 67, 71, 74, 77, 81, 82–83, 95, 97, 99, 100, 102, 103, 104, 105, 107, 109, 111, 114, 148, 151, 219, 220, 222, 331
Welles, Orson 9, 51, 53, 54
Wells, H.G. 49, 50, 51, 52–53, 54, 55, 56, 57, 58
Wister, Owen 199–200, 202, 204, 244, 251, 261, 291, 297, 302